GLOBALISATION, JUSTICE AND DEVELOPMENT

GLOBALISATION, JUSTICE AND DEVELOPMENT

C. NARASIMHA RAO

SERIALS PUBLICATIONS
NEW DELHI (INDIA)

First Published - 2007

ISBN : 81-8387-071-6

Published by

SERIALS PUBLICATIONS
4830/24, Prahlad Street, Ansari Road
Darya Ganj, New Delhi-110002 (India)
Phone : 23245225. Fax : 91-11-23272135
E-mail: serials@satyam.net.in

CONTENTS

FOREWORD

'Globalisation' - a mouthful-to the novice, a global village with peace, prosperity and happiness all round. How deceptive this picture is and how cruel the fall-out of its implementation is the tale unfolded in this volume. The Centre for Scientific Socialism of the Acharya Nagarjuna University organised an International Seminar in February, 2005 the subject being "Globalisation: Opportunities and Challenges". Papers read on the occasion and the speeches delivered have been compiled into this work and I must say that the theme has been discussed threadbare in all its facets.

Unlike elsewhere, the focus has been on the different spheres affected by the phenomenon and the wealth of details available in this book is a treasure for the discerning. The bibliography annexed to every paper/speech is by itself a wealth that has gone into the contributions made by distinguished persons whose works appear herein.

A much used term-much abused, would be the proper description globalisation has been dissected and considered in relation to the concept, the divide between the fib and fact, the promise and reality in regard to agriculture, the idea's strangulation of the small sector industries, its impact on the services sector, that on workers, the menace of water being cornered by the transnationals, its effect on Women and Education etc. It does not stop at that. There is an expose of the Guilty who have been traded the country's security, concluding with an impassioned denunciation of the false claims advanced by the collaborators, by no less a person than S.P. Shukla, a former Secretary to the Union Government. The contributors work is preceded by a theme paper which contains a preview of what is to come. Most interesting therein is what leading theoreticians and those in the field have to say of globalisation. George Soros-yes, rub your eyes, it's the same Soros whom one would expect to be in the opposite corner, describes the phenomenon as 'the development of global financial market, the growth of transnational corporations and their increasing domination over national corporations and their increasing domination over national economics'. What therefore Dr. Mahatir, the former Prime Minister of Malaysia said about the role played by finance speculators was not untrue and here we have corroboration from one of the targets chosen by Mahatir to describe the forces behind the wreckage of the economics of Malayasia and other South East Asian countries at a critical juncture of their history. The theme paper has selected quotes from different writers on the subject and a short introduction to what each essay has to say on the subject probed in it. Interestingly, some Western writers have defined globalisation in terms hardly complimentary. Joseph Stiglitz calls it an 'agenda of the rich countries'. James Petras and Henry Veltmeyer say it is 'the new name for imperialism in the 21st Century'. Echoing Lenin, it is observed that 'globalisation is the political project of a transnational capitalist class'. The theme paper points out that globalisation has led to (1) A wave of Mergers and Acquisitions (M & As) thus wiping out smaller and weaker industries, (2) Aggressive expansion of the market and tighter control over backward countries to extend their markets and seize more and more of their cheap raw materials. Prabhat Patnaik of the Centre for Study of Economics & Planning, Jawaharlal Nehry University (JNU) rightlly describes 'globalisation of finance as being at the core of current phase of imperialism'. In the past it was said that the North-South hiatus lay in Capital from the North, not choosing to move from the North to the South and the inability of Labour from the South to move to the North. Globalisation was said to have solved the problem by moving finance into the South from the North, thus enabling labour of the South accomplishing in its home country what it could not do earlier. Theoretically attractive; but in reality a myth. This was untrue for it glossed over the truth which lay in a distortion of deliberately confusing the mobility of finance for the mobility of productive capital. This is a recurring theme in most of the papers and it needs repetition for the credulous have been really taken in by the glib lies invented by the advocates of globalisation. The expression 'neo-liberal' appears repeatedly in the work. I submit this is a misuse for liberalism-a beneficial ideology in the main should be replaced by the correct term-0'neocon' or 'neo-reac' (neo-conservative or neo-reactionary). Be that as it may, Prof. Patnaik reveals a perception far too common amongst the protagonists of the concept by drawing attention to the 'paradox of a country with a huge starving population undertaking massive export of foodgrains'. He also points to the fibs told by the supporters of globalisation parroting two widely-held and erroneous perceptions: That poverty in India has been declinging when the truth is that it has increased in the post-liberalisation period. Next that increasing accumulation of stocks in foodgrains indicates an economic improvement in the condition of the masses who were now taking to a diversified diet-comprising possibly fruits, dry and wet and vegetables. As a matter of fact the decline in absorption of foodgrains was due to squeeze on the population, specially the rural population. He speaks of increasing poverty being utilised and successfully by the fascists to increase bitterness amongest the masses on grounds like religion, race and ethnicity. Last is the truly profound observation that's there is a basic contradiction between the adoption of neo-liberal policies and the preservation of democratic institutions.

Kamal Nayan Kabra in his essay on globalisation it has appraised in the parameter of Justice and Development, reveals that in 1980, the disparity amongest the rich and the poor was a mere 79 per cent but after globalisation's advent had widened to 117 times. The much talked of trickles-effect was a myth for it did not materialise in the domestic economy-leave alone on the global scene. The truth about Globalisation, could best be said in the words of a Zinoist-Imperialist Thomas Friedman, who confessed that the market forces could never work without the hidden fist of America-comprising its Army, Navy, Air Force and Marines, that kept the world safe for the Silicon Valley's. And this is the author of several articles and a book lauding

Capitalism and Imperialism in the name of spreading Democracy. That old Fox, Henry Kissinger has been much more forthcoming in accepting that globalisation was another name for United States dominating the World. The Indian Economy's performance since 1990 has been appraised by J. Mohan Rao and Amitava Krishna Dutt. K. Ashok Rao construes the National Electricity Policy (NEP) in the background of the clamour for making electricity more market oriented. A widely-held belief is that the losses accruing in this sector are the result of large scale thefts in the processes of transmission, distribution and billing the thieves being the poor. Now it is an open secret that it is only the rich and the powerful whether in the rural or the urban areas, who have benefited by these manipulations. In a telling phrase the NEP is pointed out to be a 'classic case of privatising profits and nationalising losses'. The Enron mirage which so dazzled the Maharashtrian political class, rightly comes up for severe castigation. The trial of Kebneyh Lay and his cronies has at least begun in America. As against this not one word has been uttered against the many politicians in Maharashtra and even the NDA Government of 13 days for the burden cast on the starving millions of Indians. These unfortunates will have to pay or forego Rs. 35,000 crore for a non-performing junk powerhouse because the governments had taken the plea that they did not have the resources to solve the power crisis in the country. 'While visits of the skin-clinging tight dresses of Rebecca Marc to Matoshree (Bal Thackeray's residence) and the Government's Mantralaya were reported time and again when the project was being touted as the solution to the State's power crisis, all this has been now forgotten by the media scrambling for tidbits to score points over one another-and a silent watchdog suits the powers-that-be'.

An appraisal by G. Sreedhar titled "Globalisation and Agriculture in the Developing Countries", reminds me of the fast vanishing apples from the orchards of Himachal and Jammu-Kashmir. It is now supplanted by the costlier imported variety which requires us to pay two and half times more than the native and rots as fast-but comforts the craze for things 'phoren'. The writer concedes that there has been a slight increase in merchandise trade, the quantum being a mere half of what it was in 1980. Developed countries have not concealed their concern to protect the producer of agricultural products in their regions. In the United States the protection is about 20per cent, 46per cent for the European Union, 52per cent for Canada and 82per cent by Japan. This causes a loss of about 45 billion dollars per year to the developing countries. The benefits do not go to farmers, but to agro-industry giants. These mega concerns include Cargil and United Fruit Company. The WTO permits developing countries to have tariffs upto 10per cent. Our Governments, to teach us the virtues of asceticism, has tariffs of a far lesser per centage. The nation's interests would be better served by enhancing the domestic market support to our farmers by way of increased infrastructure and State investment in the farm sector at least in proportion to the subsidies given by the richer nations. The good Prof. rightly says that Trade is a game that involves moves and countermoves-what he implies but does not put bluntly, is that our governments policy is the imposition of sacrifices on the long-suffering farmers as also consumers-all in the name of a fad. Ramesh, Chennamaneni takes a look at the comparative performance of agricultural cooperatives in Germany and India. He rightly believes that co-operatives have more to offer than other forms of economic ventures and this despite the laws and Government inertia haven't been all that helpful to the co-operative movement in India.

Former Secretary to the Prime Minister K. R. Venu Gopal asserts that after the liberalisation process began there has been an increase in any number of situations where the poor have gone hungrier and been thrown out of their livelihood and employment. He refers to trade liberalisation enthusiasts wanting to know why we need to produce food when we can import the same? This, he says, betrays an elementary ignorance of three basic pillars of food security as defined by the FAO:availability, stability and access. Pointing to the duplicity of the United States and EU pursuing their selfish interests and misuse of the mechanism of the WTO, he observes that trade liberalisation is not some sort of manna from heaven, which is nothing but pure good. In a telling three words he observes 'It is not'. A sound Food and Nutrition Policy, is made up of several strands , the basic being the twin concept of the Right to work and the Right to Food being mandatory. The neo-

react policies advocated by pointing out to the masses the true position so that food and nutrition security become a reality for the Indian people and remain so for all time to come. A. Annadurai assesses The Impact of Globalisation on our Small Scale Industries. He points out that this sector gives more than 40per cent of the gross turnover in manufacturing activity and exports of manufactured products in the country-in terms of value worth Rs. 7,42,021 crore and Rs. 80,919 crore respectively . They utilise local resources and skills, meeting needs of the local market. This is despite the fact that the Plan outlays right since 1950-51 has never measured up to even 1per cent of the investment in any plan period. Growth rate pre-reform has been quite satisfactory, though it has started declining since the craving for liberalisation was translated into governmental priority from 1990.

The liberalisation enthusiasts go weak in the knees when speaking of the effects of Globalisation on the Services sector. The appraisal by M.V. Lakshmi and Meena Rao partly justifies the euphoria, though it is well to remember that it is at the cost of a severe strain on the working personnel-in particular those employed in the I T sector. Next it is early days to make a correct assessment, which can serve as a long time planner.

K.L. Mahendra essays the impact of globalisation on workers and finds a dismal record. The gap between the world's poorest and the richest has widened consequent to globalistion. He quotes a Human Development Report to establish the oft-ignored conclusion that economic growth per se does not automatically lead to poverty alleviation. The high-income countries have cornered the largest share, leaving a niggardly 3 to 4per cent for the low income group of nations. Free cross-border movement of capital has aggravated economic inequalities and social justice. Out-sourcing has created rifts among workers of the world whom Marx urged to unite so that their chains would crumble. The diversion created by the capitalists in the developed countries had become an instrument to divert the people's wrath against ethnic minorities and immigrant workers. Growing unemployment in India was attributable to a serious decline in the job creating potential of the Indian economy since 1993-94. Most affected were the workers in the agriculture sector. Public expenditure on social services was grossly inadequate as compared to developing countries. The allocation for education was lower than that in East Asian countries. On health the allocation by India was the lowest among South Asian Countries. Incoming foreign funds were mostly going to the 'take over' of existing Indian industries, the least to Greenfield projects. Disinvestment pursued with an unholy zest by the government there hardly being any difference between NDA and the UPA in this matter has resulted in serious looses. Sterlite was sold for Rs. 500 crore though it has assets worth Rs. 5000 crore. Tatas took over VSNL for Rs.1400 crore when it had a reserve of 1200 crore-immediately transferred by the new owners to other purposes. Privatisation yields were used to cover budgetary deficits – a case of family silver being sold to meet current revenue deficits. Workers in the unorganized sector constitute 92per cent of the work force but were not covered by any social security measures. The high salaries in the IT sector were at the cost of all night work to enable the developed world beneficiaries have the output on their tables, the moment they arrived for work the next morning. Female workers were the greatest sufferers. There has been an increase in the profits of the corporates, but at the cost of downsizing of labour with a gradual decline in their incomes. The judicial outlook was also being influenced in favour of industry.

A.V.Nachane considers Globalisation in the context of water. The unregulated flows of capital daily had turned the world into a global casino. Water, a principal sources of profit-an area to be conquered for accumulation of private capital. Trade in water presently stood at 400 billion dollars and expected to rise to 1000 billion dollars. Only 10 per cent had been commercialised the MNCs craving for privatisation of the rest and that fast. There would be no recession in this trade and no wonder the private sector coveted the ubiquitous brittle plastic container replacing public faucets. India did not need this phenomenon at all. It had an annual rainfall of 4000Bn. cubic metres of which only 40 billion cm went into drinking and other domestic use. Remedies to overcome the periodic shortages lay in water harvesting, equitable sharing of water based on need rather than financial clout and afforestation on a vast scale. Water was a social asset and its transformation into a commodity was an aberration arising from market fundamentalism. Access to water was a fundamental right of every inhabitant which could not be bought, sold or quoted on the stock exchange, traded or swapped.

Naierossadat Dameshvar from Iran takes a look at women in the context of globalisation. Views conflict vis-à-vis the impact –one, believing that the millennium has arrived and the other that the females already groaning under a burden will suffer greater strain in the days to come. Female employment may increase being easier to exploit. In the services sector, only the skilled will find employment and their proportion is very low in developing countries. Lack of recognition of women's contribution in the informal sector will continue. Women more particularly, the poorer sections-will continue to suffer from additional vulnerabilities like malnutrition, sexually transmitted diseases, pregnancy complications, domestic violence and sexual abuse.

M. Sundara Rao considers the impact of globalisation on the country's New Economic policy (NEP). The discovery is that less developed countries suffer when they impose Quantitative Restrictions(QRS) as the developed succeed in getting these removed. This has led to a surge in the Indian market for consumer goods much fancied by the middle and upper classes. The opening of the floodgates will result in a loss of work income by artisans, marginal and small farmers and SSIs lakhs of small units will close. There will be an increase in the import bill nullifying the slight improvement in the export sector. The exporter will no longer get the sops he has become used to for the WTO regime will eradicate them fast and completely. The cost will be Mergers & Acquisitions (M&As) of Indian companies by MNCs, closure of small and medium level industries and displacement of workers both in the rural and urban areas.

The Impact on Education is appraised by Sadegh Bakhtiari. To contribute to and benefit from globalisation, people need knowledge, skills, capabilities and rights. This is essentially a public sector function. Our Govt. does not believe in the theory. It wants education to become commercialised so that only the rich and/or influential can send their children to the portals of learning. In the process the politicians who have now taken to it in a big way, can fatten themselves as learning barons, having dry-pumped sugar, cotton, hospitals et al. Education rightfully worked can do wonders to remove all manner of differences amongst the countries and peoples of the world. The growth of the IT sector can efface the divides of time, space and cultures. But if this is to be the entitlement only of those who can afford to pay God help our future generations. Education deficits even in developed countries is a matter of concern. In developing countries the deficit, wide enough has become more pronounced and ineradicable. Social exclusion and too wide a gap between wage/income diffentialsals can be calamitous. Neglect of educating the masses will adversely affect the countries concerned.

M.K. George goes further into this subject and poses the challenge as the need for globalisation to make education an equalizer rather than create a neo-colonialist bunch aping the west. He refers to H.G. Wells quote of history becoming more and more a race between education and catastrophes.

M.V.S. Koteswara Rao and B.P.C. Bose narrate a biography of the Guilty. What compelled the Government to sign on IMF agenda's dotted line comprises misguided planning process, neglect of agriculture, mismanagement of the public sector, failure to control black money and the non-performing assets of banks'. The list is not complete, but the authors reveal a mind-boggling complicity at high levels destroying valuable assets built up by hardworking masses.

In the last two decades a number of self-annointed champions of national security have been prattling about the importance of defence in contradistinction to national security the most visible face of this being our President. A country's security depends far more on a contented population than citizens being thrilled by marching armed forces in well-drilled formations and to the accompaniment of patriotic music. A contented people require a rough measure of equality in access to food, health, education, work and opportunities. Security further require a well-crafted foreign policy which gives primacy to the true interests of the country rather than a me-too coyness with the only superpower now extant. The authors rightly emphasise the need for security embracing equity, modernization and environmental features as being of importance-as important as new technology to fine-tune the security measures for India.

S.P. Shukla, a Former Secretary of the Government of India was called for delivering the valedictory address and his experience, erudition and eloquence has led to a product truly amazing. The paper should be made compulsory reading for all those led into the unthinking adulation of the ignorant and the deceitful ones. He sees redemption and so do most of us in the gathering Anti-globalisation sentiment, worldwide movements and agitations against wars staged by imperialists and the condemnations proclaimed from the platform of the World Social Forum. A coalition will emerge according to Mr.Shukla and it will 'launch the movements on the trajectory of establishing the foundation of a truly global society which is just, harmonious and peaceful. 'Amen'say all those who think alike.

I commend the sponsors of the Seminar, the participants and those who have contributed their valuable time and effort to bring out this most readable account on a subject of vital importance.

S.M. DAUD

PREFACE

People in developing countries lived in relatively self-sufficient communities before the colonial rule by planted rice and other crops, fished and hunted for other food. They have used the local resources and indigenous skills and also to some extent satisfied with available housing, clothing and other needs, which they have produced through village and cottage industries. The modes of production and life style were largely in harmony with the natural environment.

Colonial rule imposed new economic systems, new crops, the industrial exploitation of minerals and participation in global market changed the social and economic structures of developing societies. Developing world grew more and more dependent upon global trading and financial systems. Trans-national corporations setting up trading and production basis and selling products in developing countries. IMF, World Bank and Trans national banks etc., were loaned billions of dollars to these poor countries to import highly capital intensive technologies.

The developing countries were sucked deeply into the whirlpool of the world economic system and consequently loosing their indigenous skills, their capacity for self reliance, and their confidence. The transfer of resources from developing countries to the developed countries taking place through many channels. There is a transfer of physical resources and there is also a transfer of financial resources. Due to unequal terms of Trade and fall in commodities prices, the developing world loosing billions of dollars. In human terms, this means drastic cuts in living standards, massive retrenchments of workers, and big reduction in government budgets in many developing countries. "The new Imperial order and the promotion of the interests of the dominant economic institutions through neo-liberal policies have profound consequences for democracy and society". A growing divide between haves and have-nots has left increasing numbers in the third world in dire poverty, living on less than a dollar a day.

In this back ground, an International Seminar has been organised at Acharya Nagarjuna University, Guntur in which academics and scholars from India and abroad have presented their papers and participated in depth discussions. I feel the seminar proceedings may certainly help to understand the challenges and opportunities before the globalisation.

C. NARASIMHA RAO

ACKNOWLEDGEMENTS

The Centre for Scientific Socialism of Acharya Nagarjuna University on the occasion of its Bi-decennial celebrations has organised an International Seminar on "Globalisation: Opportunities and Challenges" during 11-14th February 2005. This International Seminar is sponsored by the ICSSR, UGC, Lanco, Kondapalli Pvt. (Ltd) the Chamber of Commerce, Vijayawada and Guntur. The proceedings of the seminar are published in this volume. It contains twenty papers presented by eminent academicians from India and abroad. I express my sincere thanks to all those who presented their papers in this International Seminar.

I wish to express my sincere thanks to Professor Prabhat Patnaik and Prof. Kamal Nayan Kabra for their valuable presentation of key-note addresses. I am very much thankful to Sri. S.P. Sukla, who delivered the valedictory address on this occasion.

I wish to express my sincere thanks to our beloved Vice-chancellor Prof. L. Venu Gopal Reddy, M.Com, Ph.D., who extended utmost help in organizing this International Seminar. I am thankful to the Chair Persons who chaired different sessions and rapporteurs for recording the proceedings of the seminar and presenting the reports in the plenary sessions of the International Seminar. My hearty felt thanks to Prof. K. R. Chowdry who helped us day in and day out to successfully organize this International Seminar and also to bring out this publication.

I am also equally thankful to justice Daud, Retired Justice of High Court of Mumbai for writing valuable foreword to this volume.

I must place on record that but for the financial grant of ICSSR, New Delhi, UGC, New Delhi, DRDL, Hyderabad and Defence Labouratories, Gwalior we cound not have organised this International event, for which we remain thankful to these organisations.

My hearty felt thanks to Lanco, Kondapalli Power (Pvt) (Ltd) who generously came forward to be one of the the co-sponsor of this International Seminar. And I am also equally thankful to thePresident Sri Gaddam Subba Rao, Chamber of Commerce, Vijayawada and the President Sri Atukuri Anjaneyulu, Guntur respectively who agreed to be the other co-sponsors of this International Seminar. We also thankful to Tobacco Board, Guntur, R. Rama Swamy of Vikram Publishers, Vijayawada, Nagalla Siva Ram Prasad, Vijayawada, ASSIST, Ongole and Siddhartha Academy of General and Technical Education who helped us in different ways in organising this event.

I am highly thankful to my colleagues N. Anjaiah, K. Soma Sekhar and V. Divya Thejomurthy, the students, scholars and the supporting staff who spent sleepless nights to successfully organize this International Seminar. I am also thankful to Serials Publications, New Delhi, who published the proceedings of this International Seminar.

CONTRIBUTORS

C. Narasimha Rao and N. Anjaiah, Centre for Scientific Socilism Acharya Nagarjuna University, Guntur.

Prabhat Patnaik, Centre for Economic Studies Planning, Awaharlal Nehru University, New Delhi.

Kamal Nayan Kabra, Former Professor, Indian Institute of Public Administration, New Delhi.

J. Mohan Rao, Department of Economics, University of Massachusetts At Amherst (USA).

Amitara Krishna Dutt, Department of Economics, University of Norte Dame.

K. Ashok Rao, Convener, National Working Group on Power Sector, New Delhi.

Konrad Hagedorn, Humboldt University, Berlin, Germany.

Ramesh Chennamaneni, Humboldt University, Berlin, Germany.

G. Sreedhar, Professor of Rural Development, S.K. University, Anatapur, A.P. - 515003.

K.R. Venu Gopal, IAS (Rtd), Former Secretary to the Prime Minister and Special Rapporteur National Human Rights Commission.

A. Annadurai, Lecturer In Economics, Madras Christian College, Tambaram, Chennai-59.

M.V. Lakshmi, Associate Professor, Institute of Foreign Trade, Gitam, Visakhapatnam.

B. Meena Rao, Professor, Department of Politics and Public Administration, Andhra University, Visakhapatnam-530003.

K.L. Mahendra, President, W.F.T.U. Hyderabad, A.P.

A.V. Nachane, General Secretary, All India L.I.C. Employees Federation, Mumbai-400001.

Naierossadat Daneswar, Azad University, Khomeinishahr, Iran.

M. Sundara Rao, Professor of Economics, A.U.P.G. Centre Etcherla, Srikakulam (DT).

Sadesh Baktiari, Associate Professor, Isfahan University, Iran.

M.K. George, Principal, Loyola College of Social Sciences, Tiruvananthapuram, Kerala India-695017.

U.P. Thakur, Defence Research Development Organization, Hyderabad.

K. Soma Sekhar, Faculty Member, Department of Rural Development, Acharya Nagarjuna University, Guntur-522510.

V. Divya Thejomurthy, Faculty Member, Department of Rural Development, Acharya Nagarjuna University, Guntur-522510.

S.P. Shukla, Former Secretary, Ministry of Commerce and Trade, Government of India, New Delhi.

GLOBALISATION: OPPORTUNUTIES AND CHALLENGES
(THEME PAPER)

C. Narasimha Rao & N. Anjaiah

Globalization has become a buzz word for the last two decades with a lot of explanatory, analytical, apologetic and critical literature coming out from various social science and humanities disciplines as well as policy pronouncements of international agencies and national governments. People's movements, non-governmental organizations (NGOs), independent intellectuals and journalists have also contributed to the growth of literature on globalisation. A cursory glance at any of the documents from either international agencies like the United Nations, the World Bank, the International Monetary Fund (IMF), the World Trade Organization (WTO) or national governments or people's movements and NGOs provides a multitude of definitions, interpretations, defensive arguments and wild criticisms in favour of and against globalisation. It is estimated that more than a thousand scholarly publications and over 10,000 research articles are emerging on the subject every year. A simple search for the word globalisation points to millions of web pages. Almost every community in the world has been going through this process and almost all members of intelligentsia have been expressing some or other views on globalisation. However, this proliferation of information has not led even to a broad consensus on the theme of globalisation and there are as many divergent opinions.

As a scholar on globalisation has put it, "after all, globalisation is an uneven process, meaning that people living in various parts of the world are affected very differently by this gigantic transformation of social structures and cultural zones. Hence, the social processes that make up globalisation have been analyzed and explained by various commentators in different, often contradictory ways. Scholars not only hold different views with regard to proper definitions of globalisation, they also disagree on its scale, causation, chronology, impact, trajectories, and policy outcomes."

Even as the divergence is so vast in terms of the globalisation's scale, causation, chronology, impact, trajectories, and policy outcomes, all the diverse viewpoints on the subject can be broadly classified into two major camps at the extremes–one emphasizing the opportunities and benefits that can be reaped out of the process and the second, alerting about the challenges and threats involved. In between, there are several arguments accepting and rejecting some aspects from both the camps. Thus the current seminar has taken these two extreme aspects of *Globalisation–Opportunities and Challenges*–as its focus.

There are also different opinions on whether globalisation is a process or a state of affairs or a system or a force or an age. There are different views on whether the process helps the developed world or the developing world. It is also questioned whether the process leads to integration of all economies into a single global market or disintegration and marginalization of some sections of the economies or people. The process is differently comprehended as one imposed by the well-entrenched imperialist forces in general and Multi National Corporations (MNCs or Trans National Corporations—TNCs) in particular on one hand and a conscious choice embraced by the third world governments on their own on the other.

There have been a number of studies by a variety of organizations from the International Labour Organization to the local activist groups discovering the ill effects of the globalisation process. While one extreme point of view treats globalisation as a new nomenclature to the old, exploitative imperialist system, the other states that the process provides a win-win situation to both the developed and developing countries. Even some of the protagonists of globalisation have realized the negative side of the process and began arguing in favour of adding "human face" to globalisation. The existing body of literature is a testimony to both positive trends in some parameters of growth and negative impacts on some social sectors. Both sides have put forth enormous amount of incontestable data to substantiate their respective standpoints.

GLOBALISATION–PROBLEMS OF DEFINITION

In this complex scenario, it would be quite difficult to arrive at a universally acceptable and reasonably comprehensive definition of globalisation. Several authors who worked on the subject expressed their inability to do so and remained contented with their own working definition, with a number of qualifications and exceptions, resulting in hundreds of definitions.

"The term globalisation is used in so many ways and in such varied contexts that it seems almost futile to attempt a universally acceptable definition for it. Speakers and writers have discussed the impact of globalisation on practically every aspect of human existence, namely, politics, economics, religion, culture, knowledge and science," said Amiya Kumar Bagchi.

Arguing that "given these competing labels have very different meanings, their indiscriminate usage is often obscures and invites confusion", Steger suggests to define globalisation as "a multidimensional set of social processes that create, multiply, stretch and intensify worldwide social interdependence and exchanges while at the same time fostering in people a growing awareness of deepening connections between the local and the distant."

Though Steger's definition tried to encompass a broad spectrum, it leaves out economic and financial aspects of globalisation, which are far more crucial in the opinion of some other scholars. As Steger himself recognized, "one of the central tasks for globalisation researchers consists of devising better ways for gauging the relative importance of each dimension without losing sight of the interconnected whole. But it would be a grave mistake to cling to a one-sided understanding of globalisation."

Anthony Giddens looked at globalisation as a spatial integration in the sphere of social relations when he said: "Globalisation can...be defined as the intensification of worldwide social relations which link distant locations in such a way that local happenings are shaped by events occurring many miles away and vice versa."

In contrast, there are authors who viewed globalisation in purely economic terms and defined it in financial, trade and market realms. George Soros, for example, referred to globalisation as "the development of global financial market, the growth of transnational corporations, and their increasing domination over national economies."

Samir Amin said, "the advance of globalisation has not been confined to trade....It also affects productive systems (auto-centric national systems are progressively dismantled to be reconstituted as part of an integrated global productive system), technology (specific national technologies make way for universal technologies), financial markets, and many other aspects of social life. A simultaneous phenomenon is the integration of Third World countries that have embarked on industrialization."

"Globalisation can be described as the process which involves growing economic interdependence of countries worldwide...The present globalisation process is characterized by five major developments: (a) rapid growth in international financial institutions; (b) fast growth in trade, especially among TNCs; (c) surge in foreign direct investment, largely contributed by TNCs; (d) the emergence of global markets; and (e) the diffusion of technologies and ideas through rapid expansion of a globalized transportation and communication system," said Kavaljit Singh.

Former economist of the World Bank and Nobel laureate, Joseph Stiglitz, criticized globalisation in scathing terms. He analyzed globalisation in terms of briberization (privatization), hot money cycle (capital market liberalisation), IMF riot (market-based pricing or raising prices on food, water and cooking gas) and opium wars (free trade) and said this four-point formula destroys national economies and is an agenda of rich nations.

Globalisation policies are being imposed on the governments of the third world countries through structural adjustment policies as conditionality when the governments seek assistance from international financial agencies. Michel Chossudovsky analyzed structural adjustment as "conducive to a form of economic genocide which is carried out through the deliberate manipulation of market forces. When compared to genocide in various periods of colonial history (for example, forced labour and slavery), its impact is devastating."

There are yet others who explained globalisation in cultural terms and defined it so. Some scholars tried to analyze globalisation as McDonaldization, Westernization, Marketization, Commoditization, Monoculture, Cultural Imperialism, etc and expressed concern on its cultural ramifications. Some scholars looked at the process from the angles of governance and law and debated whether it would lead to more democracy or law and lorder or anarchy and more crime. Further, a number of scholars looked at globalisation from the perspective of a marginalized section and defined it in terms of social or economic upward mobility or decline in the economic status.

Francis Fukuyama said, "the level of economic development resulting from globalisation is conducive to the creation of complex civil societies with a powerful middle class. It is this class and societal structure that facilitates democracy."

Among Indian commentators on the process, CT Kurien was one of the first economists to analyze globalisation and his argument goes as follows:

> If 'globalisation' means the coming closer together of the national economies of the world, then this is not happening. On the contrary they are getting more distanced. The gap between the North and South has increased, and, in terms of trade, since the 1980s, national economies have been becoming more isolated. The Northern countries, in particular, have been closing themselves off in different ways. The accent on multilateralism that was started after the Second World War has been turning into various shades of minilateralism and, indeed, not-so-subtle forms of unilateralism. That all this should be happening in the name of free trade, 'opening up', liberalisation and market friendliness is one of the major ironies and, indeed, perversities of our time. It also shows how frequently used terms, including technical ones, can become highly charged ideological expressions. Globalisation is the mother of all such contemporary expressions.

There is one sense (and only one) in which economies across the world are getting more closely linked: the speed and the relative ease with which 'quicksilver' capital is moving about. If that has any connection with trade, that trade is only between claims on capital, including different national currencies which have become the most frequently traded item in the 1980s and 1990s. In other words, 'trade' is now primarily the vehicle for the circulation of capital and has very little to do with the transfer of goods among national economies. Yet, the case for contemporary globalisation is usually based on the theory of international trade put forward by David Ricardo in the early nineteenth century.

GLOBALISATION–IMPERIALISM'S NEW NAME?

James Petras and Henry Veltmeyer, in a very influential book, argued that the process is only a new name for imperialism in the 21st century and sought to "unmask" globalisation:

> "Globalisation is at the centre of diverse intellectual and political agendas, raising crucial questions about what is widely considered to be the fundamental dynamic of our time–an epoch-defining set of changes that is radically transforming social and economic relations and institutions in the 21st century.

Globalisation is both a description and a prescription, and as such it serves as both an explanation–a poor one, it has to be said–and an ideology that currently dominates thinking, policy-making and political practice. As a description, "globalisation" refers to the widening and deepening of the international flows of trade, capital, technology and information within a single integrated global marker. Like terms such as "the global village", it identifies a complex of changes produced by the dynamics of capitalist development as well as the diffusion of values and cultural practices associated with this development. In this context, reference is often made to changes in the capitalist organization of production and society, extensions of a process of capital accumulation hitherto played out largely at the national level and restricted to the confines (and regulatory powers) of the state.

As a prescription, "globalisation" involves the liberalisation of national and global markets in the belief that free flows of trade, capital and information will produce the best outcome for growth and human welfare. When the term "globalisation" is used, whether to describe or prescribe, it is usually presented with an air of inevitability and overwhelming conviction, betraying its ideological roots.

How the before mentioned epoch-defining developments and changes are interpreted depends in part on how "globalisation" is conceived. Most scholars see it as a set of interrelated processes inscribed within the structures of the operating system based on capitalist modes of global production. Others, however, conceive of it not in structural terms but as the outcome of a consciously pursued strategy, the political project of a transnational capitalist class, and formed on the basis of an institutional structure set up to serve and advance the interests of this class.

We have here a major divide in analysis and theoretical perspective. On the one hand, those who view globalisation as a set of interrelated processes tend to see it as inevitable, something to which necessary adjustments can and should be made. This is even the case for analysts like Keith Griffin on the left of a well-defined ideological divide within the field of development studies, a well-known proponent of "human development" as defined by the United Nations Development Programme (UNDP) and a declared advocate of radical change or social transformation. From the inevitability-of-globalisation perspective, the issue is how a particular country, or group of countries, can adjust to change in the world economy and insert themselves into the globalisation process under the most favourable conditions. Griffin, for one, believes that such integration and adjustment is both necessary and possible. The issue, he argues, is how the forces driving the globalisation process can be harnessed to serve the requirements of human development.

On the other hand, those who view globalisation as a class project rather than as an inevitable process tend to see the changes associated with it differently. In the first place, "globalisation" is regarded as not a particularly useful term for describing the dynamics of the project. It is seen, rather, as we do – as an ideological tool used for prescription rather than accurate description. In this context it can be counterposed with a term that has considerably greater descriptive value and explanatory power—imperialism.

Using this concept, the network of institutions that define the structure of the new global economic system is viewed not in structural terms, but as intentional and contingent, subject to the control of individuals who represent and seek to advance the interests of a new international capitalist class. This class, it is argued, is formed on the basis of institutions that include a complex of some 37,000 transnational corporations (TNCs), the operating units of global capitalism, the bearers of capital and technology and the major agents of this order, which also include the World Bank, the International Monetary Fund (IMF) and other international financial institutions (IFIs) that constitute the self-styled "international financial community", or what Barnet and Cavenagh prefer to call "the global financial network". In addition, the New World Order is made up of a host of global strategic planning and policy fora such as the Group of Seven (G-7), the Trilateral Commission (TC) and the World Economic Forum (WEF); and the state apparatuses in countries at the centre of the system that have been restructured so as to serve and respond to the interests of global capital. All of these institutions form an integral part of the new imperialism–the new system of "global governance".

From this alternative perspective, "globalisation" is neither inevitable nor necessary. Like the projects of capitalist development that preceded it–modernization, industrialization, colonialism and development–the new imperialism is fraught with contradictions that generate forces of opposition and resistance and that can, and under certain conditions will, undermine the capital accumulation process as well as the system on which it depends. The recent crisis of the Asian economies (of Indonesia, South Korea, Thailand, Malaysia, etc) was deeply rooted in their integration into the world's financial markets and the highly volatile movement integration into the world's financial market and the highly volatile movement of international capital.

Globalists emphasize the constraints placed on government policy or the action of social group, the strategies pursued by diverse social organizations and the possibility of significant of substantial (systemic) change.

Critics of globalisation, on the other hand, emphasize the opportunities and emergence of social forces for change provoked by the social contradictions of the imperialist system–development that chronically disrupts all areas of life under capitalism. At issue in this controversy are the conflicting interests at play, the forces of opposition and resistance generated, and the practical political possibilities for mobilizing these forces.

The "inevitability" of globalisation is a critical issue. But a more critical issue, perhaps, is what the discourse on globalisation is designed to hide and obfuscate: the form taken by imperialism in the current, increasingly world wide capitalist system for organizing economic production and society."

OPPORTUNITIES

The proponents and executors of globalisation have been claiming that the process unveils tremendous opportunities for the developing world through integrating those economies with the international economies. The integration helps acquire more access to the markets of the developed world for the producers of goods and services from the developing world, they claim. Based on the philosophy of trade as engine of growth, the globalisation supporters advocate every economy to embark on trade and export-oriented path.

The arguments in favour of globalisation have been succinctly recapitulated in a report by Werner Sengenberger:

> "Standard economic wisdom tells us that globalisation enriches every participating country. Net gains accrue from economic integration, even though within a country there may be winners and losers. With liberalized foreign trade and investment, funds will flow to the poor countries where capital is scarce, and hence, the return on investment will be higher than in the developed industrialized countries. Capital inflows may come in the form of loans or portfolio investment, supplementing domestic savings and loosening the financial constraint on national public budgets and on additional investment by local companies. Or they may take the form of foreign direct investment (FDI), which is expected to bring about greater efficiency as a result of more intense competition, trade specialization in accordance with local comparative advantages and the transfer of technology and superior management techniques. If a developed country that produces skill intensive products trades with a less developed country producing commodities with low skill content, both countries are said to benefit. According to the

standard economic theory on trade – first developed by David Ricardo, and more recently elaborated in the Heckscher-Ohlin and the Stolper-Samuelson theorems – trade will entail factor cost equalization which will diminish the economic disparities between nations and eventually let them converge at the same level of income."

During the last two decades, the arguments in favor of globalisation have made at least five claims:

1. Globalisation is about the liberalisation and global integration of markets.
2. Globalisation is inevitable and irreversible.
3. Nobody is in charge of globalisation.
4. Globalisation benefits everyone.
5. Globalisation furthers the spread of democracy in the world.

CHALLENGES

The opponents of globalisation are spread across a wide spectrum—from the extreme right wing national exclusivists to the extreme left anti-imperialists. People like former World Bank official Joseph Stiglitz, former IMF official Davison Buddhoo, trader in global financial markets George Soros, Nobel economist Amartya Sen have also expressed discontent over the way globalisation is pursued along with parliamentary left, Greens, Marxist rebels from Mexico to the US, and Europe to India. Various kinds of NGOs also joined the bandwagon of anti-globalisation. The anti-globalisation protests have grown in strength and were able to scuttle or weaken the process of globalisation.

The critics of globalisation have refuted each of these claims with substantial data. They argued that globalisation has not integrated the global markets but helped the rich nations and TNCs to the detriment of the growth of poor nations and marginalized communities. Stating that the present globalisation process is nothing but a new name for imperialist domination, the critics argued that it is neither inevitable nor irreversible. Refuting the claim that there is nobody dictating globalisation, the critics have shown that how the process was initiated by rich nations and MNCs and forced it on the vulnerable third world governments. Demonstrating the volume of resource transfer and spread of the markets, critics have argued that the process is not a win-win for everybody but substantially benefits MNCs and their collaborators in the third world. The critics have also punctured the claim that globalisation helps democracy grow by showing a number of examples where the globalisation forces strengthened military dictatorships and undemocratic governments.

GLOBALISATION'S PRESCRIPTION TO INDIA

In the context of Indian economic reforms, globalisation or liberalisation is defined by a commentator as consisting of the following key features. Though the analysis is dated and needs some revision, it is worth mentioning:

- **Liberalising the financial markets** through deregulation and allowing speculators a free hand in our stock and foreign exchange market. Although Capital Account Convertibility has been shelved for the moment after the South East Asian disaster, the government is unwilling to change the course of financial liberalisation. The demand for autonomy of the Reserve Bank of India has to be seen in this context.
- **Liberalisation of trade** with lifting of quantitative restrictions on a large number of importables including agricultural products and luxury items. While this move has an adverse impact on the domestic economy, export-oriented agriculture under the liberalized trade regime is further threatening our food security. It is also to be noted that our export performance has remained far from being satisfactory in the post reform period.
- **Roll back of the state** from the productive sectors and aggressive privatization of public sector enterprises. The higher growth rates which were expected to follow from

greater private sector participation and increased efficiency in the post reform period has remained elusive. Industrial growth has widely fluctuated throughout the '90s with periods of stagnation and unemployment has been increasing. While the loss making public sector was castigated for inefficiency and being a burden on the state exchequer, those that are being privatized are the most profitable blue chip ones like GAIL, ONGC, Indian Oil, etc.

- **Paranoid over fiscal deficits** and unjustifiable fiscal restraint. While the government's spending on crucial areas is being cut back, huge tax concessions are being given to private business and foreign capital. On the other hand, despite having surplus stocks of foodgrains, the government refuses to provide any fiscal stimulus for generating employment or eradicating poverty.
- **Retreating from the path of self-reliant development**. Strategic sectors like power, telecommunications, insurance and banking are being opened up to private participation including foreign investments. Apart from a rise in the cost of these services which would necessarily follow privatization, the implication for our self-reliance and developmental needs are also grave. The government has also virtually absolved itself from the responsibility of building infrastructure, especially for rural development.
- **Attacks on the livelihood of the poor** through de-subsidization. While the growth of food output is precariously low the government is out to cut back subsidies on essentials. The hike in prices of food and fertilizers while poverty is once again on the rise in our country would further marginalize the poor who are already on the brink of their subsistence.
- **The erosion of the social sectors**. The negligence of the social sectors is too stark to be mentioned. The state of human development in a country with millions of illiterates, malnourished and ailing people cannot be

improved without active government intervention. Economists, as distinguished as Prof. Amartya Sen, have been at pains to convince policy makers to step up investment in health and education in our country. However, the government does precious little except paying lip service to the cause. The privatization of higher education considering it as a non-merit good is another retrograde policy, which undermines the intellectual self-reliance of the country.

A HISTORICAL PERSPECTIVE ON GLOBALISATION

To quote the highly respected authority on imperialism Harry Magdoff: "By the end of 1990, foreign direct investment–that is, investment in manufacturing, real estate, raw materials extraction, financial institutions, etc., made by capitalists of all lands outside their national borders–reached over $1.5 trillion. Actually, this official estimate grossly understates the case because it is based on book values. But even as a minimum estimate, what is significant about this number is not only its size but the unprecedented speed with which it has grown in the last two decades: the amount directly invested in foreign lands nearly tripled in the 1980s alone. Moreover, this investment went far beyond manufacturing and the extraction of raw materials. To an ever larger extent foreign capital spread to such fields as finance, real estate, insurance, advertising, and the media.

This upsurge and diversification of globalisation has been introducing new economic and political features in the countries of both the periphery and the core. In the periphery, foreign capital has penetrated more widely and deeply than ever before. In the core, the change of direction has helped produce in the world's key money markets an extraordinary spiralling of credit creation, international flows of money capital, and speculation.

This new stage of globalisation has meanwhile given rise to questions about its longer-run significance. A widely accepted theory visualizes the erosion of national sovereignty at the centres of capitalism, presumably to be replaced by an "international" of capital that will make and enforce the rules of international relations. The more thoughtful members of the ruling capitalist class are well aware how chimerical the notion of a rising international of capital is. It is true that in view of the growing complexity and the many pitfalls in the world of global finance, they seek ways to strengthen, or create new, international institutions which can help minimize the potential chaos they face. But as much as the need is understood in the abstract, and as many steps as have been taken in the hope of greater cooperation, there is no let up in the drive of nations to acquire more power and wealth. The upshot is that the speeded-up globalisation of recent years has not led to harmony. On the contrary, it is itself a product of growing disharmony. Contrary to widespread expectations, sources of tension among the leading capitalist powers have increased side by side with their growing interdependence. Nor has the geographic spread of capital reduced the contradictions between the rich and poor nations. Although a handful of third world countries, benefiting from the globalisation process, have made noteworthy progress in industrialization and trade, the overall gap between core and periphery nations has kept on widening.

For the sake of perspective, it is worth recognizing that the recent splurge in globalisation is part of an ongoing process with a long history. To begin with, capitalism was born in the process of creating a world market, and the long waves of growth in the core capitalist countries were associated with its centuries-long spread by conquest and economic penetration. In the past as in the present, competitive pressures, the incessant need for capital to keep on accumulating, and the advantages of controlling raw material sources have spurred business enterprise to reach beyond its national borders. The tempo and nature of expansion has of course varied over time, influenced by change in political and economic conditions and the available technology for making war, transporting goods, and communicating.

While the expansion of capitalism has always presupposed and indeed required cooperation among its various national components–with respect to transportation facilities, weights and measures, monetary and credit arrangements, etc.–there never has been a time when these same national components ceased to struggle each for its own preferment and advantage. Centrifugal and centripetal forces have always coexisted at the very core of the capitalist process, with sometimes one and sometimes the other predominating. As a result, periods of peace and harmony have alternated with periods of discord and violence. Generally, the mechanism of this alternation involves both economic and military forms of struggle, with the strongest power emerging victorious and enforcing acquiescence on the losers. But uneven development soon takes over, and a period of renewed struggle for hegemony emerges."

"The internationalisation of finance capital is a notably distinguishing attribute of the modern globalisation process. It is true that between the last quarter of the nineteenth century and the start of the First World War, European money markets, and most especially the City of London, experienced an hitherto unheard of degree of internationalization. But looking backward, one can see that international financial markets were then still only in their infancy. By the 1980s, under the impact of changing economic and political pressures, and assisted by new electronic and communication technology, a totally new stage of global finance had emerged–one with "the freest-flowing and most sophisticated (that is, complicated) financial markets the 'world has ever known...Currencies, commodities, government and corporate bonds all are now issued and traded around the clock and around the world."

GLOBALISATION–AN INDIAN ANALYSIS

'Globalisation' is basically a crisis-management programme to retrieve the imperialist economies from the recurrent recessions hitting them. After the post-World War II boom, the Oil Shock of 1973 shook the world capitalist system...and since then, the tremors in the economy continue to recur. Simultaneously, the US' involvement and defeat in Vietnam and the resulting devaluation of the dollar led to the collapse of the Bretton Woods agreement of fixed exchange rates. In quick succession it faced two more severe crises, in 1980-81 and an even more severe crash in 1991-92. Though there have been intermittent and partial recoveries, the overall depression is only deepening, as can be seen by the 1997 events in South-East Asia and then Russia, the decade-long stagnation in Japan, the complete crash in the economies of Argentina, Ecuador, Turkey and now Brazil, and the ongoing recession in the major economies of the world.

'Globalisation', 'neo-liberalisation', etc. are the imperialist answers to the crisis–that is, a restructuring of their economies in order to face the crisis. It has two basic aspects: first, to restructure capitalism by a wave of mergers and acquisitions to form bigger conglomerates, and to increase surplus value (profit) through massive attacks on the working classes in their home countries. Second, by an aggressive expansion of their market abroad, with greater controls over their wealth and cheap labour resources. Though it is the second factor that affects backward countries like India, the two are inter-related and inter-dependent.

First, the question of restructuring. In the home countries of the imperialists, the massive wave of Mergers and Acquisitions, creating ever more gigantic conglomerates, has resulted in the elimination of smaller and weaker industries. The M&A wave, which is now slightly reduced, had, two years back, reached the astronomical figure of over $1 trillion a year. Through this process, the bourgeoisie was able to get over the immediate effects of the crisis. First, faced by shrinking markets (and over-production) it was able to extend its markets by capturing those of the company acquired; second, the large stock of accumulated capital, which was unable to find an outlet in new (or expanded) production due to shrinkage of the market, was now utilized (in the acquisition of the other company/companies). And third, through mergers, 'rationalization' of production was achieved by introduction of high technology and big cuts in labour–thereby restoring the falling rate of profits. Together with this restructuring of their capital and production, there was a simultaneous attack on the working class–through huge cuts in the labour force, de facto wage freeze, big utilization of part-time and contract labour, extension of hours of work, outsourcing of production to low wage areas, gigantic cuts in government's social welfare, etc.–resulting in not merely restoration of the rate of falling profits, but in a windfall increase in profits.

Now, the second aspect of 'Globalisation'–the aggressive expansion of their market and tighter control over the backward countries, and also many of the ex-socialist states. With the collapse of Soviet Social Imperialism, much of its markets throughout the third world had been replaced by the Western (and Japanese) imperialists. Besides, the markets of the ex-Soviet Union and East Europe too opened out to them. With the collapse of China and a setback in the international communist movement, not only has the Chinese market been opened to imperialist loot, but an aggressive policy of hegemony and domination of the underdeveloped countries of the world is being adopted, to enhance the existing loot ten-fold. In these backward countries, under the banner of 'globalisation', TNCs are gobbling up large parts of private industry, public sector industries, finance, banking and insurance, small scale industry and also their natural resources (agriculture and mining). Trade is becoming even more distorted, leading to a huge invisible out-flows of wealth to the imperialist countries. And enormous manipulations on the financial markets have led to windfall profits to international speculators, while simultaneously destroying local currencies and stock markets.

These then, are the two major aspects of globalisation. The second is being facilitated by the governments and ruling classes of the backward countries, who, acting as conscious betrayers of their country's interests, are introducing extensive reforms in policies, laws, regulations, rules etc. in order to allow this brazen robbery.

And so it is with India. It matters little which government is ruling at the Centre or in the States, all have been prostrating before their new god–the Dollar...So we find 'globalisation' of the Indian economy taking place at break-neck speed.

Besides, the imperialist system had been in a state of continuous crisis since the two oil shocks of the 1970s. The crisis deepened in the 1980s. Drastic solutions were sought. This resulted in the three-pronged attack already mentioned–that is, an attack on the working-class in their own country to increase the rate of exploitation and raise profits through what came to be known as Reganomics and Thatcherism; next, a massive reorganization of capital through an unheard of wave of Mergers & Acquisitions (M&A), whereby big capital became giant in size; and third, a new offensive against the backward countries of the world, to further extend their markets, seize more and more sources of cheap raw materials, and increase their loot ten-fold.

By the late 1980s and early 1990s, it was this latter phenomenon that came to be called globalisation. 'Globalisation' is nothing but a nice-sounding word for the ruthless offence of international finance capital on the backward countries of the world. Earlier, the colonialists termed their despotism as the civilizing rule of the whites over the darks. Today, these new colonizers have their own Rudyard Kiplings, in the form of the Fukuyama's End of History, that give a sense of inevitability to the new form of banditry. Besides, the vast leaps in technology, bringing world-wide events to every home through out the world by means of TV and Internet, gives a false image of the so-called global village. Villages there are, and that too most backward ones throughout the world, but it is the metropolis that dominates and runs them, particularly the US.

The already weakened economies of the backward countries through decades of colonial and neo-colonial loot were utilized to batter them further in the name of 'aid'.

Their battering ram was the IMF-World Bank combine (later the WTO), which bulldozed these economies with Structural Adjustment Programmes (SAPs). So, India too, caught in a Balance of Payments crisis, first in 1981, and again in 1991, also fell into the trap. And as our 'leaders' keep repeating, there has been no looking back to the economic reforms since initiated, no matter which party is in power at the Centre or in the States. In the name of globalisation, international finance capital, particularly that of the US, has, in just this decade, increased its octopus-like grip, not only over all spheres of the Indian economy, but also over every aspect of the socio-political life of the country.

FOCUS OF THE SEMINAR

Having stated the two sides of the coin, this seminar attempts to throw light on both the diametrically opposite viewpoints to arrive at a reasonably substantial conclusion. As already noted, it is a difficult process, but then the seminar, with contributions from learned scholars, would like to present as many and diverse viewpoints as possible, to have wider understanding. Since the subject is so vast, the seminar is attempting to take it up in the following four sub-themes:

(a) Macro-economic, financial and trade sectors

(b) Agriculture, industry, services, resources and technology

(c) Impact of international institutions on socio, economic, cultural and political sectors. Impact of globalisation on workers, peasants, weavers, middle class, women, children, dalits, tribals, minorities and other social groups. And the impact of globalisation on equity and justice, language, literature, people's arts, media and culture, human rights, democracy, national laws and governance, national sovereignty and imperialism.

(d) Emerging issues: biotechnology, genetic engineering, and GM crops, food security, safety and nutrition, application in agriculture, industry and pharmaceuticals, ecology and environments.

MACRO-ECONOMIC ISSUES, FINANCIAL AND TRADE SECTORS

The seminar would like to discuss the issues of the economy at the national macro level which include growth of GDP, trends in per capita, trends in exports and imports, inflow of foreign direct investment, fiscal aspects like budget allocations and deficit, infrastructure building, balance of trade, foreign exchange reserves, banking sector reforms, financial markets, capital and current account convertibility, etc.

AGRICULTURE, INDUSTRY, SERVICES, RESOURCES AND TECHNOLOGY

Globalisation policies, as discussed above, have resulted in significant changes in various social and economic sectors including agriculture, industry, services, resources and technology. Any of these sectors has witnessed thorough transformation during the last 15 years. Changes that occurred in each of these fields could be studied in detail and already various scholars have generated thought-provoking literature.

IMPACT ON AGRICULTURE

The imperialist grip on India's agriculture, as on other sector of the economy, is tightening. Falling yields of foodgrains and their soaring prices, the ever-rising costs of production, the ecological and environmental damage, the erosion of genetic wealth, the making of food a play-thing in the speculative international market, the pauperization of large masses of peasants, the stark reality of more hunger and more malnutrition – all these and more, the prices the people are paying for the policies which India's ruling classes are pursuing to serve imperialist masters and to serve themselves.

IMPACT ON INDUSTRY

A 1999 report of the most authoritative source on Indian business and economy, Centre for Monitoring the Indian

Economy (CMIE) said, "TNCs are on an M&A rampage. Almost all the major sectors of the economy have witnessed the entry of TNCs. Instead of setting up fresh Greenfield capacities, they have preferred to either acquire existing companies or existing capacities. An increasing number of Indian corporates unable to withstand the fiercely competitive environment, have found an easy and lucrative way out by selling their assets to the TNCs....Eight years since the reforms had set in, we see the sell-out to the TNCs as the fastest and most significant 'globalisation' of the Indian business houses."

Major effects of globalisation on agriculture can be seen in:

(i) Forced opening up of the Indian market to agricultural imports;

(ii) Further reduction in the already abysmally low investments in agriculture;

(iii) Wrecking of food security approach in agricultural production; and

(iv) Dismantling of public sector procurement and price support operations and public distribution.

As a result of globalisation, Indian industry has seen:

(i) Public sector disinvestment and de-industrialization;

(ii) Massive unemployment;

(iii) Threat to small scale and indigenous industrial segments;

(iv) Collabourations, mergers and acquisitions to make Indian industrial class into comprador; and

(v) Creating huge market for TNCs.

Service sector will be impacted in the following way with globalisation:

(i) Banking, insurance, aviation, communication, will be thrown open for TNCs.

(ii) Media, advertising, culture, entertainment industries will be dominated by foreign values and capital.

(iii) Local and indigenous service segments will be throttled.

Indian resources and technology will be either rendered useless or commoditized to bring profits to MNCs.

IMPACT ON WORKERS

In order to maximise the profits of TNCs and their local partners, the globalisation process had aimed its attack on working class in particular. Liberalisation of labour laws and the formal and informal introduction of Exit policy and various retrenchment, retirement policies, right to hire and fire at will for the employers, contract labour policies, piece-rate and putting out methods instead of wage rate and regular employment have been introduced as part of globalisation. Even the World Bank documents in the early 1990s stipulated that "giving companies greater freedom to make investments, enter new lines of production and expand, may be of only modest effect, if firms are not concurrently given greater freedom to adapt to market forces by retrenchment, merger and/or closure and sale of assets."

IMPACT ON PEASANTS

A large number of peasants have committed suicides in the Indian countryside beginning from the later part of the 1990s when the full impact of globalisation became pronounced. The tying up of Indian agriculture with the international market and forcing or luring Indian farmers to grow export-oriented marketable crops for the benefit of international agri-business companies led to vulnerability of Indian peasants. As a result, Indian peasant was unable to withstand the huge cost involved in growing such crops and market failures. Already Indian farmer was dependent on vagaries of weather and then the rapid fluctuations of market prices was added to the farmer's woes. The new WTO regime forced the Indian farmer to compete on equal terms with the giant agri-business corporations of the world. Whatever small subsidy Indian farmer used to get was withdrawn or reduced. All the input prices have gone up. The poor and landless peasants have also been marginalized further by globalisation and corporate and contract farming started to swallow their lands.

IMPACT ON WEAVERS

The major thrust of the government in the context of neo-liberal reforms has been on orienting the handloom sector to the globalisation process as a principal strategy for its survival. What is in the process lost sight of is the strength of the handloom sector, which lies in the acceptance of and demand for its products in the local market. The specificity and specialty of handloom products is largely determined by the local needs governed by the local traditions and customs. The community skills, techniques involved in different stages of production are historically evolved and are the property of the community, owned and imparted communally. For this reason, the handloom production is characterized by its region-specific diversity. Thus, it cannot be reduced to or understood only in terms of abstract demand and supply principle of market.

The recurrent crises in the handloom weaving sector due to globalisation process have led to destabilization of the entire segment that is the second largest occupation in India. The crises resulted in starvation deaths and suicides of hundreds of weavers across the country.

The most visible victims of the economic policies launched as part of the liberalisation drive are those sections of society who are disorganised and whose community support base is weak. The plight of handloom weavers is illustrative to the unfolding grim prospect for the vulnerable communities in our society. Their fragmentation in such that in spite of the fact that they have been victims of the greed of master weavers, traders and moneylenders and the apathy of the state, the weavers have remained mute spectators to the crisis they are in. Even when they have undertaken certain forms of collective action, sporadically and locally, the dominant interests in the handloom sector, closing their ranks, have seen to it that the brittle organization gets broken.

IMPACT ON MIDDLE CLASS

Globalisation has affected middle class both positively and adversely. While a section of the middle class was able to grab the opportunities thrown by globalisation and began chasing dollars and dreaming and achieving upward mobility, vast sections of middle class began feeling the pinch of globalisation. They lost their employment in government, quasi-government and PSUs. They had to face retrenchments, lay-offs, wage cuts, DA freeze, scrapping of bonus payments, etc. While the employed middle class had these shocks, the number of unemployed among the middle classes began bulging. On the other hand, consumerism fostered by TV and other media raised the aspirations among the middle class resulting in a huge gap between the reality and aspirations. This situation has led to socially explosive situations, at times resulting in rise suicides and crime due to desperation.

IMPACT ON WOMEN

With globalisation, women have been marginalized further, patriarchal values are sought to be strengthened, commodification of women increased and their second-rate citizen status has further deteriorated. The decreasing job opportunities and massive retrenchments have pushed women back to their homes. Increasing economic hardships added to the enormous burden of looking after home. The rise of media and creating woman icons have led to consumerist culture resulting in looking at woman more as a commodity rather than a human being.

IMPACT ON DALITS

Thanks to globalisation, the small gains made through reservations have been reversed. While employment itself is diminishing, there is no scope for getting a just and proper share in employment. Bulk of the dalits are landless and land reforms is a key question for their development. But globalisation has not only avoided the agenda of land reforms but also it has substituted it with corporatisation of farming for global agricultural market by agri-business corporations. With privatization of education, dalits lost their right to have a good education.

IMPACT ON TRIBALS

As with the dalits, the systematic cuts in welfare expenditure, the privatization of public sector, drop in investment in agriculture, dismantling of the PDS, etc have hit the tribals very hard. With nothing to turn back to and with no money even for medicine, thousands of tribals, including a large number of children, are dying of starvation, malnutrition and simple diseases. In order to give the forest resources and mineral resources to the TNCs, the governments have been denotifying tribal areas and offering vast forest areas to foreign companies and their partners. Laws of the land that protect tribals and their land rights are being repealed and tribals are further pushed into interior forests.

IMPACT ON MINORITIES

The obtaining economic situation naturally leads to fascism and instigating enmity against religious minorities is a part and parcel of the fascist trend. Further, since the globalisation forces world wide are spreading Islamophobia across the globe, their prejudices and class interests have combined with the ruling class interests in India also. Gujarat carnage is but one example of how globalisation forces and Hindutva forces can join hands against minorities.

FOOD SECURITY

While starvation deaths are closely related to the policies of distribution and food security, farmers' suicides are closely related to the policies of agricultural production and procurement. Starvation is basically a crisis of the distribution system. Starvation can be eradicated only by providing the poor with increased access to food, ensuring food security, offering employment opportunities, increasing wages and thus, eradicating poverty. As the crisis is all pervading, the processes of production and distribution cannot be viewed as watertight compartments. Farmers' suicides and starvation deaths are two sides of the same coin, i.e, agrarian crisis. In the background of increasing crisis in agriculture, we cannot stay away from taking a closer look at a major section, the agrarian and rural labourers who remain the backbone of agriculture on the country.

QUESTIONS THAT BEG FOR ANSWERS

The seminar would attempt to raise, discuss and answer some of the following questions:

- What is the marked difference between the policies adopted before and after globalisation?
- What is the exact point of departure for studying globalisation?
- Where do we locate globalisation in the history of capitalism and imperialism?
- What is the specific nature of the world economy in the post-WWII phase that led to the evolution of globalisation in the late 1970s?
- What is the correlation between the economic policies of Ronald Reagan and Margaret Thatcher on one hand and emergence of globalisation on the other?
- What are the determinants of globalisation policies, both in local and international terms?
- Have the policies helped improve the macro economic situation and financial sector of the developing countries?
- Whom does the global trade favour?

- What is the impact of globalisation on production, distribution, exchange and consumption of various commodities and services?
- What is the effect of globalisation on natural resources, bio-diversity and bio-piracy?
- How globalisation affects ecological balance and environmental safety?
- How does bio-technology, especially genetically modified crops, affect the food safety and livelihood security and sovereignty of nations?
- What are the measures required to face global market forces?
- How the distribution or redistribution of global and national resources takes place under the impact of globalisation?
- How does the new patent mechanism help or harm the interests of farmers of developing countries?
- What happens to the small and medium entrepreneurs in the developing countries with the onslaught of big and major industry from abroad?
- What happens to the artisans and people living on service sector, if foreign companies are allowed free entry into the service sector?
- With the ever growing innovative technologies being imported from outside what will happen to the native talent and exploratory urges?
- What is happening to the democratic governance and sovereignty after the international agencies started imposing their conditionalities?
- How does one relate a host of emerging problems like workers losing their livelihood due to privatization and closure of industrial units in the third world, peasants facing problems in the markets dictated by international price fluctuations, weavers losing their markets due to

the conditionalities of the international agencies, social sector feeling the pinch of lowered budget allocations– to the process of globalisation?

- With the emphasis on an integrated market, which includes uniform culture and language, would there be a threat to the pluralist culture and is cultural diversity endangered?
- Since the post-colonial legislation across the globe had imposed restrictions on colonial economic and political interests, the present globalisation is seeking to liberalize those stringent laws. What will be the effect of the liberalisation on laws of the land? Is it going to lead to recolonisation as some critics suggest?
- Is globalisation with human face an empty phrase or does it have any meaning?
- What are the options before the people of the third world to overcome the difficulties of globalisation?

THE MEANING OF CONTEMPORARY GLOBALISATION

Prabhat Patnaik

"Globalisation" is the term under which imperialism presents itself in its current phase. The term however is a misnomer, since its implicit suggestion, that the degree of freedom of commodity and capital flows of the present epoch is something unprecedented in the history of capitalism, is not tenable. Not that the present epoch is not *sui generis*, but what is unprecedented about it is something altogether different, namely an immense "globalisation" of finance, and a communications revolution which *inter alia* has made such globalisation of finance possible.

Of course, global financial flows themselves are nothing new, and authors like Hilferding, Hobson and Lenin had discussed them at great length for the pre-First World War period. But the present "finance capital" differs from that of the earlier epoch in being detached from its specifically national moorings (and hence not being part of some *national* capitalist strategy), in being also detached from any specific links with industrial capital, and hence representing a highly volatile force buzzing around in quest of speculative gains in a world not marked (thanks perhaps to the immense pressure of this finance capital itself) by any significant barriers to capital movement arising from inter-imperialist rivalries (Patnaik 2000). It is the emergence of this new form of international finance capital, and the "globalisation of finance" brought about by it, which is at the core of the current phase of imperialism.

I

There are two very common misconceptions about this process of globalisation of finance. The first relates to its nature, and the second to its implications. The fact that we speak of a new form of finance capital, and of the associated "globalisation of finance", does not mean that somehow the process of production under capitalism has ceased to be relevant, or that the multinational corporations engaged in production, which used to be so much talked about in the context of imperialism earlier, have become secondary. Lenin (1975; 114-5) had talked of "monopoly" as constituting a "superstructure" on old capitalism, giving rise to a "mosaic reality". In the same vein we can talk of the new world of finance capital as constituting a "superstructure" erected on the earlier structure of monopoly capitalism giving rise to a "mosaic reality". The MNCs have not ceased to be important; they have become enmeshed with this world of finance, with the process of globalisation of finance, with the quest for speculative profits, and with the quest for the cheap acquisition of assets all over the world as a result of this "financialisation" process. (The case of ENRON, a huge MNC whose executives over-reached themselves in their speculative activities, underscores the point). To talk in the old vein of MNCs as the key actors in contemporary imperialism, as if nothing had changed since the decade of the sixties, would be wrong. To talk of MNCs as if they themselves had remained unchanged in their attitudes and behaviour would be equally erroneous. And not to talk of MNCs at all on the grounds that all that mattered today was purely speculative finance capital would be even more wrong. We have to talk about a new "mosaic reality" where globalisation of finance is superimposed on the older, pre-existing capitalism, and the new form of international finance capital that presides over this process is not an entity separate from the MNCs but one with which they are enmeshed.

The second misconception lies in the belief that for any economy, especially a third world economy, opening up to this globalisation is good for growth. This belief, in the case of the third world, is sustained by the argument that the international mobility of capital in the current epoch results in a migration of capital from the "North" to the "South", setting up productive enterprises in the latter and overcoming, at long last, the phenomenon of uneven development in the world economy which had arisen precisely because labour, traditionally, *could* not move from the South to the North while capital, traditionally, *would* not move from the North to the South. This earlier reluctance of capital to move from the North to the South, despite the lower wages prevailing in the latter (and hence despite the greater profitability of locating production in the latter) is apparently being overcome at last. And several pronouncements emanating from the North (including of late from Senator John Kerry, the Democratic Presidential candidate in the US) buttress this feeling that globalisation is at last overcoming the North-South dichotomy historically associated with capitalism, by ushering in more rapid growth in the South.

The mistake here lies in confusing the mobility of finance for the mobility of productive capital. Notwithstanding what people like John Kerry have to say, the mobility of productive capital from the North to the South continues to be extremely limited. (Even in the case of China, the usually-cited "success story" for productive capital inflows, the bulk of such inflows are from overseas Chinese, and not from the "North", strictly speaking). There are no doubt individual micro instances of such mobility which is what people like Kerry seize upon, but in macro terms the magnitude of productive capital movement from the North to the South (of which DFI inflows, *other than in the form of take-overs or conversion of debt into equity*, would be the appropriate index) is still limited. When we additionally consider the fact that not all fresh DFI inflows are necessarily growth-promoting (indeed such DFI which merely substitutes for the domestic investment that would have occurred in its absence, is likely to be growth-reducing, since it constitutes an implicit form of de-industrialization), it is clear that the gains in terms of higher growth in the third world from opening up to the globalisation process, would, from this source at any rate, be rather meagre.

On the other hand, however, opening up to globalized *finance* has a distinctly growth-retarding effect, since it invariably brings in its train a process of deflation of the economy via reduced State expenditures (U. Patnaik 2002). Finance capital is always opposed to an "activist State" in matters of employment and welfare promotion. But when finance capital is globalized and the State continues to be a nation-State, its opposition acquires a spontaneous effectiveness: any State that dares to be activist, overriding the opposition of finance capital, would find itself confronting a capital flight, with adverse consequences for the economy. To avoid these consequences and hence to prevent possible capital flight, the States make every attempt to ensure that the "confidence of the investors" in the economy, which basically is an euphemism for the "confidence of the speculators", is not undermined. And they do so by eschewing any activist role in employment promotion, and subjecting the economy to a deflationary process which reduces the growth rate.

The opposition of finance capital to State activism in employment promotion cannot be explained by any legitimate economic fears. True, at high levels of employment and activity, the prospects of inflation loom large, as do the prospects of a significant widening of the current account deficit of the balance of payments. Both these factors give rise to fears of an exchange rate depreciation which has adverse consequences for the profitability of globalized finance. But such fears do not constitute an adequate explanation. The opposition of finance capital to employment stimulation by the State becomes manifest even when the economy operates at a level of activity which is so low as to rule out any genuine fears about inflation and exchange rate depreciation. (In the late twenties for instance, the British Treasury, under the influence of the City of London which was a major financial centre of the capitalist world, had rejected Lloyd George's proposal for a Public Works programme to overcome unemployment, even though the level of unemployment, at 10 per cent at that time, was already so high that an increase in activity at that juncture could not conceivably cause inflation or depreciation).

The source of the opposition of finance capital to State activism in matters of employment lies elsewhere. Writing in 1943, Michael Kalecki had said that the fact that employment, in the absence of State intervention, depended on the so-called "state of confidence" of the capitalists, gave the latter a "powerful indirect control over Government policy: everything which may shake the state of confidence must be carefully avoided because it would cause an economic crisis. But once the Government learns the trick of increasing employment by its own purchases, this powerful controlling device loses its effectiveness (Kalecki 1971; 139)." State activism on employment in other words undermines the social power, and with it the social legitimacy, of the capitalist class. And if this is true of capitalists engaged in production, then how much more true must this be of the rentier class, whom Keynes (1946) had characterised as the "functionless investor" and which is typified by finance capital?

There is an additional factor. Deflation is typically associated with the selling off of public enterprises at throwaway prices of which the capitalist class in general, and finance capital in particular, are the beneficiaries. Deflation in other words acts as a mechanism of primitive accumulation of capital. When enterprises built out of the savings of the people at large are handed over virtually *gratis* to a few members of the international financial oligarchy, the effect is exactly the same as the direct expropriation of many petty producers by a few capitalists that Marx had captured under the rubric of primitive accumulation. It is instructive that this process of primitive accumulation is sought to be justified by a piece of utterly bogus theorising (based on a complete confusion between stocks and flows) which holds that "disinvestment" is a perfectly legitimate means of closing a fiscal deficit.

Of course, the benefits of deflation for finance capital are not exhausted with this. Since deflation, via the recession it generates, drives several small producers out of business, their assets, or at the very least the space occupied by them, become available to large capitalists, and in particular to finance capital. Needless to say, when assets change hands, they do so usually at throwaway prices.

Deflation enforced by finance capital restricts domestic demand and hence contributes adversely to the pace of economic growth via this channel. It does so in another way as well. Since in the era of globalised finance deflation is a pervasive phenomenon afflicting not just third world countries but those of the advanced capitalist world as well, the entire world capitalist economy experiences relative stagnation, which in turn gets imported into the domestic economies of the third world under the regime of trade liberalisation. For both these reasons third world economies when they open up to "globalisation" in the current epoch experience a retardation of growth rather than acceleration.

The protracted stagnation and double-digit unemployment which the advanced capitalist world has been experiencing, in the decades following the post-war boom aided by Keynesian demand management, the absolute decline in per capita incomes over much of Latin America and Africa over the last two decades, and even the slowing down of the dramatic growth rates, achieved earlier by the East and South East Asian countries, since the beginning of the nineties when they opened themselves up to global financial flows, are all indicative of this profound tendency towards stagnation which characterises the current epoch of "globalisation".

Of course, it may be argued that India and China illustrate the opposite of this claim, since they apparently have witnessed higher growth since opening themselves up to "globalisation". But in the case of China, it is questionable if she has opened herself up to "globalisation", since she is insulated from global financial flows and retains a degree of (implicit if not always explicit) trade restrictions.

In the case of India, which is more open to financial and trade flows, despite not having full capital account convertibility, the growth rate of the material commodity producing sectors has come down since the introduction of economic "liberalisation", and particularly so in the last quinquennium neo-liberal policies had gathered momentum. The high growth claims are based entirely on the performance of the service sector and hence are quite dubious, given the theoretical and statistical problems associated with the growth rate figures of this sector. (Even in the case of China the growth rate figures are likely to represent an exaggeration). Besides, the adverse impact of the openness to globalisation on a range of material indicators impinging on welfare, is quite indubitable in the case of India, as we see below.

II

The impact on employment of this global stagnation, arising from the globalisation of finance, is scarcely ever recognized, especially in the advanced capitalist world, where the accent instead is on the "export of jobs" to the third world. This works to the advantage of international finance capital: while one section of workers, those of the third world, is pitted against another section, those belonging to the first world, the role of international finance capital, the significance of its hegemony, goes completely unnoticed. Both these stances, viz. the promotion of a rift between the workers, and the silence on the hegemony of finance, contribute to a perpetuation of this hegemony.

The view that highlights the "export of jobs" as the primary cause of unemployment would have some credibility if the total number of jobs was incapable of being augmented.

This, however, is far from the case. State intervention of *an appropriate kind* can counter the current deflation and enlarge the level of activity in the world economy as a whole. True, no individual nation-State caught in the vortex of globalised finance, with the exception perhaps of the U.S., can pursue employment-augmenting policies (it can do so only if it ceases to be a part of globalised financial flows by putting restrictions on such flows, for which however it would have to pay a certain price, on which more later, arising from imperialist hostility). The exceptional position of the U.S. arises from the fact that its currency (notwithstanding the recent strength of the Euro) is looked upon wealth-holders everywhere as a stable medium of holding wealth, almost "as good as gold". A capital flight from the U.S., even if its government pursues an expansionary policy, remains an unlikely event (as is being demonstrated now with the widening fiscal deficit under the Bush administration). The U.S. therefore has the capacity to act as a "locomotive", pulling the entire world capitalist economy out of stagnation through the expansionary fiscal policy of its own State. But, from its *national perspective,* the U.S. has little to gain by acting as such a "locomotive", since that would entail a larger *national debt* of the U.S. for the purpose of expanding employment elsewhere in the world. Since the U.S. State cannot rise above its *national perspective*, it cannot, despite its exceptional position, pursue employment-promoting policies *for the capitalist world as a whole*.

But even though an expansionary policy by the U.S. alone for promoting employment in the capitalist world is not likely, a *concerted expansion* by several capitalist States is both possible and can achieve the same end. Indeed even during the great Depression of the 1930s, there were many plans, e.g., the Kindersley, Francqui, ILO and Keynes Plans, which had suggested precisely this, namely a coordinated expansion among a group of leading capitalist countries. The real hurdle to this plan today, as it was during the 1930s, is the opposition of finance capital, expressed above all as an objection to fiscal deficits which a large number of academic economists, journalists and pamphleteers are made to articulate in an ethos where finance capital has ideological hegemony. Thus, the hurdle to employment promotion, and hence the factor underlying persistent and large-scale unemployment, is the hegemony of finance; the argument about "export of jobs" is a convenient camouflage.

We can look at the issue in the following way. There are two very distinct hurdles to the pursuit of employment - promoting policies by States in the current epoch. The first is the fact that finance capital opposes such policies; and the second is the fact that while the States are nation-States, finance capital in today's world is international finance capital. If instead of nation-States there was a global State then the second of these reasons would have ceased to be operative. Since there is no actual global State it would have to be a *surrogate* global State that can at all contemplate pursuing employment-promoting policies for the world economy as a whole. The State of the leading capitalist country, the U.S., though it is capable of acting as such a surrogate global State, *and does play this role in certain respects,* is nonetheless too much of a nation-State to take on the employment-promoting role of a possible global-State. It would therefore, have to be a whole group of nation-States acting in concert that can act as a surrogate global State for purposes of employment-promotion. But even if such a group of nation-States could be persuaded to act in concert to promote global employment, it would still have to confront the opposition of globalised finance capital, i.e. the first hurdle mentioned above. It is not surprising therefore, that globalised finance capital uses a whole gamut of weapons to prevent employment-promoting policies, by an entire group of nation-States acting in concert, from taking effect. And one important weapon is to shift the focus to the so-called "export of jobs" to the third world.

III

Let us now consider the impact of globalisation upon the different classes within a third world society. Deflation reduces the employment opportunities in such an economy, especially within the rural sector, a phenomenon that has occurred in India in the period of neo-liberal reforms, notwithstanding the claims about high growth. Between 1993-04 and 1999-00, the two years of large sample surveys by the NSS, rural employment increased by a mere 0.58 per cent per annum, which was far below the growth of rural population. There was a drop in the work participation rate observed over this period; but this is likely to have been the outcome of the "discouraged worker effect" of higher unemployment, rather than a reflection of any genuine withdrawal of potential workers for purposes such as education. Numerous micro studies also point to a sharp increase in rural unemployment, as does, to a limited extent, the current-daily-status unemployment rate.

Associated with rising unemployment is a restriction on the purchasing power in the hands of the rural population. Ironically, despite a reduction in per capita output of foodgrains in the period since 1990-91, per capita absorption has dropped even more precipitously, so that an average Indian absorbs about the same amount of foodgrains today as he or she did on the eve of the Second World War (U. Patnaik 2004). If the difference between output and absorption even shows itself at the level of the all-India data, then one can legitimately conclude that for rural India it must have been even sharper. The other side of this difference between output and absorption has been a massive increase in food grain stocks (nearly 65 million tonnes prior to the recent drought), which *inter alia* have been dumped on the world market at throwaway prices. This paradox of a country with a huge starving population undertaking massive exports at throwaway prices is a singular contribution of the deflation associated with the neo-liberal policies.

Between 1990-91 and 2003-04 (BE), the ratio of Central government expenditure (including transfers and loans) to GDP at factor cost went down sharply, from 20.54 per cent to 17.41 per cent. This has been a consequence largely of the decline in Central government tax revenue to GDP and also, to a certain extent, of the decline of the ratio of the fiscal deficit to GDP. And one of the sharpest cuts has been in rural development expenditure, which, from being 14 per cent of the GDP on average during the Eighth Plan period, has come down to less than 6 per cent of late.

An argument is often advanced of the following kind: since much of the rural development expenditure, even when intended for the benefit of the rural poor, really gets into the hands of the rural rich, a reduction in it is of little consequence as far as the poor are concerned. This argument is erroneous: it does not take into account the multiplier effects of the government's rural development expenditure. Even when such expenditure is cornered by the rural rich, its multiplier effects generate some employment for the rural poor, and hence are of some indirect benefit to them. To be sure, if the expenditure was not cornered by the rural rich but actually came into the hands of the rural poor, that would be most desirable. But even when this does not happen, expenditure undertaken is still far better than expenditure not undertaken.

Cuts in government expenditure also affect the level of demand for the industrial sector. Together with import liberalisation which in practice has a demand-constricting effect (once the pent-up demand for a variety of hitherto not-available luxury goods is catered to through the setting up of domestic productive capacity with the help of liberalised imports), such cuts precipitate industrial stagnation and recession, affecting especially the small-scale sector. Industrial employment is affected adversely at the same time that the "social wage" is cut, catching the industrial workers in a pincer move. The virtual disappearance of the cotton textile industry in its old centres like Bombay and Ahmedabad, and the absolute impoverishment of lakhs of workers who are thrown out of employment as a consequence, is only one striking illustration of a pervasive phenomenon.

But it is not just the traditional petty bourgeoisie, the small capitalists, and the workers both urban and rural, who become victims of neo-liberal economic policies. The peasantry too, not excluding even the rich peasantry, is pushed into great adversity, which is now getting reflected in a spate of suicides by peasants all over the country. Secular stagnation in the world economy, on account of the pervasively deflationary policies being followed, results in a secular fall in the terms of trade for primary commodities vis-à-vis manufacturing. While the terms of trade fluctuate a great deal from year to year, the trend through these fluctuations is a downward one for primary commodities, especially agricultural products. A second factor, of more recent origin, also contributes to such a decline. And this has to do with the secular depreciation in their real exchange rates which third world countries experience when they enter into the process of financial liberalisation. Let us consider this closely.

Wealth-holders, whether in the first or in the third world, do not generally consider third world currencies as safe mediums for holding wealth, a judgement that does not get altered no matter how much deflation is undertaken in the third world economy to make its currency more attractive. As a result, opening up the economy to free capital flows usually leads to a secular decline in the value of the third world currency as capital slowly drains out of the country; and this decline itself fuels the belief that the currency is not a safe medium for wealth-holding. There are to be sure fluctuations in the real exchange rate with occasional bursts of speculative capital inflow pushing up the currency value, but through these fluctuations the secular trend is downwards. This entails a reduction in the relative values of commodities, typically primary commodities, which these economies export, since the money wages are fixed in terms of the local currencies, providing an additional cause for the adverse movement in their terms of trade.

In India the peasantry had been insulated against a decline in its terms of trade, arising from factors such as those mentioned above, because of the system of public procurement and distribution that had been in place for quite some time. But with liberalisation this system became substantively inoperative. Moreover since there were only a few crops which were covered under this system, the changes in cropping pattern that occurred, as agri-exports gathered momentum under liberalisation, took the peasantry out of the ambit of this system even as world prices were crashing. At the same time, the prices of inputs such as electricity and fertilizers increased as subsidies were sought to be cut in the new deflationary environment; and the entitlement to credit from institutional sources which agriculture enjoyed in the *dirigiste* period disappeared as foreign banks (which were averse to lending to the peasantry) were allowed to operate, and even the domestic nationalised banks were asked to keep an eye on their profits rather than get carried away with "social responsibility". Caught in the grip of these factors, and having to confront, for the first time, multinational seed companies, with their vast monopoly powers buttressed by intellectual property rights enshrined under the WTO, the peasantry experienced an unprecedented squeeze, which necessarily had an impact on other rural classes as well, especially the labourers.

While a vast segment of the population was thus adversely affected by neo-liberal policies, a certain section, consisting of the domestic rentier class, professionals engaged in the burgeoning service sector, a section of the capitalist class that could grab public assets, large capitalists who benefited from the decline of the small producers, the local agents and employees of foreign companies, governments, aid agencies, NGOs, and Bretton Woods institutions, and a whole range of fly-by-night operators, speculators and middlemen mediating the newly opened up and rapidly expanding "foreign connection", gained from the phenomenon of globalisation.

This essential divergence between the fortunes of the many and the fortunes of the few gets camouflaged by two widely-held erroneous perceptions. The first asserts that poverty in the Indian economy has been declining. This is sought to be established by referring to the consumer expenditure figures thrown up by the NSS 55th round. While it is admitted by everybody that the data thrown up by this round are "contaminated", the argument put forward by several economists (with the blessings of the World Bank) states that after proper adjustments are made, a decline in poverty is still quite indubitable. This has been challenged by independent scholars (Sen 2004) who, after careful scrutiny of the data, have concluded that no conclusions can be reached one way or the other on the poverty question with the existing data. A more potent line of attack questions the very methodology of existing poverty estimates. Since the "poverty line" criterion was meant only as a surrogate for a calorie norm (in terms of which basically poverty is defined in India), and since calorie absorption data are directly available, there is no reason to go through the rigmarole of updating the poverty line and using the NSS expenditure data to estimate the poverty ratio. It would be far better to go to the point directly and see from calorie absorption data what the percentage population below the calorie norm for poverty would be. On doing this exercise it turns out that this latter percentage exceeds that calculated on the basis of the "poverty line" approach by a huge margin in recent years, which suggests that *any poverty calculation on the basis of consumption expenditures is fundamentally flawed and that poverty as originally defined has, far from coming down, actually increased in the post-liberalisation period*.

The second erroneous perception relates to food absorption. It is argued that the reason for the large accumulation of foodstocks lies in a change in consumption habits of the people entailing a diversification away from foodgrains. It would follow from this that far from being indicative of a decline in living conditions of the mass of the people, the accumulation of foodstocks actually indicates the contrary, namely some improvement in their living standards where they can even afford to enjoy more diversified consumption. The idea that with an improvement in per capita incomes, societies consume less of foodgrains per capita, is utterly wrong. True, they may consume less foodgrains *directly*, but their *indirect* consumption of foodgrains (in processed forms and as inputs for the animal products that are consumed) goes up. Taking direct and indirect consumption together, per capita foodgrain consumption increases with per capita incomes, and is associated with an improvement in the people's living standards. Thus, the per capita foodgrain consumption, taking both direct and indirect consumption together, was nearly a tonne per year in the former Soviet Union. It is close to that figure in the US, and only slightly less in the other advanced capitalist countries. So, when in India we find a decline in per capita total absorption of foodgrains, and that too accompanied by a decline in daily calorie intake, the conclusion is inescapable that there is a squeeze on the population, especially the rural population. The question then arises: how can such a squeeze be sustained, especially in a society characterized by robust electoral politics?

IV

There are at least three safety-mechanisms which international finance capital acquires for itself to ward off any threats to its global dominance. The first has already been mentioned above, namely a division between the workers in the North and those in the South, which ensures not only that there is no global unity among workers against globalised capital, but also that any potential challenge to the hegemony of finance capital within the North itself is warded off by placing the blame for the economic ills upon a distant group of hapless workers.

The second, briefly mentioned earlier, consists in the fact that any stepping out of a neo-liberal regime entails costs of transition which are so large that most political formations within any country do not have the strength to undertake it. Even the prospects of a political formation with an alternative agenda coming to power triggers off capital flight, an exchange rate depreciation resulting in inflation (to the detriment of the very masses in whose interests the alternative agenda was conceived to start with), and a threat of bankruptcy. All this is quite enough to unnerve the political formation that had dared to espouse an alternative agenda; it usually falls in line by declaring that it too is "pro-reform", that it too is full of the best possible intentions towards "foreign investors".

Sometimes however a political formation with an alternative agenda may come to power unexpectedly. In such a case, even if it is intrepid enough to put in place immediate capital controls to ward off capital flight, it would still have to deal with the issue of inherited foreign debt which has to be rolled over; and such rolling over becomes impossible without the "co-operation" of international finance capital, the Bretton Woods institutions and the States of the advanced capitalist countries, especially the "super-imperialist" US State. But even if the new domestic government carries its intrepidity several steps further by announcing a unilateral debt moratorium, or even if the debt overhang is not significant enough to cause much worry for the new government, nonetheless any departure from the neo-liberal agenda brings retaliation from the entities just mentioned. Together with this comes a clamour of criticism, from those with vested interests in neo-liberalism, from "intellectuals" serving these interests, and from the media both domestic and foreign (which in any case have come very close to finance capital in the current epoch), about declining living standards of the people (which, even if true, is caused by imperialist retaliation itself), about the unwisdom of the "doctrinaire" economic policies being pursued by the government, about "violation of human rights", and about alleged tales of "nepotism" and "corruption". These are sometimes made into excuses for imposing sanctions (pushed through a pliant Security Council) and, in the last analysis, for armed intervention, by proxy or even directly.

The third mechanism springs from the divisions among the people of a third world country that the pursuit of a neo-liberal trajectory of development inevitably generates. The impoverishment of the people creates conditions where different sections among them often struggle against one another even more fiercely, as has been happening in many parts of Africa, of which Sudan is the latest example. The tragedy of this fierce struggle for dwindling means of livelihood, is portrayed by the so-called "liberal" opinion (especially when the regime concerned is not a client of imperialism), only as an instance of "bloody-mindedness" leading to "genocide" which it is the "White Man's Burden" to put an end to. Likewise, situations of unemployment, as is well-known, are conducive anyway for the exacerbation of communal, ethnic, religious and racist divisions among the people. Reliance upon the inflow of direct foreign investment for growth also produces secessionist tendencies, and in the process breeds much bitterness among the people, because of the belief that being on its own would enable a region to draw more foreign funds. In short, the epoch of globalisation also generates very strong tendencies towards a fragmentation within the ranks of the deprived, which naturally helps international finance capital consolidate its hegemony.

There is however a further implication of these divisions, namely they are capable of being used by fascist forces to counter the prospects of the coming together of the people against imperialism. Third world societies, especially in the epoch of liberalisation, become sites for a struggle between secular, democratic and egalitarian tendencies on the one hand and fascist tendencies (allied to imperialism) on the other. This may sound strange at first sight, since most *fundamentalist* outfits, especially in the Arab world, are today giving anti-imperialist slogans. *But fascism must not be confused with fundamentalism*; the former is characterised above all by proximity to finance capital and is concerned with making the poor acquiesce in their exclusion rather than rise against the system for overcoming their exclusion, which, by contrast, certain types of fundamentalism advocate, though no doubt in a most inchoate fashion.

We have seen that neo-liberalism works to ensure that those who want a change of trajectory are enfeebled by considerations of the costs of transition. Even when the people vote for a change therefore they continue to remain trapped within the same trajectory. At the most a few verbal concessions are thrown towards them, such as "liberalisation with a human face" but these lead to no substantive changes. But additionally even if perchance a democratic government takes charge which has sufficient courage to embark on a new trajectory, then the fascist elements can always be unleashed upon such a government.

In short, there is a fundamental contradiction between the adoption of neo-liberal policies and the preservation of democratic institutions. We in India are currently witnessing before our very eyes a situation where the democratic compulsion of providing some relief to the poor clashes with the commitment of the new government to the agenda of globalisation. And if this clash leads to a denial of relief then the disillusionment among the people may well work to the benefit of the fascist forces. Fighting domestic fascism and fighting imperialism in other words are part of the same project. And this fight can be carried forward only by uniting the people on a broad front, preparing them for the costs of transition, and working to put in place in all earnestness an alternative development trajectory.

REFERENCES

Chandrashekhar C.P. and Ghosh J. (2002), *The Market That Failed*, Tulika Books, Delhi.

Ghosh J, and Sen A. (1998), "Capital Flows and Macroeconomics: A Historical View" in D.Nayyar ed. *Economics As Ideology And Experience: Essays in Honour of Ashok Mitra*, Cass, London.

Kalecki M. (1971), *Selected Essays on the Dynamics of the Capitalist Economy1933-1970*, Cambridge.

Keynes J.M. (1946), *The General Theory of Employment, Interest and Money*, Macmillan, London.

Kindleberger C.P. (1987), *The World in Depression 1929-1939*, Pelican Books.

Lenin V.I. (1975), *Selected Works* (in 3 Volumes), Vol. 3, Progress Publishers, Moscow.

Patnaik P. (2000), Introduction to V.I. Lenin *Imperialism the Highest Stage of Capitalism*, Leftword Books, Delhi.

Patnaik P. (2002) "Globalisation of Capital and Terms of Trade Movements", in V.K. Ramachandran and Madhura Swaminathan ed. *Agrarian Studies*, Tulika, Delhi.

Patnaik P. (2003), *The Retreat to Unfreedom*, Tulika, Delhi.

Patnaik P., Chandrashekhar C.P., and Ghosh J. (2004), "The Political Economy of the Economic Reform Strategy: The Role of the Indian Capitalist Class" in M. Mohanty ed. *Class, Caste and Gender*, Sage, Delhi.

Patnaik U. (2002), "Deflation and *Déjà vu:* Indian Agriculture in the World Economy", in V.K. Ramachandran and Madhura Swaminathan ed. *Agrarian Studies*, Tulika, Delhi.

Patnaik U. (2004), *The Republic of Hunger*, Sahmat Publication, Delhi.

GLOBALISATION, JUSTICE AND DEVELOPMENT

Kamal Nayan Kabra

I

INTRODUCTION

Every age tries to define itself. It defines itself with such aplomb, self-righteousness and self-indulgence as may make it depart from the reality by a big margin and outdo similar earlier attempts. They are powerful and telling examples of the power of language in the service of specific interests and objectives. The hegemonic power centres are likely to be endowed with notably sharp proclivity to be hyperbolic for a variety of material and socio-psychological reasons. Apart from helping them to win widespread legitimacy and help manage their operations without undue hiccups, such characterisations are used for distinguishing the present from the past and for showcasing it as a distinct improvement contributed by those who are steering the course of development. Such self-definitions may be couched in terms of either an accentuation or extension of some trends already underway, or may represent a sharp break from the prevailing situation. The element of apotheosis in such characterisations fulfils some functional as well as ideological roles. Particularly in situations when the stability and sustainability of the emerging order are contested and face actual or potential threats to their existence, the characterisation is given multifarious, emotive, vague and opaque connotations in order partly to camouflage the real meaning and implications of the way things are organised and managed and partly to use it as an ideological weapon against the opposing forces. Thus it often happens that the overall characterisations of the dominant or desired trends and directions of emerging developments, even amounting to perpetration of a neologisms, become highly wonder many different interpretations of the term appear to be simultaneously valid and operationally relevant controversial. It no longer remains clear whether they are a shorthand, concise description of reality, or such a mixture of reality, value judgements, advocacy of certain lines of policy and action and implicit denunciation of the real and imagined opposition and counteracting forces, or, an amalgam of these all. Little

GLOBALISATION: BEGINNING OF THE STORY

It can be said that the above formulations seem to apply to the present day buzz word globalisation in no small measure The beginning of the 1970s saw the end of the Post-Second War golden era of world-wide capitalist industrial growth. This period's high growth rates under conditions of near full employment and liberal rewarding of the working class in the rich countries was experienced in the wake of the new world order under the aegis of the Brettonwoods arrangements. Certain other factors like the Keynesian macro-economic management, the super-power rivalry based cold war which restrained the unhindered pursuit of narrow national commercial interests by the major trading and financial powers of the world, the growing clout of the trade unions, and the success in making the third world adopt the catching-up mimetic industrialisation as their very own agenda of development too contributed their bit to the high noon of world capitalism. The end of the golden era coincided with the collapse of the on-going attempts to reconcile modern, post-war capitalism with the interests and aspirations of the larger civic society, especially the domestic numerically large social groups like the industrial workers in the early industrialised, rich countries. Much before the existing socialisms fell to pieces towards the end of the 1980s, there occurred the unceremonious disintegration of the welfare, social, regulated capitalisms in the advanced industrialised nations under the onslaught of the Thatcher-Reagan backlash. This extreme, one-sided pursuit of their sectional agenda by the dominant groups and classes in the North went a long way to make the general public believe the neo-classical resurgence in ideology, policy underpinnings and restructuring of the international economic relations as the only viable, historically proven option. With both the attempts to either reform or replace the capitalist world order meeting their waterloo, the neo-classical philosophy and policy regime labelled globalisation seems to be enjoying a free run. Those who link up the present phase of what they christen as globalisation tend to make too much of the death and demise of the Soviet socialism and that of its satellites. They forget that within their own societies a great change of equally, if not of more, momentous proportions took place in the form of the end of liberal, social democratic and accommodative market system This coincided with the counter-revolution in development theory and policy and the beginning of the era of structural adjustment in the image and along the lines of the Washington Consensus. It seems at this stage; a new phase began on the world scene. In order to capture and glorify this change, a relatively obscure and undefined term globalisation started making rounds in popular writings, public discussions as well as in policy councils and academic discourse no less than in many raging controversies in social sciences. The emerging age and its apostles, its commanding forces and interested and disinterested advocates gave themselves and their pursuits, goals, values and dreams a name: globalisation. Ever since then, in fairly explicit manner and from the very outset with a rather torrential speed, it was taken to be the name of what all is happening as also the direction, destination as well as the motor power and means for getting there, the globalised world. Its power, elan, sweep, range, depth, even its antecedents and theoretical foundations and philosophical justification were taken to be self-evident and out they're for every one to see for oneself. It was treated as the end of history and promptly was declared to be irreversible as also something for which, it was claimed, 'there is no alternative'.

The information, communications, electronic and media revolutions were counted among the wellsprings of, or, to be precise, technological enabling factors leading to globalisation. Quite interestingly, these very 'revolutions' were pressed in to the service of globalisation for portraying and propagating it as the supreme reigning reality of our time, and the inescapable destiny and *summum bonum* of the world. Thus an all-embracing category has been found which is believed to have won open or tacit support of so many groups and classes. This is the result of the all-pervading hegemony of the rich countries and their ruling/dominant elite. Globalisation has been lapped up by the dominant and powerful ones, spread across nearly all continents, countries and cultures, who have managed to make it acceptable, with or without reservations, with or without common, shared understanding and a broadly comparable degree of commitment. Even those who would be at the receiving end of these processes of globalisation are often found to fall in line with the dominant view Truly,. at least the term globalisation has been globalised, that is ,at least for the present. Whether in support of it, or in opposition to it, whether as active and predominant beneficiaries of it or its vocal or silent victims, globalisation as the dominant theme of the current global concerns has come to acquire an unprecedented wide currency and central place in the public sphere. It covers fields as diverse as diplomacy or demography, religion or celebrity gossip, ecology or ethnography or entertainment, consumerist indulgence or conservationist moderation, technological leapfrogging and imitation or clinging to primordial identities in brief, name what you will, it is made to relate to variously understood globalisation. Not only the mundane humdrum of daily existence, but even the subtle and sublime creative arts, culture and literature, which had their strong local roots in the lives, living and, inner being and imagination of the masses and had strong localism as their characteristic forte from which spring the deep universal meanings and durability of these endeavours, are today humming the tunes of globalisation; may be with heavy and irrecoverable costs, may be in a state of semi-conscious stupor, but as hard facts of life nevertheless.

Globalisation penetrates the inner essence, motivation and actual operation of national and international politics. With its strong centralisation in the economic, political, military and informational fields, paradoxically, it is supposed to be consistent with the somewhat divergent trends towards more effective federalisation and decentralisation of politics, giving credence to the quip: think global, act local in the interest of good governance. What is often described as a unipolar world is also portrayed by some to be an essential ingredient of globalisation. However, the putative spread of democracy across countries and the pursuit of democratisation of the international institutions, whether inter-governmental or related to international business or that arising from the emerging global civil society institutions are also often supposed to be consistent with the creed of globalisation.In brief, globalisation is among those unique terms which do not have any unique meaning. It is made to encompass a great deal of diversity, differences, antagonistic elements and lack of clarity. Little wonder, it forms a part and parcel of the contemporary and historical inquiries as a real portmanteau category which cuts across paradigms, disciplines, layers and forms of reality, and sharply polarised real, palpable interests and ideologies. Increasingly it has come to be treated as an area of research, advocacy and derision by a whole array of institutions and agencies standing in diametrically opposing, combatant positions. These uncomfortable and confusing aspects of the wildly popular concept of globalisation appear to be both its positive and negative strengths, giving rise to the irony that it does not disappear from academic and practical discourse, because even in the face of theses infirmities and oddities, the debates around it remain both light-bearing and fruit-bearing,

The power, sweep and influence of globalisation are there for every one to see and experience. It is certainly true that the market fundamentalists make use of globalisation for their partisan ends. But to dismiss it as a myth and a figment of the imagination of the market fundamentalists, may be as a reincarnation of some age-old phenomenon, would amount to an ostrich-like refusal to accept globalisation as an objective thought- real which is incredibly influential and is capable of diverse interpretations.

One need not dwell more on the inchoate, diffused and partisan character of globalisation. On the basis of the foregoing, it may be reasonable to infer that there is something about globalisation which enables it to hold a centre stage position. This is so notwithstanding the fact that it is such a complex, multifaceted, vague, opaque, multi-disciplinary concept; that it is mired in the thick of controversies and refers at one and the same time to some major aspects of the putative and extant reality, ideas, policy ensemble as an instrument of ideological mobilisation, centre point of advocacy, derision and denunciation of a particular world–view and solid manifestation of the interests and hegemony of certain forces at the apex of the world's economic, political, military and so-called cultural might. One may simply allude to a variety of alternative ways in which the reality and ideas coming under the rubric of globalisation have been captured by many analysts by using a number of synonyms. These include: corporate capitalism, capitalist world system, neo-liberalism, recolonisation, transnational capitalism, market fundamentalism, globalism ,totalitarian market order, neo-imperialism, free market world, global free market integration, Americanism, hegemony of the USA, North-centric and South-centric globalisation, free and intensified global exchange of ideas, universal brotherhood in the style of *Vasudhaiva Kutumbakam*, etc Evidently, the term globalisation cannot unequivocally and simultaneously convey what all these different but inter-connected terms mean to convey. One wonders whether such vagueness is deliberate and is a factor behind its popularity. What is material is that an analysis of the processes, forces, impact and counter mobilisation against globalisation is capable of taking one around a conducted tour of the major contemporary issues, especially if one is interested in the fate of development of the third world in its external and internal dynamics and what happens to the lofty ideals of enlightenment like democracy, justice, peace, solidarity and widely shared prosperity.

II

NEO-LIBERAL FOUNDATIONS: FACTS AND FICTION

In order to understand the phenomenon of globalisation, we devote some attention to the foundations on which the concept stands. On this basis we proceed to analyse the forces, processes and real life effects produced by it. We make use of the two yardsticks of ensuring national development of the present day weak, poor and exploited countries, and, social justice for those against whom the prevailing social order incessantly operates for the purpose. A common thread seen across all the diverse concepts of globalisation is the large-scale, growing and unhindered free flow of resources, goods and services, ideas, natural and legal persons, financial claims in the form of various old and new instruments characteristic of the present day corpulent and predominant, financial sector across national boundaries, whether in fact or as preferred courses at the level of policy permitted options. Thus it appears that the essence of globalisation is a borderless world—a virtual global village. In this concept, clearly the unit of analysis is, of course, the nation-state. But at the ground level the preponderate proportion of activities which constitute international economic relations do not have the nations as the operative, directly decision-making units. All these formerly controlled and regulated and now under globalisation free cross-border activities are the activities of either natural or legal persons, who are the primary entities making decisions and, as a consequence, gaining or losing from them. True, the nation- state provides the legal and policy framework for these activities the same way as it does for the domestic activities except for the complications arising from separate national origins of the entities involved. Thus the nation state enters the picture for determining the external sector policies and procedures, while the operational, micro decision-making entities are the natural and legal persons .Apparently, this mismatch has not emerged accidentally and has identifiable implications.

MULTI-NATIONAL ENTERPRISES AND GLOBALISATION

For quite sometime now, there is a growing realisation in the attempts to make sense of the phenomenon called globalisation to zero in on the activities, role and behaviour of the large multinational enterprises(MNEs) who despite their size, power and close intertwining with the state, do not, mercifully, by themselves constitute the state, The large, multi-unit, multi-location vertically integrated common ownership and control MNEs are involved in huge international transactions, including those between their subsidiaries and the principal and between the subsidiaries, which are, by definition, internal to them and hence can not be treated as market transactions in any sense of the term. These intra-MNE transactions are not governed by the laws of demand and supply. How the so-called free international trade, the very soul and heart of the neo-liberal concept of globalisation ,can be treated free, market-determined and unregulated when the intra-MNE, non-market exchange or transfers, decided by the management of the MNEs have become a very large part of the world trade, remains a rarely asked question.

An overwhelming proportion of the activities of the MNEs are confined to the rich countries, say the OECD countries. but the gospel of globalisation proceeds as though it is the nations and the national perspectives, needs and motivation and control over resources and capabilities which determine the course of those economic activities which cross national boundaries without any hindrance by the nation states! The growing tendency is towards the formation of regional economic cooperation groupings, like the EU, NAFTA, etc., which account for as much as 70 per cent of the international trade. They are relatively more integrated compared to the rest of the world and tend to have common international policies. This factor goes to detract from the hypothesis of market-led, all-encompassing global integration in a big way in so far as it is regionalisation and not globalisation which has acquired prominence. The evidence regarding persistence of price disparities beyond the transport costs and staggering income differentials flying in the face of factor-price equalisation in a globalised world with market-determined economic decisions are too uncomfortable facts for the neo-classical diehards who generally seem to be believing that if the world does not function according to their theoretical understanding, it must be a distortion, if not worse.

Thus the conceptual basis of globalisation seems to be erring on two counts. First, it takes the nation-states to be the players in the borderless world, while the actual players are a variety of natural and legal persons, who function under the legal framework of the nation states. Second, the whole exercise is based on the assumption of market-mediated cross-border economic contacts. But the fact is that the MNEs as the major players on the international arena who carry out a substantial part of their activities crossing international boundaries as non-market internal, intra-firm transactions. Moreover, most of these transactions take place among the entities belonging to the OECD countries, many of them are tied together under regional groupings. Why does such a gross oversimplification and misrepresentation enter the concept of globalisation? Probably a line of inquiry can be found in the following formulation advanced by Noam

Chomsky: "The fantasy that the nations are the actors in the international arena is the standard doctrinal camouflage for the fact that within the rich nations, as within the hungry ones, there are radical differences in privilege and power." (*World Orders, old and New. 1994, 5*) By taking the nations as the operative units operating on the global scene, the myth of "free" exchange among sovereign, equal nations is sought to be given at least some formal validity, because the disparities between the entities within the nations are a bit too glaring and without any juridical fig leaf to be sustained even for a moment.

The fact of the matter is that it is no less a fiction that all independent, sovereign nations are equal and inter-relate on an equal footing in the global supermarket. Thus even in its oversimplified garb, globalisation understood as another name for the borderless world, is inherently asymmetrical. It seems to be inevitable that the world, as it stands today, at the end of its historical evolution, has become increasingly asymmetrical. Nothing has happened or has been done to undo the inherited and on-going disempowerment and the resulting agonies of the poor countries. The expected processes of convergence of the poorer countries as a result of following the industrialisation, capital formation, technological up-gradation path to development, as tried in the pioneer industrialised countries, have generally turned out to be counter-productive. Growing international and intra-national divergence and disparities may truly be regarded as the hallmark of the processes of international interaction as witnessed over the past five centuries or so.

IS EAST ASIA AN EXCEPTION?

The specially propped up relatively successful emulation by the East Asian newly industrialised countries is often cited as a living example of global socio-economic convergence. Apart from their sui generis, non-replicable special circumstances and favourable factors, they have turned out to be non-sustainable, excessively economistic and extracted quite unconscionably high social, political, cultural and nationalistic costs from their citizens. The globalisation of the East Asian tigers and their integration largely with the economies of the OECD countries followed in many ways a highly nationalistic course in the initial years, combining elements of import-substitution and export orientation (as a part of the strategy of the high labour cost economies of the North to use them as exclaves) along with capital controls(as concessional external borrowing went a long way to supplement their rather high domestic rate of savings) enforced by means of highly authoritative, undemocratic regimes surviving on the basis of the mighty presence of foreign armies on their soil, which, along with many other factors, reduced them to the status of virtual semi-colonies.

GROWING ASYMMETRIES

The pertinent question is: are the asymmetries likely or expected to be reduced or enhanced as a result of the incipient or well-established processes of globalisation? A positive answer is possible only by choosing to ignore the history of nation states and their interactions, especially over the last 500 years or so when the colonial rule, loot, one-way unilateral free trade and exploitation were rampant and their lingering legacy persists in various forms even to this day. These processes and the resulting structures are made stronger by the use of a number of subtle and not-so-subtle devices, including most distressingly by means of making the former colonies fall prey, with the active collabouration of their modernising elite, to the trap of catching-up, mimetic industrialisation as the only effective means of opening the golden gates of progress and prosperity. The point is not that the modern science and technology should have been spurned lock, stock and barrel, as they are of foreign origin. That would be an absurd xenophobic proposition. The pertinent point to question is the blind imitation of the so-called advanced, industrialised nations without a critical examination of the feasibility and desirability of this path from the point of view of the needs, capabilities and aspirations of the poor and hungry toiling masses of the former colonies. Given the significance of the development experience of the North, the fact of vastly different domestic conditions and qualitatively changed character of the global conjuncture facing the poor countries, a critical and people-centric examination of the development challenges would surely suggest significant departures from the European and North American path. The vested interest of the North to perpetuate dependence of the late arriving nations have led them lately to devise a new instrument in the form of the WTO. How the same old game has been played is best illustrated by the ridiculous and absurd manner in which the connotation of trade has been broadened in the WTO agreement "to include production, distribution, marketing, sale, and delivery" (Shukla, S.P., 2002, 271) as though trade is synonymous with all the economic activities in general! In view of these factors, can one treat unregulated economic and other inter-relations, called globalisation a fair, equitable and effective policy course for ensuring development ?

The last few decades over which the present phase of globalisation is supposed to have been in operation have seen worsening of the development reality and prospects. Similarly, the global inequalities, both between nations and among the various socio-economic groups within the nations all over the world have become disgustingly wider and sharper. The distressing facts on these issues are made widely known on a regular basis by the annual Human Development Reports of the UNDP and the World Development Reports of the World Bank, as also by numerous publications of the UNCTAD, ILO, etc. Many scholars have given an historical account of the intensifying global inequalities. (see References and Bibliography). The severity of the growing inequalities can be gauged by the fact that "the 400 highest income earners in the United States make as much money in a year as the entire population of 20 African nations—more than 300 million people" (Robert Weissman, Multinational Monitor, July-August, 2003) The magnitude of the problem is reflected in the following passage: "Global Inequalities persist at staggering levels. The richest 10 per cent of the world's population's income is roughly 117 times higher than the poorest 10 per cent, according to the calculations performed by the economists at the Economic Policy Institute, using data from the International Monetary Fund. This is a huge jump from the ratio in 1980, when the income of the richest 10 per cent was about 79 times higher than the poorest 10 per cent. Excluding fast growing China from the equation, the disparities are even more shocking. The income ratio from the richest 10 per cent to the poorest 10 per cent rose from 90:1 in 1980 to 154: 1 in 1999." (Ibid).

One can supplement these facts by those on poverty, food insecurity, malnutrition, incidence of morbidity and mortality, more specifically of infant mortality, illiteracy, unemployment, international indebtedness of the poor countries, the reverse and perverse transfer of financial resources from the poor to the rich nations, worsening terms of trade of the poor, primary goods exporting countries, violent volatility of financial flows to the poor, newly industrialising countries, growing fiscal impotence of the states, the iniquitous character of the WTO provisions, specifically its provisions regarding intellectual property rights, trade related investment measures, agricultural exports, trade in services and the further items on the negotiations block, called the Singapore issues. (RIS: World Trade and Development Report, 2003). In addition to these glaring facts which provide but a fleeting glimpse of the deeply embedded inequalities as the hall mark of the present world order, made worse by the ever increasing resource base and the resulting clout of the family controlled mega MNEs (about 80 per cent of them are under family control), the hyper growth and mind-boggling size of the international financial flows, mainly very short-run speculative, hot money flows, nearly totally unconnected to the real economy, tend to show the unjust and anti-development character of much of what is happening by way of global inter-relationships, specially the capital inflows from the large financial markets to the poor countries as the much trumpeted basis for initiating the processes of their convergence with the rich and industrialised countries. A new threat in the form of international crime syndicates has assumed menacing proportions as a result of the combination of domestic deregulation with global scale free play of the MNEs, motivated by the narrow financial calculus of their controlling families under the symbiotic protection of the political- administrative classes. Now that it has become clear that the expected trickle-down effects of the growth of GDP do not materialise even in the domestic economy, let alone on the global scale, even with the helping hand of the pull-up programmes and their international counterparts in the form of ODA and the so-called international development cooperation, it is rather naive to expect that such convergence can become a reality via the operation of the trickle-down and spread effects across national boundaries.

INTERTWINING OF THE INTERNAL AND THE EXTERNAL FACTORS

What needs to be specially underlined is that both external and internal peripheralisation are closely inter-connected. Peripheries have been defined as "regions where conditions in the field of politics, economy, social structure, religion and ideology are organised in favour of people living in other regions". (Hans-Heinrich, Nolte, 2003, 51). Obviously, colonial rule and the institutionalisation of similar processes after the end of formal occupation, say, e.g., in the form of dependence of the poor countries on the early industrialised nations, rather on their large companies controlling the production of capital goods and their high level, sun -rise technologies, as also for meeting the critical shortfalls in savings and foreign exchange required for this kind of industrialisation, contributed in a large measure to the processes of peripheralisation of poor nations, regions and classes of people This is how there emerged the well-known dependency syndrome. These processes and their outcomes gave the indigenous capitalist classes new opportunities for cementing their industrial and economic power within the domestic economic and political space, based on a love-hate relationship with the metropolitan MNEs.. Similar processes are continuing under globalisation, understood as a multifaceted, complex phenomenon related to the totality of international relations which have strong links with the internal power structure in every inter-linked, externally dominated country. This kind of dominance of the external factors can be seen even in the economies which are basically inward-oriented with a relatively small size of the external linkages. This is explicable mainly in terms of the strong impact of the historical legacy of post-colonial economic structures, the initial conditions and the strong-arm policies of the North for guiding their relationship with the third world in order to serve their narrow, partisan, non-global objectives. The stylised facts and what we have just discussed on some limited aspects of global inequalities, mentioned earlier, show that the processes of centralisation and concentration unleashed by the processes of capitalist industrialisation in a highly inter-linked framework in the third world countries owe themselves in no mean measure to the domestic power structures as well.

To understand this relationship between the internal and external peripheralisation vis-à-vis the core or metropolitan centres, it is useful to recall how this complex relationship has been brought out in a very telling, realistic and effective manner by Johan Galtung. According to his analysis "the impact of the rich upon poor nations can best be understood if the global political economy is viewed as the relationship between a 'Centre' (the developed countries) and a 'Periphery'(the less developed countries), each of which is further subdivided into its own 'centre'(the governing elite) and 'periphery'(groups without much power or wealth)," (Mahler,V.A.,1999,384)The pattern of their mutual interaction involves the exercise of power over these countries even after they attained their political independence not so much directly or through the agency of the so-called multilateral agencies like the World Bank and its affiliates, the IMF, WTO, etc, but "indirectly by means of a two stage process in which the centre of the Centre nation structures the options of the periphery of the Periphery nation itself." (Ibid) Describing the working of this mechanism of exercising remote and indirect control by the North over the South on the basis of the experience of Latin America, a scholar expands on the theory of Galtung. He maintains that in addition to the co-option and active utilisation of the centre of the Periphery, the middle classes too become a part of the bridgehead of the centre of the Centre nations. He says, "The middle classes of Buenos Aires, Rio de Janero,and Santiago de Chile, who completely accept the European and North American standards of consumption........live about as well as , or better than the middle class persons who live in the advanced countries. But the poor of Brazil, Argentina and Chile are poor by the grim standards of the poor in Latin America." (Karl Deutsch quoted by Hans-Heinrich,op.cit.,385) It may be pointed out that none of these countries are isolated. Instead they are rather closely 'integrated' with the economies of the North, more specifically with that of the USA.

To sum up so far ,the incongruities and oddities contained in the concept of globalisation as a result of taking the nations as the relevant units, ignoring the internal entities and their interface with the global factors and the neglect of the historical legacy of large initial, inherited inequalities (leading to non-recognition of the many asymmetries and their implications for so-called free and unfettered global interaction networks) are not the only problems one would have with the exaggerated claims made regarding the real character and implications of globalisation. The real entrepreneurs, the small formal and informal units, can hardly operate beyond the local level. This is so notwithstanding the much talked about flexible specialisation and networking and the information and communications revolution, especially in view of the monopolisation of the bulk of the socio-economic space by the giant MNEs and the relative resource poverty and weaker bargaining strength of the small formal and informal entities.

Moreover, in this view of globalisation there is only some faint and fleeting recognition of the non-economic elements that force their way in the otherwise highly economistic perspective, like for instance in the form of calling attention to what is termed social capital. In fact, in the tradition of neo-liberalism which provides the foundations of the generally prevalent concept of globalisation, the economy is taken to be what Karl Polyani called a socially disembedded entity i.e. a practically autonomous economy which exists and operates as though the other spheres of life hardly matter. This theoretical basis makes globalisation nearly exclusively an economic phenomenon, economic ideology, economic policy package and an ensemble of all these. That this is an artificial construction, an apologetic, ideological device which is not sustainable either on theoretical grounds or on the basis of the empirical evidence regarding the joint, non-separable functioning of the economy from the rest of the elements of society. As a corollary, globalisation too cannot remain confined merely to the economic domain. This is a very serious, meaningful, realistic and powerful re-discovery of globalisation as it operates and at the normative level is sought to be popularised and imposed on the whole world. For facilitating an assessment of the meaning and implications of globalisation for development and its inalienable component, justice, this re-discovery goes a long way. The point we intend to make on the basis of this discussion, therefore, is that the mechanics of globalisation can hardly be appreciated unless the intra-national entities involved in the dealings with the entities in the other countries in many diverse spheres are brought into the picture, more particularly in order to see how globalisation impacts the development of the poor countries and the nature and degree of justness of its mechanism and outcomes.

The fact nonetheless remains that predominantly as an economic category which operates in close association with the political and cultural processes, which are sought to be captured by the ideology termed "globalism" (Steger, M.B., 2002), and a neo-classical market-determined and dominated policy package, globalisation is an objective, though partial and fairly age-old reality. It can be seen in the form of multifarious intensified direct and indirect relationships between the citizens of different countries. Tall claims are made by its protagonists about its capacity to provide solution to all the problems the world at large faces. They loudly proclaim its invincibility and irreversibility, as though it exhausts all the options which can be thought of or exist. It has managed to win the sanction and support of the powerful states, their MNEs, most political formations either exercising political power or are in close proximity to power centres in different parts of the world ,as an accepted set of cure-all state policies in all the major countries. It has managed to become the darling of those who control and dominate the media, cultural outfits and other elite opinion-makers. It is true that many incisive, intellectually impressive, tightly argued and convincingly well documented political economy critiques of this brand of globalisation have appeared in current social science For instance, Manfred Steger (2002.47-79) discusses the following five central claims made in order to sell globalisation and shows their vacuity:

1. Globalisation is about the liberalisation and global integration of (national) markets.
2. Globalisation is inevitable and irreversible.
3. Nobody is in-charge of globalisation, as though it is a natural , elemental and spontaneous development and being nobody's doing, like for example of what Thomas Friedman call the electronic herd and the global supermarket (The Lexus and the Olive Tree, 2000) nobody can be blamed for its selective and discriminatory effects.
4. Globalisation benefits everyone which is possible only by assuming it to be based on symmetrical relationships

or philanthropy on the part of those who are in a position to command the processes of international inter-connectedness.

5. Globalisation furthers the spread of democracy in the World.

Based on many critiques of globalisation in its different but inter-related connotations, the world is witnessing many widely networked, vocal even militant and expanding ground level and joint international movements involving a growing number of global, national, local and mixed civil society institutions. The latter are stridently and doggedly exposing this brand of globalisation for what it is by mass mobilisation, especially of the growing army of those on whom a heavy load of miseries is regularly heaped by the relentless pursuit of its highly sectarian agenda. However, the forces of globalisation continue to maintain their upper hand. This may be related to the close equation between the content of globalisation and the interests of those who are controlling the commanding heights in the largest and most powerful countries of the world in economic, financial, technological, political, cultural and ideological spheres, The resulting clout helps its protagonists to acquire a position of great influence in moulding public opinion and setting the agenda of the day. Moreover, there are some objective factors which either work or are deftly made to work in support of the neo-liberalism based globalisation.

In order to make sense of these pro-globalisation factors, one has to recognise that growing extensive and close inter-connectedness has become an incontrovertible fact of life across the globe. This has been facilitated to an unprecedented extent by the revolution in the means of transport, communication, information gathering, processing, storage and dissemination as also substantially easy and not too unaffordable access to these by at least the vast middle-income groups. The global inter-connectedness and close interaction are spread over many aspects of people's lives, with both positive and negative implications. Among these, one may randomly make a mention of space, economy, life style and consumption patterns, cultural symbols, political participation, national and international travel, entertainment, migration, exposure to ecological and environmental crises, threat of nuclear annihilation, homogenisation of aspiration and values, sway of crass individualism, decline of communitarian ethos and ethics, mass poverty and deprivation in the midst of the growth of super-high productive potential and its large-scale actualisation in at least some countries. One can go on to add ever more items concerning which the whole world has shrunk, come closure and is facing shared challenges and opportunities. Of course, this is accompanied by grossly iniquitous sharing of the costs and benefits and a sharpening realisation of the chasm between what could be available to people at large, and what is actually obtained by the tiny minority at the apex and the vast multitudes of people below. In this respect the neo-liberal publicists tend to give a highly exaggerated list of the matters in which the world has come closure together, implying as though the potential is also the real. and further that what has become available to some is going to become available to everyone at least to a modest extent only if these processes are allowed to continue for a reasonable but foreseeable length of time Clearly the neo-liberal universe is highly exclusionary. According to their world view derived from social Darwinism, those who fail to jump on to the globalisation band wagon do not ultimately matter and are socially dispensable.

It is also rarely factored in that continuous expansion of the spatial-geographical frontiers of mankind is an age-old process and the present phase is its latest phase, but certainly is far from being the humane, just, participatory and inclusionary with healthy concern for the environment and the future generations. Nor have we reached a stage to justly maintain that no more or better globalisation can be achieved. As an aside it can be mentioned that it is a tribute to the positive ambience generated by the word globalisation that instead of discarding the present partisan and iniquitous globalisation, alternatives are proposed as South-centric globalisation or globalisation from below.

Let us call attention to the multidimensional expansion of the network of human social interactions and increasingly wider spatial inter-connections which have been growing ab initio in order to see how the present globalisation is similar to and/or different from similar earlier processes. The expansion of the society, polity and markets from the local to the regional to the national and to the global has taken many centuries but is yet to incorporate the majority as participants in the decision-making processes and consequently as their beneficiaries rather than remaining passive recipient of its mostly negative consequences as far as most of the humanity is concerned. Such an extension has, moreover, not been consecutive but has moved on simultaneously and the wider level of spatial linkages do not render the earlier narrower ones ineffective or unimportant. The emergence of the national does not, for instance, necessarily marginalise the regional and/or local. Similarly, despite the strides made by the international inter-connectedness, even in most non- autarchic countries, the local and intra-national linkages far outweigh the international linkages. This is correct even for the most powerful and industrialised rich countries championing globalisation. Long distance trade, setting up of empires spanning many continents, spread of religion and ideologies like wild fire across many countries and continents, financial transactions and movement of precious metals as medium of exchange as well as store of value between the residents of many countries, shifting of residence and habitats in the form of mass exodus, etc., are historical events and processes which were not given the name of globalisation but are, in effect, close cousins of what is presently projected as globalisation . However, even if the global inter-connections and mutual dependence are not entirely new and fair, the subjective realisation of this objective fact is far more widespread today than possibly ever before.

For a better part of history the antecedents of global, cross border multifaceted relationships were without governmental restrictions, though the cost and risk of giving effect to the long spatial movements were a formidable barrier. Apart from collecting entry/exit taxes, one has not seen any of the plethora of restrictive measures in the pre-capitalist era, except for the serfs under certain types of feudalism. It has often been pointed out that the extent of international inter-linkages among different nations from the initial years of the industrial revolution up to the First War were, in fact, more than those seen after the 1970s. But the present public policy stance of permitting the growth of global linkages without undue restrictions (more by way of loud pronouncements and for adoption by others, while departing from these free norms in their national interest by the powerful countries at will in many open and dubious ways rendering the claims regarding 'free' movement hypocritical) is also not entirely new, though stands in contrast with what was witnessed during the inter-war years and which continued to an extent right up to early 1970s. In many ways the legacy of protectionism persists even after the WTO by the trading majors in many diverse ways.

Then what is so special about the globalisation of the last few decades of the 20th century which is continuing with added gusto? The classic analyses of the capitalist development in the Marxist tradition have demonstrated the inherent tendency of internationalisation of capitalist accumulation to which international movements of labour too contribute a great deal. Thus neither in theory nor in actual conditions evolving in different countries, there is any thing out of the ordinary or unusual in so far as global economic, social, political and environmental interdependence is growing. The tendency was there; it has picked up speed or has been made to move faster and, of course, in the directions, like the financial assets and instruments, preferred by those who are in the commanding positions.. After all even the earlier big spurts in cross–border dealings owed a great deal to the dramatic technological advances of the respective periods. .Not only that, the policy of free trade versus protectionism has all along been highly controversial. Then one wonders why is there so much song and drama about the present phase of largely public policy-induced freer and larger flow of goods and services, factors of production and daily financial claims of astronomical size along with diminished movement of natural persons. That the composition of the basket of tradables changes and requires a different policy configuration to sustain itself is understandable. This happens because the leading sectors change, technological change acquires a different complexion and with higher incomes, changed distribution of income, wealth and social power and more pronounced role of the hidden persuaders, the composition of both demand and supply changes.

As maintained above, globalisation is portrayed as much as a short and crisp name for the existing reality,though hardly as its differentia specifica, as also in order to capture the ideology behind it but by a soft, pleasant and non-offensive term which helps create favourable ambience. It is considered useful in silencing and /or confusing the critics. and opponents. Capitalisms of different historical times and of different countries have been known variously, as free economies, market economies, liberal-democratic countries, laissez faire systems, atomistic systems, etc. Their usage did not arouse so many and so intense debates and controversies as have greeted the characterisation of the present phase of capitalism as globalisation. Clearly, it is not the name, the term globalisation which arouses so much passion, intellectual opposition and deep antagonism. What invokes opposition is the drive to push a highly sectarian policy package as a universally beneficial and desirable one.

Before we deal with this question, it may be helpful to try to understand the tactics adopted by the protagonists of globalisation in order to protect their turf. This involves attempts to blunt the criticism against globalisation by sidetracking the real issues and misrepresent the criticisms.

Let us take one instance. It is certainly intellectual dishonesty to criticise the critics of globalisation for being narrow-minded, like the frogs in a well, *koop mandooks*, as we in India say, or chauvinistic, who want to erect high walls around themselves in order to insulate themselves from the free flow of ideas from outside the walls they themselves have put up out of their sheer myopia or worse. No, not so much of humanity, from around the globe, including the crème de la crème, cutting across differences and diversity, and with the best of motives similar to any which have spawned enlightened movements in history, could have mobilised themselves into concerted, multifaceted action if globalisation were to mean free, open and unhindered movement and contest of various views, theories, ideologies, scientific and technological knowledge.

In so far as the WTO brand of globalisation is wedded to the measures like Trade Related Intellectual Property Rights which also sanctifies the attempts by the MNEs to improperly appropriate the traditional knowledge systems of the indigenous people and their regional bio-diversity, it is the protagonists of globalisation who are putting up barriers against free flow of ideas as a part of their drive to forge global monopolies. Such mobilisations and intellectual ferments are an indication that having seen so much which is akin to the reality of global inter-connectedness and what have you as concrete-real in the past as well it is the ideological and policy content of the present wave of globalisation and globalism which is inviting opposition. It is evident that globalisation, as understood in the current discourse has nothing whatsoever to do with free flow and interchange of ideas, ideologies and policy debates. In fact, it is the votaries of globalisation who deny and deride the existence of alternatives and pompously declare that with the collapse of the opposition to the US dominance of the world by a more or less equally powerful super power and the ideology it claimed to uphold, the resulting uni-polar world has become devoid of alternatives: according to them, it is the end of history ! A serious exercise is called for in order to understand the vocal, well-meaning and intellectually powerful opposition to what is called globalisation and the reasons for which and the devices by means of which it is sought to be imposed on the whole world as the only course available to it. As we proceed, we intend to show that it is the anti-development and anti-justice thrust of globalisation, and the resulting insecurity and nervousness of the perpetrators of this unjust sytem, especially following the post-1970 slow-down of the major capitalist countries,among other factors, which are fuelling the powerful anti-globalisation movements across the globe. Truly, just as the term globalisation has become globalised, so is the opposition to it truly global !

Is it possible that the pro-statist forces are opposing globalisation as the pro-liberalisation-globalisation forces intend to roll back the state? This seems a facile and mistaken view. The controversy over the role of the state in the economic sphere arises from an ahistorical, unrealistic, narrow and mistaken view of the economy as a socially disembedded entity, because market exchange is considered the sole mechanism available for organising and co-ordinating human social affairs. The moment the historical and contemporary facts regarding the simultaneous occurrence of and reliance on reciprocity, redistribution, house holding are recognised for social organisation and motives other than the pursuit of material prosperity are treated as relevant for the social human beings, the state-market dichotomy and polar opposition fall in place and come out in their true colour. The issue then no more remains whether the state is active in the economy or withdraws or is reduced to a minimalist position. But the issue then is transmogrified into what kind of role the state plays, how and for whose benefit, at least predominantly if not entirely. Viewed in such a framework, one finds that the issue between the protagonists and antagonists of globalisation is not whether the state participates in the economy, (which has invariably been the case) but whose game it would play, how and at what cost to various sections of society, i.e., who would yield the stick of state power to further economic interests and who would be made to foot the bill.

For one thing, none of the earlier phases emerged and survived without a powerful backing, even a catalytic role of the state. Karl Polyani showed the emergence of laissez faire regimes, exploding the myth of self-regulated markets as the organising mechanism of capitalist economies. Similarly the states of the North, he international institutions they dominate and the academic establishment under their tutelage worked together to administer deadly blows to the state-regulated, reformist and welfare capitalism in Western Europe and North America with their stillborn social markets in order to make place for the present day, supposedly market ruled globalisation. That is to say, globalisation owes itself in no small measure to state's active role, though, of course, in a highly selective manner. The state activities which find favour with the globalists are those which facilitate and encourage cross border, unrestricted movements of goods, services and financial resources according to the present economic needs of the rich, industrialised countries, mainly the G-7 countries and the big MNEs originating and controlled from them. Their shifting comparative advantage, the compulsions arising from the structural changes in their economies and their relative competitive position in the world economy determine the nature, extent and areas of free movements of goods and services and factors of production they require. For instance, when the productivity gains of the newly industrialised economies of East Asia started posing a threat to the US industry, and the services sector, mainly in R&D and the financial sector became the leading sectors of the US economy around mid-1970s, the whole game plan was changed in favour of what is presently known as globalisation. In these changes the MNEs play a very active role in order to use the state power for moving ahead with their agenda. It may be clarified that the so-called multinational or transnational companies are very much the corporate citizens of their mother countries. The MNEs and their mother countries reinforce each other's power as a result of which global economic, social, political, cultural and military power has become heavily concentrated and centralised. The close symbiotic relationship between the global business corporations and their mother countries comes out quite vividly in the following view expressed by Thomas Friedman, the author of one of the best-sellers on globalisation : " the hidden hand of the market will never work without a hidden fist—the hidden fist that keeps the world safe for Silicon Valley's technologies is called the US Army, Air Force, Navy and Marine Corps." (Quoted by Gindin,Sam, 2002,8) It is for such reasons that Henry Kissinger described globalisation as another name for the US domination of the world. It is this kind of exclusionary and asymmetric character of the present day globalisation which invokes growing resentment and opposition.

Even in the economic sphere, instead of the real economy, it is the financial sector with its astronomical size of daily cross border transactions (apparently the leading sector of the presently reigning globalisation) which is the heart of the present day globalisation. These speculative, casino-like financial supermarkets are the play -grounds of the rich mainly from the rich OECD countries, but with a very volatile and mercurial presence in some select poor but large economies. Everywhere these financial markets are dominated by the electronic herd (i.e. "millions of investors moving money around the world with the click of a mouse" like " faceless stock, bond and currency traders sitting behind computer screens all over the globe moving their money around from mutual funds to pension funds to emerging market funds , or trading on the Internet from their basements."—Thomas Friedman, 13 and 109) It is mammon-worship by these speculators who could not care less about the real economy implications of their games.

The dominant economic activity of the present day globalised world takes place in the financial sector (where mega profits of the MNEs too are parked and deployed). As a concomitant of this feature, the rule of the real economy

MNEs, no more unconcerned exclusively with the real economy and ,as business entities ,unconcerned with the fate of the real toiling human beings spread over the shrunk global village, too has become secondary to that of the speculative electronic herds largely operating in the secondary stock markets. These casinos generate by their daily transactions worth trillions of dollars huge flows of income and stocks of wealth without producing an extra blade of grass or additional employment in the farms and factories anywhere, including for the periphery of the Centre. In fact, the threat of moving their capital and enterprises around in the search for cheaper sources of inputs, including labour becomes a weapon in the arsenal of big business to impose compliance on the working classes. On the contrary, this diversion of potentially productive resources from the real to the financial sector and concentrated in ever fewer hands restricts the growth of demand for wage-goods and other goods and services capable of enhancing the quality of life for the deprived majority of humanity in remote god forsaken regions of the world. The state supported control over the R & D industry in the hands of the MNEs has a bias against encouraging labour use and goes to build technological bias against employment expansion, not to speak of the environment hostile and culturally deprived life style and values fostered by them. To the extent new technologies lead to the introduction of new products with heavy draft on energy and natural resources and belong to very high price ranges beyond the reach of the vast majority, they lead to pollution, exclusion and social discontent. In this information age and a shrunk world the victims of the financial market volatility, super unearned financial gains neither know who are wreaking havoc on their lives and living nor are in a position to find out the sources from which these thunderbolts strike them with erratic regularity.

It would be too much for the present to give an exhaustive treatment to the subject to show how sectarian, narrowly focused, exclusionary and unjust the present processes of North-centric-globalisation are. What has been briefly examined is enough to show what is its essential thrust and why. The controversies surrounding the popular concept of globalisation can be attributed to its working and results. These negative features represent an intensification of the normally obtainable unjust effects of a capitalist economy but with the abolition of its welfare and social security measures and the replacement of Keynesian approach towards fuller employment by labour market flexibility, meaning in simple words, sacrificing the welfare and rights of labour on the altar of the profits of the big business. The unsung and unwept liquidation of the reformist structural and policy initiatives by the triumphalism of the Reagan-Thatcher Anglo-American counter- revolution has made the sea rough and stormy for the smooth sailing of globalisation.

III

GLOBALISATION AND DEVELOPMENT

Let us give some specific attention to the impact of the presently existing globalisation on the processes and prospects of development of the third world. In this entire analysis, one has to sharply distinguish the present phase of globalisation with the earlier periods when similar internationalist trends and relationships, elements of a veritable international economic system, were no less visible. As Polyani has said with reference to the last quarter of the 19th century, "Only a madman would have doubted that the international economic system was the axis of the material existence of the human race." But during that period, these international linkages were not picked up for defining the essential character of the time, nor went to the extent of denying the presence of alternatives. The 19th century globalisation imposed itself on the third world in the form of a long period of imperialist rule, and contributed in a major way to the disempowerment of these countries leading to a high degree of internal disarticulation and disparity. Is the present late 20th century-early 21st century globalisation qualitatively different from its predecessor and likely to produce a different kind of outcome? It would apparently be reasonable to expect a different kind of outcome from the present phase and form of globalisation in view of the fact that the third world has wrested political independence, is consciously pursuing the path of progress with the active support and under the guidance of the former colonial masters and is supposed to be enjoying the 'advantage' of late start. This putative advantage is supposed to arise from the view which suggests that the late-late-late industrialisers do not have to reinvent the wheel and can fall back upon not only the lessons the early developers learnt at the school of hard knocks but can also count upon the physical, technological and financial resources of the rich countries with whom the poor countries now can relate as sovereign nations. The first flush enthusiasm and bonhomie regarding the cooperative pursuit of developing the laggard regions could not last beyond the 1970s when both the groups of countries that were supposed to be working as "partners in progress" reached an impasse. The attempts at architecting a "New International Economic Order" (NIEO) by the third world were related to the enthusiasm generated by the success of the OPEC countries to raise the oil prices. The NIEO was intended to increase the space available to the poor countries and correcting some of the inequities they were made to suffer. But it came to nothing. In fact these exercises met their denouement in the form of the supposed helplessness of dozens of third world countries to accept the structural adjustment programmeme (SAP). In a way, the SAP replaced the stillborn NIEO.

The SAP, consisting mainly of liberalisation, privatisation and globalisation (LPG), is the face of the present era of globalisation the third world has been confronted with as the new development policy they are coaxed, coerced and cajoled to adopt. Once again this time around too the development tool kit for the third world has been manufactured, packed, shipped and sold to the poor countries by the intellectual workshops of the world located in the G-7 countries, mainly the USA with active collabouration by the compradore intellect workers of the poor countries. One purpose for which it was designed and handed down to the debt—ridden poor countries was to integrate them, covetously christened 'emerging markets', with the economies of the rich countries who happen to be their main trading partners (what with weak or practically non-existent South-South relations) and suppliers of capital in various forms to meet their savings,foreign exchange and technology gaps. The other was to speed up their rate of growth by freeing them from the unsuccessful statist growth-retarding policy and planning trap and the associated democratic political compulsions to do something at least for the wider social constituency. Repaying the past debts mainly by fresh and enlarged external borrowing or by luring in short-term portfolio funds by rather 'sexist' make-up of their external face, and open-arm welcome of foreign capital by giving them as national treatment as given to deregulated domestic capital (considered the key elements for keeping the confidence level of the electronic herd high as reflected in the country credit-rating by basically mercenary credit-rating agencies) were considered effective enough for attaining market-determined high speed and efficient growth. In order to mask these growth fundamentalist policies with a 'human face' as a politically correct framework for implementing the new globalisation package without injuring the fragile electoral democracies, having a rather high degree of manageability of the popular verdict by the resourceful, it was thought that the poor and deprived were to be taken on board by a combination of trickle–down effects supplemented by liberally funded pull-up programmes. This latter course of action, otherwise burdensome in view of the fiscal crunch, was to be made feasible by the supply side response of a low tax rate regime.

This SAP based development intervention by the globalised regime can be examined either in the light of the outcomes seen over the last two decades or on and a priori basis. As far as the former approach is concerned, so much negative evidence from across the World has accumulated that the originators of the Washington Consensus, who fathered the SAP, have come out with disclaimers to the effect that they did not say so, or that they were misunderstood. No country in the third world has come out with flying colours even with respect to the growth fundamentalist sectional agenda: So many miracle economies of yesteryears seem to have ended up not with a bang but with a whimper One thing is clear. The structure, institutional ensemble and global equations of the third world needed a thorough redoing along with the introduction of a series of positive policies and programmes on the basis of internal regeneration, reassessment and restructuring rather than superimposition of a mimetic, catching-up agenda with continued dependence and asymmetric relationships with the rich world and the absence of meaningful and substantial. mutual cooperation among the poor and disempowered countries. Both the earlier economics of development and the later day counter-revolution in development economics and the interventions based on them fail to recognise that the growth of a diseased structure can not lead to the emergence of a healthy system, unless correctives to remove the malignancy, malfunctioning and malaise are undertaken at least simultaneously. In spite of wide-ranging socio-economic changes, expansion, diversification, role and place in the world economy, introduction and applications of many advances and fruits of science and technology, expansion of modern socio-economic infrastructure facilities on a scale not seen before, establishment of many new institutions of 'modernisation', etc, in most of the third world countries, a multi-dimensional crisis has engulfed most of the third world countries in. varying proportions. The crisis has become acute in so far as it is becoming increasingly intractable by the application of the battery of conventional measures of more of the same variety, even though with changed composition. True, there has taken place a sizeable increase in the absolute number of those who have derived net benefit in the conventional terms from the process of economic expansion: they live longer. and their consumption of goods and both public and private services is higher and more varied than ever before, though not necessarily in more secure and eco-friendly environment and possibly with more acute psychological disquietude. But the number of those who do not have livelihood security, and in one word, are made to bear a disproportionately large share of the costs and negligible share of its benefits and in many cases remain uninvited to the high table of development is not only uncomfortable large and growing but is threatening the sustainability of such partisan, partial and unjust growth. It remains unsustainable not only owing to the ecological disturbance and heavy costs but because of the growing disjunction between various aspects of social existence at macro and micro levels both within the nations and internationally.

In short, the intentional endeavours for development under the present package of globalisation policies, which are in many ways a continuation of the statist development policies but with a more open adoption of market and capital-friendly policy instruments (made respectable by the state failure to withstand the onslaught by the market forces), remain incomplete, unbalanced, iniquitous, mimetic rather than based on a real exercise of internally evolved choices in an open, democratic set of social relations capable of overcoming the pangs and costs of centuries old disempowerment which was imposed on large sections of humanity in the most inhuman manner. That even substantial and sustained rate of growth of national income remains an unrealised dream by most of the third world countries shows the inappropriate foundations and policy design derived from the SAP. Whether, the free and open-door policies based current phase of globalisation under the corporatist framework or the earlier statist forms of attempts to link up with the advance industrialised economies in order to catch-up with them on improved terms compared to the legacy of colonial domination, the essential difference was mainly with respect to the choice of the instruments and policies and not concerning the substance and content of 'development'.

It has been argued that the SAP is basically designed to inspire the confidence of the international financial markets in the safety and profitability of their financial resources made available to the poor economies in various forms as also for ensuring sustained growth of demand for the fast accumulating vast financial resources of the investors from the rich countries, additionally supplemented now by the reverse inflow from the poor to the rich countries and their on-going recycling. (Bienefeld, M. 1993). The manner in which despite rapidly growing external indebtedness and yawning and expanding trade and current account deficit in absolute terms, of about 15 to 20 billion dollars per annum, the inflows of foreign finance is embarrassingly racing in India to breach the mark of US$ 100 billion before long by way of foreign exchange reserves is a telling piece of evidence of the success of the globalisation policy package as a debt-collection and debt-market expansion policy for the corpulent financial markets of the rich countries. After all, one stated reason for going in for the present globalisation path of development in India was the strong, supposedly national honour based urge to avoid the shame and embarrassment of defaulting on the nation's external debt-servicing obligations. That one has to borrow in the international markets on extremely difficult terms even for financing non-foreign exchange requiring activities and projects was apparently not considered a matter of national shame ! Whether and how far the objectives of the creditor nations and their international organs like the World Bank, IMF, etc., to serve the interest of the international financial oligarchies by means of propagating and virtually imposing the SAP package are capable, at the same time, to satisfy the national urge and need for sustained and substantial broad-based growth along with a whole host of social and nationalistic objectives can easily be imagined. The outcomes produced by these policies across the World do not seem to justify the presumed harmony of the interests and objective of these two sets of countries

Let us not forget that the life of the present brand of globalisation in operation since about mid-1970s has been practically equally long compared to that of the earlier period's non-de-linking based mimetic, state-led growth approaches, (say from about the end of the Second World War to the first oil price hike by the OPEC countries). The latter gives some inherent advantage to the early industrialisers. What is implied is that so long as the content, parameters and meaning of development remain externally derived or given, in the context of an unsavoury legacy of the long dark period of continued, many-sided disempowerment of the third world, its largest sections of people would not be able to participate and become co-sharers in the processes of modernisation and industrialisation. This is likely to be an inevitable feature of these processes unless conscious mobilisation and even small micro-level beginnings are made to overcome the enfeeblement of the small and moribund communities, occupations and remote and deprived regions. The reason is not far to seek. The processes of globalisation give rise to the possibility of convergence and divergence in varying proportions. Both are likely and are not mutually exclusive. It depends on the actual course and content of development approach whether in a given situation convergence or divergence turns out to be stronger and asserts its supremacy basically by way of auto-centric development. The actual resolution of this conflict between the processes of convergence and divergence involves the entire political economy of development. What we have seen and is relevant for our present discussion is that the centre of the Centre, in close association with the centre of the Periphery, and by incorporating the intermediate strata by means of arousing their hopes and aspirations, has imposed on the world a market totalitarianism and presented it to the World as some kind of benign and inexorable necessity. Thus what is taking place in the name and garb of globalisation is a mal-integration of the poorer societies on highly asymmetric and injurious terms and for fulfilling an agenda which is exogenous and non-responsive to the needs and aspirations of the people and nations who have been denied, deprived and disempowered by the processes of social Darwinism unleashed on the global scale by the new social system which emerged in the wake of, among other factors, the scientific and technological revolutions of the last 500 years or so Thus the really existing globalisation the world is witnessing represents the very antithesis of development understood as real and effective collective self-empowerment of the people and, by the same token, works to deny justice to the poor and deprived. Collective self-empowerment, which is what development is all about, can become the agenda of the day only by doing away with the reigning globalisation as the ideology, agenda and be-all of the MNEs and the states of their home nations which, of course, has to be supplemented in a big way by dethronement of the domestic turf allies and collabourators of the pernicious globalisation which has so quickly disillusioned so many all over the World. It is for the third world social scientists to take up the gauntlet in order to get rid of the universal mal-development that has so unfortunately been imposed on the humanity all over in the name of globalisation.

REFERENCES AND BIBLIOGRAPHY

Aghion Philippe & G. Williamson Jeffrey (Eds) (1998), Growth, Inequality and globalisation : theory, history, and Policy, Cambridge: Cambridge University Press.

Amin, Samir, (1997), *Capitalism in the Age of Globalisation: The Management of Contemporary Society.* London: Zed Books.

Bauman, Zygmunt, (2000), *What is Globalisation?* Cambridge: Polity Press.

Bienfeld, Manfred (1993), Structural Adjustment: Debt Collection Device or Development Policy? Tokyo, Sophia University, Institute of Comparative Culture.

Brandt W. (1980), *North-South: A programmeme for Survival, Report of the Independent Commission on International Development Issues*, London and Sydney, PAN Books.

Bryan, Lowell, and Diana Farrell (1996), *Market Unbound: Unleashing Global Capitalism.* New York: Wiley.

Buelens, Frans (2000), *Globalisation and Nation-State, Northampton*, MA: Edward Elgar Publishing.

Cable, V. (1999), *Globalisation and Global Governance*, London, The Royal Institute of International Affairs.

Carroll, William, Radhika Desai, and Warren Magnusson (1996), *Globalisation, Social Justice and Social Movements: A reader, Victoria*, ON: University of Victoria.

Chalam, K.S. (1999), Rexaings in Political Economy, Hyderabad, Orient Longman.

Chomsky, Noam. (1999), *Profit Over People: Neoliberalism and Global Order*. New York: Seven Stories Press.

DeMartino, George F. (1999), *Global Economy, Global Justice: Theoretical Objections and Policy Alternatives to Neoliberalism.* London: Routledge.

DeMartino, George F. (2001), *Democratizing the Global Economy: The Battle Against the World Bank and the IMF. Monroe, ME:* Common Courage Press.

Falk, Richard A. (1999), *Predatory Globalisation: A Critique.* Cambridge: Polity Press.

Freemen, R.V. (Eds) (2002), Inequality Around the World; NewYork, Palgrave Macmillan.

Friedman, Thomas (2000), *The Lescus and the Olive Tree*, New York, Anchor Books.

Germain, Randall D. (2000) *Globalisation and Its Critics: Perspectives from Political Economy*. New York: St. Martin's Press.

Gilpin, Robert. (2000) *The Challenge of Global Capitalism: The Wold Economy in the 21st Century*. Princeton, NJ: Princeton University Press.

Gindin, Sam, (2002) Social Justice and Globalisation: Are they Compatible ? Monthly Review, June.

Golding Petter & Harris Phil, (Eds) (1997), *Beyond Cultural Imperialism: Globalisation, Communication and the New International Order,* London: Sage.

Gray, John. (1998), *False Dawn: the Delusions of Global Capitalism.* New York: New Press.

Griffin Keith (Eds) (1996), *Studies in Globalisation and Economic Transitions, London:* Macmillan Press.

Hans-Heinrich, N. (2003) "*Why is Europe's South Poor A chairs of International Peripheries.*" Review, 26 (1).

Hart, Jeffrey A. and Aseem Prakash (2000), *Coping with Gloibalisation*. London: Routledge.

Hoogvelt Ankie (Eds) (1997), *Globalisation and the Postcolonial World: the New Political Economy of Development,* London: Macmillan.

Iwasaki, T. and Others (1992), *Development Strategies for the 21st Century,* Tokyo, Institute of Developing Economies.

Kabra, Kamal Nayan (2002), "Globalisation and Governance: Cloning the New Millenium" in Reddy, N.D., Singh, S. and Arora, Dolly (eds.) Political Economy of WTO Regime: Some Aspects of Globalisation and Governance, New Delhi,Indian Political Economy Association AndRainbow Publishers.

Lechner, Frank J. and John Boli (Eds) (2000), *The Globalisation Reader*. Oxford: Blackwell.

Lindberg Staffan & Sverrisson (Eds) (1997), *Social Movements in Development: The Challenge of Globalisation and Democratization*, London: Macmillan.

Mark Lewis & others (1996) *The Growth of Nations: Culture, Competitiveness, and the Problem of Globlisation*, Bristol: Academic Press.

Martin, Hans-Peter, and Harald Schumann (1997), *The Global Trap: Globalisation and the Assault on Democracy and Prosperity*. London: Zed Books, 1997.

Mask, Rupert (1997), "Contesting Hegemony: American and Far-Right Ideologies of Globalisation in Constituting International Political Economy (Eds), Burch K and Denemark R.A. Boulder, London, Lynne Rienner Publication.

Munck Ronaldo and O'Hearn Denis (Eds) (1999), *Critical Development theory: Contributions to a New Paradigm,* London: Zed Books.

Nayyar, Deepak (Eds) (2002), *Governing Globlisation ; Issues and Instititution*, New Delhi Oxford University Press.

R.I.S, (2003), *World Trade and Development Report, 2003*: Cancun and Beyond, New Delhi, Academic Foundation.

Rahnema, M. and Bawtree, (Eds) (1997), *The post-Development Reader*, London, Zed Books.

Rodrik, Dani (1997), *Has Globalisation Gone Too Far?* Washington, DC: Institute for International Economics.

Rupert, Mark (2000), *Ideologies of Globalisation: Contending Visions of a New World Order.* London: Routledge.

Schuurman, F.J. (Eds) (2001), *Globlisation and Development Studies; Challenges for the 21st Century,* New Delhi, Vistaar.

Soros, George. (1998), *The Crisis of Global Capitalism: Open Society Endangered.* New York: Public Affairs.

Steger, M.B. and Boulder (2002), *Globalisation*, London, Rowman & Littlefield Publication.

Strange, Susan (1997), *Mad Money: When Markets Outgrow Governments.* Ann Arbor: University of Michigan Press.

Tabb, William K. (2001), *The Amoral Elephant: Globalisation and the Stuggle for Social Justice in the Twenty-First Century.* New York: Monthly Review Press.

Thimmons J. (Eds) (2000), *From Modernisation to Globalisation: Perspectives on Development and Social Change*, Malden: Blackwell.

Tomlinson, John (1999), *Globalisation and Culture.* Chicago: University of Chicago Press.

Tony S. (Eds) (1996), *Globalisation and world Society,* Cambridge: Polity Press.

Wilber, L.K. and Johnson K.P. (Eds) (1992), *The Political Economy & Development and Underdevelopment,* Fifth Edition New York, McGraw Hill. Inc.

World Bank (1998), *Global Economic Prospects and Developing Countries: Beyond Financial Crisis,* Washington, World Bank.

World Bank (2001), *Globlisation, Growth & Poverty: Building & Inclusive World Economy* 'Washington, D.C.

A DECADE OF REFORMS: THE INDIAN ECONOMY IN THE 1990S

J. Mohan Rao & Amitava Krishna Dutt

INTRODUCTION

Since mid-1991, India has undergone wide ranging economic reforms which-in the words of its government-aim to liberalise and globalise the economy. Not unlike many other developing and transitional economies, the reforms were undertaken following a foreign exchange crisis that brought India to the verge of default on its foreign loans. Besides a stabilisation programme, both internal and international economic activity have been de-regulated and liberalized. Internal liberalisation included the dismantling of a complex industrial licensing system, opening up to private investors a number of sectors previously reserved for the state, some divestment of stock in the public sector, decontrol of administered prices, and financial liberalisation. External liberalisation measures included removal of non-tariff barriers to imports, reduction in import tariffs, incentives for foreign direct investment and technology inflows, allowing Indian firms to borrow abroad, and the opening up of Indian stock markets to foreign investors.

As might be expected, the reform programmeme has evoked a variety of responses, some based on a priori theoretical expectations and others citing the trickle of empirical evidence. These responses range from euphoria about freeing a caged tiger from *dirigiste* shackles to ride the crest of free markets, to dogged mistrust about free markets among those enamoured with autarkic, state-led development. Others hold guardedly optimistic expectations for certain aspects of the reforms. Many are concerned with their "social" impact which encompasses effects on employment, poverty, income inequality, and the quality of life for the majority of people. Table 1 places some examples of these diverse views along two axes in terms of their potential longer-term impact: economic growth and social outcomes.

Table 1
Alternative Views on the Effects of Economic Reforms

		Social Outcomes		
		Positive	*Neutral*	*Negative*
Growth Impact	Positive	Official view Bhagwati & Srinivasan (1993) Bhagwati (1994) Joshi and Little (1996) World Bank (1998)	Dreze & Sen (1995)	Kumar (2000a)
	Neutral			Bhaduri & Nayyar (1996)
	Negative			Patnaik (1997) Nagaraj (1997, 2000a)

Reform-minded governments and economists such as Bhagwati and Srinivasan (1993) view globalisation as not only quickening growth but also promoting mass well-being. Compared with India's *dirigiste* and autarkic policies, they argue that foreign competition and foreign direct investment will improve allocative and production efficiency. For them, trade liberalisation increases the demand for semi-skilled and unskilled workers, increases their wages, and thereby reducing poverty and improving income distribution. Higher growth also augments fiscal resources for health, education and other social needs. Furthermore, the reforms can release any foreign exchange or aggregate demand constraints on economic growth, although these effects are not typically emphasised in neo-liberal eulogies of reforms.

An alternative view has it that the reforms, while desirable for promoting growth, are largely orthogonal to the trajectory of social outcomes. Dreze and Sen (1995) argue that reforms which increase growth will not automatically expand opportunities to lead a normal span of life, to live in good health, to read and write, and not to go hungry. Rather, their social impact depends on whether reform benefits are channelled towards improving the conditions of the poorest, to breaking down caste and gender hierarchies, and in generating employment. They therefore, argue that the "removal of counter-productive government controls may indeed expand social opportunities for many people. However, to change the circumstances (such as illiteracy and ill-health) that severely constrain the actual social opportunities of a large part of the population, these permissive reforms have to be supplemented by a radical shift in public policy in education and health" (Dreze and Sen, 1995, p. 16).

A third view, articulated by some economists such as Kumar (2000a) and social activists, is that even if they have a positive or neutral growth effect, economic reforms will have an adverse impact in social terms. A primary concern here is that globalisation will slow down employment growth if it succeeds in improving the rate of technological change, even if output growth increases. Slow employment growth, especially that of unskilled labour, will increase economic inequality. Even the sectoral changes that are supposed to ensue from the reforms are likely to cause employment losses for the many who are ill-equipped to find employment in expanding sectors. Second, a shift in employment towards unprotected and low-paid informal, casual, labour is feared as employers try to respond to the pressures of reforms by reducing labour costs. Third, if reforms shift the terms of trade towards agriculture, the rise in the price of food will reduce the real income of the poor. Lastly, cuts in social spending which accompany liberalisation and globalisation will also reduce the disposable income of the poor and government services available to them.

A final view (see, for instance, Patnaik, 1997) is that the reforms have a negative effect on both growth and mass well-being. First, increasing inequality along the lines just discussed will depress aggregate demand and slow down industrial growth. Second, trade liberalisation will increase imports but not significantly affect exports, thus reducing aggregate demand further. Third, cuts in government spending which accompany the reforms, especially on infrastructural investment, will further reduce industrial demand, and have adverse consequences on industrial and agricultural growth from the supply side. Fourth, agricultural investment and growth will not respond to price incentives, especially in the absence of land reforms which are not on the reformist agenda, and in view of declining infrastructural investment. Finally, liberalisation of capital inflows is unlikely to increase direct foreign investment much, given the low level of development, the low educational levels of unskilled workers and political uncertainty, while portfolio flows, if they increase, are likely to increase economic uncertainty and lead to intermittent foreign exchange crises. High interest rates for attracting such capital flows will also have an adverse effect on investment and growth.

This paper examines the record with a view to assessing these diverse views about India's globalising reforms. In Section 2, we examine the content of reforms undertaken, clarify the meaning and significance of the term "globalisation" and describe how we will explore the effects of globalisation in the following sections. Section 3 looks at some macro-economic dimensions of performance including the realised effects of openness on external transactions, on economic growth and other macro-economic indicators, and on trends in the rural sector which remain the mainstay of employment. Section 4 summarises trends in employment and its distribution across sectors and the formal/informal divide. Section 5 examines the evidence and controversies relating to the assessment of changes in income distribution and poverty under the impact of reforms. Section 6 turns to government policy toward social safety-nets. Section 7 concludes.

THE REFORMS, OPENNESS AND GLOBALISATION

Reform Planks: India's post-colonial governments pursued determinedly interventionist and autarkic policies. Apart from high walls of tariffs and quotas, the accumulation regime rested on the twin pillars of state-led investment and state-led coordination of economic activity. The public sector grew from small beginnings to acquire a GDP share of one quarter and an investment share of one half in the late 1980s. Significant parts of the private, especially formal, sector were controlled through an industrial licensing system, financial and credit controls, price and distribution controls, and labour laws. In addition to extensive quantitative restrictions on foreign trade, foreign direct investment (FDI) was heavily restricted as to both sectors and the equity share of participation.

After the crisis of June 1991, the self-professed policy of the government has been liberalisation and globalisation. Although this policy change was not an altogether abrupt one-through the late 1970s and the 1980s, there were attempts at reducing state control and autarky by successive governments-the reform of 1991 was unprecedented in scope. In July 1991, immediately following the general elections, the balance of payments crisis, and the imposition of IMF conditions, the new government of Narasimha Rao announced a radical policy overhaul in its Industrial Policy Statement. The changes included the removal of most non-tariff restrictions on imports of capital and intermediate goods, the broadening and simplification of export incentives, and the elimination of state trading monopolies. A negative list of restricted imports was drawn up to include items of national sensitivity (chiefly defense and health-care), and some capital goods and most consumer goods (the number of which has subsequently been reduced) for protectionist reasons. The import of all other goods was allowed except those still reserved for import through the government's canalising agencies.

The percentage of products covered by non-tariff barriers, using the harmonised system o trade classification, came down from 90 per cent in the pre-reform period to 44 per cent by 1995 (Mehta, 1997), being phased out for all tradables other than consumer goods. Tariff rates have also fallen. According to the WTO, the (weighted) average nominal tariff fell from 87 per cent in 1990-91 to 20 per cent in 1998-99, the highest rates falling from 355 to 200 per cent. The average economy-wide effective rate of protection has been estimated to decline from 87 per cent in 1989-90 to 62 per cent in 1993-94 and further to about 30 per cent in 1995-96 (Mehta, 1997). The ratio of import duties to the total value of imports fell from a peak of 53 per cent in 1987 to 22 per cent in 1997, though rising slightly in 1998. However, the dispersion in import tariffs remains high (Mehta, 1997), and there has very recently been some back-pedaling on tariffs for products such as automobiles in response to industry pressures.

The rupee was devalued by 20 per cent against the US dollar in July 1991 and further in February 1992 when an official dual exchange market was created. Since the inflation rate was about 14 per cent in 1991-92, the depreciation of the real exchange rate was by 7.89 per cent. In August 1994, a unified, floating exchange rate regime was adopted with the rupee becoming fully convertible on the current account. Figure 2 shows movements in the rupee price of the dollar, which has increased steadily since 1994.

Restrictions on FDI inflows have also been reduced considerably. Departing from the earlier restriction of 40 per cent required by the Foreign Exchange Regulation Act (FERA), foreign equity holding of up to 51 per cent was allowed in 34 high priority industries requiring large investments and advanced technology. Foreign ownership of up to 74 per cent was allowed in 14 additional infrastructure and high-priority industries, and 100 per cent foreign ownership on an automatic basis is allowed in ports, roads, and full ownership status is also given to NRI investors in priority industries. A Foreign Investment Promotion Board is allowed to approve up to 100 per cent foreign ownership in cases involving transfer of high technology, export-oriented projects, energy and infrastructure projects, and consulting and trading companies, and is required to do so expeditiously and transparently. To encourage technology transfers, the government announced that it would provide automatic approval for technology agreements related to high priority industries within specified parameters.

Portfolio capital inflows have also been deregulated. NRIs and foreign institutional investors (FIIs) such as pension funds and mutual funds were allowed to own stock in the corporate sector subject to some limits (which were gradually relaxed), with full repatriation rights and without restrictions on volume of trading or lock-in period and favourable tax rates. Subsequently, the markets for debt and for government securities were also opened up to FIIs. Larger Indian firms were allowed to obtain long-term low-cost financing from international capital markets, subject to government approval. However, many types of capital account transactions are still banned or restricted (Nayyar, 2000). Commercial borrowing on international capital markets is restricted to selected, longer, maturities and the rest requires case by case approval. Commercial banks are not allowed to accept deposits or make loans denominated in foreign currencies, with a few exceptions. Apart from capital outflows associated with capital inflows, the regime of capital outflows has not been significantly liberalised.

Sweeping measures of internal deregulation have also been implemented, which complemented the external liberalisation measures and made the economy more open. India's byzantine licensing system was dismantled by abolishing the licensing requirement for industrial investment in all but 14 specified industries (on grounds of environmental hazards, national security or social well-being). Industries and services, including infrastructure such as telecommunication, roads, power generation and petroleum refining, that were earlier reserved for the public sector were opened up to private (including foreign) investors. Restrictions on investments by large industrial houses (and foreign companies) under the Monopolies and Restrictive Trade Practices Act were abolished. A phased programmeme of privatisation of public sector enterprises (PSEs) has been launched, shares in PSEs have been sold, and over the last year or so a limited amount of actual privatisation has occurred. The financial sector has also been drastically liberalised. Banking reform gave permission to new private sector banks including foreign joint ventures, and private non-bank financial intermediates are also allowed. The Capital Issues Control Act was repealed, and the regulation of a liberalised capital market has been entrusted with a newly created Securities and Exchange Board of Trade, and online trading and dematerialised trading has been introduced. Moreover, a programme of economic stabilisation has accompanied the above measures: in particular, the fiscal deficit was reduced by over a third.

Successive governments have expressed their intention of carrying these reforms further. It has been announced that import tariffs will be reduced to international levels, quantitative controls removed ahead even of initial schedules, and the rupee made fully convertible by opening the capital account (though this last step seems to have lost support in the aftermath of the Asian financial crisis).

Globalisation and Openness

Much of the literature and common parlance in India even more, uses openness and globalisation synonymously. In this paper, however, we reserve the term *openness* to refer to policies that aim to bring about economic integration with international markets, and take *globalisation* to be some measure of increased external integration actually achieved. The reason for distinguishing between the two terms, despite the close relation between them, is that openness may not go hand-in-hand with globalisation, as defined here.

The importance of openness and globalisation in India's economic reforms is obvious. As noted earlier, the official case for the reforms relies on both positive and negative arguments. The key positive arguments are: (1) that trade liberalisation will improve allocative efficiency by shifting resources from capital-intensive to labour-intensive sectors; (2) that reduced protection will raise technical efficiency by exposing Indian firms to foreign competition; and (3) that lowered barriers to foreign capital inflows will speed up capital accumulation and raise productivity levels through technology upgrading and spillovers. The official case also takes aggregate demand and foreign exchange constraints on growth to be the consequences of an autarkic policy orientation, the remedy for which lies in openness and globalisation; this constitutes the negative case for the reforms. Each of these arguments makes external integration-or globalisation-the engine of economic growth, and openness the centrepiece of policy. As described above, the reforms also involve internal de-regulation and liberalisation, and the adoption of other elements of domestic policy orthodoxy. However, these are viewed as *economic pre-requisites*, or at least facilitators, for pursuing a successful policy of openness for increasing globalisation and, in turn, the likely *political consequences* of a policy of openness. Therefore, openness does indeed constitute the focal point, and globalisation the touchstone, of the new regime as it is perceived by its architects.

Since our purpose is to examine the consequences of globalisation, we will focus mostly on import liberalisation, removal of restrictions to capital flows and on technology imports-which are the main elements of greater openness. However, we will also take into account domestic policy changes-internal liberalisation as well as those involving general macroeconomic policy-given that these reforms are inextricably linked to, and flow from, the logic of globalisation.

Methodological remarks

To assess the growth and social impacts of globalisation we compare trends before and after the onset of the reforms in 1991. It is important to be forewarned of the problems of this method.

The "before/after" method is problematic because the year 1991 witnessed a harvest failure and a severe payments crisis which obliged the government to undertake stabilisation measures which are not necessarily part of the structural reforms. Moreover, as we have seen, the government not only embarked on external liberalisation but also on reforms liberalising domestic activities all of which may not be related to openness. Finally, the economy has been subjected to a number of shocks-such as the East Asian crisis and economic sanctions-which are arguably independent of the reform process. Given that the post-1991 outcomes are likely to be affected by all of these changes, it would seem impossible to attribute the differences solely to policy changes affecting external economic relations. We will guard against this problem by examining causal mechanisms linking aspects of the reform to economic performance in addition to general trends relating to growth and the social sector.

It may be thought preferable to examine the effects of "globalising" reforms using a suitable computable general equilibrium model to consider the effects of changes in parameters which reflect foreign-sector reforms alone. This has the virtue of isolating the effects of external policy changes. However, it is problematic because it ignores the close relationship between external and domestic policy changes alluded to earlier: the requirements of consistency might force domestic policy changes to conform with external policy changes and as "domestic" policy changes affect the level of "globalisation". For instance, the dismantling of the licensing apparatus, usually thought of as an internal liberalisation measure, may make exports more competitive and the economy more attractive to foreign investors.

A second issue is whether 1991 is an appropriate date for our comparison. It is generally accepted in the Indian discussion that the most important policy discontinuity occurred in 1991. However, some have argued that since liberalisation started in the 1980s and even earlier, it is not appropriate to compare the period before and after 1991 to measure the effects of reforms. We take the view that 1991 is the crucial divide for three reasons. First, despite some degree of liberalisation during the 1980s, the process never gained real momentum. After Indira Gandhi's return to power in 1980 there were some cosmetic changes. After Rajiv Gandhi became Prime Minister following her assassination in 1984 there was some amount of reform, but in 1987, after some political setbacks, the thrust towards economic liberalisation slowed down (Kohli, 1990, p. 305-24). Second, during the decade the most important policy reforms concerned reducing internal barriers to entry which allowed large business houses to have a larger role in industrial development, and not so much external liberalisation. Regarding the external sector, there was significant rationalisation and some liberalisation of imported raw material imports and component imports (by shifting importable items from restricted lists to what was called the Open General License), easing of technology imports, and some very limited liberalisation of capital goods imports. But even in the middle of the decade Indian nominal tariffs were among the highest in the world (Ahluwalia, 1991, p. 27). As shown in Figure 1, import duties as a percentage of imports increased through most of the 1980s, exceeding 50 per cent in 1987 and 1988, before coming down especially after 1991 (though a part of this increase reflects a shift from quantitative to tariffs restrictions). Third, most observers attribute the higher growth of that period, especially in the industrial sector, to expansionary fiscal policies, infrastructural investment, and foreign borrowing. Even pro-reform observers like Ahluwalia (1991) and Bhagwati (1993,

p. 92), who argue that the micro-economic reforms of the 1980s may have made some contribution to the higher growth, agree with this conclusion. It has therefore become established practice, in recent discussions and appraisals of reforms, to consider 1991 as their real beginning (see, for instance, Ahluwalia, 1995, Bhagwati, 1998).

A third issue concerning the before/after method is that the beneficial effects of external integration take time to be felt and too few years have passed (and fewer still for which relatively complete evidence is available) since 1991 to judge these longer-term effects. While there is some merit in this argument, especially in a large country like India, it can be overemphasised. A decade has already passed since the reforms were initiated. Moreover, we propose to examine both events immediately following 1991 and those occurring subsequently to distinguish the shorter and longer terms.

OPENNESS AND ECONOMIC GROWTH

To analyse whether economic opening has had any identifiable effect on economic growth and related macro-economic indicators we first discuss the extent to which the Indian economy has become more globalised under the new regime, and examine mechanisms by which these changes affected the economy. We then turn to the overall macro-economic indicators, and to the agricultural sector which is home to over three-fifths of the labour force and an even higher fraction of the poor.

Increased Openness and Globalisation

Trade Flows

India's foreign trade as a fraction of GDP has grown significant, from around 15 per cent in the 1980s and 17 per cent in 1990-91 to about 25 per cent in the late 1990s. However, there has been a marginal fall in the ratio since the peak of 1995-96, despite continued import liberalisation. Whereas India's share of world exports fell consistently from about 2 per cent in the 1950s to about 0.6 per cent in the

1970s, and then stayed at around 0.5 per cent from 1973 onwards through the 1980s, the share has now risen smartly to 0.8 per cent in the post-reform period. In growth terms, the dollar value of India's exports increased annually immediately after the reforms at 12 per cent between 1990-91 and 1995-96, which is significantly higher than the 7.5 per cent growth rate for world trade. By any standard, this must be reckoned rapid globalisation. But these trends conceal some problems.

1. The growth of exports does not appear to be sustained. After growing annually in 1993-94 and 1995-96 at around 20 per cent in dollar terms, in 1996-97 and 1997-98 growth was at 5.3 per cent and 4.6 per cent, and there was actually a decline by 3.9 per cent in 1998-99. The sharp acceleration has been attributed both to a rapid growth in world trade and to a sharp real depreciation of the rupee in the early 1990s (see Marjit and Dasgupta, 1997, and Srinivasan, 1998), which can be said to be a direct result of economic reforms. The subsequent slowdown can be partially explained by the slowdown of world trade and the East Asian crisis (and the resulting sharp depreciation of East Asian currencies). However, the real exchange appreciation in the mid 1990s, at least in part due to capital inflows which resulting from reforms, also arguably had an impact (see below).

2. The import-GDP ratio has increased even faster than the export-GDP ratio, reaching a level of about 14 per cent in the second half of the 1990s. This implies that the trade deficit (as a percentage of GDP) has worsened for much of the 1990s, presumably due to liberalisation, although there has been some recent improvement. Further, reductions in import taxes and removal of non-tariff barriers on consumer goods, as planned, are likely to further widen the trade deficit.

3. While there was a shift in the composition of imports between 1980-81 to 1990-91, no further shift occurred during the post-reform period (Mehta, 1997). This is

surprising considering the large changes in the structure of protection, and suggests that changes in trade policy affecting the relative competitiveness of import-competing sectors may have been neutralised by other policy shifts.

4. Econometric evidence does not support the conventional conjecture that changes in competitiveness have increased India's exports; nor do the reforms appear to have had an appreciable impact on exports as measured by post-reform dummy variable (Mehta, 1997).
5. As with imports, the composition of India's exports has not changed significantly in the 1990s, while it did so between 1980-81 and 1990-91 (Mehta, 1997). Kumar (2000a) has argued that India's export competitiveness has been affected adversely by the failure to diversify exports. India's export growth acceleration appears to have been caused by a shift in export composition towards relatively dynamic Asian markets.

FDI Inflows: After stagnation in the 1970s, the inflow of FDI has recently increased, following limited liberalisation, the FDI stock nearly tripled in 1980s. In the wake of the policy changes of 1991, approvals of FDI inflows increased spectacularly: compared to $200 million in 1991, about $17 billion worth of FDI proposals was approved in 1997. As Figure 5 shows, actual inflows also increased rapidly, although considerably smaller than approvals. FDI as a percentage of Gross Domestic Investment and GDP has also grown rapidly between 1991-92 and 1997-98, as shown in Figure 6, although it should be noted that all FDI does not represent capital formation (see below).

Despite this rapid expansion, however, FDI inflows to India remain low compared to other LDCs in Asia such as China, Malaysia, Thailand and Indonesia, and also far below that of all LDCs in relation to GDP-a ratio which increased from 0.8 per cent in the early 1990s to 2 per cent in 1997, according to World Bank estimates (compared to India's peak level of 0.85 per cent in 1997-98). Cumulative FDI into India in the 1990s decade has been around \$15 billion, compared to China's inflow of \$238 billion during 1994-1999. Moreover, it is unclear to what extent that increase in FDI will be sustained. As Figure 5 shows, FDI inflows fell in both years after 1997-98, reversing the upward trend since 1991-92.

There is also some doubt on whether the spurt in FDI was caused by the liberalisation policy. Kumar (1998) has pointed out that India's share of FDI inflows from Germany, France and the US do not show any significant change, which suggests that liberalisation has not had a major impact. India seems to have merely benefited from the dramatic expansion in FDI flows from advanced countries to developing countries in the 1990s, which can to a large extent be explained by conditions internal to advanced countries. However, to the extent that the increase in this FDI was due to less restrictive policies in developing economies in general, it can be argued that India's reforms at least enabled it to maintain India's share in these higher flows.

Has the increase in FDI had (or likely to have) a positive effect on growth in India? FDI is supposed to foster growth by increasing capital accumulation, inducing technological change and greater efficiency, and by improving the balance of payment directly and by increasing exports. Regarding capital formation, we have seen that the FDI-GDI ratio has remained small. In fact, the state-through the financial institutions that it controls-has remained the principal financier of local enterprises, in both public and private sectors,. The share of foreign firms in fixed asset formation in the corporate sector remained unchanged at about 10 per cent in the 1990s. Moreover, foreign firms used a smaller fraction of their investible resources in physical investment than Indian firms. During the five years since 1991-92, the ratio of gross fixed assets to total uses of funds for the foreign private sector was about 13 per cent lower for foreign compared to indigenous private firms (Nagaraj, 1997). It appears that FDI largely represents the acquisition of managerial control of existing firms, rather than representing new capital formation. During 1997-99 nearly

40 per cent of FDI inflows have taken the form of mergers and acquisitions of existing Indian enterprises, reversing the trend till 1990 when nearly all FDI inflow took the form of greenfield projects (Kumar, 2000b). Regarding technological change, the evidence provides little support for the widely-held expectation that the new liberalisation of FDI will help upgrade technology, enhance product innovation and transfer management skills. The growth rate of productivity for industries with relatively high advanced foreign technology inflows is not significantly greater than that for other industries (Goldar, 1993). Moreover, since a large portion of FDI takes the form of mergers and acquisitions, the extent of technological inflows and diffusion of knowledge within the economy is likely to be low. Kumar (2000b, p. 2855) points out that in many cases TNCs have bought up profitable enterprises to obtain distributional channels, where managerial and technological improvements have been negligible. In fact efficiency in these enterprises may have declined because of inappropriate new management practices and technology (as suggested by a fall in the market share of firms taken over by TNCs). Since TNC acquisition has also largely taken the form of buying out joint ventures-previously important conduits for knowledge inflows-the effect on technological change is negligible, and that on the future of technological diffusion, arguably negative. While greenfield investment can increase competition, mergers and acquisitions by TNCs-mostly of a horizontal rather than a vertical nature-has tended to increase industrial concentration (Kumar, 2000b), with possible adverse effects on efficiency, especially due to the recent relaxation of antitrust laws. Mani and Bhaskar (1998), Goldar and Ranganathan (1998), and Basant (2000) find that there has been a decline in the trend of in-house R & D in the corporate sector in the 1990s, arguably due to easier access to foreign technology. To the extent that the effectiveness and speed of technology transfers depends on domestic technological capability, the effect of this trend on technological change is arguably negative. Domestic technological capability can also

be adversely affected by competition faced by domestic firms from foreign firms due to brand and trade names which put domestic competitors at a disadvantage (Kumar, 2000a). Finally, the shift in sectoral composition of FDI flows-from high technology manufactures to services, infrastructure and low technology manufacturing sectors. Regarding the balance of payments, Kumar (2000b) points out that a significant portion of investment by TNCs does not involve net inflows of foreign capital. In about 27 per cent of the deals associated with TNCs in India between April 1993 to February 2000, acquisitions have been made by Indian affiliates of TNCs, often with their internal fund accruals and domestic borrowings. Taking into account the repatriation of profits to foreign parent firms, the effect of this on the balance of payments is likely to be negative. The effect on exports is also likely to be negligible, given that the bulk of FDI in India is directed to the home market, with TNCs and their affiliates acquiring domestic firms to take over established domestic distribution networks (Kumar, 2000a). Overall, there is little evidence that growth has been positively affected by FDI inflows. Measuring FDI as a ratio of GDP, we find that there is no evidence that either FDI or growth Granger-cause each other, even at the 10 per cent level of significance.

Portfolio Investment and Foreign Currency Bank Deposits: Total foreign portfolio investment in India expanded rapidly, from $6 million in 1990-91 to over $3 billion in 1999-2000. Indeed, the growth was initially much more rapid than the growth of FDI, so that portfolio investment constituted the bulk of total foreign investment until 1996-97. Foreign currency deposits in banks have also increased rapidly, including non-resident Indian (NRI) deposits. Despite these rapid increases, the magnitude of the flows has been small, both in relation to the size of the economy and in comparison to many other Latin American and East and South East Asian economies.

The increased flows of foreign capital were expected to promote higher saving, investment and capital formation, thereby increase the rate of growth. However, the expected growth effects of portfolio flows and bank deposits appear not have been fulfilled.

The deregulation of the stock market and its opening up to international capital flows did produce an enormous growth in the market (see Singh, 1998) with market capitalisation ratios increasing dramatically in the early 1990s. However, according to some estimates the volatility of stock prices also appears to have increased in the 1990s, partly due to the growing influence of the FIIs, a direct consequence of deregulation (see Roy, 2001). Kohli (2001a) finds that correlation measures between portfolio capital flows and stock price indices are strong and positive, and that these influences are clear during the capital market surge in the 1992-95 period.

While market enthusiasts hoped that stock market stimulation from foreign inflows would help bump up the saving rate, no such connection appears to have materialised. While the volume of household savings held in the form of shares and debentures and in units of the Unit Trust of India (a public sector mutual fund) has risen 35-fold since 1980-81, the overwhelming part of this reflects a shift from bank deposits to stocks. After the sharp fall in stock prices following the boom, the share of stocks went down again in favour of bank deposits (Pal, 1998). Moreover, a large proportion of these inflows did not contribute to fixed capital formation in manufacturing since the ratio of Gross Fixed Capital Formation to the supply of long-term funds available to that sector fell significantly during 1992-96 (Nagaraj, 1997). Nagaraj argues that the resources were more important for inter-corporate investment, financing mergers and takeovers, and to fuel the real estate boom. Mumbai's real estate prices increased by between and 4 and 6 times from 1991 to 1996 and the cost of office space reached levels well beyond those in New York, London, Tokyo or Hong Kong, but declined sharply after that to levels 60 per cent lower than peak prices in 2000. Though Mumbai's experience was extreme, it reflects trends in other major cities in India (Nijman, 2000). It is likely that a significant part of the demand surge was fuelled by capital inflows, even if foreign inflows were not directly responsible for financing real estate purchases. To the extent that the stock market did supply funds for capital formation, this increase was compensated by a fall in internal corporate funding, possibly due to lower profitability (Singh, 1998). Pethe and Karnik (2000) find that there is weak causality running from the index of industrial production to stock prices, but not the other way around. Roy (2001), using a number of variables to measure economic activity, also reports that there is no long-run stable relationship between stock price and the macro-economy. Thus, there is little evidence that a rise in stock prices translated into higher industrial investment and growth by reducing the cost of finance or improving business expectations.

The volatility of these hot money flows seen elsewhere in the world is also reflected in Indian experience since 1991. Portfolio flows, subject to 'sudden reversal', are more volatile than FDI. Kohli reports that the standard deviation of portfolio investment between 1990 and 1999 is 5163.2, as compared with 4592.3 for FDI taking for annual figures, and the difference increases when measured at higher frequency, that is, quarterly and monthly. The fact that absence of full convertibility of the rupee on the capital account has partially shielded India from the crises which has affected East and South East Asia. Nevertheless, the volatility of portfolio flows is obvious from Figure 7.

When inflows are high, the rupee tends to appreciate, eroding the competitiveness of Indian exports. Impulse response analysis shows that a one standard deviation positive shock to net inflows of foreign currency causes real exchange appreciation by 0.14 per cent in the next quarter (Kohli, 2001a). The Reserve Bank of India (RBI) has tried to contain the effects of capital inflows on exchange rate appreciation by intervening in foreign exchange markets. Following the heavy capital inflows in the 1993-95 period, and again in 1997-98, the RBI purchased dollars to prevent an appreciation of the rupee. The consequence of this has been a large increase in foreign exchange reserves, with the result that the stock of international reserves in 1999-2000 is 552 per cent higher than the 1991 level. In periods of high capital inflows, the RBI has tried to lean against the wind by raising the discount rate and by increasing cash reserve requirements, with open market operations having a small role because of the limited ability of bond and equity markets to absorb government securities (Kohli, 2001b). Thus, interest rates have occasionally been increased when capital inflows have increased, as in 1993-94 and 1996-97, when both nominal and real rates increased.

When capital flows are reversed, pressures are created on the balance of payments, requiring import compression and restrictive government policies that reduce the growth of the economy. These outflows can be caused by factors exogenous to the economy, such as political disturbances in India, contagious effects due to problems elsewhere in the world, as occurred during the East Asian crisis which led to a sharp decline in 1997-98.

Economic Growth and Other Macro-economic Indicators

Growth: Leaving out the high-growth year of 1988 and the crisis year of 1991, Figure 8 shows that real GDP growth fluctuated between 3.5 per cent and 8 per cent during the 1980s and 1990s. As such, it is difficult to come to any clear conclusion about trends before and after 1991. On the one hand, the highest rate of growth for a single year occurred before the 1991 reforms. On the other hand, between 1994 and 1996 the economy grew consistently above the 7 per cent level, a feat not achieved in the pre-reform years. This high rate of growth, however, has not been maintained thereafter: in 1997-98, it fell to below 5 per cent and was just above 6 per cent in 1998-99. As the recession continues GDP growth was officially estimated at about 4 per cent in 2000-01. The advance estimate for 2001-02 is put at 5.4 per cent, despite a very strong harvest (with industrial growth at 2.3 per cent during April-December 2001).

Average and trend growth rates are more revealing. According to the new series of GDP that makes the comparison more favourable for the post-reform period, average GDP growth was 5.6 per cent between 1991-92 and 1998-99 compared to 5.9 per cent in the 1980s. However, if one leaves out the bad year 1991-92, the average for the post-reform period becomes 6.4 per cent. Thus, the rate of growth for the post-reform period is higher than that of the previous decade if one leaves out 1991-92, but lower if one includes it (in both cases excluding the recent recession years). Nagaraj (2000a) examines GDP data for the1980-81 and 1999-2000 period using a dummy variable for the post-liberalisation period to find that there is no statistically significant break in the trend growth rate of 5.7 per cent after 1991-92, and this result holds even when the year 1991-92 is excluded. It has been argued that the recent slowdown has been caused by exogenous factors such as the East Asian crisis, economic sanctions following the nuclear tests, and war in the region, and does not reflect long-run trends, which makes the comparison even more favorable for the later period. However, to the extent the recent slowdown reflects an industrial recession (which continues in full swing at the time of writing) triggered mainly by a slowdown in public investment (see Kumar, 2000a) it is arguably a consequence of reforms.

At a disaggregated level, there is some disagreement about rates of growth differences before and after reforms, depending on what series one examines. Table 2 provides data from the Government of India's *Economic Survey*, on annual average growth rates of several sectors in the pre-reform period, which it takes to be 1980-81 to 1991-92 and the post-reform period, which it takes to be 1992-93 to 1999-2000. The data show a decline in the rate of growth of agriculture, not only in all crop production, but also in food grain production. There is also a decline in industrial production, as well as in total manufacturing. Of the manufacturing sectors shown in the Table, only intermediate goods and consumer goods sectors reveal an increase in the growth rate in the post-reform period, while there is a sharp decline for capital goods. In terms of GDP (value added) in manufacturing, however, there is an increase in the rate of growth in the post-reform period. Turning to trend rates of growth, Nagaraj (2000a) using National Account Statistics data finds no statistically significant change in the trend growth for the primary sector or the tertiary sector during this period, and a modest though significant reduction in the growth rate for the secondary sector. The tertiary sector has grown no faster in the post-reform period than earlier, but given the slow-down in the growth rate of the secondary sector, it has emerged as the fastest-growing sector. At an even more disaggregated level, none of the industry groups (the one digit level) has experienced an increase in the growth rate, while two sectors-that is, manufacturing, and public, social and personal services-constituting about 30 per cent of GDP in the 1990s-have registered a statistically significant slowdown.

Table 2
Sectoral Rates of Growth

	1980-81 to 1991-92	*1992-93 to 1999-2000*
Agriculture and Allied Sectors	3.9	3.6
Agriculture (all crop)	4.2	3.7
Foodgrains	2.9	2.0
Industrial Productiont	7.8	6.0
Manufacturing	7.6	6.3
Basic Goods	7.4	6.1
Capital Goods	9.4	5.9
Intermediate Goods	4.9	9.1
Consumer Goods	6.0	6.3
GDP-Manufacturing	6.1	7.4

Source: Government of India, Ministry of Finance, *Economic Survey*, 2000-01.

One consequence of the tertiary sector becoming the fastest growing sector of the economy is that its share in

GDP has increased by virtually 1 per cent point every year from 41 per cent in 1990-91 to about 49 per cent in 2000-2001, and issue to which we will return below.

Saving and investment: Figure 9 shows trends in domestic saving and investment rates. It reveals that domestic saving and investment rates, as well as the fixed investment rate fell after the reforms, presumably due to the economic contraction resulting from the stabilisation programme, but then increased steeply up to 1995-96. These increases, however, were reversed in 1995-96. Though domestic saving and investment rates recovered somewhat afterward, fixed investment has fallen consistently as a share of GDP since 1995-96. Gross fixed capital formation as a share of GDP in the private corporate sector has also fallen steadily since 1995-96. Overall, however, gross fixed capital formation grew at the faster rate of 6.9 per cent during the 1990s than in the 1980s, when it grew at 4.2 per cent, and the average gross domestic fixed investment as a percentage of GDP was higher in the 1990s than in the 1980s.

While this increase may be counted as a positive payoff to the financial (internal and external) liberalisation, it has not resulted in higher growth, so that the added accumulation seems to have contributed to increased capital intensity in the economy rather than to income growth. Data on actual capital-output ratios confirm this: the net fixed capital to output ratio for the economy, after falling from 2.63 in 1980 to 2.38 in 1990, increased in the 1990s to 2.46 in 1994. The net capital-output ratio in industry, after showing a declining trend in the 1980s, has risen from 5.6 in 1990-91 to 7.1 in 1998-99. Whatever the relative influence of wage growth, technology upgrading, or exposure to foreign competition, this belies the expectation that external liberalisation would reduce capital intensity.

Government finance: As shown in Figure 10, the gross fiscal deficit of the Central and State governments increased in the 1980s, from 7.5 per cent of GDP in 1981-82 to over 11 per cent in 1990-91. Fiscal stabilization was the key feature of the stabilization programme adopted after the crisis, so that there was a declining trend (with a brief reversal in 1993-94) till 1996-97, when it fell around 7.5 per cent. Since then, however, the ratio has increased, going above the 10 per cent mark by the end of the decade. This increase has been due to an increase in the revenue or current account deficit of the Central and State governments. The interest burden on the Central budget has continued to rise throughout the 1990s, its share in current expenditure increasing from 29 per cent in 1990-91 to 36 per cent in 1999-2000, with its level as a proportion of GDP increasing from 3.8 per cent to 4.7 per cent. While this is the primary source of the fiscal squeeze, another source of revenue squeeze, especially noticeable during the last half of the 1990s, is import tariff revenue. Customs revenue as a ratio of total Central Government revenues fell from above 33 per cent in 1991 to below 27 per cent in 1999-2000. The effect of this on tax revenues can be seen from the fact that in 1999-2000 gross tax revenues have declined by 0.9 per cent of GDP, composed of a fall in indirect taxes by 1.6 per cent and a rise in direct taxes by 0.7 per cent. The effect on the government budget deficit can be seen by comparing the actual Central Government deficit to GDP ratio to what it would have been had the 1991 ratio of customs to total revenue been maintained, as shown in Figure 11.

One predictable consequence of this fiscal squeeze is that public capital formation has slowed down during the 1990s. As shown in Figure 10, the Central Government's capital expenditure as a proportion of GDP has declined from 5.6 per cent in 1990-91 to 2.6 per cent in 1999-2000. It is widely acknowledged that one of the major explanations of India's strong growth performance in the 1980s is the increase in infrastructure investment, especially in railways and power generation (Ahluwalia, 1991: 85-87). Such investment not only has a positive supply-side effect, but there is also evidence that there is a positive demand-side effect as government investment "crowds in" by private investment, both in the industrial and agricultural sectors. There is a consensus that between the declining fiscal capacity of the state and the unresolved regulatory complexities surrounding privatisation, the infrastructure sectors loom increasingly large as a constraint on economic growth, especially given India's low level of infrastructure development (World Bank, 1996). Many argue that the industrial recession after 1995 has been in major part a consequence of the decline in government investment. Public sector capital formation slowed down to just 3.4 per cent per annum (from 5.5 per cent in the 1980s). In particular, Gross Fixed Capital Formation growth in electricity, gas and water fell from 7.9 per cent per annum in the 1980s to just 4.8 per cent in the 1990s.

Prices: Figures 12 and 13 show trends in inflation and in interest rates (the real rate of interest referring to the prime lending rate adjusted for inflation measured by the GDP deflator). The sharp spurt in prices in 1991 is the combined effect of the drought, monetary restriction associated with the stabilisation programme, increases in administered prices and in the issue prices of government-subsidised foodgrains, and subsequently, the extraction of an export surplus from the economy. Bank rates were jacked up to curb inflation, to entice capital inflows and as part of a programme of financial liberalisation. With the cooling of inflation, interest rates fall, and indeed they have fallen 2 to 3 points below where they had been prior to liberalisation reflecting the massive growth of the primary issues market after 1994. The real interest rate, however, increased again, although it has recently fallen as a result of rate cuts attempting to overcome the recession.

The rate of inflation, measured by the GDP deflator or the CPI has been somewhat lower than in the pre-reform period. Measured by the CPI, it fell from an annual average of 8.9 for the 1981-82 to 1990-91 period to 8.5 in the 1992-93 to 1998-99 period, while in terms of the GDP deflator it fell from 8.4 to 7.3 per cent. However, the inflation rate has fluctuated in the recent period, and in 1998-99 almost reached the high level of the crisis year of 1991-92. An additional trend is that the CPI inflation has been higher than that in terms of the GDP deflator (and also of wholesale prices). The main reason for this divergence is the higher weight of the food group in the CPI, though the costs of other items of mass consumption, such as housing and medical care, have also shown significant increases.

The growing relative price of food is also reflected in the relative price of agricultural products, which increased from 113 in 1992-93 to 129 in 1999-2000, with 1981-82 as the base, as shown in Figure 14. Although the relative price shown refers to wholesale prices, and this price need not affect the market price of foodgrains given India's subsidised public food distribution system, the market price of food has generally followed procurement prices in the 1990s (see Balakrishnan, 2000), implying that the consumer price ratio has shown a trend similar to the wholesale relative price. There is some evidence that this trend in the relative price of agricultural products, although determined by policy, has been affected by the performance of agricultural growth relative to demand growth. Measuring the latter by the difference between the real rate of growth of agricultural value added and the real rate of growth of GDP at market prices, we find a negative correlation between the relative price of agricultural products and the lagged relative performance of agriculture for the 1970-1998 period. There is also evidence of Granger causality from relative growth to the relative price at the 10 per cent level of significance, so that slow agricultural growth may have caused a rise in the agricultural terms of trade. These changes in the relative price of agricultural products and food, in turn, have important implications for the debates concerning economic reforms on agricultural growth and poverty, to which we will turn later.

Another price relevant for the discussion of India's reform is the relative price of traded goods to non-traded goods, which can be measured by the real exchange rate. As shown in Figure 15, although the nominal trade-weighted exchange rate has increased for most of the 1990s, the real exchange rate has not shown a similar pattern. There was a significant real depreciation of more than 80 per cent between the mid-1980s and 1993-94, after which there was some appreciation, with fluctuations around the 160 mark (with 1981-82=100).

Growth constraints

We next turn to three sets of factors that can act as constraints on the rate of growth of the economy, namely, aggregate demand, total factor productivity growth (*TFPG*), and foreign exchange constraints.

Aggregate demand

The concern with aggregate demand as a determinant of growth has been lately drowned by the focus on supply-side cures implicit in the reformist agenda. However, we believe aggregate demand remains highly relevant in stimulating investment, and raising utilisation in the oligopolistic non-agricultural sectors of the formal economy, and thereby output and savings (see Dutt, 1996). The role of different components of aggregate demand - private investment, government spending and export - in stimulating growth is analysed in Figure 16. X is total supply (GDP plus total imports), I is private investment, G is total government expenditure (including government investment), E is exports, and s, t and m are the ratios of private saving, taxes, and imports to total supply. X, I, G and E have been deflated by the GDP deflator and expressed in real terms. Following Godley and McCarthy (1997), we take I/s, G/t, and E/m to be the contributions of investment, government spending and exports to GDP (since they show the real levels of these components multiplied by the respective "own" multipliers); X is therefore a weighted average of these three contributions0. We find that government spending has, since the 1980s, always been the major expansionary component of demand, since G/t consistently lies above the X line. The domestic private sector has more or less played a neutral role, since I/s has been close to X, while exports has consistently played a depressive role, since E/m is consistently below X. This pattern, strongest during the

1980s, confirms the importance of government fiscal policy in generating growth in the 1980s. The contraction of fiscal spending during the crisis of 1991 is reflected in the data, as is the contraction in the private domestic sector and the expansion in the role of exports. However, soon thereafter we find the fiscal factor recovering its role, though leveling off between 1993-94 and 1996-97 as the role of the private domestic sector and exports has grown. Despite these changes, however, the basic pattern remains that of fiscal policy being the major expansionary component of aggregate demand even after the reforms. Given the recessionary tendencies since 1996-97, this analysis finds further confirmation in the growing clamor for fiscal boosts to the sagging growth of industry and in the resultant increase in G/t.

Productivity growth

Turning to the supply-based approach, we use the simple and popular method of calculating *TFPG* using Solow's residual, despite its well-known problems. Our estimates of the residual, using the equation

$$TFPG = g\,(Y/L) - K\,g\,(K/L)$$

where g (i) refers to the rate of growth of i, Y is real output, L is total employment, K is real net fixed capital stock and ?K is the share of capital in output, are shown in Figure 17. As expected, *TFPG* is negative in the crisis year of 1991. Leaving aside 1991 (when *TFPG* is negative), the average *TFPG* is 3.4 for 1980-90 and 2.5 for 1991-95, suggesting that there has been a decline in *TFPG* after the 1991 reforms compared to the 1980s.

Other available estimates of productivity growth performance-including those using more micro-level data-do not reveal an improvement in the post-reform period. Kumar (2000a) reviews the evidence to argue that productivity performance of Indian industries actually deteriorated in the 1990s as compared to the 1980s, and that this holds true at both 3-digit and 2-digit levels.

Balakrishnan et. al. (2000), using data from a panel of 2,300 firms spread over five industry groups at the 2-digit level for the years 1988-89 to 1997-98, find evidence of a statistically significant fall in total factor productivity growth after 1991-92. Krishna and Mitra (1998) report a statistically significant increase in productivity growth after 1991 in four select industries, a study criticised by Balakrishnan et al (2000) on account of the method used for the construction of capital and labour input variables.

Given that productivity growth in services is usually lower than in other sectors, it may also be surmised that the relative growth of the service sector (noted earlier), without an increase in its relative price, may have reduced overall TFPG. To examine this hypothesis and to examine the contributions of productivity change within sectors and structural change to overall productivity trends we turn to labour productivity figures, since the data required for total factor productivity calculations by sectors are not available. For this purpose we use sectoral real GDP, workforce, and gross value added per worker data from the most recent NSS rounds (see Sundaram, 2001). Growth rates for these over the 1993-94 to 1999-2000 period are shown in Table 3. We find a contraction in employment in the agricultural sector, a rise in manufacturing and mining, and a relatively larger rise in construction and services, confirming the relative growth of the services sector. The workforce has grown annually at less than 1 per cent, significantly below the rate of population growth. Labour productivity has grown most rapidly in mining and manufacturing, only slightly more slowly in construction and services, and total labour productivity has grown at around 6 per cent per annum. The last three columns of the total decomposes the total change in labour productivity utilising the method used by Pieper (2000). They show that over 90 per cent of total productivity change was due to changes within sectors, and less than 10 per cent was due to inter-sectoral changes in employment, primarily due to a shift from agriculture to construction and services. The more detailed sectoral

Table 3

Labour Productivity Change Decompositions, 1993-94 to 1999-2000

	Growth rate			*per cent contributions in total*		
	GDP	*Workforce*	*GVA*	*Own*	*Reallocation*	*Sector total*
Agriculture	3.08377	-0.24541	3.337365	16.8082	2.020379	18.82858
Mining and Manufacturing	7.334804	1.260611	5.998575	20.87087	0.602388	21.47326
Construction and services	8.993408	3.226636	5.586515	53.32946	6.368701	59.69816
Total	6.891888	0.840983	6.000442	91.00853	8.991468	100
Agriculture and allied activities	3.08377	-0.24541	3.337365	16.8082	2.020379	18.82858
Mining and quarrying	4.686208	-2.9436	7.861212	3.125213	-0.66949	2.455722
Manufacturing less repair services	7.738465	1.51368	6.131966	18.67442	0.343124	19.01754
Electricity, gas, water	6.833561	-4.80335	12.22407	4.564322	-1.24889	3.31543
Construction	6.348739	6.22767	0.113971	0.129523	0.939297	1.068819
Trade, hotels and restaurant	9.184884	6.22401	2.787387	8.289924	2.785044	11.07497
Transport, storage, and communications	8.728242	5.224443	3.329833	4.88077	2.432232	7.313003
Financing, insurance, etc less GDP in dwellings	12.64451	5.290468	6.984525	10.2628	4.266936	14.52974
Community & social services incl. repair services	8.462587	-1.47759	10.08925	22.25536	0.140834	22.3962
Total	6.891888	0.840983	6.000442	88.99054	11.00946	100

Source: Authors' calculations using data from Sundaram (2001).

classification confirms these trends. But it also shows that the greatest employment growth was in construction, in which productivity growth was slowest, while the most rapidly growth services sector, community and social services including repair services, lost labour and made the largest single contribution to total productivity growth. We therefore, find little evidence that services have produced a drag on overall productivity growth, although some sectors, such as construction, seem to have played some role. However, we also find no evidence of a significant sectoral shift towards traded goods sectors, such as manufacturing, which could have boosted overall productivity growth by improving intersectoral efficiency in ways expected by proponents of reform.

Balance of payments

Another potential constraint on growth is the balance of payments. If the economy is exchange constrained in the sense that of being subject to periodic shocks due to foreign exchange shortages, the rate of growth of the economy on average will be determined by its balance of payments position.

We have already discussed trends in exports and imports and seen that the trade deficit continues to be large. This problem, however, has been reduced by the invisibles account. Private transfers by Indians working abroad has increased from 1 per cent of GDP in the late 1980s to 2.5 per cent during 1993-94 to 1998-99. Invisible receipts have also increased due to booming software exports since 1993-94, which is currently at about 0.6 per cent of GDP. The information technology sector has, indeed, been seen as one of the success stories of the globalisation process, given the rapid growth of the industry world-wide (although recent troubles in the US are likely to have a dampening effect). This sector has not only increased exports and remittances by Indians working abroad, but also promises to improve efficiency in the industrial and service sectors. These items remained buoyant in the late 1990s when, as mentioned earlier, export growth spluttered, helping to keep the current account deficit within manageable proportions.

Turning to the capital account, foreign capital inflows in terms of non-debt resources-FDI and portfolio-have increased over the 1990s as discussed above. This has reduced the relative reliance on external commercial borrowing, especially short-term debt. The total capital account surplus has been at an average of 2.5 per cent of GDP during the period 1996-97 to 1998-99, which has been more than sufficient to offset the current account deficit.

The result of these trends-with the RBI intervening in the foreign exchange market to stabilise the rupee-has been a large increase in foreign exchange reserves, which stood at the $35 billion level in January 2000. The improvement in India's balance of payments can also be seen from the fall in the external debt/GDP ratio from 41t to 24 per cent between 1991-92 and 1998-99 and a corresponding decline in the debt-service ratio from 30 to 18 per cent.

Although the balance of payments situation appears to be comfortable, and growth has not be adversely affected by foreign exchange constraints in the post-reform period, a large proportion of capital inflows takes the form of volatile capital flows, including portfolio flows and short-term debt including NRI deposits. Kumar (2000a) estimates that about 61 per cent of foreign exchange reserves represent short-term debt and portfolio liabilities (such as FII stock market investment). Thus, while growth in the post-reform period has not been constrained by foreign exchange availability, the economy remains vulnerable to shocks that reverse hot money flows.

Agriculture under the Reforms

During the two decades prior to the reforms, there had been a growing belief in some quarters that agriculture had been discriminated against via policies of industrial protection and quantitative restrictions on international trade. Reformers understood the resulting "negative subsidy" to agriculture to be the principal constraint on agricultural growth and on raising rural living standards. The big moves toward trade liberalisation under the reforms were therefore, expected to confer large benefits on agriculture via reduced prices of inputs and increased prices of outputs. The Agreement on Agriculture under the WTO was also expected to work in the same direction by raising world prices of agricultural commodities and expanding trading opportunities for Indian agriculture.

Critics of the liberal programme since 1991 maintain that it neglects agriculture. They fear that structural adjustment policies of the 1990s together with the falling trend in public investment in agriculture dating from the 1980s are undermining the basis for labour-absorbing and equitable growth. At least during the early years of the reform, its defenders argued that agriculture is a prime if indirect beneficiary due to reduced protection for industry and the (partial) removal of restrictions on agricultural exports. They maintained that further movement on this reform path, including especially freeing up the food and agricultural markets and the relaxation of quantitative restrictions in conformity with the WTO agreement, could only further these benefits as India will then emerge as a major exporter in this sector.

But experience since the reforms appears to bear out the critics. Despite the highly unusual succession of normal monsoons throughout the decade, there has been a substantial deceleration in the annual growth rate of the index of agricultural production from 3.4 per cent in the 1980s to just 2.2 per cent in the 1990s. Foodgrains output growth has also decelerated from 3.5 per cent in the 1980s to a mere 1.7 per cent in the 1990s, the latter implying a declining trend in per capita supply. The decline in the rate of growth of agricultural GDP between the same two periods was considerably less, from 3.9 to 3.3 per cent. A part of the difference, some believe a major part, may be accountable by data revisions, especially in value-added in horticulture. The GDP share of agriculture at 1980-81 prices has fallen from 29.96 per cent in 1991-92 to less than 25 per cent. While one might argue that this decline reflects a healthy process of structural change, this seems distinctly implausible not merely because trade reforms, in the liberal reckoning, greatly reduced "urban bias" but also because poverty increased at least during the early years and food consumption fell. How could it be that as a "pro-agriculture" policy took root, the share of agriculture fell off so significantly? And how could continued low levels of food consumption be construed as structural progression? Perhaps, the liberal diagnosis and prescription for agricultural development are flawed.

The disappointing impact of reforms on agricultural performance cannot be blamed on adverse developments on the price front. In the case of the dominant agricultural commodities whose prices continue to be domestically determined, the steady and steep increases in procurement prices have prevented an even greater decline in the growth of agricultural GDP. According to Sen (2001), the terms of trade for agriculture were far more favourable during the 1990s than during the 1980s, reaching their highest level in 1998-99 since 1974-75. Successive grants of generous minimum support prices for wheat and rice have made their market prices rise considerably faster than the prices of most other agricultural commodities (and produced a massive accumulation of unwanted stocks). Moreover, agriculture is now protected from import competition as compared to industry since duties on most agricultural imports are significantly higher than the 35 per cent maximum on industrial products. Hence, whether assessed in terms of trends in domestic relative prices or in terms of a comparison of domestic and border prices, it is just not true any more that agriculture has been discriminated against or suffers under the burden of "negative subsidy". While agricultural performance under the reforms has been decidedly disappointing, this cannot be charged to the failure of the policy regime to conform to liberal strictures.

One intent of reforms was to prune agricultural input subsidies (for power, irrigation and fertilisers) to make fiscal room for raising public investment in agricultural infrastructure including research and extension. On the whole, however, progress in this direction has been tardy so that, by default, supply-shifting public investment has continued to be well below the levels attained in the late 1960s and the 1970s. This situation has been aggravated by the worsening fiscal situation of the states. Although private investment has been higher during the 1990s, and this despite a slackening of bank lending to the rural sector following financial sector reforms, returns in terms of output and income growth have been well below par.

While the poor record of agriculture under the reforms has disappointed reformers' expectations, informed observers had all along known that those expectations were founded on a poor understanding of Indian agriculture, especially the extravagant claim for the growth-augmenting power of prices. The restoration of fiscal allocations for agriculture and its infrastructure remains the key but this will require that policy-makers shed their neo-liberal penchant for downsizing government and their supply-side faith that lowered tax rates will enhance the fiscal take. In addition, private investment and complementary public investment will not yield higher returns if inertial elements in policy are not overcome. These elements include: (1) a continuing reliance on a high-input and high-capital intensity strategy that is evident in the heavy subsidisation of inputs, the failure to mobilise surplus labour on farm or for infrastructure building off the farm; (2) capital-intensive and environment-unfriendly programmes to augment the effective supply of land; (3) the assumption of the immutability of the particular combination of agrarian inequalities and market failures together with government policies themselves that alone can account for the low rate of labour-absorption in Indian agriculture.

External liberalisation, far from fulfilling the liberal hope that India would emerge a successful exporter of foodgrains and many other agricultural commodities, has prompted growing concerns that a flood of cheap imports will undercut domestic production and the livelihood of millions. As many as 229 of the 714 items on the recently freed list of imports are agricultural commodities and there have been steep declines in world market prices in recent years. In addition, even when pre-integration domestic supply prices can be taken to be below normal world prices, the volatility of world markets means added risks so that integration may impose a penalty on farmers rather than confer an incentive. The unequal WTO accords have imposed market access conditions on the developing world while allowing the developed countries to retain their subsidy regimes virtually intact.

The agricultural import bill is dominated by edible oils, oil cakes and pulses. Domestic production of these items is concentrated in dryland regions, particularly in the hands of relatively poor farmers. Production and yield constraints derive from the continued failure of public investment and action, especially in respect of credit, irrigation, high yield varieties and drought-proofing. Unfortunately, India's position at the WTO has been to defend quantitative restrictions solely in terms of balance of payments constraints when, in fact, considerations of livelihood, employment and food security are at least as important. The expectation is that government will be compelled to raise tariff rates on agricultural products to prevent erosion of the domestic production base. Import duties have already been doubled in 2001 in respect of coffee, tea, and edible oils. Since the WTO bound tariff rates are considerably higher for agricultural commodities than for industrial products, there is ample potential cushion against import competition at least for the foreseeable future.

Paradoxically, these developments have rejuvenated the old debate about industry versus agriculture. Notwithstanding the declining trend in public investment in Indian agriculture, the government fears that WTO ceilings on the Aggregate Measure of Support (AMS) for agriculture may be found to be binding. The extent of AMS, however, remains a contentious issue. Even the Bank and the Fund hold irreconcilable positions. According to various World Bank estimates, AMS for Indian agriculture has been negative but the negative subsidy has declined over time, from 30 per cent in the 1970s and early 1980s, to 9 per cent in the early 1990s. The continued fall in global agricultural prices during the 1990s implies a further decline in the negative AMS (Alagh, 2001). On the other hand, the IMF estimates government expenditure on agriculture at 29 per cent of agricultural GDP in 1990-93, most of this being interpreted to be a subsidy. This number is considerably larger than the WTO ceiling and compares unfavorably with, say, Indonesia (6.9 per cent) or Thailand (12.9 per cent). The presumption is that the IMF measure of agricultural support has risen further during the 1990s.

How far the government will have to go down the path of raising agricultural tariffs remains to be seen but farmers' lobbies, including those in the agriculturally prosperous state of Punjab, are girding for a fight to reverse or stall the ongoing liberalisation. An illiberal turn may well redound to the good of Indian agriculture provided government returns to a sensible programme of public investment, agrarian and institutional reforms, and environmental sustainability, and provided it can stave off challenges from the WTO while instituting its own policies in the pursuit of livelihood, employment and food security. More than the future of Indian agriculture may well depend on such a reversal.

CHANGES IN THE EMPLOYMENT STRUCTURE

Employment and wages are probably the major potential channels through which the social impact of increased openness and globalisation are felt. In this section, besides presenting the evidence on overall employment and unemployment trends, we examine trends in formal sector employment and in informalisation, and in the sectoral composition of the labour force. One should be forewarned, however, that given the preponderance of household and tiny enterprises, high rates of underemployment, very high incidence of casual-frequently part-time-work, and widespread seasonal and gender gaps in employment opportunities in spatially dispersed-often localised-labour markets, that our information base is not very reliable.

Trends in Formal Employment

Figure 18 shows the changes in employment levels through the mid-1990s in the "organised" sector, which includes all public sector employment (mostly in industry and services), and employment in private sector units that employ more than 10 persons. It shows that organised sector employment grew sluggishly during the 1980s and through the mid-1990s, and that most of this was in the public sector while private sector employment stagnated. Figure 19 shows that the growth rate of organised sector employment fell steadily over the entire period, a trend dominated by the decline in the rate of growth of public sector employment. Private sector employment growth, throughout the 1980s, was slower than public sector employment growth. Only as late as 1992 did it equal the latter. Through the mid-1990s, it fluctuated at a level that did not counter the decline in the growth of public sector employment, so that total organised sector employment growth continued to fall.

However, formal employment growth appears to have recovered after the mid-1990s. In particular, the faster growth of private sector employment in the 1990s has attracted some attention, especially in the wake of the stagnation of the 1980s, and some have been quick to attribute the growth to the reforms. Goldar (2000) uses pooled time series cross-industry data to argue that faster employment growth in the 1990s is explained by slower wage growth and a faster growth in smaller factories in response to changes in trade and industrial policies since 1991. Nagaraj (2000b), however, questions this interpretation, pointing out that the trend decline in average factory size is not a recent phenomenon, but one which has occurred for a long time and which also occurred in the 1980s when employment growth stagnated. He also questions Goldar's econometric specification, which does not appropriately take into account the relation between wages per person and days worked, and finds that employment is primarily affected by value added. He argues that slow output growth in the 1970s resulted in excess labour. When output grew in the 1980s it was accommodated by increasing hours per person rather than by increasing employment. As output growth continued in the 1990s, the labour overhang was exhausted, and employment growth recovered.

While the trend in organised sector employment is suggestive, this sector accounts for only around 10 per cent of total employment. We therefore need to examine figures for total employment, to which we now turn.

Aggregate Employment and Employment Structure

One way of measuring total employment in India is to use available figures for the total work force and applying officially available unemployment figures from the formal sector and assuming that there is no open unemployment in the informal sector. Following this approach it appears that while in the 1980s employment generally grew at a rate below population growth, in the 1990s, employment growth was somewhat higher, though much of the increase occurred in 1997. These employment figures are, however, highly dubious, since the unemployment figure actually refers to the number of persons on the live employment register and may include employed people who wish to move to a different job.

The dubious employment series can be used to obtain an estimate of the percentage of formal sector employment to total employment, as shown in Figure 20. Since this series is seen to reflect quite closely the series on the share of formal employment in the total labour force, which is also shown in the figure, we can have some confidence in the direction of changes revealed by it. The series bears testimony to the decline in the share of formal employment in total employment in the 1990s, which accentuates a trend that was present in the 1980s.

More reliable employment figures for the economy as a whole (including the unorganised sector) are available only from the *decadal* censuses and from the periodic surveys conducted by the national sample survey (NSS) organization. Census figures available for 1981 and 1991 cannot reveal any trend changes that may have been caused by the recent reforms. NSS estimates, however, are available for 1983, 1987-88, 1993-94 and 1999-2000 and for others years in the 1990s based on "thin" samples. NSS figures are disaggregated for urban and rural areas and for males and females.

Going by these estimates, the annual rate of employment growth between 1983 and 1991 averaged 2.39 per cent with organised sector employment growing more slowly than unorganised sector employment (1.73 per cent compared to 2.41 per cent). Subsequent thin survey results showed a considerable slackening of employment growth during 1990-91 and 1997-98 to a mere 1 per cent per annum with organised sector employment growing a dismal 0.6 per cent per annum (Datt, 2001), as compared to an estimated labour force growth rate of about 2.5 per cent for the decade.

The NSS 55th round (1999-2000) statistics on employment further confirms this decelerating trend in employment growth. In terms of long-term or usual status, the ratio of rural workers (as primary or subsidiary workers) to rural population fell from 44.4 per cent in 1993-94 to just 41.7 per cent in 1999-2000. There was a drop, though smaller in magnitude, for urban India as well. These findings imply a workforce growth rate of just 0.81 per cent per annum compared to a population growth rate of 1.75 per cent per annum. This reduction is independent of shifts in the age-structure and only partly due to increased school enrolment (Sundaram, 2001). It is notable that this trend contrasts sharply with a rising trend in worker/employment ratios: between 1987-88 and 1993-94, these had risen marginally for urban males and females and for rural females but significantly for rural males (from 53.9 per cent to 55.3 per cent).

The sectoral distribution of the workforce also reveals some surprises. The share of agriculture and allied sectors in total employment declined sharply from 63.9 per cent in 1993-94 to 59.8 per cent in 1999-2000 with absolute employment declining for the first time since independence. This trend out of agriculture, which had been observed during the 1980s also, had been stalled between 1987-88 and 1993-94, mostly during the early years of the reforms (Kundu, 1997). Community, social and personal services also witnessed a substantial decline in the absolute workforce while mining and utilities suffered minor absolute declines. The decline in the former is a reversal in the trend observed between 1987-88 and 1993-94.

Employment in manufacturing has risen only slightly from 10.7 per cent of the workforce in 1993-94 to 11.1 per cent in 1999-2000 with practically all of the rise concentrated in urban areas. Even this slight gain is only a recovery from the decline in the percentage of workers in manufacturing in urban areas between 1987-88 and 1993-94. The biggest gains in workforce occurred in construction and in trade, hotels and restaurants, the compound rate of growth in both sectors exceeding 6 per cent per annum (see Table 3). The latter sector now rivals manufacturing in the size of the labour force it employs. Kundu (1997) explained the loss of manufacturing employment during the early years of the 1990s in terms of jobs being sub-contracted out by large manufacturing units to smaller ones which are often household units that classify themselves as service units. While such misclassification may well occur, some of it is undoubtedly real. The virtual stagnation in the share of manufacturing employment should be seen in the light of our earlier conclusion that, for the economy as a whole, output growth has not kept pace with investment growth, both possibly manifestations of capital deepening.

As for unemployment, for both rural men and women in the labour force, the rate of (current daily status) unemployment rose sharply. Urban male unemployment rose a little while urban female unemployment actually fell.

Overall, then, the employment situation has worsened during the 1990s especially in rural areas.

There has also been rising casualisation of the workforce in the aftermath of reforms and a decline in the share of self-employment. The share of casual labour in employment rose from 31.2 per cent in 1988 to 37 per cent in 1998. The quinquennial surveys show the rise to have been from 33.8 per cent in 1993-94 to 36.2 per cent in 1999-2000 (Sundaram, 2001). It should be noted, however, that the declining trend in both regular employment and self-employment had also been observed during the pre-reform period from 1977-78 to 1987-88, and on through 1993-94, although the trend seems to have intensified after 1987-88. While growing casualisation is certainly in keeping with services accounting for the major share of workforce increments, even in the sectors of regular employment, retrenchment, closures and lockouts have risen as the price that unions must pay when they resist casualisation (Datt, 2001). The government is now seeking to boost private employers' bargaining position and increase labour market "flexibilisation" by proposing that industrial establishments employing up to 1,000 workers will no longer be obliged to seek approval from the appropriate government to fire or layoff workers. Existing provisions in the Industrial Disputes Act require such approval for all units employing more than 100 workers. The proposal, billed as a key plank in the "second generation reforms", is expected to encounter considerable political resistance.

Overall, therefore, there is enough grist in the employment trends for the reform critics' mills. First, the decrease in participation rates for rural workers is worrisome. It may be symptomatic of slowed employment growth in an economy long accustomed to high rates of underemployment disguised as non-participation. Second, the decline in formal employment growth (both public and private) below the rate of growth of the labour force over a period of nearly a decade, when formal sector output has grown at its fastest pace in history, suggests a clearly unhealthy pattern of development. When this is coupled with the increasing incidence of casual labour and the decline in self-employment, it appears that a process of *informalisation* seems to have become endemic in the Indian labour markets. This has potentially serious consequences for wages, job security, inflation protection, workers' basic rights, and the future of the Indian labour movement. It is undoubtedly a symptom of the further weakening of labour vis-a-vis capital. Third, the increasing feminisation of the regular labour force may well be a further cause of concern for the working classes. At first sight, it would seem to be a trend towards greater gender equality. But as Kundu (1997) has argued, this is probably a continuation of a trend starting in the 1980s in which female regular employment has been in low-wage, low-productivity sectors; indeed, female regular wages are often no higher, even less, than casual male wages. A final cause for concern is the stalled share of employment in manufacturing (along with a decline in agriculture) with much of the gain accounted for by service sectors. On the whole, these trends in employment structure run counter to reformers' expectations: tradable sectors (agriculture and manufacturing) have not become more labour-intensive while it is non-tradables that have enjoyed the biggest employment (and output) gains.

INCOME DISTRIBUTION AND POVERTY

Growing income inequality has been a nearly ubiquitous concern about globalisation in both rich and poor countries. In India, absolute poverty has traditionally received overwhelming attention in both academic research and policy debate long before the "globalising" reforms of 1991, and this tendency has continued after the reforms. The inattention to inequality may not be entirely, perhaps even mainly, a matter of social priority; it may also be seen as resting on the relative stability of the expenditure distribution over several decades. But as with employment statistics, statistics on distribution too leave much to be desired. Of late, even the statistics on poverty have become muddled. Sophisticated but divergent arguments concerning what large-scale surveys "really" tell us, the challenge of reconciling gaps between national accounts statistics and the surveys, and a variety of often conflicting corroborative evidence have left us with a wide range of poverty "estimates" differing by a factor of 2 or more. In what follows, we will try to tease out some conclusions about trends in poverty and inequality from such numbers as are available and attempt to link these with the reform process.

The Incidence of Poverty

The official all-India poverty line is defined by the per person expenditure required (given the pattern of actual consumption expenditures in the base-year sample) to assure a minimum food intake of 2,100 calories in urban areas and 2,400 calories in rural areas. The poverty line equalled an expenditure of Rs. 49 for rural areas and Rs. 57 for urban areas at 1973-74 all-India prices. Between 1951 and 1975, the proportion of people below the poverty line (the headcount ratio) showed sharp fluctuations but no long-run trend. Table 4 shows trends in rural and urban poverty incidence from the mid-1970s. These numbers have been refined to correct for price level variations across states and survey period following the 1993 recommendations of the Planning Commission's Expert Group on Poverty Estimation (World Bank, 1998). As the Table shows, the headcount ratio fell rapidly and fairly steadily from the mid-1970s to the late 1980s, the average annual rate of decline being 2.4 per cent (World Bank, 1998). After 1986-87 the poverty measures started fluctuating again, and registered increases after 1991, the headcount ratio rising from 36 per cent in 1990-91 to 41 per cent in 1992. Note also that the head-count ratio fell back in 1993-94.

In recent years, controversy has plagued India's poverty statistics. Poverty statistics have become something of an acid test of the success of the reforms since, barring the balance of payments situation, there is no evidence of improvement in overall growth or employment during the

1990s relative to the 1980s (as argued in the preceding sections). Unfortunately, the latest round of the NSS has aggravated the statistical and interpretative muddle. The controversy had been incipient through most of the reform period. Based on result from the large survey of 1993-94 and the succeeding "thin" surveys carried out annually by the official National Sample Survey (NSS) Organisation (shown in Table 4), a rough consensus prevailed among researchers that rural poverty-unlike urban poverty-in India as a whole showed no trend reduction. But proponents of the reforms dissented on the ground that without another large survey, firm conclusions could not be drawn about either the trend in poverty or its link to the reforms. In the normal course, the NSS 55th round (July1999 through June 2000) should have settled the matter, Since the previous large survey was carried out in 1993-94, giving a six-year period covering the key years when reforms would have taken effect. But this was not to be, owing to methodological changes incorporated in the 55th round.

Table 4
Poverty in India, 1973-1998 (Headcount, per cent)

Period	*Rural*	*Urban*
Oct 73-Jun 74	55.7	48.0
Jul 77-Jun 78	50.6	40.5
Jan 83-Dec 83	45.3	35.7
Jul 86-Jun 87	38.8	34.2
Jul 87-Jun 88	39.2	36.2
Jul 88-Jun 89	39.1	36.6
Jul 89-Jun 90	34.3	33.4
Jul 90-Jun 91	36.4	32.8
Jul 91-Dec 91	37.4	33.2
Jul 92-Dec 92	43.5	33.7
Jul 93-Jun 94	36.7	30.5
Jul 94-Jun 95	41.0	33.5
Jul 95-Jun 96	37.2	28.0
Jan 97-Dec 97	35.8	30.0

Source: Datt (1999).

Until the large survey of 1993-94 (the 50th round), respondents' consumption levels were assessed for the previous 30 days. The suspicion that the 30-day recall underestimated the true level of food consumption prompted experiments using both the seven-day recall and the 30-day recall in separate samples during the years succeeding the 50th round. Between 1994 and 1998, poverty levels in India, based on the seven-day recall method, were lower by as much as 40-50 per cent than estimates using the 30-day recall (Visaria, 2000).

The 50th round showed the rural and urban poverty ratios in 1993-94 to be 36.7 per cent and 30.5 per cent respectively whereas the 55th round in 1999-2000, based on a different survey methodology, showed steep declines in these ratios to 27.1 0 per cent and 23.6 per cent respectively. Taken at face value, therefore, the 55th round implies a compound annual rate of decline in rural poverty of 4.9 per cent and in urban poverty of 4.2 per cent. The rate of decline in national poverty is thus more than twice as large as that recorded in the 1980s.

But there is little doubt that the change in the reference period of the 1999-2000 survey from 30 days-the norm since the mid-1950s-to seven days in 1999-2000 as also the simultaneous collection of information for both reference periods from the same respondents has "contaminated" the 55th Round estimates. The justification for the 7-day recall is not only that this is the standard practice elsewhere in the world but also that recall errors would be lower than with the 30-day recall. But critics allege that estimates using the 30-day recall have lost their independent standing because they are tied to the seven-day estimates: respondents and surveyors alike would be under pressure to record consistent numbers (dividing the monthly numbers by 4 or multiplying the weekly numbers by 4). Indeed, they have correctly noted that estimates based on the seven-day recall actually show a worsening of the poverty situation. Thus, going by Visaria's seven-day recall figures, rural poverty incidence increased from 19.1 per cent in 1995-96 to 24.8 per cent in July-December 1999 and urban poverty ratios increased from 15.2 per cent to 23.4 per cent. The only thing that seems beyond reasonable doubt is that, because the last quinquennial survey did not use a seven-day recall, the latest estimates cannot be compared to the previous estimates.

Corroborative evidence has also been adduced for both the conflicting views about poverty. Consider the evidence on real wage growth. Based on the latest quinquennial round of the NSS, Sundaram (2001) finds that real wages of casual agricultural labour rose by 2.80 per cent per annum for rural men and 2.94 per cent for rural women between 1993-34 and 1999-2000. For casual labour in non-agricultural activities, the rate of rise was higher still. Despite the decline in employment ratios, estimated real yearly wage earnings per worker and per capita have risen for all categories of labour. This seems to provide a possible basis of support for the claim that poverty ratios have declined during the last six years of the 1990s. On the other hand, observed declines in employment ratios and in per capita consumption of foodgrains both point to a worsening of poverty. Moreover, the growth in real wages during the 1990s was not any higher than in the 1980s and overall inequality seems to have definitely worsened (see below). Coupled with the observation that the rate of growth of per capita income is not significantly higher in the 1990s as compared to the 1980s, these facts simply cannot support the massive trend decline in poverty that some commentators have read into the data based on the 55th Round.

The poverty line, defined as it is in terms of a base-year level of total expenditure sufficient to secure an exogenously given nutritional norm, implies a behavioural rather than a normative specification of non-food items of consumption. Updating such a poverty line by accounting for general price inflation in subsequent years does not guarantee that the resulting poverty lines will remain adequate to secure the nutritional norm. In the Indian case, in fact, the divergence between the updated poverty lines and the nutritional norm has increased since the base year 1973-74 (Mehta and Venkatraman, 2000). In 1993-94, for example, the updated poverty lines were only 66per cent and 74 per cent of the corresponding levels of expenditure "required" to secure the nutritional norm. Put differently, the updated rural and poverty lines implied actual calorie intake in the respective expenditure groups of only 82 per cent and 90per cent of the nutritional norms. With rough "corrections" for the divergence, the incidence of nutrition-based poverty is 75 per cent and 54 per cent respectively rather than the official poverty ratios of 37 per cent and 32 per cent respectively.

The divergence is basically due to a shift in consumption expenditure from food to non-food, from cereals to non-cereal foods, and from coarse to fine cereals. In a preference-based approach, these shifts would be interpreted as the revealed preferences of consumers. But this would render the nutrition "norm" quite irrelevant to the poverty measurement exercise. Another approach seeks to explain at least the greater decline in rural as compared to urban calorie consumption as due to increased agricultural mechanisation which reduces the exogenously-given calorie requirement (Rao, 2000). But mechanisation is known to reduce employment so that the decline in calorie intake may represent a decline in availability rather than in requirement (Saha, 2000).

In fact, Mehta and Venkatraman provide evidence that while cereal intake has declined significantly, expenditure shifts to non-cereal foods have meant negligible increases in their quantities, and expenditure shifts to non-food (e.g., transport) also do not reveal unambiguous gains in the quality of life. They suggest that these expenditure shifts resulted from "the foreclosing of earlier choices and a compulsive interaction with markets" (p. 2381).

Further support for this interpretation is provided by an analysis of the survey and valuation methods employed in the NSS against the backdrop of changes in rural institutions and production structures (Suryanarayana, 2000). One part of the argument is that the trend decline in measured poverty reflects overestimation of poverty in the 1950s and 1960s. The overestimation is on two counts: (a) a significant part of wage payments, made in the form of cooked meals, was recorded in the NSS as consumption of the employer; (b) while own production, a major source of consumption then, was valued at farm-harvest prices, the poverty lines were inflated because they were price-adjusted using market prices (including trade and transport margins). The first source of overestimation declined progressively with the shift to cash wages while the second declined as market purchases grew at the expense of own production. The second part of the argument is that there has been an increasing underestimation of poverty since the 1970s: the reduced availability of coarse cereals (driven by changing prices and technologies, and increasing reliance on market access) compelled substitution by the costlier fine cereals; poverty lines adjusted with base year weighted deflators thus understate the cost of the nutrition-based consumption norm. The decline in access to cooked meals also forced expenditure on necessary complements such as fuel and edible oils, and on the overhead cost of acquiring the same level of nutrition.

India's progress in the fields of education and health has been similarly tardy. At the last census, 1990-91, the literacy rate among women and men aged 7 and above was 39per cent and 64per cent respectively, up from 30per cent and 56 per cent in 1980-81. Life expectancy at birth was 59.2 years in 1990-91 compared to 50.4 years in 1980-81. Estimates for these measures after 1990-91 suggest that the upward trend is continuing. Although the improvements compared to 1950-51 (when the female and male literacy rates were 9per cent and 27per cent, and life expectancy at birth was 32.1per cent) are notable, India lags far behind other developing countries, including some Asian neighbours.

It is useful to examine the general determinants of trends in poverty before we turn to a consideration of the particular effects of globalising reforms. One route to reducing poverty is agricultural growth. Using time series data on agricultural poverty, which they obtain by modifying NSS data, Datt and Ravallion (1996) find that trends in poverty are explained mainly by agricultural growth. According to their estimates, overall growth in the economy accounts for most of the reduction in the headcount poverty measure-80 per cent for the entire period and almost 100per cent since 1970. The evidence across states, according to Datt and Ravallion, shows that poverty reduction has occurred fastest in states that have experienced rapid rural growth with strong infrastructure development (such as Punjab and Haryana) and in those that have relied on human resource development (such as Kerala). By contrast, Sen (1996) finds that, for the period after the Green Revolution, there is a rather weak link across states between the rate of per capita agricultural growth and reduction in rural poverty.

A second route to reducing poverty is through labour-intensive industrial or non-agricultural growth in urban or in rural areas. While Datt and Ravallion find no empirical support for this view, Sen (1996) reports that increases in non-agricultural incomes tend to reduce poverty in both rural and urban areas. Of particular importance in this respect is the role of increases in non-agricultural employment in rural areas not merely because it may reduce unemployment and underemployment but also because, as a number of authors have noted, it is strongly associated with rising real wages in agriculture during the 1980s. This rise in real wages seems to discredit the view that increases in rural non-agricultural employment were due to the distress needs of those pushed out of labour-shedding agriculture. It has seemed natural to suppose instead that the association between rising wages and rising non-farm employment must reflect the pull of demand. Sen (1996) has argued that rising government expenditures in rural areas, on revenue and capital account, have provided a major impetus for the growth. This view is compatible with the further observation that non-farm employment growth is broadly unrelated to the rate of agricultural growth across states. Since government expenditures in rural areas have slowed under the reforms, the presumption must be that this source of poverty alleviation has weakened considerably.

A paradox of the 1980s' experience is that the sharp decline in rural poverty and a rise in rural real wage rates occurred despite the very slow growth of urban organised sector employment and the slower growth of agricultural employment than that of the labour force. An alternative hypothesis, which departs from the assumption of full employment, and relies on an exogenous rise in rural wage rates (due perhaps to increased bargaining power of labourers) helps to explain this paradox (see Rao, 1998b). Such a wage rise can explain both the fall in the employment-output ratio within agriculture and the concomitant fall in poverty rates. A relative rise in non-farm employment can still occur provided labour demand increases due to increased government expenditure (as argued by Sen), but also because of a rise in the wage share. Sen provides evidence that real wages increased almost twice as fast as labour productivity in agriculture. The resultant increase in the wage share increases the demand for non-agricultural rural products, given a higher marginal propensity to consume (in general and for non-agricultural goods in particular) out of rural wages than out of non-wage income.

A third determinant of poverty, which has attracted much attention, is the price of food. It has been argued, consistent with all available evidence, that an increase in the price of food increases poverty by reducing the real incomes of wage earners for whom wages do not keep up with food prices. The fact that this holds for rural areas as well as urban areas is not a puzzle, since most of India's rural poor (and even some of the non-poor) are net purchasers of food. Ravallion (1998), however, argues that the correlation between the two variables is actually spurious. He finds that the movement in both the poverty rate and the relative price of food are the result of changes in a third variable, agricultural output: a bad harvest can be expected to increase the relative price of food and also increase rural (and total) poverty. Pooling time-series data for 1960-61 to

1993-94 across states, Sen (1996) finds, however, that a rise in the relative price of cereals increases poverty even if agricultural output per worker is included as a variable.

Ravallion's argument that a change in food price affects poverty via its impact on mean rural consumption but not on the distribution of rural consumption (or income) rests on erroneous inequality measures. His measures of inequality are premised on the incorrect assumption that the cost of living index is the same for the rural poor and non-poor. While his conclusion that price changes have statistically zero distributional effects applies to the nominal inequality of rural incomes, the same data nevertheless imply a worsening of real inequality (see Rao, 1998a). This last conclusion leads us directly back to the established understanding that food price increases hurt the poor through the mechanism of (real) inequality increases. It also follows that price reforms incur the risk of both transitional and permanent reductions in real wages and corresponding increases in poverty. As discussed in the following section, this is precisely what seems to have happened during the decade of the 1990s.

Critics of the reforms have attributed the rise in poverty in the initial years of the reforms to the PDS issue price increases, the consequent open market price rise and the curtailment in supplies. Suryanarayana (1996) shows that there were roughly symmetric declines in cereal availability in both rural and urban areas and that the reforms were responsible for the adverse effect on poverty. The part of food subsidies actually accruing to consumers has fallen since 1991 through a combination of price increases and quantity reductions (Swaminathan, 1996). Indeed, both open market (wholesale) prices and issue prices through the PDS have more than doubled. That this has most likely had an adverse effect on poverty can be seen from Sen (1996), which adds a relative price of food term to what is essentially the Ravallion-Datt (1996) equation discussed above, and finds that this modified equation is able to explain the increase in poverty after 1991.

Dimensions of Economic and Social Inequality

Income inequality as proxied by the Gini coefficient of consumption expenditure shows little change over the years. Table 5 shows that in both rural and urban areas this coefficient has fluctuated without a clear trend. However, the mean Gini coefficients for the "pre-reform" years (1989-91) are lower than their "post-reform" (1995-97) counterparts: these are, respectively, 28.0 and 29.5 for rural expenditures and 34.8 and 36.0 for urban expenditures. Though modest, these increases do indicate a worsening of the nominal expenditure distributions in both sectors.

Table 5
Gini Coefficient of Nominal Consumption Expenditure Distribution

Period	*Rural*	*Urban*
Oct 73-Jun 74	28.5	30.8
Jul 77-Jun 78	30.9	34.7
Jan 83-Dec 83	30.1	34.1
Jul 86-Jun 87	30.2	36.8
Jul 87-Jun 88	29.4	34.6
Jul 88-Jun 89	29.5	34.8
Jul 89-Jun 90	28.2	35.6
Jul 90-Jun 91	27.7	34.0
Jul 91-Dec 91	29.9	33.0
Jul 92-Dec 92	29.9	35.1
Jul 93-Jun 94	28.6	34.3
Jul 94-Jun 95	30.2	37.2
Jul 95-Jun 96	28.4	35.5
Jan 97-Dec 97	30.6	36.5

Source: Datt (1999).

Let us leave aside the controversial and non-comparable numbers from the 1999-2000 NSS. The fact that NSS surveys for the 1990s show that poverty did not decline despite the similarity of GDP trend growth to that in the 1980s (when poverty did decline significantly), implies that "scepticism will continue unless it is established that there was an increase in inequality" (Sen, 2000: 4501). Two points are pertinent to an informed assessment of this issue. First, the fact that growth in rural real consumption expenditure as estimated by the NSS fell well short of the growth in real income as per National Accounts Statistics (NAS) has been seized upon by defenders of the reform to discredit NSS poverty estimates (prior to the 55th round). How justified is this? Second, NSS consumption surveys are known to underenumerate the rich leading to persistently lower estimates of total non-food consumption as compared to the NAS. Hence, NSS-based point estimates of the inequality of consumption distribution understate income inequality both because savings are left out and because the rich are underenumerated. Furthermore, if the rich had gained disproportionately from the income growth of the 1990s, then, NSS mean consumption estimate would be biased downward relative to the NAS estimate while, at the same time, the NSS consumption inequality estimate would be biased downward relative to true inequality (Sen, 2000).

On the first of these points, Rao (1998a) had argued that when the key food/non-food relative price is changing, Gini coefficients based on the nominal distribution of expenditure do not measure inequality in real expenditure; the latter can only be calculated after converting nominal expenditures into real by means of class-specific deflators. Not surprisingly, Sen (2000) finds that the difference in the NSS real consumption trend during the 1990s and the corresponding NAS trend arises not chiefly from differences in estimates of nominal magnitudes but from differences in the price deflators used to derive the real magnitudes. While the NAS magnitudes are deflated by the implicit consumption deflator, the NSS consumption data are deflated by price indices for agricultural labourers and industrial workers. Both these price indices have risen faster during the 1990s than the implicit NAS deflator primarily because prices of food items, especially cereals, have risen relative to all other items which are mainly consumed by the rich. Hence, at least in an export statistical sense, the rise in the relative price of food is a principal factor explaining why poverty did not decline in the 1990s.

Thus, even ignoring the under-enumeration of the rich, Sen (2000) concludes that (1) urban nominal expenditure inequality which had no trend in earlier periods trended up during the 1990s; (2) rural nominal inequality which had been declining earlier reversed course during the 1990s; and (3) there was also increased disparity between rural and urban areas. In conjunction with the preceding argument that, given a trend increase in the relative price of food, the trend in nominal rural inequality understates the trend in real rural inequality, these conclusions (based on uncontaminated NSS data) indicate an unambiguous rise in real inequality during the 1990s.

Indication of changes in the functional distribution of income may be gleaned from estimates of the growth in per-worker gross value added and in "earnings per worker" per annum. Based on NAS, the annual compound rate of growth of GVA per worker over the period 1993-94 to 1999-2000 was 3.3 per cent in agriculture, 6.1 per cent in manufacturing and 6.1 per cent for the economy as a whole (Sundaram, 2001). With the GDP share of agriculture being about a quarter, the growth rate of GVA per worker in non-agriculture is approximately 7.04 per cent. Now real wages of casual agricultural labour rose 2.80 per cent per annum for rural males and 2.94 per cent for rural females while the average number of days worked per rural worker fell at the rate of 0.2 per cent per annum for rural males and rose at the rate of 0.34 per cent for rural females. Assuming that the latter figures for rural India apply equally to agricultural workers and that there is no change in the relative wages of regular workers vis-a-vis casual workers, these trends in real wages and employment per worker imply that real labour earnings per worker rose at the rate of 2.6 per cent per annum for male agricultural workers and 3.28 per cent for females. The weighted average growth rate of earnings per agricultural worker is thus 2.83 per cent per annum which is significantly less than the rate of growth of GVA per agricultural worker (3.3 per cent). Thus, assuming that the distribution of GVA between regular and casual workers remained unchanged, the share of 'surplus' (profits, interest and rents) in agriculture rose during the 1990s.

As for non-agriculture, real wages of casual non-agricultural labour rose 2.74 per cent per annum for urban males and 4.18 per cent for urban females while the average number of days worked per worker fell at the rate of 0.09 per cent per annum for urban males and rose at the rate of 0.53 per cent for females (based on figures reported in Sundaram, 2001). Assuming that these figures apply equally for all non-agricultural workers and, as before, that there is no change in the relative wages of regular workers vis-a-vis casual workers, real labour earnings per worker rose at the rate of 2.65 per cent per annum for males and 4.71 per cent for females. The weighted average growth rate of earnings per non-agricultural worker is thus 3.06 per cent per annum which is very considerably smaller than the rate of growth of GVA per worker in non-agriculture (7.04 per cent) or in the economy as a whole (6.1 per cent). Once again, assuming that the distribution of GVA between regular and casual workers remained unchanged, the share of 'surplus' (profits, interest and rents) in non-agriculture rose during the 1990s.

Given the significant excess of the growth rates of value-added over the wages bill in both agriculture and non-agriculture, these calculations strongly indicate that the income share of labour in both sectors, but especially in non-agriculture, has fallen over the years from 1993-94 to 1999-2000. While the growth in real wage rates and annual wage earnings over the six year period cannot be reconciled with the position that poverty failed to decline, the significant deterioration in the functional distribution of income and in the personal distribution of income both within and between sectors indicate that the rate of poverty reduction declined under the reforms.

For the period between 1970-71 and 1995-96, there is strong evidence of divergence in per capita real SDP across Indian states based on the trend in the yearly coefficient of variation. The divergence was especially evident in the case of agriculture whereas SDP in services were convergent (Dasgupta, Maiti, Mukherjee, Sarkar and Chakrabarti, 2000). Although the analysis suggests that there was convergence in the SDP from "infrastructure" (defined as transport, electricity and banking), it is doubtful that this can be interpreted as showing that unequal development in infrastructure is not the primary cause of divergence. For one, convergence was evident only in the case of banking; in respect of both transport and electricity, there was divergence. For another, the constructed "infrastructure" variable does not include elements of public services (e.g., research and extension, education and health) that may be highly productive especially in the case of agriculture which is identified as the leading sector underlying overall income divergence.

During the post-Independence era, agricultural growth has depended on central initiatives despite agriculture being a state subject. Over the past decade and more, inter-state variation in agricultural performance has widened, in part due to the steep rise in current input subsidies overwhelming the growth of public investment. As a result, the share of public investment in agriculture has fallen to just 25 per cent today. Whereas the coefficient of variations for rural and urban poverty ratios in the states fell during the 1970s and 1980s, they have risen during the 1990s. This seems to be a consequence of the devolution of resources and decentralization of policies and programmes from the center to the states brought on by the reforms.

The poor in India are concentrated among the landless, among members of scheduled castes and tribes, and households in which all members are illiterate (World Bank, 1998). These are not disjoint groupings. The vast majority - 74 per cent - of the Indian poor make their living in the rural, still mainly agricultural, economy. A recent study of the incidence of poverty among socially disadvantaged groups such as scheduled castes (SC), scheduled tribes (ST) and female-headed (FH) households provides graphic evidence of the economic differentiation imposed by social disadvantage (Meenakshi, Ray and Gupta, 2000). Going by per capita total expenditure unadjusted for family size, poverty rates are higher among SC and ST households than among all households in virtually all states, the excess incidence varying typically between a quarter and a half. But surprisingly, unadjusted poverty incidence is significantly lower among FH households. However, when per capita expenditure is adjusted for family size (to reflect economies in consumption), the differential incidence of poverty among SC and ST households rises further while the apparent advantage of FH households is reversed.

Aspects of Social Policy

Past experience suggests that government policy regarding the "social sector" has an important influence on the incidence of poverty, the distribution of income, and the availability of social opportunities to the mass of the population. Given India's low level of achievement in terms of poverty alleviation and in expanding social opportunities, and given the unequalising socio-economic impact without any acceleration in income growth consequent upon the globalising reforms discussed above, government policy has an important role in the future. In this section, we examine trends in public social spending and the robustness of existing social safety-nets in the face of the reforms.

TRENDS IN GOVERNMENT EXPENDITURE

Several studies have argued that the reforms had adverse effects on government spending on the social sector (see Guhan, 1995): for instance, expenditure on rural development and social services declined by 0.4per cent of GDP between 1990-91 and 1992-93. Considering a longer span of time and including both central and state governments, Nagaraj (1997) finds that government final consumption expenditure as a percentage of GDP (at factor cost) has declined from an annual average of 11 per cent for 1986-91 to 10.1 per cent during 1992-95. However, the expenditure on health, education, housing and social services -which include, but are not confined to, spending on items which benefit the poor-stayed the same over the two periods at 2.9 per cent of GDP, and was in fact higher than the 2.4 per cent level for 1981-85. Defense and economic services bore the brunt of the cuts. For the same two periods, government current expenditure as a percentage of GDP fell from 19.4 to 17.9 per cent, and government capital expenditure fell from 7.5 to 5.7 per cent. Here, current expenditure on health, education, housing and social services as a percentage of GDP fell slightly, from 6.1 to 6.0 per cent, but capital expenditure stayed the same; the losers again were defense and economic services.

These budgetary figures show that government social spending did not decrease as a percentage of GDP except immediately after the crisis. However, this does not imply that the benefit the poor received did not fall since this depends on the effectiveness of the programmes funded by these expenditures, the extent to which the poor actually benefited, and changes in relative prices affecting the real delivery of services (this is considered below). Nor does it imply that globalising reforms had 'no effect' if the counterfactual would have allowed increases in these expenditures from increased revenue mobilisation rather than the fiscal compression that was actually pursued. The need for increased social expenditures and their potential for raising both living standards and economic growth may be judged rather from the evidently low levels of social opportunity both before and after the reforms. The tradeoffs imposed by globalising reforms arguably consists in the failure to cultivate this complementarity between growth and social opportunity.

Social Safety-Nets

Recognizing social security as an obligation of provincial and Central governments, the Indian Constitution calls upon the state, within the limits of its capacity, to make effective provision for 'public assistance in the case of unemployment, old age, sickness, and disablement, and in other cases of undeserved want' and for maternity relief. Since Independence, social security legislation has been extended in several directions by acts relating to retirement funds, maternity benefits, family pension schemes, deposit-linked insurance schemes, and medical, disability and, employment injury benefits (see Guhan, 1992). Organised labour is covered under these various enactments, and public and quasi-public employees are covered by non-legislated directed benefits. Social security expenditures are estimated to be less than 3per cent of GNP (see Guhan, 1992).

However, social security for over 90per cent of workers, who are in the unorganised sector or are self employed, is extremely meagre, being confined to some 'means' tested old-age pension, and accident, group life and hut insurance schemes for specific groups. Moreover, the legislation suffers from shortcomings which thwart the effectiveness of the programmes, allowing evasion by employers in providing contributions. Areas in which benefits are provided by state governments show enormous differences in coverage. No western-style unemployment relief is offered in India, which is a severe problem for self-employed and unorganised sector workers for whom no employment security exists. Some relief from unemployment, particularly in drought-affected regions, is offered in rural areas through schemes of employment creation to which we now turn.

EMPLOYMENT GENERATION SCHEMES

The highly successful Maharashtra Employment Guarantee Scheme, which was established to provide relief during severe droughts in rural Maharashtra in 1970-73, has become a country-wide model. The scheme had a wide coverage (its daily attendance reaching a seventh of the total rural population at its peak) was well targeted (since the very cash wage allowed the programme self-select the poorest), and it had the clear objective of providing (Joshi and Little, 1996, p. 235). Given its success in reducing widespread misery, starvation and death, the scheme continued beyond the droughts, but with the wage increasing steadily and with reduced funding, it became progressively less successful, and the amount of employment it generated declined.

All-India public employment generation schemes are similar to the Maharashtra. The biggest of these schemes, the Jawahar Rozgar Yojna (JRY), was established in 1989 by merging two previous programmes. Its main aim was to create additional employment for the unemployed or underemployed below the poverty line who lived in rural areas, but its additional aim was to create rural assets, especially those which would benefit scheduled castes and tribes. Among the programme's stimulations was that the wage could not be below the prevailing legal minimum wage rates. Portions of the JRY are confined to backward areas. The JRY and its various components take up as much as 60 per cent of the Central government's budget on rural development and social expenditures.

The JRY provides an average monthly employment of five persondays per beneficiary family. However, the employment provided in the larger poorest states was much lower. Moreover, its ability to reach the poor within states is also limited. In 1992, 57 per cent of participants were from families above the family poverty line and only 18 per cent fell in the category of the very poor or worse (partly because the higher wage removed the self-selection advantage enjoyed by the Maharashtra programme) The net transfer to the poor, taking into account the fact that other work is reduced, has been estimated at only about 14 per cent of expenditure (Joshi and Little, 1996, p. 238).

Education policy

Despite the stated objective of providing free and compulsory education up to the age of 14 (one of the directive principles of the Constitution urged the state to provide such education by 1960!), compulsory education has not been implemented anywhere in India. As noted above, literacy rates are low, lower than in China, lower than in many east and south-east Asian countries more than thirty years ago, lower than in the average for low-income countries other than China and India, and no higher than in sub-Saharan Africa. There are great disparities in literacy rates by regions and by sex. The student teacher ratio for the 6-10 age group is 58, out drop rates are extremely high, and public expenditure on education remains low by international standards with a strong bias against primary education. Some improvements in the 1980 seems to have gone to higher emoluments, not to increasing the number of teachers. Structural adjustment measures in the 1990s slowed down education expenditure growth and even caused a decline in the number of primary and upper-primary school teachers between 1991-92 and 1992-93 (Dreze and Sen, 1995, 111-23). These trends, however, have subsequently been partially reversed.

Public Distribution System (PDS) for Foodgrains

The PDS is a public safety-net programme that buys agricultural products from farmers to protect them against excessive losses in periods of surplus production and sells them to consumers to protect them from high prices in and outside years of shortage. The PDS distributes rice, wheat, edible oil, kerosene and sugar at subsidised prices through a network of 400,000 shops in urban and rural areas all over the country. The implicit subsidy under the PDS has been stable at around 0.5 per cent of GDP. Retail prices are fixed by each state government taking into account local distribution costs and retailer margins, besides the issue price fixed by the Food Corporation of India, and some states provide additional subsidies.

The ability of the PDS to provide effective protection and help to the poor has been questioned. It has been found that States making the greatest use of the PDS are not necessarily the poorer ones. The poor are not more likely to consume basic foodgrains distributed through the PDS than are the non-poor. It has been estimated that only about 40 per cent of the total quantity of wheat and 47 per cent of rice supplied through the PDS are consumed by the poorest 40 per cent of the population (World Bank, 1998, Joshi and Little, 1996, p. 233). Moreover, the costs of administering the programme are high for a number of reasons, including pilferage and inefficiency.

Public distribution of foodgrains at subsidised prices remains the single most important instrument of direct poverty alleviation available. Yet, reforms through the 1990s have worked at cross purposes in deploying this key instrument. Per capita foodgrains availability has fallen successively over the closing years of the last century. At the beginning of the reform process, the issue price of rice was raised by 30 per cent and that of wheat by 21 per cent in December 1991 and this narrowed the gap between the procurement and issue prices. Since procurement prices paid to farmers were repeatedly raised throughout the last decade, issue prices, especially for the above-poverty households, were also raised periodically. Although increased procurement followed, the decision to raise issue prices for PDS recipients above the poverty line has reduced the offtake. The upshot has been a rapid build up of stocks to over 40 million tonnes and a rise in government expenditure on the food subsidy even though consumer subsidy per se has fallen.

It has long been implicitly understood that the stabilisation of cereal price dynamics is the most important form of 'social safety-net' available in India. It is also the closest thing to an 'incomes policy' that a poor country can wield. While orthodox stabilization concerned itself with lowering the rate of inflation, orthodox structural adjustment in relation to agriculture and food (consisting in market liberalisation) was expected to lead to a rise in the relative price of food. In fact, however, the moves toward trade liberalisation have been accompanied by continuing high domestic support prices for the main food commodities. As a consequence, domestic relative food prices have risen rather than decline in sympathy with recent world market trends. As previously noted, this is the principal reason for an adverse movement in real (as opposed to nominal) inequality in rural India.

The reforms have tended, in conformity with World Bank orthodoxy, to move the PDS toward greater targeting toward the below-poverty households. Although the targeted PDS introduced in 1997 lowered prices for the below-poverty households, it also reduced the ration for these households to 10 kgs. Only later, in the budget for 2000-01, the ration was raised to 20 kgs. Moreover, targeting fails to take note of the gap between the numbers who are vulnerable to being poor and the numbers who are actually poor at any given time. This gap provides strong justification for moving in the opposite direction toward greater universality (Swaminathan, 1998). Errors of exclusion from the PDS are presumptively far more serious than errors of including those who are not vulnerable. Yet, the targeting principle has been upheld with consequent increases in issue prices and narrowing of the difference between the issue price and the open market price. While these moves have scarcely changed the food subsidy relative to GDP, the decline in PDS offtake even as open market relative prices of food commodities have been on the upswing is an indicator of increased distress among the vulnerable.

Swaminathan also notes that the primary reason for the failure of PDS to reach the intended beneficiaries has less to do with corruption and mismanagement than with wide inter-state disparities in the scale of distribution. Coverage of the relevant population is an increasing function of the overall scale of the programme at the state level. The poorer states actually had a proportionately smaller share of the total offtake as compared to the better off states. Increasing coverage under the PDS, both among poorer states and to include the vulnerable, will necessarily raise fiscal expenditures and thus require confronting the ruling neo-liberal orthodoxy at its root.

CONCLUSION

This paper has attempted an overall assessment of the impact of the economic reforms undertaken in India since the crisis of 1991. It pays particular attention to the effects of reforms, both directly and via economic growth, on mass well-being. We have argued that openness, in the sense of policies which aim at increased economic integration with international markets, has been the focal point of the reforms whilst globalisation, which we take to mean the increased external integration actually achieved, has been the touchstone of the new policy regime as perceived by its architects.

In the official view, supported by many Indian economists, policies of liberalisation and globalisation are justified as the best means to social ends such as poverty alleviation and human development. By accelerating growth, these policies can directly improve social opportunities and, by augmenting public expenditure and capability, indirectly enable government to take direct actions aimed at creating social opportunities. At the very least (even if it is supposed that neither of these linkages holds automatically), the pursuit of public action for enhancing social opportunities can proceed on a track parallel with globalising economic policies. Thus, social progress and globalising policies are at worst independent of each other and at best strongly complementary.

But it is increasingly apparent that these neo-liberal tenets have not been vindicated by the decade of experience since the reforms began. True, the balance of payments has been restored in terms of both current account deficits and foreign exchange reserves. But the promise of accelerated economic growth has not been fulfilled while industrial growth has fallen from 7.8 per cent in the 1980s to less than 6 per cent in the 1990s and is no longer leading the economy. The expected increase in economy-wide labour intensity and a consequent rise (decline) in employment (unemployment) have failed to materialise. The hope that getting agricultural prices "right" will shift resources into the rural economy has been belied. The faith in increasing external integration as the be-all of a strategy of development has been contradicted by growing internal dis-integration, in the form of increasing economic disparities across states and across the urban-rural divide. The desire to strengthen the fiscal situation through supply-side policies has been frustrated by stagnant government revenues and a continued rise in public debt. The urge to curb the food subsidy bill through reduced coverage and higher consumer prices only served to raise that bill through a phenomenal increase in food stocks. Unless one willingly reposes faith in the non-comparable evidence on poverty yielded by the National Sample Survey for 1999-2000, there is little reason to celebrate continued, let alone accelerated, progress on the poverty front. On the whole, the evidence shows increased inequality in the personal and functional distribution of real income within the rural and urban sectors, and a rising rural-urban income gap. Thus, neither direct nor indirect channels of complementarity have been realised. And the record provides sufficient grounds to doubt even the weaker expectation that social ends and globalising policies can be pursued simultaneously without trade off or conflict.

If the principal charge against earlier regimes is that they failed to set up or implement effective policies for expanding social opportunities, the new regime has not proved immune to the same charge. Without an account of this failure, scepticism seems warranted that meaningful development can be assured by the neo-liberal strategy. Such an account must be found not just in the purely economic assumptions underlying the prevalent wisdom but also in the realities of India's political economy. This general point may be illustrated in relation to agriculture. If genuinely equitable agricultural growth and rapid rural poverty alleviation are to be achieved, this will require a substantial step-up in public investment in rural infrastructure, research and thorough-going reforms in land relations and credit delivery. There is little room to believe, however, that such a programme can be pursued without producing major contradictions within the fiscal, economic and, ultimately, political priorities of the reform regime presently in place.

NOTE

Portions of this paper update and draw on an earlier paper by us (see Dutt and Rao, 2001). We are grateful to the Center for Economic Policy Analysis and the Ford Foundation for financial support, and to participants of conferences at Beijing and Hanoi, and especially to Lance Taylor, for comments and suggestions. We are also grateful to Kajal Mukhopadhyay for help with the econometrics.

REFERENCES

Ahluwalia, Isher J. (1991), *Productivity and Growth in Indian Manufacturing*, Delhi: Oxford University Press.

Ahluwalia, Montek S. (1995), "India's Economic Reforms", in Robert Cassen and Vijay Joshi, eds., *India: The Future of Economic Reform*, Delhi: Oxford University Press.

Alagh, Yoginder (2001), "WTO and India: Getting Facts Right", *Business Line,* February 9.

Balakrishnan, Pulapre (2000), "Agriculture and Economic Reforms. Growth and Welfare", *Economic and Political Weekly,* March 18, 999-1004.

Balakrishnan, Pulapre, K. Pushpangadan and M. Suresh Babu (2000), "Trade Liberalisation and Sroductivity Growth in Manufacturing: Evidence from Firm-level Panel Data", *Economic and Political Weekly,* October 7, 3679-82.

Basant, Rakesh (2000), "Corporate Response to Economic reforms", *Economic and Political Weekly,* March 4, 813-22.

Bhaduri, Amit and Deepak Nayyar (1996), *The Intelligent Person's Guide to Liberalisation*, New Delhi, Penguin.

Bhagwati, Jagdish (1994), *India in Transition. Freeing the Economy*, Delhi, Oxford University Press.

Bhagwati, Jagdish (1998), "The Design Of Indian Development", in I.J. Ahluwalia and I.M.D. Little, eds., *India's Economic Reforms and Development: Essays for Manmohan Singh*, Delhi: Oxford University Press.

Bhagwati, Jagdish and Srinivasan, T.N. (1993), *Indian Economic Reforms*, New Delhi: Ministry of Finance, Government of India.

Dasgupta, Dipankar, Maiti, Pradip, Mukherjee, Robin, Sarkar, Subrata, and Chakrabarti, Subhendu (2000), "Growth and

Interstate Disparities in India: Statistical Analysis", *Economic and Political Weekly,* 35:2413-2422.

Datta, Gaurav (1999), "Has Poverty Declined Since Economic Reforms? Statistical Data Analysis", *Economic and Political Weekly,* 34:3516-3518.

Datt, Ruddar (2001), "Where are the Jobs Mr. Sinha?" *Business Line.*

Deshpande, Sudha and Deshpande, Lalit (1998), "Impact of Liberalisation on the Labour Market in India. What Do Facts from the NSSO's 50th Round Show?" *Economic and Political Weekly,* May 30, L31-L39.

Dreze, Jean and Sen, Amartya (1995), *India. Economic Development and Social Opportunity*, Delhi, Oxford University Press.

Dutt, Amitava K. (1996), "The Role of Keynesian Policies In Semi-Industrialized Economies: Theory and Evidence from India", *International Review of Applied Economics,* 10(1), January, 127-40.

Dutt, Amitava K. (1998), "Globalisation, Foreign Direct Investment and Southern growth: Evidence from Selected Asian Countries", J.R. Chen, ed., *Economic Effects of Globalisation*, Avebury, 1998, p. 45-96.

Dutt, Amitava K. and Rao, J. Mohan (2001), "Globalisation and its Social Discontents: the Case of India", in Lance Taylor, ed., *External liberalisation, economic performance, and social policy,* New York: Oxford University Press.

Economic and Political Weekly Research Foundation (1997), *National Accounts Statistics of India, 1950-51 to 1995-96,* Mumbai: EPW Research Foundation.

Godley, Wynne and McCarthy, George (1997), "Fiscal Policy will Matter", unpublished, Jerome Levy Institute, Bard College, New York.

Goldar, B.N. (1993), "Impact of Technology and Productivity Growth in Indian industry", *Productivity,* 34(1), April-June, pp. 87-90.

Goldar, B.N. (2000), "Employment Growth In Organised Manufacturing in India", *Economic and Political Weekly*, April 1-7.

Goldar, B.N. and V.S. Ranganathan (1999), "Economic Reforms and R and D Expenditure in Industrial Firms in India", *Indian Economic Journal,* 46 (2), 60-75.

Guhan, S. (1992), "Social Security in India: Looking one Step Ahead" in B. Harriss, S. Guhan and R.H. Cassen, eds., *Poverty in India. Research and Policy*, Bombay, Oxford University Press.

Guhan, S. (1995), "Social Expenditures in the Union Budget: 1991-96", *Economic And Political Weekly*, May 6.

Joshi, Vijay and Little, I.M.D. (1996), *India's Economic Reforms, 1991-2001,* Oxford: Oxford University Press.

Kambhampati, Uma; Krishna, Pravin; and Mitra, Devashish (1997), "The Effect of Trade Policy Reforms on Labour Markets: Evidence from India", *Journal of International Trade and Economic Development,* 6 (2), 287-97.

Kohli, Atul (1990), *Democracy and Discontent. India's Growing Crisis of Governability*, Cambridge: Cambridge University Press.

Kohli, Renu (2001a), "Capital account liberalisation: Empirical Evidence and Policy Issues-I", *Economic and Political Weekly,* April 14, 2001.

Kohli, Renu (2001b), "Capital account liberalisation: Empirical Evidence and Policy Issues-II", *Economic and Political Weekly,* April 21, 2001, 1345-48.

Krishna, Pravin, and Mitra, Devashish (1998), "Trade Liberalisation, Market Discipline and Productivity Growth: New Evidence from India", *Journal of Development Economics,* 56, 447-62.

Kumar, Nagesh (1998), "Liberalisation and Changing Patterns of Foreign Direct Investments. Has India's Relative Attractiveness as a Host of FDI Improved? *Economic and Political Weekly,* May 30, 1321-29.

Kumar, Nagesh (2000a), "Economic Reforms and their Macro-Economic Impact", *Economic and Political Weekly,* March 4, 803-12.

Kumar, Nagesh (2000b), "Mergers and Acquisitions by MNEs: Patterns and Implications", *Economic and Political Weekly,* August 5, 2851-58.

Kundu, Amitabh (1997), "Trends and Structure of Employment in the 1990s. Implications for Urban Growth", *Economic and Political Weekly*, June 14, 1399-1405.

Mani, Sunil and M. Vijaya Bhaskar (1998). "A Curmudgeon's Guide to Economic Reforms in India's Manufacturing Sector", *Economic and Political Weekly,* Dec. 19.

Marjit, Sugata, Byasdeb Dasgupta and Sandip Mitra (2000), "Currency Sevaluation and Exports: Separating Actual from Statistical", *Economic and Political Weekly,* April 29, 1553-58.

Marjit, Sugata and A. Raychaudhuri (1997), *India's Exports: An Analytical Study*, Delhi, Oxford University Press.

Meenakshi, J.V., Ray, Ranjan and Gupta, Souvik (2000), "Estimates of Poverty for SC, ST and Female-Headed Households", *Economic and Political Weekly,* 35 : 2748-2754.

Mehta, Jaya and Venkatraman, Shanta (2000), "Poverty Statistics: Bermicide's Feast", *Economic and Political Weekly,* 35:2377-2382.

Mehta, Rajesh (1997), "Trade Policy Reforms, 1991-92 to 1995-96. Their Impact on External Trade", *Economic and Political Weekly,* April 12, 779-84.

Mellor, John W. and Desai, Gunvant M. (1986), *Agricultural Change and Rural Poverty: Variations on a Theme by Dharm Narain*, Oxford, Oxford University Press.

Nagaraj, R. (1997), "What Has Happened since 1991? Assessment of India's Economic Reforms", *Economic and Political Weekly,* Nov. 8, 2869-79.

Nagaraj, R. (2000a), "Indian economy since 1980: Virtuous Growth or Polarisation?" *Economic and Political Weekly,* August 5, 2831-38.

Nagaraj, R. (2000b), "Organised Manufacturing Employment", *Economic and Political Weekly,* September 16, 3445-8.

National Sample Survey Organization (1996), *Key Results on Employment and Unemployment*, *50th Round*, Department of Statistics, New Delhi.

Nayyar, Deepak (2000), "Capital controls and the World Financial Authority: What can we Learn from the Indian Experience?" Center for Economic Policy Analysis Working Paper Series III, No. 4, New School University.

Nijman, Jan (2000), "Mumbai's Real Estate Market in 1990s: De-regulation, Global Money and Casino Capitalism, *Economic and Political Weekly,* February 12, 575-82.

Pal, Parthapratim (1998), "Foreign Portfolio Investment in Indian Equity Markets. Has the Economy Benefited?" *Economic and Political Weekly,* March 14, 589-98.

Patnaik, Prabhat (1997), "The Context and Consequences Of Economic Liberalisation in India", *Journal of International Trade and Economic Development,* 6 (2), 165-78.

Pethe, Abhay and Ajay Karnik (2000), "Do Indian Stock Markets Matter? Stock Market Indeces and Macro-economic Variables", *Economic and Political Weekly,* January 29, 349-56.

Pieper, Ute (2000), "Deinstrialisation and the Social and Economic Sustainability Nexus in Developing Countries: Cross-country Evidence on Productivity and Employment", *Journal of Development Studies,* 36 (4), April, 66-99.

Rao, C.H.H. (2000), "Declining Demand for Foodgrains in Rural India: Causes and Implications", *Economic and Political Weekly,* 35:201-206.

Rao, J. Mohan (1998a), "Food Prices and Rural Poverty: Liberalisation without Pain?", *Economic and Political Weekly,* 33:799-800.

Rao, J. Mohan (1998b), "Food, Agriculture and Reforms: Change and Continuity," *Economic and Political Weekly,* 33:1955-1960.

Rao, J. Mohan (1998c), *Openness, Inequality and Poverty.* Background Paper prepared for the Human Development Report (1999). New York: UNDP.

Rao, J. Mohan and Storm, Servaas (1997), "Distribution and Growth in Indian Agriculture", in T.J. Byres (Ed.), *The Indian Economy: Major Debates Since Independence*, Delhi, Oxford University Press.

Ravallion, Martin (1998), "Reform, Food Prices and Poverty in India", *Economic and Political Weekly,* January 10, 29-36.

Roy, M.K. (2001), "Stock markets in a Liberalised Economy. Indian Experiences", *Economic and Political Weekly,* January 27, 367-76.

Saha, Anamitra (2000), "Puzzle of Declining Rural Foodgrains Consumption", *Economic and Political Weekly,* 35 : 201-206.

Sen, Abhijit (1996), "Economic Reforms, Employment and Poverty. Trends and Options", *Economic and Political Weekly,* Sept., 2459-77.

Sen, Abhijit (2000), "Estimates of Consumer Expenditure and its Distribution: Statistical Priorities after NSS 55th Round", *Economic and Political Weekly,* 35 : 4499-4518.

Sen, Abhijit (2001), "A Whole Crop of Uncertainties", *Frontline,* 18.

Singh, Ajit (1998), "Liberalisation, the Stock Market, and the Market for Corporate Control: A bridge too far for the Indian Economy?" in I.J. Ahluwalia and I.M.D. Little, eds., *India's Economic Reforms and Development: Essays for Manmohan Singh*, Delhi: Oxford University P.

Srinivasan, T.N. (1998), "India's Export Performance: a Comparative Analysis", in I.J. Ahluwalia and I.M.D. Little, eds., *India's Economic Reforms and Development: Essays for Manmohan Singh*, Delhi: Oxford University Press.

Sundaram, K. (2001), "Employment-Unemployment Situation in the Nineties: Some Results from NSS 55th Round Survey", *Economic and Political Weekly,* 36 : 931-940.

Suryanarayana, M.H. (1996), "Economic Reforms, Nature and Poverty", *Economic and Political Weekly,* 31 : 617-624.

Suryanarayana, M.H. (2000), "How Real is the Secular Decline in Rural Poverty", *Economic and Political Weekly,* 35 : 2129-2140.

Swaminathan, Madhura (1996), "Structural Adjustment, Food Security and System of Public Distribution of Food", *Economic and Political Weekly,* 31:1665-1672.

Swaminathan, Madhura (1998), *Weakening Welfare: The Public Distribution of Food in India*, New Delhi, LeftWord Books.

Visaria, Pravin (2000), "Alternative Estimates of Poverty in India", *Economic Times,* June 29.

World Bank (1996), *India. Five Years of Stabilization and Reform and the Challenges Ahead*, Washington D.C. : The World Bank.

World Bank (1998), *India. Achievements and Challenges in Reducing Poverty*, Washington D.C. : The World Bank.

CRITIQUE OF THE NATIONAL ELECTRICITY POLICY

K. Ashok Rao

WISH LIST OR RENEGING FROM CMP COMMITMENT?

The twenty-three-page document recently approved by the Union Cabinet of the Government of India cannot be construed as a policy document. At best, it is a wish list of the Government of India and at worst, a declaration that there will be no amendment to the Electricity Act 2003, Common Minimum Programme (CMP) or no CMP.

Inter-alia, the wish list consists of:

- Add about one lakh MW of installed capacity between 2002-2012.
- Create adequate reserve capacity.
- Electrify all homes by 2012 (electrify about 56 per cent of rural households, besides urban).
- Create a Rural Distribution Backbone.
- Bring loss levels to international standards by 2012.
- Automate sub-stations with SCDA.
- Remove all subsidies except for 1unit per day to those below poverty level.

Some of the above can be achieved, for some like SCADA the cost effectiveness needs to be established and some are just jargon like "Creating a Rural Distribution Backbone", "Bring loss levels to international standards by 2012" All that can be debated and discussed separately. What is of concern to us here is that essentially this implies that what could and could not be achieved since independence (58 years) would be achieved within seven years ! And with what will all this be achieved-the magic wand–Electricity Act 2003!

CHASING THE RAINBOW?

The only indication of how this wish list would be fulfilled is a statement:

> "To meet the objectives of rapid economic growth and "power for all" including household electrification, it is estimated that an investment of the order of Rs. 9,00,000 Crores at 2002-03 price level would be required to finance generation, transmission, sub transmission, distribution and rural electrification."

Where this kind of money will come from is not stated in the policy document, other than an assurance to the private sector of guaranteed returns and a hope that consequently investments would flow:

> "Capital is scarce. Private sector will have multiple options for investments. Returns on investment will, therefore, need to be provided in a manner that the sector is able to attract adequate investments at par with, if not in preference to, investment opportunities in other sectors. ... An appropriate balance will have to be maintained between the interests of the consumers and the needs for investments.... The Central and State Government need to develop workable and successful models for public private partnership. This would also enable leveraging private investments with public finances."

POLICY DOCUMENT OR IDEOLOGICAL ASSERTIONS

The policy document does not seem to take note of the fact that private investments are drying up-having fallen substantially in recent years, from a peak of $50bn in 1997, investment in power projects with private participation in developing countries fell to around $7bn in 2002. The World Bank evaluation report in 2003 noted that by 1999 the WB's power lending portfolio had been recognised as one of the Bank's worst performers, with continuing problems of political and financial risk noted in South and East Asia. The report also observed that the WB became centered on privatisation to an even greater extent than was stated in its own policies, and with poor results: *"subsequent to the 1993 Policy, and without explicitly enunciating it as a major strategic change, the Bank mostly advocated privatisation, as well as private participation through management contracts, as a means to achieving commercialisation. This shift led to a highly reform-intensive power portfolio, which ultimately performed poorly overall during most of the 1990s"*. Inspite of all this evidence, that the Indian Government is distorting legislation and policy obsessively soliciting privatisation and the illusive FDI.

The policy document is more ideological than even the World Bank:

> "Private sector participation in distribution needs to be encouraged for achieving the requisite reduction in transmission and distribution losses and improving the quality of service to the consumers."

Such an assertion is not borne out from the experience of Orissa and Delhi, the two states that have privatised distribution. On Orissa the Kanungo committee recorded:

> "The private sector partners of the DISTCOs, neither brought superior management skills into the companies nor did they arrange financial support by way of working capital for the companies. All that they gave was the fund they had brought for acquisition of shares at the time of privatization. When we pointedly asked about infusion of working capital, we were told that infusion of capital into the DISTCOS need to be viewed as joint responsibility of both the partners, not the private sector partner alone We find this attitude difficult to accept, particularly having regard to the clause 8.I in the Shareholders Agreement executed at the time of privatization ......

The DISTCOs are in dire need of capital, working capital in particular. Instead of using the good offices of BSES Ltd. to secure working capital in accordance with the Shareholders Agreements for the three DISTCOs under their control, they have persistently defaulted in the payment for power they purchased from GR1DCO and thereby have over exploited GRIDCO's misplaced generosity in permitting them to use as working capital"

On Delhi the Comptroller and Auditor General (CAG) in its report states:

1. The Delhi Electricity Reforms Act which vests the authority to frame the scheme (for privatisation and transfer of assets and manpower) in the Government. Section 2 (d) of the Act stipulates that "government" means the Lt. Governor of the NCT of Delhi. Hence, any substantial changes in the terms of transfer scheme should have been re-submitted to the Lt. Governor for his approval. The Audit report suggested that the Government might obtain post-facto approval of Lt. Governor to the modifications made in the Transfer Scheme.
2. A scrutiny of the note (Government's note on the valuation of assets) indicated that the general methodology had been explained, the basic figures adopted, the weightages given and assumptions made were not indicated and hence the basis of arriving at the final figure of Rs. 3,160 could not be verified.
3. At the time of Request for Proposal (RFP), the total loss was to be reduced by 20.75 per cent for DISCOM 19.25 per cent and I for DISCOM II and III. At the time of Share Acquisition Agreement, consideration of collection efficiency was included in the calculation of AT&C and requirement for reduction of AT&C losses was diluted to 17 per cent over a period of five years. Audit scrutiny revealed that if we consider the collection efficiency along with technical losses as allowed by the Delhi Electricity Regulatory Commission and the technical consultants,

the loss on these two factors viz., technical loss and collection efficiency was 18.63 per cent. Taking into account the acceptable technical loss of 7.3 per cent, the extra loss allowed to the DISCOMs on account of technical loss and collection efficiency was 11.20 per cent. The non-technical loss viz. primarily theft reduction and misuse which was one of the primary objectives of privatisation was thus only 5.80 per cent in five years viz. 1.1.6 per cent per year as against 3 pre cent per year on an average envisaged in the RFP. This resulted in a significant dilution of the loss reduction targets as originally envisaged in the RFP.

4. By reducing loss reduction level from 20.75 per cent for DICOM I and 19.25 per cent for DISCOM II and III to 17 per cent for all, TRANSCO is deprived of an accrual of Rs. 3,929 crores...The support level envisaged was Rs. 2,600 crore, but even a support of Rs. 3,450 crore was not adequate to compensate for the loss that would be incurred by TRANSCO in view of the assumption made for increase in consumer tariff every years @ 10 per cent...Enhancement of moratorium period (for repayment by DISCOMs) will result in depriving the holding company of interest amount of Rs. 339.84 crore which would have accrued after the third year. Moreover, it enables utilisation of loan amount of Rs. 1,1416 crore for an additional two years without interest.... There is a difference of Rs. 3,107.62 crore between the figure of total receivables depicted in the Balance Sheet ending 31 March 2002 of DVB and that worked out by the consultants...

5. The gross difference in the amounts paid to (the consultant) SBI CAPs and subsequently to ASCI was not justified given the work actually involved.

A study by Prayas indicates even old and well-established private distribution companies like Tata and BSES in Mumbai, CSES in Kolkatta have not shown greater efficiency or reduction in losses etc. than the comparable

Pune municipal area of MSEB. There is no evidence anywhere else in the World either; studies suggest that in transmission and distribution, there is *"no significant difference in technical efficiency between the two ownership types."*

The policy document is full of assurances to private investors. But in respect of the Public Sector the only major role envisaged is:

> "Public Services obligation like increasing access to electricity to rural households and small and marginal farmers have highest priority over public finance."

Indeed, a classic case of 'privatising profits and nationalising losses.'

In any case the share of power sector in total outlay of both Central and State governments has been systematically brought down from 18.33 in 1991 1991-92 to 13.09 in 2000-2001. And the share of the power sector in the total outlay of the States has come down more drastically from 26.09 in 1991-92 to 17.81 in 2000-01.

MORTGAGING THE FUTURE

The policy document states:

> "The Electricity Act 2003 has put in place a highly liberalized framework for generation. There is no requirement of licensing for generation. The requirement of techno-economic clearance of CEA for thermal projects is no longer there."

The Government of India does not seem to have learnt anything from the Dhabol fiasco. The Dhabol Power Plant (Stage I of 748 MW) has now remained shut for more than 40 months after Maharashtra State Electricity Board (MSEB) charged it with violation of its contractual obligations. The Stage II of the plant is unfinished and construction halted midway, the entire plant of 2,192 MW is now junk. The Indian financial institutions IDBI and IFCI that had advanced loans are now helplessly watching over Rs. 10,000 crore (more than US $ 2000 million) turn into non-performing assets. The Government of India has been sued for $ 110 million (Rs. 500 crore) to compensate OPIC for the political risk insurance claims paid to the new owners of Dhabol GE and Bechtal, "The concerted actions of the Indian Government have effectively deprived Dhabol Power Company (DPC) and its investors and lenders of their fundamental rights, interests, use, benefits and control of their investments in Dhabol project in violation of Government of India's obligations under public international law." This claim has been made under the USA–India bilateral trade agreement. Under the Indo-Mauritius trade treaty (since Dhabol is owned through a Mauritius based intermediary Enron Mauritius) GE and Bechtal are suing the Government of India for another $ 1.2 billion (Rs. 5,520 crore) and at the end of November 2004 another case under the Indo-Dutch bilateral trade treaty (because Enron is owned by another intermediary company, Overseas Power Production, which is registered in the Netherlands) for $ 3.9 billion compensation (Rs. 17,940 crore). The starving millions of Indians will bleed for more Rs. 35,000 crore for a non-performing junk powerhouse, because the Government had taken the plea that they did not have the resources to solve the power crisis in the country.

What is most dangerous is that the policy document endangers future generations by allowing long-term commitments without a clear assessment of their impact. There is no fuel policy or an assessment of the energy balance of the country. In UK, as a result of the power policy, the entire Coal industry was virtually destroyed. Even if one ignores concerns like employment etc., what in India, would be the long-term implication for foreign exchange requirements due to:

> "Imported coal based thermal power plants, particularly at coastal locations, would be encouraged based on their economic viability...Imported LNG based power plants are also a potential source of electricity and the pace of development would depend in their commercial viability."

The investors, would not only enjoy legislative freedom without any checks and balances, but would also be allowed to enter into long-term contracts, as assured by the policy document:

> "Generating companies may enter into medium and long –term fuel supply agreements specially with respect to imported fuels for commercial viability and security of supply".

Since each investor would be concerned only with the viability of his particular project, which agency would be responsible for the cumulative impact on the nation-its foreign exchange and energy security? Suppose, for the sake of argument, most of the investors find imports fuels LNG or coal or any other commercially viable and enter into long-term contracts, would the Government of India have unlimited foreign exchange to finance the imports? Would it be unconcerned about the fate of the coalmines and millions of workers? What would happen to the energy security of the nation? The policy document is silent on these issues.

Hydropower site is a gift of nature. And there are only a finite number of sites. Privatising hydropower implies that the state loses the right to commercially exploit the site. Hydropower is available in states that have very little industry and other revenue earning sources. The prosperity of Himachal Pradesh is largely due to state exploiting Hydropower.

COSTLY POWER FOR THE CONSUMERS

And what does the policy document give the consumer?

1. End of all subsidies.
2. Ensure recovery of the cost to serve.

To anybody familiar with the power system this is nothing more than what the policy documents itself admits,

> "there is an urgent need to correct this imbalance (of cross-subsidies) without giving tariff shock to consumers."

There is however no roadmap on how the tariff shock will be avoided. The most critical of all is what happens to affordable price for supply to agriculture. Would for example replacing Section 59 of the Electricity (Supply) Act 1948 (requiring State Governments to ensure a 3 per cent rate of return to the SEBs) with Section 65 in the Electricity Act 2003 wish away the compulsions on the State Governments to violate the law and not abide by the resolution of Chief Ministers on a minimum agricultural tariff. Why was the "reformist" Government defeated in election on the promise of free power to the farmers. The policy document does not explain on what basis is this economic and political reality wished away.

In exchange for loss of subsidies the consumer is promised of competition, which by definition has to benefit the consumer. The term Competition is bandied about as being something like the competition between grocery shops in the neighbourhood. The policy document does not explain, how competition would be achieved when the dice is loaded in favour of cherry picking (with instruments like non discriminating open access and second distribution license etc.) besides one sided power purchase agreements.

The consumer is promised the freedom to chose his source of supply as if there were no price tag attached to such a choice. In UK for providing competition "*the software to allow retail competition cost more than $1.2bn (paid by consumers) to install and operate and has also been highly problematic. Competing for retail consumers is expensive. In 1990 before retail competition for small consumers was allowed in Britain, about 5 per cent of domestic consumers' bills went to meet the costs (billing, meter reading etc) of the retail supplier. Now those costs include marketing, cost of switching, incentives for switching etc, and suppliers' costs now represent about 30 per cent of domestic consumers' bills.*" In a country like Japan with 216 GWh of consumption there are about 2000 consumers who consume more than 2 MW, in India that number may not be even in three digits. Besides all these serious concerns the policy document does not even answer a simple question, how does competition become operational under conditions of shortages?

CONCERN FOR THE WRENCHED OR JUST USING THEM?

The policy document bemoans the fact that:

> "As per the Census 2001, about 44 per cent of the households do not have access to electricity. Hence meeting the target of providing universal access is a daunting task requiring significant addition to generation capacity and expansion of transmission and distribution network."

It is obvious that the lack of universal access has been used to justify large scale expansion, for which obviously there are no funds and therefore the urgent need to open all doors and liberalise everything to attract the much needed private and FDI funds. Either the authors of the policy document are unaware of the state of the Indian people or are just playing the World Bank style game of 'polemics of poverty reduction'.

Millions of people In India are living on the margins. A study suggests

> "It is observed that 44 out of the total 59 regions (in the major states) have >30 per cent of the poor households living under severe poverty. These households, under severe poverty, have consumption level less than 75 per cent of the normative consumption at the poverty line. What is of more concern is that about 44 regions have >40 per cent share among the households belonging to the category of severe or 'very poor'.
>
> The recent evidence capturing the post liberalisation period between 1991-1997, clearly suggest that despite significant increase in per capita income, rural poverty did not decline in any considerable manner. This is mainly due to the increased inequality not only vis-à-vis the urban areas but also within the rural population. As a result, the real per capita consumption of the bottom 40 per cent of rural population has experienced either negligible or even negative growth during the same period."

Prof. Utsa Patnaik's analysis emphasises the seriousness on the food front:

> In the course of the last five years (1998 to 2003), the population of the Republic of India has been sliding down towards sharply

> lowered levels of per capita foodgrains absorption, levels so low in particular years that they have not been seen for the last half century. Between the early 1990s when economic reforms began, and at present, taking three-year averages, the annual absorption of foodgrains per head has come down from 177 kg to 155 kg Such low absorption levels were last seen in the initial years of World War 11-from where they had fallen further still. Again, after some recovery, the very first few years after Independence half a century ago and the food crisis of the mid-1960s, are comparable to present average absorption levels.
>
> Forty years of effort have been lost in the last decade of neo-liberal economic reforms, with over four-fifths of the loss taking place in the last five years alone. The most remarkable and disastrous feature of the last five years of NDA rule in India has been the slide-back to the low level of 151 kg per head food absorption in rural areas by 2001, a level not seen for fifty years. Reports of starvation, farmer suicides and deepening hunger, should cause little surprise when we consider the recent trends in the official data on foodgrains output and availability. If we exclude the abnormal drought year 2002-03 and consider the average output of the preceding two years, we find that net foodgrains output per capita has fallen by about 5.5 kg compared to the early nineties, owing to a slowing of output growth. This fall in per head output had been anticipated by this author (Patnaik 1996): as agriculture was opened up to the pull of global demand, 8 million hectares of foodgrains growing land has been diverted to exportable crops between 1991 and 2001, and yield has not risen enough to compensate, leading to a sharp decline of annual output growth which has fallen below population growth (even though the latter itself has been falling): hence we see fall in per head output.

To these starving millions the policy document promises:

> "A minimum level of support may be required to make the electricity affordable for the consumers of very poor category. Consumers below poverty line who consume below a specified level, say 30 units per month, may receive special support in terms of tariff which are cross-subsidied. Tariff for such designated group of consumers will be atleast 50 per cent of the average (overall) cost of supply. This provision will be further re-examined after five years."

The Government of India would do well to ensure food to the starving rather than give slogans of 'power for all' and use their wretchedness to justify neo-liberal demands.

REWRITING THE FEDERAL CHARACTER OF INDIA

Even though the policy document mentions:

> "Electricity being a concurrent subject, a well co-ordained approach would be necessary for development of the power sector".

But the State Governments are given no alternative option. Unbundling of the State Electricity Boards is presumed and the policy document states:

> "For ensuring financial viability and sustainability, State governments would need to restructure the liabilities of the State Electricity Boards to ensure that the successor companies are not burdened with past liabilities".

The Government of India has internalised the methodology of the World Bank of 'output-based aid'. The policy document states.

> "The Central Government would also assist the States, which develop a clear road map for turn around, in arranging transition finance from various sources which shall be linked to pre-determined improvements and efficiency gains aimed at financial viability and putting in place appropriate governance structures".

The message to the State Governments is clear, if you want any funds either from the Central Government or transition finance from various sources (read World Bank) unbundle the State Electricity Boards and create privatisation enabling conditions.

THE INDIAN PEOPLE WANT ANSWERS

The most important questions the people want to know are.

WHY is there no enquiry into the enormous loss to the Nation due to the Dhabol Power Project? WHY is no individual responsibility fixed? (If in spite of being one of the biggest funders for Bush's election, the officials of Enron can go to jail in USA, why are the patrons of Enron not in jail in India?)

WHY is there no enquiry into the privatisation in Orissa and Delhi in spite of the Kanungo Committee report and the findings of the CAG ? WHY is no individual responsibility fixed?

India is a land where 70 per cent of the peopie depend on agriculture. What the people want is a policy document of the Government of India that answers the following questions:

- What are the compulsions that caused state governments to violate Section 59 of the Electricity Act 1948 (that has placed a statuary obligation on Governments to ensure a 3 per cent rate of returns to SEBs)?
- How would the violation stop merely by replacing Section 59 of the 1948 Act Section 65 of the 2003 Act (that requires the State Government to pay in advance for grant of subsidy?)
- What is the cost of all the incentives, guarantees, concessions, comforts given to the private firms in generation and distribution? How does it compare to the subsidies given to Agriculture and Domestic consumers?
- How will purchase of high cost power from Private Sector generators (IPPs) bring down the price of power? and how will cherry picking through instruments like captive power plant, second distribution license, non discriminating open access provide relief to the retail consumer?
- Would the cost of canal irrigation water be increased to match the cost of groundwater?
- Would the disparity between the cost of canal irrigation and groundwater irrigation based on high power tariffs be sustainable?
- What would happen to the viability of Indian agriculture?
- What is the long-term feasibility of Governments riding on two stools–undertake World Bank-led "reforms' and

give free power to farmers? Which of these options will be jettisoned and why?

And in the context of multilateral agreements on Agriculture that need answers are:

(a) Is the objective of the World Bank to achieve, through the Electricity reforms, that which WTO agreement on Agriculture was unable to achieve?

(b) Would Indian Agriculture be able to compete (March 2000, the Government of India withdrew Quantitative Restrictions on 714 items out of 1429 items) against highly subsidised European and American farmers in a global free market economy, if the subsidy to Indian farmers is withdrawn?

(c) By making Electricity costly would Indian agriculture be moved from food grain crops to cash crops to serve the Multinationals through large contract farms?

A MODEL BEING REJECTED IN OTHER ASIAN COUNTRIES

The World Bank and its counterparts enforced similar legislation and policy in most of South and South East Asian countries. In Bangladesh, ADB drafted the Electricity Reform Bill. The World Bank together with the ADB drafted the Power Sector Restructuring Policy of Indonesia in 1998 that was the basis of the Electricity Act No. 20/2002. ADB drafted the legislation–EPIRA–to privatise NAPOCOR amidst a scandal of payoffs to parliamentarians.

The Constitutional Court of Indonesia annulled on Wednesday Electricity Law No. 20/ 2002, ruling. The Court held that it was against Article 33 of the 1945 Constitution that stipulated that "economic sectors that are important and crucial for the welfare of the people must be controlled by the state and must be developed to give the maximum benefit to the people". The Court held that "since electricity was an important commodity pivotal to the lives of many people, electricity should remain under the government's control."

We, the people of India, having solemnly resolved to constitute India into a sovereign socialist secular democratic republic enshrined Article 38 in the Indian Constitution that states:

The State shall in particular, direct its policy towards securing:

(a) That the ownership and control of the material resources of the community are so distributed as best to subserve the common good;

(b) That the operation of the economic system does not result in the concentration of wealth and means of production to the common detriment;

Where does the Government of India get the legal power to violate the Constitution of India?

COINCIDENCE OR COMPLIANCE

The entire policy document paragraph after paragraph states with "The Act provides." "The Act mandates..."; "The Act enables..."; "The Act prohibits..." "Under the Act..." and so on. Essentially what is passed of as a policy of the Government of India is nothing more than a paraphrase of two documents (i) The Electricity Act 2003 and (ii) Operational Guidance for World Bank Group Staff-Public and Private Sector Roles in the Supply of Electricity Services–The World Bank The Energy and Mining Sector Board- February 2004.. Given below in a tabular form, are a few examples of comparision between the two documents. Are the similarities a coincidence or mere compliance by a client? You decide.

CONCLUSION

It is unfortunate that the Union Cabinet of the United Progressive Alliance (UPA) Government should approve such a document as a National Electricity Policy. That the UPA government is uncritically pushing legislation piloted and passed during the previous National Democratic Alliance notwithstanding a common minimum programme is a great betrayal of the Indian people.

WHOSE POLICY IS IT ANYWAY?
Coincidence or compliance?

Government of India *National Electricity Policy*	*World Bank* *Operational Guidance for WB Staff*
The Central Government and the State Governments need to develop workable and successful models for private public partnership. This would also enable leveraging private investment with public sector finances.	It is important to consider the full range of options for public-private partnerships.... It should be remembered that the public sector can have a financing and/or a risk bearing role in all of these arrangements.
Necessary institutional framework would need to be put in place not only to ensure creation of rural electrification but also to operate and maintain...through appropriate arrangements with panchayats, local authorities, NGOs and other franchisees.	Governments may seek to introduce new, local service providers into the rural electrification business in particular whether it should be provided through existing facilities like SME development windows and NGO supported micro-finance and business development entities.
Private sector participation in distribution needs to be encouraged for achieving the requisite reduction in transmission and distribution losses and improving the quality of service to the consumers	The private sector has shown that it can deliver efficient investments and improved services to customers of the power sector provided that the right business incentives are in place to attract investment.
... except for lifeline support to households below the poverty line who need to be adequately subsidised, subsidies should be properly targeted at the intended beneficiaries in the most efficient manner....	In general, targeting subsidies at connections would be preferable to subsidising consumption. Staff should assess, along with the government, the extent to which proposed subsidy schemes would benefit the poor and

Contd....

Government of India *National Electricity Policy*	*World Bank* *Operational Guidance for WB Staff*
A minimum level of support may be required to make the electricity affordable for consumers of very poor. Consumers below poverty line who consume below a specified level, say 30 units per month, may receive special support in terms of tariff, which are cross subsidised. Tariffs will be 50 per cent of the average cost of supply.	whether there is sufficient fiscal space for these subsidies… staff should discuss and agree with clients measures to focus subsidies on lower income consumers.

TRANSITION IN AGRICULTURE: THE CASE OF PROPERTY RIGHTS REFORM IN CENTRAL AND EASTERN EUROPE

Konrad Hagedorn

INTRODUCTION

In this paper, processes of privatisation and restructuring of agricultural land in Central and Eastern Europe will be considered as phenomena of institutional change which can only be controlled to a limited extent. This is in contrast to the view that such institutional innovation was actually following pre-designed concepts which could be precisely implemented by political and administrative actors. Accordingly, just focussing on conventional policy recommendations by saying "what governments should do" without having gained sufficient knowledge on the particular actors and institutions in the country in question may be more detrimental than helpful. The ability of internal and external political actors to govern and to control real changes in institutions, that means not only formal ones such as new laws which are often insufficiently implemented, is rather low in transition counties. In addition, some political elites in several transition countries have developed a culture of extreme "rent seeking", sometimes also characterised by the terms "the grabbing hand" (Shleifer and Vishny, 1998) or "the roving bandit" (Olson, 1995, 2000). This means that the activities of such powerful actors are not automatically and primarily oriented towards policies and institutions that improve the well-being of their society (Hanisch, 2003: 97). Certainly, this does not equally apply to all transition countries and to all political actors in these countries.

This paper is organised as follows: first, we will draw an outline of analytical approaches that emerged at the beginning of the transition period to find the determinants of land privatisation and agricultural restructuring. In this phase, a distinction was made between historical factors and determinants originating from the property rights formation process itself. Then a more complex conceptual framework based on theories of institutional economics and political economy is presented, which was applied in a comprehensive research project. The results from this research phase are based on empirical studies on institutional change conducted in selected transition countries. Finally, issues of lack of social capital in the transformation process as a field for further research is discussed.

FIRST APPROACHES TOWARDS AN UNDERSTANDING OF AGRICULTURAL TRANSFORMATION

Similar to transformation studies for other parts of the economy, those on agricultural transformation mostly were normative at the beginning of the transformation process. The underlying assumption was that privatisation of agricultural land and other agricultural assets and restructuring of farms should be determined by the aim of economising transaction costs within the farm firm (see Schmitt, 1991). Conse-quently, two main questions were discussed:

(a) Which farm size-as a proper target of privatisation and restructuring–will prove superior? To what extent will digressive production costs be accompanied by likewise digressive transaction costs or, in contrary, be outweighed by progres-sively increasing transaction costs?

(b) Which organisational structure of the privatised and restructured farms will be the most competitive, if production cooperatives are compared with family farms, for example?

However, already at the beginning of the nineties, Swinnen (1992, 1993, 1994) argued that it may be sufficient just to look at the farm unit as a transaction-cost saving entity if we are in a well developed, stable farm economy which is not affected by major changes due to structural adjustment or reform policies. In a period of fundamental transformation of the farm sector, however, the whole network of relationships between the actor and organisations in the agricultural sector has to be taken into account, including the (changing) rules they are based on. Thus, several additional factors had to be included into the analysis:

– The particularities of the starting situation regarding farm organisation and agricultural structures, e.g. size of the plots belonging to land owners and availability of capital.
– Relationship to other institutions related to agriculture such as access to inputs, marketing cooperatives, extension services, credit institutions, information systems, etc.
– The Political Economy of agriculture, especially with regard to different interests, special constraints and emerging conflicts due to privatisation and de-collectivisation policies.
– The evolutionary characteristics and potential path dependency which may come into being during the transformation process and may lead to different routes of change.

"Consequently, the policy advice for the restructuring of CEE agriculture should not ignore the existing structure and/or the institutional and policy environment and should not limit the relevant variables to the initial and final equilibrium situation. Rather, it should explicitly include the process of change in the analysis" (Swinnen, 1994: 4). Thus, there are reasonable arguments which show that the isolated (and static) perspective of only the farm unit is an "approach in a vacuum" (Swinnen, 1994: 12). These initial insights into the complexity of the transformation process indicated the necessity of more systematic attempts.

BASIC ELEMENTS FOR A SYSTEMATIC EXPLANATION OF INSTITUTIONAL TRANSFORMATION

One of the main institutional questions reform politicians had to deal with was whether and how private property rights in land should be re-introduced. There were two conflicting answers to this question:

- Ownership rights in land should be given back, i.e. land restitution in historical boundaries should be supported in order to do historical justice.
- Land restitution in historical boundaries should be avoided because it leads to inefficient agricultural structures. Instead, land should be sold or distributed by a voucher system.

The Central and Eastern European countries have made very different decisions with regard to these options (see Swinnen, 1994, 1996, 1997; Swinnen and Mathijs, 1997; Swinnen et al., 1997; Hagedorn, 1997, 1998; Lerman et al., 2004).

THE DIVERSITY OF TRANSFORMATION PROCEDURES IN TRANSITION COUNTRIES

Restitution of land to previous owners was a general rule of privatisation in Central and Eastern Europe. However, there are manifold exemptions as the following examples illustrate:

Russia / Ukraine: Restitution was not feasible because the previous borders were no longer available. Land was distributed to the rural population on a per capita basis. Privatisation remained incomplete with regard to the extent of effective rights actually transferred to individuals.

Baltic States: Restitution to former owners was accepted as a general rule, but only for ethnic Estonians, Latvians and Lithuanians; ethnic Russians were excluded from land distribution.

Romania: Restitution of land to former owners was combined with per-family distribution of some land. Land expropriated prior to 1947 was not restituted.

Bulgaria: Restitution of land to former owners in historical boundaries was initiated after 1990 by means of a bureaucratic procedure, but the process proceeded only slowly and was frequently modified by changing governments.

Albania: After an initial period of "wild privatisation" land was distributed on an equal per-capita basis. The political forces, which preferred this strategy, were stronger than those politicians who represented the interests of former owners (mainly the nobility).

Hungary: Priority was given to voucher privatisation, by which two thirds of the land owned by the collective farms were distributed. This strategy supported the survival of large farms.

Slovenia: To a large extent, the small family farms had not been collectivised or nationalised. Land was returned to former owners, but Italian citizens were excluded from land restitution.

Czechoslovakia: Land expropriated prior to February 25, 1948, was not given back to previous owners. Collectivised land was returned to the original owners. After the country was divided into the Czech and the Slovak Republics, some differences in the privatisation strategies came up. In the *Czech Republic*, land formerly owned by the Catholic Church was not restituted. In the *Slovak Republic*, the government changed the date of reference in a way that allowed for restitution to the Catholic Church.

Poland: The major part of agricultural land in Poland is operated by family farms, which were neither collectivised nor nationalised. Most of the nationalised land belonged to Germany before World War II. Poland avoided restituting it to Germans; state-owned land has been leased or sold.

Germany: No restitution of land and other property to former owners expropriated during the so-called land reform from 1945-1949 took place. This land has been pre-privatised by long-term lease contracts and is sold at approximately half the market prices by a land acquisition programmeme. In contrast, land expropriated or collectivised later than 1949 was restituted.

Non-land assets were usually not restituted. Instead, they were privatised by a voucher system or transformed into capital shares in the reformed cooperative farms.

HISTORICAL DETERMINANTS EXISTING AT THE STARTING POINT OF TRANSITION

At least some of these differences can be explained by historical factors that influence the process of privatisation and restructuring but cannot be considered as being endogenous to the process. During this process, conflicting goals played a role, mainly economic efficiency and income distribution. The goal of income distribution can be differentiated into two objectives that have not always been compatible in the process: equity as a social concern and doing historical justice as a legal demand. In countries like Bulgaria, exhibiting rather egalitarian land distribution prior to collectivisation, these objectives were more or less compatible. In countries with unequal distribution of pre-reform land ownership, like in Albania, they were conflicting. Some of the conflicts involved in land restitution can be explained by the following determinants:

- The ownership-status after collectivisation or nationalisation.
- The ethnicity of asset ownership prior to the socialist era.
- The equality of asset distribution before collectivisation or nationalisation, and
- The persistence of social values, human capital and informal institutions.

1. If we look at the impact of the legal asset ownership after collectivisation, we must distinguish between land and other assets. Both kinds of property are usually treated differently. The first reason is that land is still physically available. Its quality may have been changed, e.g., by investing in drainage or irrigation systems, and it may no longer lie adjacent to a road, due to land consolidation which was connected with the collectivisation process. But it can still be given back as a physical unit. This is not true with regard to other assets like cattle or machines. At the beginning these assets were collectively used, but after collectivisation they were still privately owned. However step by step, they were replaced by new assets, i.e. by new machines or by other animals. Therefore, it is impossible to return the original assets to the former owners.

   In the case of land, people often still held the *formal* ownership rights, although they were no longer allowed to decide on the use of the land, i.e. they did not have *effective* property rights. In this case, privatisation does not mean the transfer of legal ownership rights, rather than the transfer of effective property rights. It was impossible for the government to choose a different privatisation procedure in these cases than land restitution. Otherwise they would have taken away the legal ownership rights from the formal or legal owners. Swinnen (1996) emphasises that it would have been extremely ironical if private ownership rights, after having survived forty years of collectivisation and state control, would be confiscated by governments that were democratically elected.

2. The impact of ethnicity results from the fact, that the privatisation policy affects the distribution of assets between ethnic groups (which may live inside or outside the country). For example, most of the countries did not restitute land to foreigners and have even restricted land sales and land renting to foreigners. Poland does not sell

the land of the state farms formerly owned by Germans to foreigners, and the same is true for land formerly owned by the Sudeten-Germans in the Czech Republic. In Slovenia, Italians owned some of the land that was nationalised after World War II, and they were also not restituted. In the Baltic states, Russians as a large ethnic minority were not integrated into the process of privatisation. By restricting restitution to former owners, they were excluded, because former owners were all native Latvians and Lithuanians. In this way, the restitution policy secured land ownership only in the hands of native citizens.

3. Distribution of land ownership before collectivisation is important as a determinant of the privatisation process, because it determines to what extent the objectives of "historical justice" and "social equity" are conflicting or compatible. If pre-collectivisation land ownership was egalitarian as it was, for example, in Bulgaria, restitution of land is promoting historical justice as well as social equity. However, if it was more unequal distribution, then historical justice and social equity became conflicting objectives. Albania is a good example for this (see Cungu and Swinnen, 1999). Here two different political parties which both belong to the anti-communist group represented these conflicting objectives. Both strongly supported privatisation and de-collectivisation, but one of them favoured land restitution to former owners and the other one wanted land to be distributed among farm workers. In Albania, land distribution was very unequal prior to collectivisation. In the best agricultural regions of the country, the land was owned only by a few families, while a large part of the population was working as hired labour in agriculture. Therefore, land distribution on an equal per-capita basis favoured a large number of voters, which seemed to be a more influential political factor than the interests of the former landlords.

4. Social values and human capital represent important reasons for the persistence of informal institutions. Formal institutions can suddenly be changed in a process of revolution. However, informal institutions such as social customs and norms do not change so easily. Privatisation and land reform may effectively destroy and break up the previous formal arrangements, but this may be different with informal institutions and human capital. For example, in some post-socialist societies like in Russia, private ownership of land is not very popular because it is often considered immoral (Schulze et al., 1999). This could be one reason why the revival of very large private farms to be observed here (Koester, 2003) may provoke social conflicts in rural areas.

DETERMINANTS ARISING FROM THE INTERACTION BETWEEN POLITICAL DECISION MAKERS AND OTHER ACTORS INVOLVED IN THE PROCESS OF PROPERTY RIGHTS FORMATION

Whereas the above-mentioned factors appeared to be rather clear, less progress could be made in explaining political and administrative determinants. Some observations and hypotheses were discussed:

1. If formal ownership rights are transferred to individuals, this does not auto-matically mean that these individuals also have received effective property rights. For example, restitution does not always take place in original boundaries, but it is usually also allowed to give the previous owner a comparable piece of land, i.e. restitution in comparable boundaries. It may be difficult for the new owner, to get his plot of land out of the reformed collective farm because it usually was assigned by the management of the reformed farm. Provided that the claimant has access to the legal system, he can go to court if he does not get his land or disagrees with the assignment. "Restitution in comparable boundaries" has important impacts on the bargaining power between collective farm

management and the person who wants to retrieve his or her land. In the presence of transaction costs, formal property rights that are restituted may not or only insufficiently become effective (see Swinnen, 1996).

2. Another reason why formal or legal ownership rights may be incomplete are implementation problems and obstruction occurring at the level of local administration and the level of collective farms. Usually, governments face principal-agent problems as far as their relationship to the implementing agencies is concerned. Particularly, governments in transition countries have to deal with considerable difficulties in monitoring and controlling the implementation of the reforms (see Section 4).
3. The tasks of the staff working in the ministries and other administrative units in Central and East European countries have changed fundamentally. Formerly, they were involved in the process of central planning and needed predominantly technical knowledge. Now they had to implement agricultural policies for structural adjustment, privatisation, environmental protection, social security, etc., and this often requires new knowledge and procedures.
4. After 1990, there were opportunities for reform politicians in transition countries, i.e. they could decide for reform-oriented policies without facing serious opposition. However, soon the costs and social hardships of the reforms became obvious, and the groups who were negatively affected protested against the new policies. This also contributed to the recovery of the so-called "old forces" in some of the countries. For example, in Bulgaria the liquidation committees established to transform collective farms were replaced by new administrative units. Which political coalition will dominate in the long run, crucially depends on the political economy of the trans-formation process. One possibility to achieve a reliable basis of political support may be to create "a large group of property owners in society" that "will result in

a long-term constituency for 'reform-minded' politicians and parties" (Swinnen, 1994: 10). These landowners will then support those politicians and parties that will help them to obtain the highest returns to their property. However, there is also the opposite way to build a long-term constituency that can make anti-reform politicians and parties more competitive than reform-minded. By stabilising old structures, like large-scale collective farms, a group of voters can be addressed whose social and economic well-being depends on agricultural policies.

A COMPREHENSIVE CONCEPTUAL FRAMEWORK BASED ON THEORIES OF INSTITUTIONAL ECONOMICS AND POLITICAL ECONOMY

This discussion on the *"endogenous factors of privatisation and restructuring"* raised more questions than answers. As a consequence, additional research was initiated, for example, the KATO project (Hanisch et al., 2001), which focused on the transition process in three Central and Eastern European countries. In Poland, the Czech Republic and Bulgaria, processes of liberalisation and market development, privatisa-tion and property rights changes, as well as restructuring and path dependencies were analysed. The results can be attributed to three analytical levels: (1) the empirical design for analysing rapidly changing and evolving institutions in transition economies, (2) the suitability of different theoretical approaches for understanding transition, and (3) policy recommendations targeting better governance and an improved institutional framework.

RESEARCH FRAMEWORK FOR THE ANALYSIS OF PROPERTY RIGHTS REFORM:

The KATO project explored main areas of agricultural transition to create an understanding of the process of agricultural transition. Three types of studies were selected which can be classified according to Williamson's concept of "four levels of social analysis" (LSA).

1. **Property rights formation (LSA 2):** For analysing the process of property rights formation in agricultural land and non-land assets, selected hypotheses from Public Choice and Transaction Cost Theory and from the Theories of Social Conflict and Collective Action were combined to explore the explanatory power of the different hypotheses (Hanisch, 2003; Milczarek, 2002; Schlüter, 2001).
2. **Governance structures (LSA 3):** Based on transaction cost theory, restructuring/ downsizing of post-socialist agricultural firms (Brem, 2001) and contracting forms in the hog supply chain (Boger, 2001) were studied.
3. **Efficiency of resource allocation (LSA 4):** The influence of market competition on the technical efficiency of different types of organisation (Curtiss, 2002), the technical efficiency of different organisational forms of farms (Kaneva, 2000), the effectiveness of investment support programmes (Czerwinska-Kayser, 2000) and the impact of different reform policies on economic growth (Pavel, 2001) were analysed.

Between these three groups, the studies differed in terms of their research questions, empirical methodology and theoretical concepts. However, the group of studies dealing with the formation of property rights in land and agricultural assets in Bulgaria, Poland and the Czech Republic followed a homogeneous approach. They focussed on the question of what factors determine the formulation of property rights (LSA 2), and how the resulting institutions become socially accepted rights of action in the process of implementation and coordination (LSA 3 and 4) (Hanisch, 2003; Milczarek, 2002; Schlüter, 2001). Public Choice and Positive Political Theory approaches were used to analyse the political process that led to the choice between alternative forms of asset privatisation and land reform measures. Actor constellations at different levels of social analysis were identified for investigating the decision-making processes responsible for the formation of economic rights and rules.

The analyses of land privatisation and property rights reforms were based on a qualitative case-study approach that focused the empirical analysis of decision-making processes and actor constellations. The actor- and process-oriented case studies included the links and interactions between different levels of social analysis. This approach, which used in-depth interviews with numerous relevant actors, proved particularly useful for obtaining detailed information on the process of law-making. As these reform laws affected the situation of many actors involved and defined their economic rights of action at the level of private ordering, the empirical approach paid special attention to the distributional characteristics of these impacts.

As the research subject is both complex and dynamic, Hanisch (2003) designed a research framework (see figure 1) which was "taking an actor-based, rational choice perspective" (Scharpf, 1997: 36-50). Each actor is considered as a decision maker and, each decision is analysed in the context of potential alternatives and of other actors' decisions" (Hanisch, 2003: 120-123). This actors-oriented framework reflects the process of property rights formation during the transition process (as shown in figure 1). It employs a rational choice model for analysing the *Choices and Actors in Charge* as regards both their individual and collective decisions. "To the left of each actor there is the *Pool of Alternatives* to consider while analysing decisions. *Results* from choices at the political level (A1) turn into restrictions (slashed arrows) on the choice of alternatives on the subsequent levels of decision making, as appears on the level of reform implementation (A2) and the level of private ordering (A3). Here governance structures arise and the perceived income distribution feeds back to the constellation of political actors (policy cycle). The slashed arrows point in two directions. This means that decisions on a higher level are constrained by the respective political and implementation costs which consequently arise and which allocate a price to each political and administrative decision" (Hanisch et al., 2001).

Level A1: For explaining political decisions on land reform and privatisation of agricultural assets, the political influence of the rural electorate and the specific features of the discussed choice alternatives (reform packages) are taken into account. The hypotheses about the objectives of actors are derived from Public Choice Theory and refer to the motivation of defending political power, or following certain party ideologies (Swinnen, 1997). The efficiency of reform policies is evaluated in view of 'The Pool of Alternatives' and the cost of consensus building and implementation.

Level A2: These bureaucratic decisions can be explained by the cost of implementation and the principal-agent problems between government and administration. Formal rights and reform policies have to be interpreted by bureaucracies. The options open to actors are constrained by budgets available or written laws, and by the tools that control bureaucrats. Transaction cost and principal-agent hypotheses concentrate on the objectives and elbow room of important actors involved the incentives to carry out or boycott implementation, or those who extract money through corruption.

Level A3: After property rights reform, two general questions arose for the local actors: first, what should they do with their formal land rights? Second, what should they do with their vouchers on physical assets? The new formal property rights had to be exchanged to become rights of action (Barzel, 1989: 2). Concrete decisions, for example, setting up a single contract for renting land or the establishment of whole agricultural firms, have to be conceived of as the real process of forming new property rights. In this process income is generated, distributed and protected and the value of each actor's share of income from exchange and coordination reflects the nature of the property rights involved.

A METHODOLOGY FOR THE ANALYSES OF POLITICAL INTERACTION

Such a framework enables the researcher to investigate the property rights process at different decision-making levels

Figure 1
A comprehensive research concept

Government
Political Top
Ranks
Shock
1989
- Mandates
- Restrictions
- Resources
Appointments
Choices and Actors in Charge
Pool of Alternatives
Result
Reform Packages
A1: Politicians, Advisors,
Leading Prominents People
Formal Property Rights Central Reform Agenda
Regulations + Budgets
A2: Lawyers, Ministries
Regional/Local Administration
Effective Procedures for
Reform Implementation
Lobby Organizations
Individual Evaluation Experience
A
Local Agenda:
Privatization Scenarios, Legal Organizational Forms.
Credit-, Factor-, Management- Service-Market

A3: Locals

A
B

Economic Rights of Action
"Effective Property Rights"

B
A1: Public Choice and Beyond
A2: Agency Theory, Theory of the Bureau
A3: Transaction Cost Theory, Distributive Bargaining, Sociological Analysis of Power.

Source: Hanisch (2003)

similar to those suggested by Williamson (2000: 597). The components of this system can be considered as "intellectual bins" (Miles and Huberman, 1994: 13), and the relations between them can be described by hypotheses taken from various fields of Rational Choice Theory, as pointed out in detail by Hanisch (2003: 124-125). "At the top of the graph are politicians influenced by lobby groups ... and constrained by economic data and elections as well as by mental models and their ideological orientation. At the middle are bureaucrats in charge of reform implementation, and at the lower level are locals determining how to organise and perform transactions. Each group of actors is placed before an informal background between the pool of available alternatives at the time of decision making and other actors' decisions" (Dixit, 1996: 35).

In particular, the relationship between higher and lower levels is relevant during the transformation process. If a political system is stable, political actors are sufficiently constrained, for example by pressure from competing interest groups or demands from international organisations. Actors at a superior level are able to influence the alternatives of actors at the subsequent level (Eggertson, 1990: 7-9), and vice versa. In other words, the scope for deviating from the preferences of citizens and voters is rather limited. In contrast, "the less constrained the government is by competing pressure groups like trade unions, students, the army, foreign organisations (IMF) or powerful trade partners, the more probable bandit-like behaviour is (McGuire and Olson, 1996: 72-96). ... In times of political instability, the options open to bureaucrats are less constrained and the perspective of all actors becomes short term with regard to economic decisions (Broadman and Recanatini, 2000; Koford, 2000: 307-338). Each actor's incentive to grab as much as possible, as quickly as possible is augmented, and state control of the outcome of policy implementation is reduced. Coupled with delayed development of markets and little competition among actors on the level of market transactions, state influence on the choices of low level actors and the effectiveness of formal property rights may be comparatively small. In this situation, actors cannot credibly rely on the state as a third power for conflict settlement. They have to bear the costs of dispute settlement action on their own (Williamson, 2000: 599). Economic rights of action will deviate from formal property rights (Barzel, 1989: 2). In times where markets cannot fulfil the task of providing cheap business alternatives, market entrance and exit, the resources to protect one's property, to credibly threaten others or to wait for better deals become valuable to influence the property rights process" (Knight, 1992: 133-136) (Hanisch, 2003).

Admittedly, such a framework is too complex to be filled with empirical information in one step. Accordingly, complexity has to be reduced by decomposing the difficult causes-effects cycles. Hanisch (2003), for example, divides the various stages of the property rights process into "sub-games" which can be understood as basic units of interaction embedded in an extensive political economy game. The contributions to property rights formation achieved by the interplay of actors at each level of the system can be interpreted as being "sub-game equilibrium solutions". By means of "backward reasoning along the equilibrium path of action" (Bates et al., 1998: 239) explanations of the property rights process are constructed. These can be successively substantiated and gain in validity by employing the methodology of "analytic narratives" (Bates et al., 1998; Greif, 1998; Levi, 1998; Weingast, 1998; Rosenthal, 1998).

The main results achieved by the application of the theories and methodologies outlined above can be summarised in three points (Hagedorn, 2000):

- "Efficiency and competition" as compared to "distribution and conflict resolution" and "ideology and mental models" are not the main driving forces of privatisation.
- "Privatisation" should not be conceived of as an isolated process of establishing merely private property rights, but the heterogeneity of property rights reform should be taken into account.

- "Shared mental models", conceptions on innovation, learning processes and access to networks seem to be particularly important for institutional change which suggest that social capital deserves more attention in transition research.

These results will be explained in the following sections.

DRIVING FORCES OF PROPERTY RIGHTS REFORM

The first point we have to make when talking about efficiency as a potential driving force of privatisation is that the meaning of efficiency itself depends on the presumed institutional environment and arrangements, for example, in terms of distribution of actual income and entitlement to future opportunities. "Efficiency for whom?" (Bromley, 1989: 4) therefore is one of the main issues in the process of privatisation, because the institutional changes may favour the involved groups differently, for example, groups of reform-oriented politicians and the networks of the former nomenclature, former managers of state and collective farms or new private farmers and former state farm workers.

However, we could argue that privatisation does not necessarily mean inventing new institutions but just implementing a transfer of institutions well-known in many other countries. Since generally accepted definitions of efficiency are available then, the Theory of Exchange and Competitive Selection as an efficiency-oriented explanation for institutional change might be applicable (Knight, 1992: 106). This approach includes two main aspects: economising on transaction costs as a motivation of actors in individual exchange, and competitive pressure as a selection mechanism for efficient institutions. The latter seems to be more important for our topic. However, the KATO privatisation studies provide only little support for this approach:

At the *level of Central Government*, in all countries under investigation direct institu-tional competition, i.e., the emergence of alternative concepts for land privatisation rules and their selection via the influence of factor or product markets, did not play a role, because these markets were still to be developed. Secondly, pre-institutional competition also did not become effective for various reasons that differed between the countries. In the Czech Republic, the policy arena was dominated by attitudes against former communism, and the structure of parties and their programmes were still not organised and failed to offer the citizens sufficient opportunities to express more detailed preferences by voting (Schlüter, 2001). In addition, privatisation in agriculture did not enter the arena of general transformation policies and therefore did not become an issue that attracted the attention of voters. The choices were left to the policy network within the agricultural arena that made the policy choices dependent upon their bargaining capabilities and power resources.

In Bulgaria, the Central Government may sometimes be motivated to do what the rural electorate want them to do. However, all governments, which came into power after 1990, more or less failed to harmonise their concepts on land restitution and privatisation of farm collectives with the preferences and the needs of the voters in the rural areas. Instead, conflicting ideologies as a means to shape the profile of parties and the reputation of politicians dominated the decision-making process. Most urgent reform problems–such as how to make ownership rights more secure, provide credit for private land users, to increase the machine capacity in the countryside, to organise markets, and to privatise the processing industry-were not seriously tackled. Even the revival of the cooperatives failed to create more sympathy among the rural electorate, as the expectations of people did often not fulfil, for instance when agricultural machinery was monopolised (Hanisch, 2003). Since the governments were also not able to communicate a convincing vision of Bulgarian agriculture to the rural electorate, the overaged rural population did not believe that the reforms would be able to improve their situation. Thus, a minimum level of trust and credibility, as a basic prerequisite of a democratic system was lacking and the elections did not become an institution to control politics. Of course, this deficiency was reinforced by political instability resulting from changes in government and implementation staff.

In Poland, political circumstances were different from the other countries mentioned above for the following reasons: first, the protest movement, which started long before 1990, had already established a new and strong democratic tradition. Second, most of the land had remained in private hands during the socialist era, i.e., only state farms had to be privatised. Third, agriculture was divided into two groups5 that were geographically and politically separated and had unequal resource endowments regarding the production of political influence. Although party competition and electoral control were sufficiently institutionalised, it did not play a major role for the choice of the privatisation strategies. This was due to lack of relevance of state farm privatisation for the electorate as a whole (Milczarek, 2002). Instead, the differences in lobbying capacities of the three main groups of stakeholders-the Peasant Party, the managers of former state farms, and former state farm workers–offer an explanation of the process and its outcomes.

At the *local level*, direct institutional competition also played a minor role. In the Czech Republic, for example, markets for restitution shares, buying and leasing land and services did not exist. Pre-institutional competition could be observed–a general assembly decided on the future legal form of a farm-but the resulting conflict was more or less dominated by the negotiation power of the managers (Schlüter, 2001).

In Bulgaria, those who were successfully appropriating the scarce assets necessary to use land, such as machines and buildings, were also the most successful to appropriate the land. For this purpose, the former agricultural elite has often used practices which were far from competition-oriented behaviour or fair behaviour. For example, farm assets were supposed to be distributed in auctions by the land privatisation law, but this did not take place. Cooperatives often trade machine services for land. Rents are paid according to the willingness of the cooperatives, and in many cases lessees do not receive any payment. Even within the cooperatives, competition is not working as a selection mechanism, because general assemblies do not meet and take decisions, i.e. control of the management by the members is lacking (Hanisch, 2003).

In Poland, direct institutional competition was very limited although a land market evolved and, in principle, nationalised land was offered to all groups of farmers. However, the geographical distance between the majority of the farmers and the land offered by the Agricultural Property Agency (APA), non-cooperative strategies of the APA towards private farmers willing to buy smaller areas of land and restrictions on buying and leasing land, e.g., in auctions organised by the APA, were serious constraints.

If "efficiency produced by competition" is not the driving force of property rights reform, what else could be considered an appropriate explanation? The Theory of Social Conventions is not a convincing alternative. This approach implies the conception of salience (Knight, 1992: 102), i.e. institutions are selected through the salience of focal points and established by repeated social interactions. This implies that "the rule evolves arbitrarily. The evolutionary process is unconsciously driven by whatever salient factor focuses the attention of the actors. The interest of any particular actor or group of actors does not determine the nature of the final institutional arrangement: that is, the distributional differences produced by different rules will not be invoked by the explanation" (Knight, 1992: 102).

In contrast, the Theory of Bargaining and Distribution explains institutional change "as a by-product of strategic conflict over substantive social outcomes" (Knight, 1992: 107). As pointed out in detail by Schlüter (2001) and Hanisch (2003), this theory focuses on social interaction between actors seeking to achieve their distributional objectives. This is influenced by the differences in "action resources" the actors can make use of, such as information asymmetries between actors, education and skills, personal power, sanction power, credibility of their commitment, individual risk aversion, exit options, time preferences, etc. Although Knight only applies this approach to decentralised institutional change, most of its components also seem to be relevant to institutions that are centrally designed and are also treated by the Public Choice Theory of Institutional Change (Weimer, 1997).

There are numerous empirical observations in the KATO privatisation studies that support this explanation. For example, in the Czech case the managers of former collective farms, due to their education, had better exit possibilities than the members of cooperatives and farm workers. Family farmers were more vulnerable by time-consuming negotiations than the managers, because they urgently needed assets to make their living. Similar differences were observed as regards credibility for being a successful farm manager in the future, the ability to organise as a group, and information asymmetries. The managers were endowed with positional power in the information network, because they were located between the local and the central level (Schlüter, 2001).

In Bulgaria, the former agricultural nomenclature dominated for similar reasons in designing the changing organisation of farm production (Hanisch, 2003). However, due to the particular situation in the country, which suffered from political instability and lacking democratic structures particularly in the rural society, the power asymmetries between actors were even more extreme and enabled the rural leaders to monopolise, e.g., land, machinery services, trade and processing activities.

In Poland, the managers of former state farms can also be considered as winners in the conflict over the distribution of nationalised land, because they could influence the bargaining process through power resources like information, skills from higher education, positional power and abilities to organise as a pressure group (Milczarek, 2002). In addition, they had better access to government agencies, credit organisations and advisory services than small farmers.

WHY "PRIVATISATION" IS NO ADEQUATE CONCEPTION OF PROPERTY RIGHTS REFORM

However, these empirical observations not only reveal that the Theory of Institutional Change based on Bargaining and Distribution (including similar phenomena in political processes) offers better explanations than other approaches, but also shows that a process of privatisation driven by the desire of groups of actors having unequal power resources to appropriate "a piece of the cake", often took place in a way that cannot be considered "efficient" for society. This questions a conception popular in economics that associates efficiency with private property rights and analogously suggests that "privatisation" in the sense of merely establishing private property rights is equivalent to increasing efficiency. "There is a need, ... , for a more careful consideration of institutions and of institutional change than a model that regards one particular institutional form (private rights) as universally responsible for economic efficiency, stewardship, and higher civilization" (Bromley, 1989: 18).

Property rights theory is often misunderstood as an approach explaining the definition and distribution of disposition rights focussing on physical entities (Hagedorn et al., 2002). Strictly speaking, actors attribute (positive or negative) values to a physical good because the holder of the right is favoured by benefit streams or, in case of a duty, is burdened by cost components that are connected with the physical good. Bromley (1991: 189ff.) calls these nature components "countryside and community attributes". A natural resource, like soil, is usually considered to carry only one homogeneous property title. However, such rights cannot only be classified according to the conventional division into (a) the right to use, (b) the right to alter and (c) the right of alienation. What is more, categories of property rights can be separately defined for numerous economic or ecological properties of the physical piece of nature, each of them related to particular costs and benefits. For each of these differentiated rights components, the institutional design of the right or duty can differ: private, collective and state property regimes are imaginable, and also the absence of property rights definition in the sense of open access.

In addition, property rights on such attributes of natural or physical capital require adequate governance structures, because they must be supervised and sanctioned to become effective instead of only remaining formal in nature. The discrepancy between formal and effective property rights (see Section 3) is a well-known problem as a problem of privatisation in transition countries (Swinnen and Mathijs, 1997: 344). Those governance structures may not only consist of private ordering but also require collective or political arrangements.

In other words, concepts of property rights reform are only complete and consistent if:

- All main attributes of a physical or natural object are subjected either to private property rights or other property rights regimes if these are superior, and
- Governance structures for each component of this bundle of rights are developed, not neglecting the required political and administrative structures for decision-making and implementation.

Tornell (1999: 2), who calls the implementation of such additional restrictions to the opportunity sets of owners of privatised state owned enterprises "privatising the privatised", mentions three conditions for complete privatisation: "First, re-establishing property rights within the firm, so that new owners enjoy full residual rights of control in their firm. Second, outside the firm, facing new owners with hard budget constraints so that they do not have the power to either extract fiscal transfers, or obtain bailouts. Third, establishing a non-corruptible juridical system, and transparent bankruptcy procedures that are free from political pressures". When these pre-conditions are missing, reformers may hope that the "newly privatised firms will create a demand for good laws" (Tornell, 1999: 2). However, this crucially depends on whether or not the firms consider such a demand actually as being in line with their interests, and secondly, whether or not the state is able to supply the legal framework regarding the political economy mechanisms involved. In well-established democratic systems this may be feasible, but in countries in transition it may be impossible.

The KATO privatisation studies provide many examples for the problems that arise if decision-makers follow the above-mentioned misconception of privatisation. Thus, evidence was provided of the sanctioning of private farmers in the Czech Republic in order to keep their competitiveness and their reputation on the land market low. Another example was the monopolising of land, machine services and the processing industry in Bulgaria. The nature of this problem may be even better illustrated by the experience that privatisation concepts usually neglect environmental protection and ecological sustainability (Gatzweiler and Hagedorn, 2003). Exhausting soil fertility and destructing irrigation equipment during the process of restitution or privatising large livestock units without regulating manure pollution, etc. - all these practices show that property rights on nature components and corresponding governance structures were given low priority in the institutional reforms.

SHARED MENTAL MODELS AND LEARNING FOR INSTITUTIONAL CHANGE

When the centrally planned economies collapsed, the shared mental models (SMMs), which had been developed during the socialist era, could no longer fulfil their tasks. Individuals and groups depend on meaningful mental models for the purpose of reducing complexity (North, 1990: 24). As a consequence, people were seeking new cognitive schemata to understand and to explain their changed world. In particular at the beginning of the transformation period, when the system in transition was characterised by a high degree of insecurity, reduction of complexity was urgently needed. Since this basic function of SMMs is of major relevance in this confusing situation, ideologies have played an important role in all countries under investigation. They provide people with plausible notions on how the world works and how it should work (North, 1990: 28; Eggertson, 1993).

When old SMMs are not valid any longer and new ones are not available for the time being, individuals will of course resort to quite heterogeneous cognitive schemata. We must expect that there were extremely diverse mental models in society in the period that immediately followed the revolution, because a general consensus especially on normative principles had not been achieved yet. After a period of communication and consensus building, provided that this successfully leads to well-established SMMs, the latter may decisively help to reduce the cost of finding collective agreements on future institutional change (North, 1988: 54). On early stages of the transformation process, the societies as a whole may not have arrived at sufficiently stable SMMs yet. However, these SMMs may have already existed within certain groups that are thus able to make use of their common understanding of problems and, in this way, can reduce their transaction costs of decision-making and can achieve their particular group objectives more easily. Like institutions in general, SMMs serve as conceptions to structure human behaviour and to form and stabilise actors' expectations in social interaction. Above all, communication within groups is facilitated and requires fewer resources.

A SMM determines for a group what it conceives of as being its institutionally designed and, therefore, legitimate opportunity set. Such perceptions may substantially differ, for instance between a farmer, who has experienced forty years of socialist agriculture, and a farmer from the western world, who has operated a family farm for a similar period of time. One of the main features of an SMM is that it defines binding constraints on the opportunity sets attributed to the members of various groups, thus determining many of their rights and duties. Hence, it does not come as a surprise that the ability to shape people's SMMs proves to be an effective power resource in the bargaining process regarding new institutional arrangements.

This is particularly true if new mental models are required as a basis for new strategies. Privatisation studies have shown that there is obviously a variety of institutional choices for problems of institutional change, in general, and for transition, in particular. However, the mere fact that such solutions might exist will be of little practical use if actors or actor groups either do not know about the solutions, lack the creativity to find them, do not have sufficient resources to develop and to discuss innovations, are unable to communicate new institutional concepts in order to arrive at joint conceptions of the problems or are unable to organise collective action and participation of stakeholders. Collective learning processes combined with the evolution of new SMMs seem to play a fundamental role for institutional innovation.

The KATO privatisation studies have provided detailed empirical evidence for the relevance of SMMs. In the Czech Republic, for example, the debate about the Land Act at the national level was strongly influenced by ideological controversy being rather dogmatic in nature. One party, the "Democratic Citizens Party", which supported the restituents, favoured the ideal of small family farms, simultaneously considering land as the main source of wealth. The other party, i.e. the "Social Democratic Party", preferred the conception of industrialised agriculture organised in large production units. Its considerations focused on labour and capital required to maintain and develop such large production units. The second party was clearly dominating at the local level, i.e. in the villages. For example, introducing a land rent to be paid to the landowners was perceived of as a strange phenomenon, even for the restituents, and had to be fixed in the law.

In Bulgaria, up to now no reconciliation of the contradicting SMMs preferred by the competing parties has been achieved. This has repeatedly led to radical changes of the fundamental principles of privatisation between "The Red" and "The Blue"-these colours reflect the two main political groups6. Even in the villages this division in "The Red" and "The Blue" has strongly shaped the rural society, and even regions and villages can be classified according to this political distinction. Being red or blue has proven to be an important determinant of the privatisation process.

Poland has undergone a much longer period of transformation than the other two countries. The Polish society has been fundamentally shaped by the reform movements which started long before 1989. As a consequence, discrepancies regarding SMMs may be less relevant here. However, the question arises to what extent such conceptions do account for the dualistic structure of Polish agriculture with large farms operating on formerly nationalised land, on the one hand, and small family farms whose structure has been more or less frozen by the socialist system, on the other. Obviously, the dominating perception of this problem does not sufficiently reflect the opportunity to use privatisation of state-owned land for the structural improvement of the family farm sector.

Unfortunately, our knowledge on how SMMs evolve and how they influence institutional change is rather limited. How this kind of knowledge can be increased is shown by the excellent work of Verdery (2003) on land distribution in Romania. In her study she characterised the relations between locals (who received land) and venits (who have not got land). She cites, for example, a venit who replied to the offer of a local to "sharecrop land for him, 'We won't work for you 'aristocrats', *for chiaburs*'. Working for the collective was one thing, and it ought to entitle them to land, but working for locals was something else again. I heard the same idea in discussing with venits how they thought they would get by without land if they lost their factory jobs. 'Will you sharecrop for the people with land?' I asked, receiving the following kind of answers, always in a heated tone: 'We don't want to be serfs for the local nobles!' 'I am not going to make *someone else* a gentleman!' 'You think I look like a servant? People with lots of land are waiting for us to come and support them while they rest in the shade. Some people here have 20 ha, while others have none at all. If we go and work for them, it will be just like the days of serfdom! No way!' " (Verdery, 2003: 175f., italics in original).

SOCIAL CAPITAL AS A BOTTLENECK IN THE TRANSITION PROCESS: THE NEED FOR FURTHER RESEARCH

Many of the results pointed out above are related to phenomena like trust or opportunism, shared mental models and the properties of networks of actors. This supports the hypothesis that both the quantity and the quality of social capital in transition processes are for the success of transformation. The autocratic political design of the communist governments tried to avoid peoples' free participation in public affairs, requiring a process of learning and reorientation as an essential part of reform in those societies. Societies will only be able to cope with such demanding and sometimes disappointing changes if sufficient social capital will be accumulated (Ostrom and Ahn, 2003).

As a result of the historical development of their societies and their personal experience in their respective countries, people are differently predisposed to form relationships with one another. "This depends on social norms and the prevailing social structure. Within the CEE, the presumption of low levels of social capital is explained in the literature either by: an increase in general mistrust brought about by experiences within a planned economy (Swain, 2000); the dictatorship theory of missing social capital (Paldam and Svendsen, 2000) which eroded or destroyed voluntary cooperative engagement, and when individuals associated their political leaders with corruption and merely having self-serving interests (Lang, 1999); an increase in mistrust brought about by the 'grabbing' strategies that emerged from certain individuals in the period immediately after new institutions were rapidly introduced in the early 1990s (Sik and Wellman, 1999); or a high reliance on family and kinship networks in countries with 'weak' formal institutions

(Theesfeld, 2003; Greif, 1994). All these factors impose constraints on the formation of social capital in the post-communist states. At times, they have resulted in a break-down in communal spirit by the move to a more market-oriented economy, leading to a loss of trust and an increase in opportunism."

Paldam and Svendsen (2000) have pointed out that social capital deteriorated during the socialist era and has not sufficiently accumulated during the transition process as well. Weakness of non-profit organisations and lack of trust as a pre-requisite for collective action can be considered as important indicators for such deficits in social capital (Rose-Ackermann, 2001). Similarly, several case studies conducted in the frame of the CEESA project8 (Gatzweiler and Hagedorn, 2003) revealed that property rights reform, agricultural restructuring, political decision-making and implementation, and the management of natural resources often suffer from a lack or an unfavourable nature of social capital. Theesfeld (2003: 263-268; 2005), for example, impressively illustrates this phenomenon by her analysis of the trans-formation of the Bulgarian irrigation system. Her results show that rural citizens have "almost no trust in the parliament, the government, the courts (0 per cent), and the district administration. The trust in local authorities is higher than in any of the formal authorities at the national level, but, in general, it is low in both. Interestingly, trust in the mayor is even lower than trust in the police, both being the only two formal authorities representing the state at village level. ... Only trust in the 'blue' cooperative reaches a share of over 50 per cent. ... a share of 46 per cent of the interviewees does not trust any authority at the national level and 19 per cent do not trust any local actor" (Theesfeld, 2003: 264). Similarly, the majority of members of the parliament, especially of court members, are considered corrupt by the citizens. "... 26 per cent named the mayor, 33 per cent the water guard and 43 per cent the 'red' cooperative manager as corrupt" (Theesfeld, 2003: 264).

Such deficits regarding social capital may act as serious obstacles against institutional innovation, in particular introduction of cooperative arrangements or self-organised mechanisms of conflict resolution as well as co-production and co-management between government agencies and social groups in policy implementation. However, there is still too little knowledge on the structural properties of social capital, the relationships between its elements and the causalities behind its changes. Accordingly, reliable concepts of how social capital can be intentionally built are still lacking. There is urgent need for empirical research contributing to the development of the theory on social capital and enabling policy-makers and other actors to support accumulation of social capital.

CONCLUSIONS

Anyone who intends to give recommendations regarding the future "design" of the transition process should be aware of the limited opportunities of politicians and administrators to influence such processes of institutional change. This holds especially true for external actors, such as the EU, neighbouring countries or inter-national organisations, as foreign aid experiences have also shown (see, for example, Ostrom et al., 2001). Furthermore, we have to keep in mind that many decisions on privatisation and restructuring have not only been made long before but have been frequently revised as well. Consequently, the main task is to re-orient past implementation procedures and decisions in order to achieve stability of land policy and reliability of land institutions and cope with the consequences of past inadequate decisions and undesired outcomes of implementation processes.

Recommendations solely focussing on new policy instruments or technical solutions (for example, reducing land fragmentation by land consolidation schemes) may produce adverse effects if they are not able to predict how they will affect rent-seeking strategies and power resources of the main actors involved. Deficiencies in actors institutional structures, e.g., their political property rights and their governance structures, may provide only ineffective constraints against opportunistic behaviour. For such reasons, the institutional pre-requisites of proper decision-making and implementation processes should be prioritised, investigating the relationships between proposed policy instruments and the emergence, strengthening or weakening of democratic and participatory institutions. As the political and administrative systems are often imbalanced and sometimes suffer from corruption, the support of self-organisation may contribute to a more balanced power structure, more pluralism and increased participation. Thus, it may help to create more security for economic actors, e.g. farmers, who hesitate to invest into their enterprises.

Of course, this requires, first of all, a well-functioning administrative system. From the perspective of external agencies, it is very important to extend and to improve implementation capacities as regards monitoring and enforcement. However, it is equally important that such systems do not only serve the interests of state hierarchies (or international organisations), but would also be rooted in the rural society and would enable rural people to participate in and contribute to processes of decision-making and implementation. Building social capital in the rural society is of fundamental relevance for land reforms and land policies. This may be even more relevant for regions with major conflicts among groups, which may have unequally benefited from the privatisation process, particularly when such conflicts have an ethnic component.

External decision-makers should not exclusively interact with the administrative and professional elites, but pay attention to the involvement of rural people. Particularly in transition countries, policy processes and policy results look different at the various levels of decision-making and implementation. Monitoring and communication concepts should reveal on-site findings and should elucidate whether people are actually provided with access to information, policies, common pool resources, extension services, and the legal system. Special attention should be paid to the problem of postponing tasks of the transformation process, which are not immediately profitable, in favour of other tasks that offer private benefits, such as economic profits or political positions. The former, for example, applies to cultural and environmental values. Generally, any land policy has to be aware of the fact that land and other natural resources are complementary, both in economic and ecological terms.

REFERENCES

Barzel, Y. (1989), Economic Analysis of Property Rights. Cambridge University Press. Cambridge.

Bates, R.H., A. Greif, M. Levi, J.L. Rosenthal and B.R. Weingast (eds.) (1998), Analytic Narratives. Princeton University Press, Princeton: 194-230.

Boger, S. (2001), Agricultural Markets in Transition–An Empirical Study on Contracts and Transaction Costs in the Polish Hog Sector. In: Beckmann, V. and K. Hagedorn (eds.) Institutional Change in Agriculture and Natural Resources. Vol. 4. Shaker, Aachen.

Brem, M. (2001), Landwirtschaftliche Unternehmen im Transformationsprozess. Ein Beitrag zur Theorie der Restrukturierung im Übergang vom Plan zum Markt. In: Beckmann, V. and K. Hagedorn (eds.): Institutional Change in Agriculture and Natural Resources. Vol. 1. Shaker, Aachen.

Broadman, H.G. and F. Recanatini (2000), Seeds of Corruption: Do Market Institutions Matter? Discussion Paper Series VII. The World Bank, Washington, D.C.

Bromley, D.W. (1989), Economic Interests and Institutions: The Conceptual Foundations of Public Policy. Basil Blackwell, Oxford.

——— (1991), Environment and Economy: Property Rights and Public Policy. Cambridge Massachusetts.

Cungu, A. and J. Swinnen (1999), The Significance of Politics and Institutions for the Privatisation and Decollectivisation in the Albanian Agriculture. In: Frohberg, K. and P. Weingarten (eds.): The Significance of Politics and Institutions for the Design and Formation of Agricultural Policy. Vauk, Kiel: 238-250.

Curtiss, J. (2002), Efficiency and Structural Changes in Transition. A Stochastic Frontier Analysis of Czech Crop Production. In: Beckmann, V. and K. Hagedorn (eds.): Institutional Change in Agriculture and Natural Resources. Vol. 12, Shaker, Aachen.

Czerwinska-Kayzer, D. (2000), Investments and Finance in Private Family Farms: An Analysis of Polish Agricultural Transformation. Paper presented at the KATO Symposium, November 2-4, 2000, Berlin, Germany.

Dixit, A.K. (1996), The Making of Economic Policy: A Transaction-Cost Politics Perspective. The MIT Press, Cambridge, Massachusetts, London.

Eggertson, T. (1990), Economic Behaviour and Institutions. Cambridge University Press, Cambridge.

——— (1993), Mental Models and Social Values: North's Institutions and Credible Commitment. In: *Journal of Institutional and Theoretical Economics* 149 (1): 24-29.

Gatzweiler, F. and K. Hagedorn (2003), Institutional Change in Central and Eastern European Agriculture and Environment: Synopsis of the CEESA Project. In: Institutional Change in Central and Eastern European Agriculture and Environment. Vol. 4. FAO, Rome.

Greif, A. (1994), Cultural Beliefs and the Organisation of Society: A Historical and Theoretical Reflection on Collectivist and Individualist Societies. In: *Journal of Political Economy* 102 (5): 912-950.

——— (1998), Self-Enforcing Political Systems and Economic Growth: Late Medieval Genoa. In: Bates, R.H., A. Greif, M. Levi, J.L. Rosenthal and B.R. Weingast (eds.): Analytic Narratives. Princeton: Princeton University Press: 23-63.

Hagedorn, K. (1997), The Politics and Policies of Privatization of Nationalized Land in Eastern Germany. In: Swinnen, J.F.M. (ed.): Political Economy of Agrarian Reform in Central and Eastern Europe. Aldershot, Brookfield USA, Singapore, Sidney: Ashgate: 197-236.

——— (1998), Concepts of Institutional Change for Understanding Privatisation and Restructuring of Agri-culture in Central and East European Countries. In: Frohberg, K. and W.R. Poganietz (eds.): The Importance of Institutions for the Transition in

Central and Eastern Europe-with Emphasis on Agriculture and Food Industry. Vauk, Kiel: 51-64.

——— (2000), What to Learn? Evaluating the Privatisation Experience in Transition. Paper presented at the KATO Symposium, November 2-4, 2000, Humboldt University Berlin, Germany.

Hagedorn, K., K. Arzt, and U. Peters (2002), Institutional Arrangements for Environ-mental Cooperatives: a Conceptual Framework. In: Hagedorn, K. (ed.): Environ-mental Co-operation and Institutional Change: Theories and Policies for European Agriculture. Edward Elgar, *Cheltenham,* UK, and Northampton, MA, USA: 3-25.

Hanisch, M. (2003), Property Reform and Social Conflict. A Multi-Level Analysis of the Change of Agricultural Property Rights in Post-Socialist Bulgaria. In: Beckmann, V. and K. Hagedorn (eds.): Institutional Change in Agriculture and Natural Resources. Vol. 15. Shaker, Aachen.

Hanisch, M., V. Beckmann, S. Boger and M. Brem (2001), In Search of the Market: Lessons from Analyzing Agricultural Transition in Central and Eastern Europe. Paper presented at the ISNIE Conference in "Institutions and Governance", September 13-15, 2001, Berkeley, CA, USA.

Kaneva, K. (2000), Institutional Reform, Organizational Restructuring and Efficiency of Bulgarian Agriculture. Paper presented at the KATO Symposium, November 2-4, 2000, Berlin, Germany.

Knight, J. (1992), Institutions and Social Conflict. Cambridge University Press, Cambridge.

Koester, U. (2003), A Revival of Large Farms in Eastern Europe? How Important are Institutions? Proceedings of the 25th International Conference of Agricultural Economists (IAAE), August 16-22, 2003, Durban, South Africa.

Koford, K. (2000), Citizen Restraints on "Leviathan" Government: Transition Politics in Bulgaria. In: European Journal of Political Economy 16 (2): 307-338.

Lang, S. (1999), Communication and Public Participation in Rural Development Processes in Eastern Europe. Problems and Solution Strategies. Riga: WWF Latvia.

Lerman, Z., C. Csaki, and G. Feder (2004), Agriculture in Transition: Land Policies and Evolving Farm Structures in Post-Soviet Countries. In: Lerman, Z., C. Scaki and J. Swinnen (eds.): Rural Economies in Transition. Lexington Books, Maryland.

Levi, M. (1998): Conscription: The Price of Citizenship. In: Bates, R.H., A. Greif, M. Levi, J.L. Rosenthal and B.R. Weingast (eds.): Analytic Narratives. Princeton University Press, Princeton: 109-147.

McGuire, M.C. and M. Olson (1996): The Economics of Autocracy and Majority Rule. In: Journal of Economic Literature 34 (1): 72-96.

Milczarek, D. (2002): Privatisation as a Process of Institutional Change. The Case of State Farms in Poland. In: Beckmann, V. and K. Hagedorn (eds.): Institutional Change in Agriculture and Natural Resources. Vol. 11. Shaker, Aachen.

Miles, M.B. and M.A. Huberman (1994), Qualitative Data Analysis: an Expanded Source-book. Sage, London.

Murray, C. (2004), Social Capital and Cooperation in Central and Eastern Europe – A Theoretical Perspective. IDARI conceptual paper. At: 1/25/06, download from October 15, 2004.

North, D.C. (1988), Theorie des institutionellen Wandels. J.C.B. Mohr (Paul Siebeck), Tübingen.

——— (1990), Institutions, Institutional Change and Economic Performance. Cambridge University Press, Cambridge.

Olson, M. (1995), Why the Transition from Communism is so Difficult. In: Eastern Economic Journal 21 (4): 437-462.

——— (2000), Power and Prosperity. Outgrowing Communist and Capitalist Dictatorship. Basic Books, New York.

Ostrom, E. and T.K. Ahn (2003), Soziales Kapital und kollektives Handeln: Eine sozialwissenschafliche Perspektive auf soziales Kapital (German translation of "A Social Science Perspective on Social Capital: Social Capital and Collective Action"). In: Deutscher Bundestag (ed.): Bürgerschaftliches Engagement von Unternehmen. Enquête-Kommission "Zukunft des Bürgerschaftlichen Engagements", Schriftenreihe. Vol. 2. Leske + Budrich, Leverkusen, Germany.

Ostrom, E., C. Gibson, S. Shivakumar and K. Andersson (2001): Aid, Incentives, and Sustainability. An Institutional Analysis of Development Cooperation. Workshop in Political Theory and Policy Analysis. Sida Studies in Evaluation 02/01. Bloomington.

Paldam, M. and G.T. Svendsen, (2000), Missing Social Capital and the Transition in Eastern Europe. University of Aarhus, Aarhus.

Pavel, F. (2001), Success and Failure of Post-Socialist Transition. Theory and Application to Bulgaria. In: Beckmann, V. and K. Hagedorn (eds.): Institutional Change in Agriculture and Natural Resources. Vol. 2. Shaker, Aachen.

Rose-Ackermann, S. (2001), Trust and Honesty in Post-socialist Societies. In: Kyklos 54 (2/3): 415-444.

Rosenthal, J.L. (1998), The Political Economy of Absolutism Reconsidered. In: Bates, R.H., A. Greif, M. Levi, J.L. Rosenthal and B.R. Weingast (eds.): Analytic Narratives. Princeton University Press, Princeton: 64-108.

Runge, C.F. (1981), Institutions and Common Property Externalities: The Assurance Prob-lem in Economic Development. Ph.D. Dissertation, University of Wisconsin-Madison.

Ruttan, V.W. (1984), Induced Institutional Innovation. University of Minnesota, St. Paul (mimeo).

Scharpf, F.W. (1997), *Games Real Actors Play. Actor-Centred Institutionalism in Policy Research.* Westview, Boulder.

Schlüter, A. (2001), Institutioneller Wandel und Transformation. Restitution, Transforma-tion und Privatisierung in der tschechischen Landwirtschaft. In: Beckmann, V. and K. Hagedorn (eds.): Institutional Change in Agri-culture and Natural Resources. Vol. 3. Shaker, Aachen.

Schmitt, G. (1991), Why is Agriculture of Advanced Western Economies still Organised by Family Farms and Will this Be also in the Future? In: European Review of Agricultural Economics 18 (3/4): 443-458.

Schulze, E., P. Tillack, O. Dolud and S. Bukin (1999), Eigentumsverhältnisse landwirt-schaftlicher Betriebe und Unternehmen in Rußland und in der Ukraine–Befragungs-ergebnisse aus den Regionen Nowosibirsk und Shitomir. IAMO Discussion Paper no. 18. Halle/Saale.

Shleifer, A. and R.W. Vishny (1998), The Grabbing Hand. Government Pathologies and their Cures. Cambridge, MA and Harvard University Press, London.

Sik, E. and B. Wellman (1999), Network Capital in Capitalist, Communist and Post Communist Countries'. In: B. Wellman (ed.): Networks in the Global Village. Life in Contemporary Communities. Westview, Boulder: 225-253.

Swain, N. (2000), The Rural Transition in Post-socialist Central Europe and the Balkans. Working paper No. 9. Max Planck Institute for Social Anthropology, Halle.

Swinnen, J.F.M. (1992), The Development of Agricultural Policies in Eastern Europe. An Endogenous Policy Perspective. The Leuven Institute for Central and East European Studies Working Papers, No. 2: 1-9.

——— (1993), The Development of Agricultural Policies in Central and Eastern Europe. In: Food Policy 18 (3): 187-191.

——— (1994), Overview of Policy and Institutional Reform in Central European Agriculture. In: Swinnen, J.F.M. (ed.): Policy and Institutional Reform in Central European Agriculture. Avebury, Aldershot: 1-30.

——— (1996), Three Determinants of the Choice of Privatization Policies in Central and East European Agriculture. LICOS, Leuven.

——— (ed.) (1997), Political Economy of Agrarian Reform in Central and Eastern Europe. Aldershot, Brookfield, USA and Ashgate, Singapore, Sidney.

Swinnen, J.F.M., A. Buckwell and E. Mathijs (eds.) (1997), Agricultural Privatisation, Land Reform and Farm Restructuring in Central and Eastern Europe. Aldershot, Brookfield, USA and Ashgate, Singapore, Sidney.

Swinnen, J.F.M. and E. Mathijs (1997), Agricultural Privatisation, Land Reform and Farm Restructuring in Central and Eastern Europe. In: Swinnen, J.F.M., A. Buckwell and E. Mathijs (eds.): Agricultural Privatisation, Land Reform and Farm Restructuring in Central and Eastern Europe. Aldershot, Brookfield, USA and Ashgate, Singapore, Sidney: 333-373.

Theesfeld, I. (2003), Constraints for Collective Action in a Transitional Economy: The Case of Bulgaria´s Irrigation Sector. In: World Development 32 (2): 251-271.

——— (2005), Transition of a Common-Pool Resource. Determinants of Institutional Change for Bulgaria's Postsocialist Irrigation Sector. In: Beckmann, V. and K. Hagedorn (eds.): Institutional Change in Agriculture and Natural Resources. Vol. 21. Shaker, Aachen.

Tornell, A. (1999), Privatising the Privatised. National Bureau of Economic Research, NBR Working Paper 7206. Cambridge, MA.

Verdery, K. (2003), The Vanishing Hectare. Property and Value in Post-socialist Transylvania. Cornell University Press, Ithaca and London.

Weimer, D.L. (1997), The Political Economy of Property Rights. In: Weimer, D.L. (ed.): The Political Economy of Property Rights. Institutional Change and Credibility in the Reform of Centrally Planned Economies. Cambridge University Press, Cambridge: 1-14.

Weingast, B.R. (1998), Political Stability and Civil War: Institutions, Commitment, and American Democracy. In: Bates, R.H., A. Greif, M. Levi, J.L. Rosenthal and B.R. Weingast (eds.): Analytic Narratives. Princeton University Press, Princeton: 148-193.

Williamson, O.E. (2000), The New Institutional Economics: Taking Stock, Looking Ahead. In: Journal of Economic Literature XXXVIII (3): 595-613.

GLOBALISATION AND INSTITUTIONAL CHANGES IN AGRICULTURE: A COMPARISON OF COOPERATIVES IN GERMANY AND INDIA

Ramesh Chennamaneni

INTRODUCTION

Tomatoes from Israel at the supermarket in Berlin, capital city of Germany, cost Rs. 70 Rupees or about 1.4 Euro per kilo. This is a very good price and people are happy to purchase them. So also different agricultural products such as milk, butter, cheese, pork, potatoes and cabbage from domestic german production, chicken from Italy, onions from Egypt or eggs from Poland. But what is the reason that a hard working farmer in Kurnool in India can only get 5 paise for kilo tomatoes, a price which is not even enough for the package charges of the product ? At the same time, consumers in Hyderabad have to pay Rs 5 per kilo of tomatoes. The products in the supermarket in Berlin such as tomatoes, butter, cheese, etc coming from Germany and other countries have one thing in common: All these products are grown by individual farmers and are marketed by their respective cooperatives.

But why Cooperatives? In the context of liberalisation, marketisation, and globalisation of the economy, we hear very often certain questions, such as will the cooperatives be relevant under the liberalised market oriented economy?

Will the cooperatives prove viable in the environment of competition and liberalisation? Will the Government continue supporting the cooperatives? Will the cooperatives survive without the Gov-ernment support? Regarding the relevance of cooperatives under the liberalised economy, it should be noted that, historically, the very concept of cooperatives was born in England during the 19th century in the environment of free economy, as a means of self-protection against consumers' exploitation by the traders. In Germany, the history of Raiffeisen Cooperatives show that self help motive and solidarity for the neighbour were, among others, the main motives. Today, apart from England and Germany, in most countries of the industrialised world, starting from Japan, USA and scandinavian countries cooperatives play a significant role in influencing markets. More than 50 per cent of all marketing of agricultural products is done by cooperatives in Germany making it one of the strongest institutions in Europe.

HISTORY OF GERMAN COOPERATIVES

For nearly 150 years, a tradition of agricultural cooperatives has existed in Germany. In 1862 Friedrich Wilhelm Raiffeisen founded credit cooperatives as loan bank associations which soon began trading in commodities. They were founded with the aim of utilising economies of scale (club the interests of small and marginal farmers), enabling the development of market power along the lines of a counterweight and, by working together, to accelerate innovation and implementation of technical advances in processing and marketing. Cooperatives are based on the principles of self-help, self-government, and responsibility for one's own actions. Their aim is to foster the economic well-being of their members. This is the basic foundation of the law of cooperative associations. As democratically organised enterprises, they remain clearly separate in goals, decision-making processes, and supervision from their competitors on the market. These fundamental principles have remained untouched by functional and structural changes in the farming sector and retain their validity today. Nevertheless, the image and character of the cooperatives in Germany have changed radically from self-help organisation for the poor rural population to modern, powerful institutions.

After undergoing extensive structural changes, 4221 agricultural cooperatives are grouped together under the umbrella of the Raiffeisen cooperatives. Their total current turnover is about 38 billion Euro. Around half of the total purchasing and sales turnover generated by farmers is through their cooperatives. Thus the rural cooperatives enjoy a global market share of 50 per cent. The structure of the agricultural cooperatives can be divided into three distinct levels. At the local level, there are 4184 cooperatives with three million members, of which 566 are credit cooperatives with commodity trade (1.9 Million members), 576 agricultural purchasing and marketing cooperatives (160000 members), 455 diary cooperatives (199000 members), 140 Fruit, Vegetable and Horticultural Cooperatives (50000 members), 278 Wine Cooperatives (66000 members), 127 Cattle and Meat Cooperatives (119000 members), 837 agricultural Cooperatives (56000 members) and finally 1205 other cooperatives (345000 members). The next level is the regional level, with corresponding regional central enterprises (70 in number) which in turn support national enterprises (5 in number) at the federal level. Associations can be found at both the regional and the federal levels.

Let us now see how these cooperatives work: Credit cooperatives with commodity trade are an exceptional form of cooperative. They can be found principally in southern Germany, where farm holdings are smaller than in the north. The cooperative finances the farmers procurement and the purchase of livestock and then helps process and market the harvest and animal produce. This system fits to our farmers structure and will be examined in detail later.

Of more importance are agricultural purchasing and marketing cooperatives, which offer a specific product range and achieve a market share of between 40 per cent and 55 per cent in the markets for cereals, fertilisers, pesticides and farm machinery. Apart from these, these cooperatives are today in a position to undertake diversification strategies and are active in retail industry for gardening, domestic and construction products, fuels as well as wholesale trade in construction materials. Dairy, fruit,vegetable and horticulture, wine, cattle and meat cooperatives have developed special packages for their members and have grown into economically viable institutions competing in the German, European and world markets.

Regarding the other mentioned cooperatives, it is to be stated that these are a range of service cooperatives for the agricultural sector, which offer member enterprises many and varied services, from chilling facilities to technical assistance. For many years, these cooperatives are active in cultivation and marketing of bio-mass (with which electricity can be produced). As also in the sector of marketing bio-diesel (diesel extracted out of rapeseed). A large number of cooperatives have completely taken over the task of providing consumer goods for rural populations.

Agricultural farm production cooperatives played a special role in the earstwhile eastern Germany, which was under communist rule up to end of 1989. These cooperatives took over all the production in agricultural sector. After structural changes, viable cooperatives-as large as 68per cent in marketing-have come up in the recent years according to their specialisation and comparative advantage. This example shows that given the commitment by the members, cooperatives can overcome political changes of any magnitude.

THE FOUR PILLARS OF GERMAN POLICY

As we have seen, farms have come together to form their own cooperative institutions to benefit from economies of scale and to strengthen their market power. Without strengthening one's market power it is impossible to have equal chance in markets, particularly for individual small resource-poor farmers. The rules of market are very cruel, as we have seen with the example of farmers who want to sell tomatoes in Kurnool. In Germany the farmers have found their own institutions to articulate their economic and social interests. There are four institutions, which act as four pillars of German agriculture:

(a) Institutions that exert influence on agricultural policy. Here farmers organisations work like watch-dogs to safeguard the interests of agriculture and their members. These are German Farmers' Association or DRV, and German Agricultural Society or DLG, and the Association of the Chambers of Agriculture.

(b) Institutions that conduct information, counselling and training functions. This group consists of the chambers of agriculture which are autonomous, professional, self-governing institutions. As corporations under public law they perform an organisational role for the providers of counselling and information services.

(c) Institutions focusing on the co-operation of farms in the joint use of the means of production in farming. These are ring organisations. These ring organisations, which are partially supported by the Government, consist of machinery and farming rings, producer cooperatives and producer rings and supervisory rings. For example machinery rings, which is the most important, are those where machinery is purchased jointly and offered to individual members for use. There are presently 292 machinery rings cultivating 60per cent of total arable land in Germany.

(d) The final group consists of institutions whose function is to foster co-operation in procurement, sales and marketing for farms. As described already above, the rural cooperatives represent important self-help institutions for the agricultural sector on the agricultural commodity markets.

The interactive effects of these institutions at political level, farm level, information and counselling level, market level guarantee the basic interests of the farmers.

A CRITICAL APPRAISAL OF COOPERATIVES IN INDIA INTERNATIONAL AND NATIONAL SCENARIO FOR AGRICULTURAL DEVELOPMENT

As has been mentioned earlier, the policy thrust being given to the agricultural sector by the Indian government since the 90's places greater reliance on the free operation of the market forces and the creation of a favourable price and trade regime. The measures that are advocated include removal of all restrictions on domestic trade as well as import and export of agricultural goods, use of incentive prices for raising production, removal of subsidies on agricultural inputs, re-vamping of the public distribution system and reorganisation of agricultural credit by restricting concessional finance facilities. This new policy package marks a clear departure from the past agricultural policies.

It is generally assumed that under the GATT scenario, reduced support levels and rationalisation of trade barriers will increase production and export of various commodities with comparative advantage in India. Diverse agro-climatic condi-tions and the existing differences in actual and potential yields strengthen this argument. Similarly, the reduction in import barriers are expected to reduce con-sumer prices in those countries where the tariff barriers are very high, which will generate strong demand and will push up imports. A number of empirical modelling exercises, such as Tyers and Anderson model, Static World Policy Simulation Model of USDA, IIASA Model, OECD Model, show that international prices will rise and so will the trade volumes, though the estimates of change in prices and trade vary from study to study (see Tyres et al. 1992; USDA 1986; Brandao et al. 1993; Gulati et al. 1994).

An important factor, very relevant for GATT scenario is that the domestic support levels in India are negative for most of the agricultural commodities, which is in sharp contrast to support levels in the developed countries, generally more than 10 per cent of the total value of their agricultural output. The product specific and non-product specific Aggregate Measure of Support (AMS) for 17 out of

22 total products for which India maintains market support programmes works out to be negative, i.e. (-)Rupees 196 billion, which forms (-)22.50 per cent of the value of agri-cultural output during the base period 1986-87 to 1988-89 and has increased in the last years to (-) 341.45 billion during 1992-93. This indicates the massive amout of "Taxation" Indian agriculture is subjected to (Gulati et al. 1994).

During the 1980's and also thereafter, Indian absolute prices were lower than world prices for rice, cotton, tobacco and bananas, whereas for wheat and sugar the domestic prices were higher (see Fig. 1). A crucial question would be, as total cultivable area is almost limited and changes in price ratios would change cropping patterns in favour of crops with comparative advantage, how far foodgrains production and

Figure 1
Indian and World Prices (Rupees per Quintal)

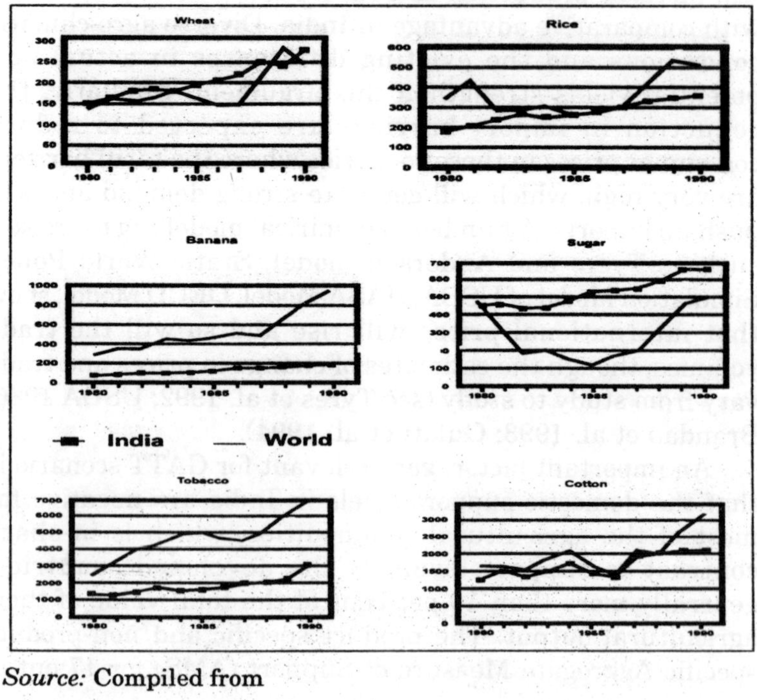

Source: Compiled from

possible trade will have implications for self sufficiency and food security goals of the country (see Chennamaneni 1997). An attempt using relative price ratios in domestic and international markets to forecast such shifts in crop-ping patterns and changes in exports shows that area under oilseeds (particularly rapeseed-mustard and groundnut), but also that of coarse cereals is likely to contract. On the other hand, area under fine cereals, rice, wheat, fibre crop and cot-ton, is likely to expand and may emerge as important export items. National Council of Applied Economic Research on the future agro-export basket of the country also supports this (Gulati et al.1994). Nayyar et al.(1994)

In view of the implications of a post-GATT scenario directed towards increased trade, agricultural and trade strategy has to gear itself to the challenges to reap maximum gains for the country. Identifying favourable commodities for exports, their likely changes and the necessary policy measures in regulation and prices, apart from infrastructure developments in storage, handling and fast track facilities as well as long-term investments in research and extension in yield and quality are crucially important to accelerate agro-exports.

As opening up trade will improve incentives by raising producer prices, non-price factors such as public investment in infrastructure, technological changes, human development and institutional reforms aiming at cooperative ventures are at least as important as prices in inducing an effective supply response, particu-larly in backward areas, so that increments in real incomes of the poor farmers can be augmented. A wide-spread literature shows that conventional cooperative marketing promoted by the government has, by and large, failed in India. More than one-third are incurring losses and have poor management capabilities (see Shivamaggi 1996). As has been already mentioned, marketing is becoming a vital infrastructure requirement and has to be developed through cooperative, public and private efforts. At the same time, it should be clear that management is a highly competitive function and could play a crucial role in protecting and pro-moting the activities of individual farmers.

HISTORICAL DEVELOPMENT

During the Independence struggle it was the dream of millions of people that after the independence, which then became reality in 1947, the country will have an economic order where one group of people will not exploit the other; which will enlist peoples voluntary participation in the process of planning and implementation of programmes of economic development, which will not lead to concentration of economic power; and which will ensure economic development with social justice. The main contents of the policy pursued by the Indian government was (a) enaction and partial implementation of land and tenancy reform laws (b) coordination of agricultural development in the economic planning and the im-plementation of government promotion measures in the frame of five year plans (c) introduction of a system of village self-government (village panchayats) and (d) development of agricultural cooperative system up to gradual introduction of ag-ricultural cooperative farms.

A blue-print for cooperative development was given by the National Development Council (NDC) in its Resolution on Cooperative Policy on November 8, 1958, and subsequently, in the recommendations of the Working Group on Cooperative Policy, set up by the Ministry of Food and Agriculture, Government of India, in January 1959 for considering the administrative and organisational ar-rangements required for implementing the above referred NDC's resolution. As it was before the independence, when a blue-print of cooperative development was given by the colonial government at the beginning of the 20th century (Bergmann 1971), the initiative for building cooperatives followed a top-down model of cooperative development. The NDC resolution has envisaged the following functions for the village cooperatives: (a) the provision of credit in close coordination with the production programmes for the village and assistance in particular to those who do not obtain credit under ordinary commercial banking principles (b) linking of credit with marketing (c) full use of irrigation facilities available includ-ing undertaking the responsibility for maintaining irrigation works for excavating and maintaining field channels (d) making adequate arrangements in the village for producing seeds and organic and green manures (e) arranging for distribution of fertilisers received for the village and their supply on credit to the farmers (f) pro-motion of animal husbandry and other programmes supplementing agriculture in-cluding village industries (g) application of improved techniques such as dry farming, contour bunding, soil conservation, etc and (h) consolidation of holdings and other works of benefit to the community.

With the adoption of cooperation as an instrument of economic development, a target-achievement oriented approach was introduced in the five-year plans for organising various kinds of cooperatives in the rural areas. The government has provided massive financial, technical, administrative and other support, directly and through state governments to achieve the targets. To accelerate the cooperative development, the government has introduced the concept of state partnership in the cooperatives, a measure which, on the one hand has strengthened the financial base of cooperatives, but on the other hand it has been misused for direct government interference in and control over the cooperatives. With all this help, the indian cooperative sector has grown to one of the largest in the world in terms of number of societies, membership and structural framework. There are in all 0.35 million cooperatives of all kinds, with nearly 170 million individual members. Its structure is broadly three-tier: the primaries federating at the district, state and national levels. The major cooperative segments (production credit, investment credit, marketing, processing, consumers, housing, fisheries, weavers, artisans, etc.) have their vertical federations for sectoral coordination. The horizontal federations, known as cooperative unions at various levels, viz., district, state and national are the spokes organisations of the entire cooperative sector in their respective areas.

One of the fundamental issue arising out of the cooperative development in India so far is weather to call these institutions cooperative as such. Cooperative theory requires cooperatives to be voluntarily set up by the members to meet needs defined by them, in the manner decided by them and managed by them democratically. Indian cooperatives, on the contrary, came into being at the be-hest of the government, which defines who should be the members, what purposes it should serve, and how. Cooperative laws across the country allow the registrar of cooperatives to refuse citizens the right to voluntarily set up cooperatives, if he/she is of the opinion that the proposed cooperative might not be viable, or that if allowed to come into existence, it will affect the business of a "cooperative" already in existence, and laws also empower the Registrar to clas-sify cooperatives, a power used by him/her to restrict, contain or expand the very raison d'etre of a cooperative, its primary objective.

PERFORMANCE OF MAJOR COOPERATIVES

As has been mentioned, cooperatives have entered into nearly all economic activities, thanks to massive government assistance. But the important questions put in the current debates going on are: How is their performance? Are they serving their members? What are their weaknesses? In this chapter, we would like to analyse the functioning of major cooperatives related with agricultural activities. One of the most important of them is the Primary Agricultural Credit Cooperatives (PACS). There are nearly 90,000 PACS covering 99.8 per cent of the villages. The total individual membership is nearly 86 million farmers with an average individual membership of 961 per PACS. PACS meet about 30 per cent of the agricultural finance. According to an in-depth study, about 52 per cent of the PACS are viable; the total share capital is about Rs 1.5 billion, the Government contribution being more than 17 per cent (Dwiwedi 1996).

In this connection, it is stated that even among the viable PACS, not many have undertaken various functions expected from them (for further analysis see Chennamaneni 1990). As the matter of viability was seriously discussed by the Government and the Reserve Bank of India (RBI) and restructuring was recommended on *ad-hoc* basis frequently, changes in the restructuring also took place from top to down approach. Small societies were amalgamated into large size, from large size to one cooperative for a panchayat area. These changes were implemented virtually by the cooperative departments, without the participation of the members in the decision making. This type of ap-proach for a country like India with large local variations has proved wrong. Members have not been taken into consent in the design and size and pattern of the cooperatives, and therefore, treated these cooperatives as not their own. Other major factors responsible for weaknesses of PACS are political interfer-ences, such as decision to waive loans upto Rs 10 000, mounting overdues, seriously declining member loyalty due to discrimination in providing services.

Regarding the marketing cooperatives, the Government have started them in 1956 with the aim of establishing one marketing cooperative society in every regulated market in the country. A network of nearly 3,000 primary agricultural marketing cooperatives and an equal number of commodity marketing cooperatives have come up. The primary objective of these cooperatives was to market the produce of members to their best advantage. However, the development of marketing cooperatives has not been even in regard to organisation, turnover, profitability and importance. Marketing of sugarcane, cotton and oilseeds for a predominant share in the total turnover of all the marketing cooperatives in the country. The activities of marketing cooperatives include commercial purchases, procurement operations, price support operations, market intervention, purchase under pooling system and pledge business. A detailed analysis is done elsewhere concerning the activities of procurement, price support to enable the public distribution system as well as the problems arising out of them for the poor consumers (Chennamaneni 1997). One of the major drawbacks regarding the performance of marketing cooperatives is the fact that these are not functioning according to the objectives of their bye-laws. According to *Dwiwedi* (1996) 30 per cent of these cooperatives are not undertaking any marketing activity and another 30 per cent are dormant and the rest are functioning marginally.

The story of agro-processing, where the cooperatives have successfully en-tered are sugar, paddy, dairy and spinning. There are 240 sugar cooperatives which produced nearly 60 per cent of total national production in 1994-95. Cooperatives have played a successful role in the development of dairy or milk processing and marketing. A three- tired organisational structure has developed whose production base comprises of primary village level cooperatives of milk producers. The key functional units consisting of district level cluster unions of such village societies and at apex level a state-level federation of cluster unions. The structure embraces production, procurement, processing and marketing of milk. There were 70 829 dairy cooperatives with total individual membership of 7.4 million milk producers in 1994-95.

By and large, the processing segment of the cooperative sector is successful because of the following reasons (see Dwiwedi 1996):

Processing created value addition, which enabled more income and better economic returns to the members.

- There is bottom-up functional integration at various levels strengthening each other.
- The structure has been built on peoples felt needs and not on governments interference.
- The involvement of members is very high and the local leadership dedicated with clear direction.
- Management was professionalised, necessary for such products processing.

RELEVANT ISSUES OF STRUCTURAL CHANGES

While a discussion on all relevant issues is not possible here, we would like to confine ourselves to two important aspects here, (a) cooperative management and (b) role of governments in promoting cooperatives.

Cooperative management has to follow the cooperative laws and rules, bye-laws of the society, international cooperative principles, the administrative deci-sions and orders of the Registrar of cooperative societies. It has to achieve the bye-law objectives, while at the same time strengthen the basic values in the cooperatives, specially honesty, solidarity, transparency, etc. Cooperative management has to deal with human aspirations and expectations. In India, however, in cooperative management according to the old law, the decision making power has been greatly curtailed by subjecting them to the approval of the Registrar of Cooperative Societies. A typical pattern of key personnel being appointed by the government out of government cadres has made cooperatives virtually a part of the establishment. Cooperative laws empower the Registrar/government to (a) amalgamate, merge, divide cooperatives, almost at will; (b) unilaterally amend the by-laws, the basic contract amongst the members, in all matters including the objectives, the activities, membership eligibility, the management of cooperative; (c) conduct and withhold elections, and nominate persons to the board of directors; (d) supersede the board and appoint anyone, not necessarily members, to manage the affairs for such lengths of time as seem appropriate; (e) decide on staff strength, recruitment, qualifications, service conditions; (f) decide on investment of funds by the cooperative, even in its own business; (g) appoint auditors and receive their report; (h) liquidate or continue the existence of a cooperative even when members think otherwise.

In this process a lot of deep-rooted vested interests of bureaucracy have developed. The management of cooperatives has also been excessively politicised, by replacing elected board of management with nominated persons, who in most cases are political people ignorant of co-operation. Elections to the cooperatives are not held and the administrators run the cooperatives. These aberrations have greatly weakened the cooperatives.

In the context of liberalisation, marketisation, privatisation and globalisation of the economy, certain questions, such as will the cooperatives be relevant under the liberalised market-oriented economy? Will the cooperatives prove viable in the environment of competition and liberalisation? Will the Government continue supporting the cooperatives? Will the cooperatives survive without the Government support? Regarding the relevance of cooperatives under the liberalised economy, it should be noted that, historically, the very concept of cooperatives was born in England during the 19th century in the environment of free economy, as a means of self-protection against consumers exploitation by the traders. In Germany, the history of Raiffeisen Cooperatives shows that self-help motive and solidarity for the neighbour were, among others, the main motives. Today, apart from England and Germany, in most countries of the industrialised world, starting from Japan, USA and Scandinavian countries cooperatives play a significant role in influencing markets. Particularly in India, where nearly 70 per cent of the population lives in rural areas, where 70 per cent of the total agricultural farms possess less than 2 ha land resources and are based on small farmer economy, apart from artisans, agricultural labourers, poor consumers, only cooperatives have the potential to safeguard their interests which will be increasingly subjected to open competition in the future.

Even the Government's policy is that the cooperatives will have their due relevance under the economic reforms undergoing now. Presently a serious discussion is going on the issue of the relationship between the state and the cooperatives. It is correctly argued that this relationship should be redefined and changed, and subsequently, the government should announce a National Policy on Cooperation. Though there are a number of factors relevant to define this new relationship, we would like to confine ourselves to the following four major issues relevant for this study.

Firstly, the cooperative laws in the country are not in the interest of the members of the cooperatives. They are in the interest of the government and the Registrar of Cooperative Societies to enable their interference in practically every aspect of the functioning. The cooperative laws have to be changed according to the recommendations of Brahm Prakash Committee of 1990. The State of Andhra Pradesh, which has enacted the first pilot law on these recommendations in 1995 and the practical implications for the new independent cooperatives, will be dealt with in later chapters.

Secondly, the main role of the government should be to build a conducive envi-ronment for the cooperatives. The cooperatives on the other hand, have to work towards the goal of self-reliance. Self-reliance does not mean that the entire finances should be contributed and raised by members themselves from their own resources. It means cooperatives should, like any other commercial enterprise, have the capacity and viability to borrow and repay out of their economic surplus. Borrowing, even from the Government institutions with capacity to repay, is not against the principle of self-reliance. This implies, however, that free cooperatives exist and work for the welfare of their members. Governments have to evolve a new policy approach under such an emerging scenario.

Thirdly, co-operation is a value-oriented concept. Its value content is most important for its distinct identity. This image has been, by and large, maligned in the last decades in India. It is high time that a new debate on public opinion on co-operation, its validity, its revitalisation, its restructuring, its redefining gains more importance. The ingredients of values, as reformulated in 1995 by the International Cooperative Alliance (ICA: 1995), such as self-help, democracy, equity, equality, solidarity, honesty, openness and social responsibility should be ele-ments of the cooperative movement and cooperative development in the learning process for the future. Combined with the value concept, it is the principles of co-operation-democratic member control, member economic participation, autonomy and independence, member education and information, co-operation among cooperatives and concern for community-which have to be followed by the cooperatives, as incorporated in the laws.

Fourthly, there should be an end to the political instrumentalisation on and control of cooperatives. It is a well known fact that it has been one of the most powerful single factors for the weakness of cooperatives in India. This again needs a consensus and commitment from all the political parties to refrain from making cooperatives making their areas of influence. The ongoing discussion by the cooperative promoters in India to amend the constitution of India to reaffirm the right of citizens to form and manage cooperatives and carry on trade and business as cooperatives is in the correct direction reflecting the necessity of their independent free functioning.

RELEVANCE OF COOPERATIVES IN TODAYS INDIA

Since India began its Five-year-Plan approach to development after Independence, cooperatives have been one of the instruments of economic development promoted by concessions, subsidies and direct government interventions. Consequently, by and large, cooperatives have failed to be member institutions result-ing in economic inefficiency, bureaucratically controlled, and tools of power for political parties. At the same time, the policy thrust being given to the agricultural sector by the Indian government since the 90's places greater reliance on the free operation of the market forces and the creation of a favourable price and trade regime. The measures that are advocated include removal of all restrictions on domestic trade as well as import and export of agricultural goods, use of incentive prices for raising production, removal of subsidies on agricultural inputs, re-vamping of the public distribution system and reorganisation of agricultural credit by restricting concessional finance facilities.

The major challenge in this scenario of globalisation for the small and marginal farmer is: Can his farming be economically viable under this new set of rules ? The answer would be NO if institutional changes are not taken up seriously by the policy makers to safeguard the interests of the vast majority of rural population. Particularly in India, where nearly 70 per cent of the population lives in rural areas, where 70 per cent of the total agricultural farms possess less than 2 ha land resources and are based on small farmer economy, apart from artisans, agricultural labourers, poor consumers, only cooperatives have the potential to safeguard their interests which will be increasingly subjected to open competition in the future.

In view of the implications of a WTO scenario directed towards increased trade, agricultural and trade strategy has to gear itself to the challenges to reap maximum gains for the country. Our farmers can reap the fruits of globalisation provided our policy makers can identify favourable commodities for exports, their likely changes and the necessary policy measures in regulation and prices, apart from infrastructure developments in storage, handling and fast track facilities as well as long-term investments in research and extension in yield and quality.

Which perspective do farmers' organisations, political leaders, social workers, NGOs have in mobilising the poor farmers for co-operation and for social change? Marketing is becoming a vital infrastructure requirement and has to be developed through cooperative, public and private efforts. At the same time, it should be clear that management is a highly competitive function and could play a crucial role in protecting and pro-moting the activities of individual farmers. In an economy where the increase of both employment and purchasing power need urgent attention, it is probably the cooperative with its decentralised, democratic, producer-sensitive and producer-controlled design which makes pos-sible and viable the pooling of small quantities of products from a large number of producers spread over a large area for cooperative marketing. The same applies also to the supply services-agricultural inputs, irrigation water, credit, education and training, housing or consumables, as the success story in Germany shows us. Our successful DWCRA experiences in Andhra Pradesh have shown that savings and credit cooperatives with their decentralised (therefore lower cost), democratic (therefore, member-sensitive) nature encourage small and large savings and bring into circulation large amounts of scattered and hidden financial resources give a boost to local capitalisation, to reinvestment, to choice in employment, to choice in consump-tion as to improved quality of life for large numbers of people.

Therefore, "The market" as such has absolutely little to offer to a large number of producers, savers, consumers and barrowers as it is the case in our rural areas. These are millions of small and marginal farmers, agricultural labourers, artisans and people working in petty business in informal sectors. In today India, cooperatives probably have more to offer to economic growth and social development than most other forms of enterprise have. This inevitably means institutional changes and the search for new institutions, such as cooperatives.

CONCLUSION

When other forms of enterprise are being given even greater freedom than they already enjoy, it was the Government of Andhra Pradesh which first accepted the challenge of liberalising its cooperative laws. In 1995 it made a conscious decision to amend the state cooperative law so that citizens freely could work together through the cooperative form of business to achieve their objectives without unnecessary controls and excessive regulations. On the first of June 1995, the Andhra Pradesh Mutually Aided Cooperative Societies (APMACS) Act, 1995 came into force, after having been unanimously passed by the legisla-tive assembly on 4th May

1995. Leaders of all political parties spoke in favour of the proposed reform. For the cooperative movement in India a new chapter began.

Broadly speaking, the principles underlying the APMACS Act of 1995 adhere to democratic member control, member economic participation, autonomy and independence, member education and information, co-operation among cooperatives and concern for community. APMACS Act offers the people of Andhra Pradesh an opportunity to set up business enterprises which are cooperative in nature, i.e. which provide services to members, give returns to them on their usage of the services, and are controlled democratically by the user-members. Control by members includes their right to define their cooperative, its membership, its services, to decide on the management structure, on the investment of funds, on liquidation, subject to only such restrictions are as reasonable and applicable also in other free economies.

However, there has not been any substantial progress since the last years in taking this message to the people and mobilise them. In AP, we have only few successful model projects with not even 2 per cent of total farmers involvement. This failure can be attributed towards low importance given to this vital sector by the government and all political parties. Also farmers organisations have failed to keep this issue on top of their agenda. It is highly questionable in this connection to give high priority to issues dealing with irrigation water which would increase productivity and agricultural activity, but to give low priority to institutional changes and institutional building such as cooperative marketing institutions, which would finally decide the economic viability of farmers through getting right prices and returns. Moreover, industrialised countries, also Germany have been debating intensively since the last years how to reduce their subsidies so that they can prepare themselves according to the new WTO Rules. Presently, also to promote cooperative sector, Germany and other developed countries will take back subsidies in trade and marketing and shift them towards direct payments to farmers for environmental and preservation of cultural landscape under the so called Green Box. These subsidy activities will not come under WTO restrictions and allow their farmers to sustain the changes occuring in global agriculture scenario.

In India, however, the domestic sup-port levels for our farmers are negative for most of the agricultural commodities, which is in sharp contrast to support levels in the developed countries generally more than 10 per cent of the total value of their agricultural output. The product specific and non-product specific Aggregate Measure of Support (AMS) for 17 out of 22 total products for which India maintains market support programmes works out to be negative, i.e. (-)22.50 per cent of the value of agricultural output in the nineties. This indicates the massive amout of "Taxation" Indian agriculture and indian farmer is subjected to. At the same time we have about 60 million tones of foodgrain reserves lying idle in a year of unprecedented drought and our public distribution system has virtually refrained to address major issues for which it has been established. Unfortunately, policy-makers in Delhi have failed to formulate a consistent agricultural policy to address the serious implications these developments will have on our farmers in general and our economy in particular under the new emerging scenario. What we urgently need is a new orientation in our agricultural policy taking fully the implications of the emerging new scenario of globalisation with a strong political commitment to support small farmer economy through institutional changes and institutional building.

REFERENCES

Andhra Pradesh State Cooperative Union Limited (APSCUL)(1995), Andhra Pradesh Mutu-ally Aided Cooperative Societies Act 1995. Hyderabad.

Bergmann, T. (1971), Die Genossenschaftsbewegung in Indien. Geschichte, Leistungen, Auf-gaben. Frankfurt A.M.

Brandao, Antonio Salzar P. Martin, Will (1993), Implications of Agricultural Trade Liberalisation For The Developing Countries, World Bank Working Paper, WPS 1116.

Chennamaneni, R. and Eisen, A. (1998), Cooperatives at Cross Roads in India: Experiences from an Enquiry into a Model Project in Andhra Pradesh, India. *Berlin Cooperative Papers*, Berlin.

Chennamaneni, R. (1990), The Role of Price and Credit Policy and their Implications on the Small Farming Sector in India, *Economic Quarterly*, 25 (January). pp. 15-27.

Chennamaneni, R. (1997), Public Distribution System and New Economic Policy in India: Policy Implications, Implementation Strategies and Challenges for the Future. In: Bauer, S. et al. (Hrsg) (1997): Märkte der Agrarund Ernährungswirtschaft. Schriften der Gesell-schaft für Wirtschafts-und Sozialwissens-chaften des Landbaues E.V., Bd. 33. Münster-Hiltrup: Landwirtschaftsverlag.

Di Gregorio, M., K. Hagedorn, M. Kirk, B. Korf, N. McCarthy, R. Meinzen-Dick and B. Swallow (2004), Property Rights, Collective Action and Poverty: The Role of Institutions For Poverty Reduction. IFPRI, Washington DC.

Dwiwedi, R.C. (1996), Role of Cooperatives in Rural Economy. In: *Indian Journal of Agri-cultural Economics,* 4(Oct.-Dec). pp. 713-727.

EC (1994), Evaluation des Projets de Developpement Rural Finances Durant les Conventions de Lome I,II et III. European Commission, Brussels.

Gulati, Ashok/Sharma, Anil (1994), Agriculture under GATT: What It Holds For India. In: *Economic and Political Weekly*, 29 (July). pp. 1857-1863.

International Cooperative Alliance (1995), *Review of International Co-operation* Vol. 88, No. 3.

Johnson N. and Berdegue J.A. (2004), Property rights, collective action and agribusiness. 2020 Focus 11. Brief 13. IFPRI. Washington, DC.

Nayyar, Deepak/Sen, Abhijit (1994), International Trade and Agricultural Sector in India. In: Economic Liberalisation and Indian Agriculture edited by G.S. Bhalla. Institute for Studies in Industrial Development, New Delhi. pp.122-78.

Shivamaggi, B. (1996), Future Strategy for Development of Cooperatives In: *Economic and Political Weekly,* 20 (May). pp. 1187-1188.

Tyres, R./Anderson, K. (1992), Disarray in World Food Markets: A Quantitative Assessment. Cambridge, New York.

United States Department of Agriculture (1986), World Commodity Markets-Government Intervention and Multilateral Policy Reform, USDA, Washington.

GLOBALISATION AND AGRICULTURE IN THE DEVELOPING COUNTRIES

G. Sreedhar

INTRODUCTION

The term 'Globalisation' gained wide currency in the last two decades. Globalisation is seen as the process of economic integration of countries throughout the globe. The process implies opening up of the economies for foreign trade and long-term capital flows. Globalisation is taken to mean the increasing depth of economic interaction among the countries reflected by (1) a rising share of imports and exports in the GDP, (2) growing proportion of foreign capital in domestic investment, (3) increased financial integration among the countries and (4) greater harmonisation of domestic laws and standards with well-established norms (Baye, 2003). Globalisation, driven by technological innovations, market forces and socio-political forces, has become an inevitable process for the developing countries.

There is a heated debate on the consequences of globalisation for the developing countries. While globalisation can throw up immense opportunities for the developing countries to accelerate the pace of their development process, it can also have certain adverse consequences for them in the wake of unequal competition in the world trade with the developed countries. It must be recognised that successful integration in global economy depends upon domestic policies of a given country in trade and financial liberalisation along with market-based structural and institutional reforms such as privatisation, legal and other regulatory systems (Nissanke, 2000). Successful participation in globalisation requires the achievement of stability in key macro-economic issues such as maintaining low inflation, sustainable budget deficits, stable and appropriate real interest rates and exchange rates (Rodrik, 1996). Mere integration into the international economy does not guarantee benefits, since globalisation is taking place in an environment of global instability, characterised by the rapid expansion of global financial markets, and the risks and costs involved in integration can be substantial for the fragile economies. The World Development Report (2000/2001) views that global trends present not only extraordinary opportunities for poverty reduction but also extraordinary risks such as growing inequality, marginalisation and social explosion.

The nature of capital flows into the developing countries would determine whether it contributes to development or not. It is important to distinguish between mobility of finance and mobility of productive capital; the latter can contribute to development because the capital would be used for production and hence promote higher growth in the economy, while the presence of the former can be felt largely in the financial markets. It appears that capital flows into the developing countries in the form of foreign direct investment (FDI) largely represent the mobility of finance rather than the mobility of productive capital. The world FDI flows have grown faster than either the world trade or the world output since the early 1980s. The flow of productive capital from the North to the South has been extremely limited. According to the UNCTAD, the world FDI flows increased by 18 per cent in 2000 to $1.3 trillion compared with only $203 billion in 1990. Much of this investment was driven by corporations buying or merging with companies in other countries, contributing to increasingly global multi-national firms.

Most FDI flows went to the industrialised countries. The FDI flows to the developing countries grew only by 8 per cent to $240 billion. However, the FDI flows to Latin America and Caribbean declined by 22 per cent in 2000 and the flows to Africa continued to decline (Bigman, 2002). More than half of the FDI flows to the developing countries were confined to East Asian countries, with little flows to Latin America and Caribbean countries and only a trickle to sub-Saharan Africa. As such, the impact of FDI flows has been limited or negligible for most of the developing countries.

A majority of the developing countries are heavily dependent upon agriculture, and hence the opportunities available for them in the world agricultural trade would determine their prospects in terms of the growth of GDP and foreign exchange earnings and their multiplier effects on development, as a consequence of globalisation. As such, it becomes pertinent to examine the trends in world agricultural trade and their implications for the developing countries. This paper examines the issues concerning globalisation in the developing countries in relation to the agricultural sector. It focuses on the consequences of the developed country protectionism in the form of production and export subsidies for farm and food products and simple manufactures like textiles and clothing, and imposing of a number of safety and sanitary regulations on the imports, for the developing countries dependent on agriculture. It examines the measures needed for protecting the economies of developing countries from the adverse consequences of globalisation and promoting agricultural growth in a sustainable fashion. It also examines the measures needed at the local and global levels to ensure that the benefits of globalisation are equitably distributed to all the countries and all the sections of population.

GLOBALISATION AND WORLDAGRICULTURAL TRADE

The Uruguay Round of General Agreement on Tariffs and Trade (GATT) negotiations in 1992 brought agriculture within its framework of multilateral trading rules, which were given greater standing through the establishment of a new body, the World Trade Organization (WTO) in 1995. The Uruguay Round Agreement on Agriculture (URAA), which came into effect from 1994, took the first step to subject agricultural trade to same rules that apply to merchandise trade and progressively reduce the interventionist policies. Its major achievement was to convert all the non-tariff barriers to trade like quantitative restrictions, import bans, etc., into explicit tariffs. It also provided for the gradual reduction of domestic support and export subsidies for agriculture. It stipulated that the developed countries should lower the aggregate tariffs by 36 per cent over a period of six years, while the developing countries should lower the aggregate tariffs by 24 per cent over a period of ten years. It also imposed limits to production and export subsidies for agricultural products stipulating that the budgetary outlays for export subsidies, the overall volume of subsidised exports and the subsidies for domestic production be gradually reduced by pre-determined rates by the developed countries in six years and by the developing countries in ten years. The Least Developed Countries (LDCs-with a GNP per capita below $ 1000) were not subject to these restrictions.

But, despite the general agreement on the need to open up the markets of the developed countries to agricultural products from developing countries, the actual progress made during the past decade has been very slow. The developed countries, especially the United Stated (US) and the European Union (EU) replaced the import bans with tariffs but the tariffs were initially set at such a high level that even after a 36 per cent reduction over the implementation period of the URRA, they remained highly restrictive. Similarly, the import quotas were replaced with equivalent tariffs that established the same restrictions. Increased market access was achieved through a formalisation of concessions to the former colonies. There have been disputes between the EU and the US over bananas, hormone-treated beef and genetically modified products, which have proved to be bitter and difficult to resolve.

What have been the implications of globalisation for the world agricultural trade in general and for the developing countries in particular? Even though there has been a boom in the world trade in the past decade, with an average annual increase of over 6 per cent in the volume of merchandise trade, the share of agriculture in overall trade has shown a declining trend. Although the agricultural trade increased in real terms in the 1990s, the share of agriculture in the total trade is only about 9 per cent or half the level in 1980. This is mainly due to the diminishing share of the value-added of several low income countries heavily dependent upon agricultural exports. For instance, the slump in prices of coffee, a crop grown by over 25 million farmers in the developing countries, has adversely affected them. Taking inflation into account, the real price of coffee now is just 25 per cent of the level in 1960 and this has had adverse consequences such as rising unemployment, deteriorating indicators for health and nutrition, and an increase in the rate of school-dropouts in a number of countries from Ethiopia and Tanzania to Vietnam and southern Mexico. Similarly, there has been a slump in the prices of other agricultural commodities. The prices of tropical oils, tea and sugar have also fallen in the recent past, resulting in severe losses to the developing countries.

Another important element contributing to losses to the developing countries is the decline in terms of trade. Primary commodity exporters have to export more and more volume to retain a fixed import capacity. According to UNCTAD, Africa's terms of trade losses since 1970 have reduced the region's share in the world trade by nearly half. One more disturbing trend is that the increase in the share of developing countries in the world trade was only modest in the past decade. The share of developing countries in agricultural exports increased from 30 to 34 per cent between 1990-94 and 1995-2000, which was slower than the rate of increase for the manufactured goods. Even this modest increase was on account of a rise in South-South trade. The world agricultural trade continues to be dominated by rich countries, which account for about three-fourths of the total trade. It is also important to note that over 50 developing countries depend upon three or less primary commodities for more than half of their exports. Any fluctuation in the prices of these commodities can either adversely or favourably affect the economies of these countries.

One of the emerging trends in agricultural trade is the growth of high value food products ranging from fruits and vegetables to dairy and livestock. The rapid rise of these products has been associated with important changes in the supply chains linking the northern consumers and southern producers. Traders, processors and retailers are taking advantage of the reduced transport costs, improved communication systems, import liberalisation and openness to foreign trade. Mergers and acquisitions have reduced the number of multi-national companies competing in the global markets, and increased the importance of intra-company trading. Supermarket chains, along with large-scale food manufacturers, now occupy a central place in the agricultural trade. There seems to be a marked trend towards concentration, as indicated by the rise of large supermarket chains in industrialised countries. The developing countries are also catching up with this trend, though to a lesser extent. All these changes have implications for the farmers in developing countries. To an increasing extent, the entry to export as well as local markets is mediated through firms linked to or owned by major supermarket chains in industrialised countries. The trend toward concentration becomes evident once again. For instance, in Kenya and Zimbabwe, two of the largest suppliers of leguminous vegetables to the EU, the top five exporters account for over 75 per cent of fresh vegetable exports.

These changes have important implications for the terms on which small producers enter world markets. Most producers have to deal with a small number of large-scale processors and traders or giant supermarket chains. One feature of the trend towards concentration in processing and retailing is the emergence of 'buyer-driven' supply chains, resulting in the transfer of a growing share of value-added from the producers in developing countries to companies in industrialised countries. For instance, the coffee supply chain is dominated by four companies, namely Nestle, Kraft, Proctor and Gamble, and Sara Lee, which enjoy the lion's share of the global market. As a result, the share of coffee producing countries in the global market declined from about 30 per cent to 10 per cent in the last ten years.

Across the food sector, the supermarkets and large processors are increasing their domination of retail markets, which enable them to exercise, if not price-fixing, a downward pressure on prices paid to farmers, in a way forcing many small farmers out of the sector. The supermarket purchasing policies such as demand for product homogeneity and compliance with safety and health standards, maintenance of post-harvest quality, short-term contracts that provide no guarantee of future markets, high rates of product rejection and delays in paying for products (up to 90 days) can certainly create huge barriers for market entry to the small producers. The continuation of present trends can throw up enormous challenges to the developing countries in poverty reduction, with the small farmers getting excluded from the fastest growing, highest value-added markets, enabling the large-scale farms, supermarkets and processing chains to enjoy a lion's share of benefits. As a result, the inequalities emerging under globalisation get reinforced.

IMPLICATIONS OF NORTHERN AGRICULTURAL POLICIES

One main problem faced by the producers in developing countries is the developed country protectionism and standardisation of farm and food products and simple manufactures like textiles and clothing. Another important problem they face is that the rich countries impose a number of safety and sanitary regulations on the imports, sometimes under the pressure of import-competing farms in those countries and reject the products from the developing countries. It is estimated that the overall protection in agriculture is about 20 per cent for the US, 46 per cent for the EU, 52 per cent for Canada and 82 per cent for Japan, and due to these measures the annual loss to the developing countries is about $45 billion (Cline, 2004). The issue of agricultural policies of the northern countries, notably the US and the EU, needs a closer look here since it has implications for the small producers in developing countries. The public policy in these countries is dominated by powerful special interest groups, large farmers and agro-industrial firms such as grain traders and by complex rivalries between national governments in the EU and state governments in the US. Both the US and the EU dominate the global markets even in respect of major agricultural commodities like wheat, corn, sugar and dairy products. It is clear that the terms in which these countries trade would have implications for not only the exporters but also the staple food producers facing competition from imports.

The agricultural policies of the US and the EU seek to achieve the twin objectives of supporting farm income by driving a wedge between world and domestic prices, and at the same time protecting their share in the world market. Income support is linked to output, with incentives for production and the generation of export surpluses, which have to be disposed on world markets, usually at prices lesser than the costs of production. The agricultural exporting firms are then given access to surplus stocks financed by public subsidies. The overall support to agriculture in terms of OECD's Producer Subsidy Estimate (PSE) stood at $311 billion in 2000-01, which is equivalent to about one-third of the value of the farm output. The bulk of this support is provided for meat, dairy products, sugar and cereals. The US and the EU account for about half of the total PSE. The PSE has not declined as a share of output during the past two decades, but has actually increased in absolute terms (OECD, 2002).

The northern agricultural policies are deficient in at least two respects. First, they are not in tune with the avowed goals of their countries, which include the protection of poor farmers, support to the environment and consumer health. Since the support levels are a function of output and land area, the benefits are reaped by the large farms and corporations. In the US, the biggest 10 per cent subsidy recipients account for about three-fourths of all transfers, while 60 per cent farms receive no support at all. In the EU, just two per cent farmers account for about half of all transfers, and the farms with the highest gross margins have largest land and receive greatest support. The current subsidy policies also hurt small farmers in other ways. They contribute to rising land and land rental values, high degree of concentration, increased mechanisation and use of chemical fertilisers and pesticides, in a way adversely affecting the environment. Second, these policies have huge costs for the developing countries, adversely affecting the poorer sections. The grain exporters are provided access to cereals at prices far lower than those received by the farmers, often below the costs of production. For the small farmers in food importing developing countries, the US export price sets the terms of competition in local markets, and that competition is unequal. As a result, the US captured a growing share of Mexican corn markets, and the rising imports from US have restricted market outlets for the Mexican farmers including those in poverty-belt states of the south where about 40 per cent live below the poverty line.

Small farmers in developing countries are denied access to domestic urban markets because the imports are cheaper. The case of Haiti where the imported rice from the US accounted for nearly half of the national consumption by the end of 1990s is an instance in point. Even though the economists point out the potential gains to consumers because of lower prices, when viewed in a broader context of poverty reduction there are two potential dangers to the developing countries. One danger is that the imports can break the link between rural and urban economies, isolating rural areas from growth and restricting the development of dynamic linkages. The other danger is that the dependence on food imports implies significant foreign exchange costs, particularly for the low-income countries, with vulnerable sections exposed to the risks associated with volatility of world prices. The food trade balance is also found deteriorating for the developing countries. In a study conducted by Ravallion and Lokshin (2004), it was found that the import of cereals led to an increase in rural poverty in Morocco since the benefits to the net consumers are outweighed by the losses to the net producers.

Subsidised over-production and export-dumping can bring down the world prices and close down the opportunities for the developing countries. For instance, the EU sugar farmers, comprising mostly the very large-scale farmers, received high guaranteed prices for 12 million tonnes of sugar, and the marginal return was sufficient to create incentives to produce another 4.7 million tonnes of non-quota sugar, which was dumped on the world market, making the EU the world's largest exporter. As a result, developing countries such as Thailand, Cuba and Mozambique lost markets and received lower export prices. The US cotton farmers, comprising very large farm corporations, received subsidies at the rate of $225 per acre in 2001-02, resulting in the depression of the world cotton prices by about 26 per cent. As a consequence, the West African countries like Burkina Faso, Mali, Chad and Benin, etc., which depended heavily on cotton exports, suffered huge losses.

The lost export opportunities and lower export prices will lead to a decline in investment in agriculture and hamper the diversification of livelihoods as well as foreign exchange earnings in the developing countries. In fact, certain adverse trends are becoming evident in some countries. For instance, Burkina Faso lost 1 per cent of GDP and 12 per cent of export earnings, while the corresponding figures for Mali stood at 1.7 per cent and 8 per cent respectively. For the countries which rank very low in terms of human development indicators, these figures signify grave losses, with adverse impact on the real income losses for the farmers. Besides, the governments of these countries had to spend huge amounts to protect their cotton sector from world price trends, implying substantial fiscal burden and diversion of resources from public spending in social sectors. Thus, the losses for these countries were much worse than what the figures suggest and it would take quite some time for them to recover from the economic shocks suffered.

POLICY CHALLENGES AND THE SUGGESTED MEASURES

It becomes clear from the above discussion that the central policy challenge is to ensure equitable distribution of benefits from agricultural trade for the developing countries. This challenge assumes added significance in the context of the problem of rural poverty, as evident from the lack of access to land, irrigation and credit for the rural poor, particularly women. Most of the poor reside in remote areas characterised by weak institutional structure including lack of quality transport and communication facilities, due to which they are required to pay more for the essential inputs such as seed and fertilisers, and at the same time the higher transport costs limit their scope to sell their agricultural produce. Thus, the small producers get excluded form global markets, and are unable to compete with the imports in urban markets. The studies conducted by Deininger and Olinto (2000) and Lopez, Nash and Stanton (1995) showed that the poor producers could not derive optimum benefits due to their lack of access to key assets and capital in Zambia and Mexico, respectively. As such, there is a need to facilitate rural poverty reduction and gender equity, and redistribution of opportunity in favour of poor producers and marginal areas in terms of access to assets, inputs and infrastructure.

To address these problems, there is a need for the fundamental changes in the distribution of public spending, and the distribution of land and other assets in countries where the ownership of land is highly skewed. The agricultural input supplies such as capital, seed, fertilisers and technologies have been adversely affected due to inefficient functioning of public sector agencies and cooperatives, and the inability of the private traders to cater to the needs of farmers, especially in the remote areas. There is a strong case for reviewing the market liberalisation policies in the developing countries as they seemed to be working against the interests of small farmers, and for strengthening the input supply system with the state intervention. There is also a neglect of rural development in the recent past. For instance, the Central government expenditure for rural development in India on an average declined from about 14 per cent of the GDP during the Eighth Plan (1992-97) to about 6 per cent now. As such, there is a need for according a high political priority to rural development in order to facilitate rural poverty reduction and create conditions conducive for the small producers to take part in world agricultural trade on equitable terms. Addressing these problems at the global level requires changes in agricultural trade system implying the need for the international organisations to function in an autonomous fashion and be responsive to the needs of the poorer countries and their growing millions. It also requires the modification of the northern agricultural policies so as not to distort the world agricultural trade.

In order to overcome the inequalities in agricultural trade, there is an urgent need for effective international anti-trust provisions to prevent collusion between the small groups of companies that dominate the food sector. The developing countries should take the help of international organisations to build international quality certification institutions for their products on a priority basis. Also, there is scope to extend the opportunities for the small producers in the agricultural trade by bringing about certain improvements in the working of the supermarkets through best practices and regulatory measures. For instance, supermarkets in the US are required to pay the suppliers within 30 days. Many governments can implement this practice in their countries so as to mitigate the sufferings of the small producers. Supermarkets, on their part, can provide for longer-term contracts. There could be regulatory mechanisms within the government to control the requirements placed by supermarkets on the farmers, which suggest the need for flexibility in the non-interventionist stance of the northern governments. Public-private partnerships could also be encouraged to enhance the capacity of small producers to meet the standards imposed by supermarkets. The governments and donor agencies can come to the aid of the small producers to invest in equipment, technology, and organisational development and deal with the supermarkets in an efficient manner. International aid can play a pivotal role in creating rural infrastructure, which would enable the small producers to enter the global markets on more equitable terms, and therefore the scale of aid from richer countries needs to be increased substantially. The terms under which international aid provided to the Heavily Indebted Poor Countries towards debt relief needs to be made more liberal as the debt repayment alone accounts for more than 10 per cent of the government revenue in these countries.

Even though the URAA stipulated a 20 per cent decline in support for production and a 36 per cent decline in export subsidies, both the US and the EU achieved these targets largely by redefining the subsidies for production and export, ensuring that the support to agriculture continued on an increased scale compared to the base period. Under the URAA, certain categories of support were considered to be outside of the WTO discipline. Direct payments provided by the US were categorised as 'Green Box' on the grounds that they had minimal effects on production. The payments made by the EU were categorised as 'Blue Box' on the ground that they include the supply control measures such as the requirement for the farmers to take land out of cultivation. Both these payments were given the status of decoupled payments on the ground that they had minimal effects on production and trade, and act only as a shield against risk and lowering of world prices during certain periods. Thus, both the US and the EU have retained the support to agriculture in the form of decoupled payments. It has to be realised that it is not possible to design subsidy programmes that do not have some effect on production decisions and trade. Therefore, for the WTO purposes, it is necessary to consider direct payments as production and export subsidies to the extent they facilitate production in excess of the domestic demand and the transfer of surpluses to the world market. The EU promotes exports through a small tax on guaranteed price paid to farmers, which is about three times higher than the world market levels and this also should be treated as an export subsidy. Other programmes of support for agriculture in these countries indicate that the area brought under cultivation is likely to increase further in future. The central problem of all these policies is their in-built support for over-production and export-dumping, with adverse consequences for the developing countries.

The northern agricultural policies have to be suitably modified so that the problems they pose to the small producers in the developing countries can be overcome. For the industrialised countries in the north, the main challenge is to de-intensify production under a new, sustainable system of production, in which support is guaranteed for low levels of output. Two measures are required to meet this challenge. Firstly, these countries should phase out the direct and indirect export subsidies for agriculture, including decoupled payments, for production levels that exceed domestic demand. Secondly, these countries should ensure that subsidies are redistributed and confined to small farmers, preventing large farmers and agri-business companies from reaping any benefits.

Simultaneously, the developing countries should undertake measures to promote and strengthen sustainable rural development with certain safeguards for the vulnerable sections. It is important that the developing countries grow sufficient food in an environmentally sustainable fashion and to revitalise the employment generation. They must take all steps to protect their food systems with necessary tariffs and quotas in order to achieve the objective of rural poverty reduction and ensuring food security for their masses. Relevant safeguards have to be incorporated in policy measures for the rural poor in times of crisis such as a spurt in imports, or a fall in import prices below the national average level. The important measures to reduce the vulnerability of the poor countries include diversification in production and skill formation, value addition to the same commodities, and arrangements for institutional insurance of farmers in poor countries at the international level. Also important are the pro-active public support programmes with the aid of international agencies to help the farmers in poor countries to adjust and coordinate their resources so as to shift from traditional crops to new commercial crops.

Two measures to remove the basic constraints of the poor in the developing countries need special emphasis. First, there is a need to tackle the fundamental problem of the poor to offer collaterals for accessing credit, and here the extension of insurance coverage to all the major crops, keeping in view the location-specific features and problems, could be a useful option. Second, strengthening market information to the farmers is crucial not only to increase their access to global markets but also enable them to derive optimum benefits.

CONCLUSION

In conclusion, even though globalisation is said to have enormous potential to promote sustainable agricultural and rural development, the benefits from globalisation have not been on equitable terms for the developing countries, especially in agricultural trade. The experiences of certain developing countries that have suffered the worst consequences of globalisation in agricultural trade should be an eye-opener to all concerned, particularly to countries like India, which are just at the beginning stage of reforms in the agricultural sector, so that they take all possible measures to protect their economies. The success of globalisation depends upon the domestic policies and institutional reforms in favour of the poor in the developing countries. The international organisations such as the IMF, the World Bank and the WTO facilitating and regulating trade liberalisation, particularly in the agricultural sector, cannot absolve their responsibility to ensure equitable distribution of benefits to all the countries and different sections of population by eliminating the scope for unequal competition. The developing countries have to embark on capacity building measures so that they can participate effectively in the international negotiations and enable the international agencies to function in a truly global manner. The industrialised countries have to modify their policies of support to agriculture in such a manner that they do not affect the millions of poor in the developing countries.

FOOD AND NUTRITION SECURITY

K.R. Venugopal

When we speak of Food and Nutrition Security we are talking about those sections of the population who are poor i.e. those who are unequally placed in asset endowment, wherever they may be living geographically. Normally a majority of these would be rural labour of all kinds and the very poor in the urban areas. Usually, and rightly, we look at it at the household level, and in particular, in the context of the child and in gender terms. So, when we talk of Food and Nutrition Security, we talk of the people and their hunger including the hunger for micro-nutrients. It is about the individual's and the household's quantitative need to satisfy hunger and the qualitative need to lead morbidity–free life, healthily and productively.

1. The point that immediately comes to mind in the context of the subject of our Seminar, which is about Globalisation: Opportunities and Challenges is:

   Has the challenge to India's household level food and nutrition security arisen only in the globalisation context and the WTO context or was it something that had long preceded them?

   The answer to this question is that ever since we became a free nation not less than at least 300 million people–may be fewer in 1947 given our population then–at any given time have been food and nutrition insecure. Their numbers have, if anything, gone up never mind what our Planning Commission says. Indian Food and Nutrition insecurity has been chronic. *Chronic because Indian political leadership over these years, especially after 1976, when we broke loose from the need to import food regularly, have shown a singular indifference to the food and nutrition insecurity of the Indian poor, even when we had the wherewithal to deal with them.*

2. Now I come to the current context of fluctuation in foodgrains production seen in recent years. The current context certainly raises the spectre of India, as a nation, as against the problem of only about 35 to 40 per cent of its population, becoming a food insecure nation, what to say of nutrition insecurity which is so much more refined than food security as a concept? For this spectre, globalisation of trade or liberalisation of trade or trade reforms as it is called is without doubt partly responsible. In that sense, it is great crisis and therefore, a challenge. The crisis or challenge is greater because the crisis is deeper. That, however, is no consolation to the Indian poor because their original misery, suffered over decades without any respite, will now deepen ever more. Only this time their national leadership will have on *international alibi* to show for their own comeuppance. Therefore, the challenge now shifts to the informed citizens of India to go to the aid of the hungry masses by way of pinning down the political leadership of India to the needs of the hungry millions, in the emerging new context. This new context thrust upon the Nation is also a moment of truth and therefore an opportunity for the political leadership to do two things: (i) to guide India properly through the WTO negotiations so that the country does not get sucked into irretrievable dependency for food and medicines and (ii) to realize at least now how sadly it neglected certain vital segments of the Indian economy like agriculture, especially in the recent decades and along with it the food and nutrition

and health security needs of the people (especially those living in the currently food deficit areas) and therefore rectify them through appropriate policies and programmes and implement them honestly.

3. Challenge and Opportunity are the two sides of the same coin. Ironically, however, the Indian State's failure over long periods, but especially in the last decade and a half, has converted the opportunity itself into a challenge, for thanks to its neglect of many vital aspects of Agriculture, at the National and State levels, farmers in States like Andhra Pradesh have been committing suicide for about 7 years now and their own hunger levels and of the rural labour dependent on them have risen alarmingly, with actually some of them dying of starvation.

4. It is against this background I wish to look at the W.T.O. opportunities and challenges in the context of the Agreement On Agriculture and what it means for the food and nutrition security of the poor. Before going any further at all it would be necessary for me to state at the very outset that the WTO itself is a challenge given the dominance of the stated and unstated agenda of the industrialized, developed, rich western nations to price open our markets for their agricultural products marketed cheap in unfair competition because of a billion dollars a day subsidy they provide their producers while at the same time waging a battle against our domestic support regimes, both of which threaten our food and nutrition security at the national and household levels. Nevertheless, even in this grim scenario there are opportunities provided India's negotiators get the country's priorities right and advocate and defend them honestly.

5. It would be nothing original if I say that Food and Nutrition Insecurity can occur even in the areas abundantly endowed with water and assured irrigation. This has been proved many times over in the past in India. All I shall try to do today is to highlight a major

area, a very major area of food and nutrition insecurity that affects people living in areas that account for 70 per cent of the cultivable area in India which have no assured irrigation with little food to eat and even less employment. *I shall look at the strategies we need in the context of these areas and then at the WTO regime and see what the latter does to the former.* While what I would say would be relevant to farmers all over India, wherever they are, if we are talking of Food and Nutrition Security in the Globalisation context, then our immediate area of attention has to be to where the most vulnerable live and what WTO may mean to them.

6. After the liberalisation process started in India, we have experienced any number of situations where the poor have gone hungrier than before and been thrown out of employment and their livelihood. What the flooding of the Chinese silk did to our own sericulture industry and threw poor women out of employment in their thousand is just one example. Free trade or trade liberalisation has been held up by its protagonists as the most desirable form of ushering in growth though no unambiguous correlation has been established between free trade, growth, poverty reduction and food security, even according to the FAO. I often meet India's own over-enthusiastic free traders who ask rhetorically: "why produce food when we can import?" though elementary common sense will tell us that any dependence on international trade- based food security contradicts all the three basic pillars of food security as defined by the FAO: availability, stability and access. Availability depends upon, among other things, the political willingness of the seller, India's purchasing capabilities over a sustained period of time, stability of prices quoted by the seller and above all "access" which the seller can determine depending upon his unipolar political preferences. Has not a nation of above 1 billion people with all its carrots of a supposedly huge market dangling before the rich world's multi-national corporate houses,

who selectively influence economic and political polices of certain super powers, been sanctioned in very recent years? Even individual Indian scientists have been sanctioned. So, what stability of access are we expecting in a world of liberalized trade? Even if you have the import capacity, where is international reliability in a world of politico-economic sanctions? There is much store set by free trade advocates in the "rules and disciplines" of the AOA and the Uruguay Round. Unfortunately, experience has shown that what matters are not "rules" but who enforces those "rules" from the way the United States and the European Union have been using these very "disciplines" to distort international trade. While these two great Economic powerhouses of the industrialized world have their own mutual problems, we know how they struck a deal on the Blue Box mechanism to limit production in their countries. Thanks to the Blue Box, these developed countries of the world need not reduce the Agriculture Marketing Support they give to their farmers to limit production. As you know, in the United States, farmers are paid not to produce whereas these very powers tell you and me how we cannot give subsidised power to our small and marginal farmers. Now, if that is not distortion of trade, what then is it? *The signals are clear. We need to fight for our agricultural, food and nutrition autonomy. Even internal papers of the FAO acknowledge that international "trade liberalisation can alter not only trade flows between countries but also the incomes of producers of goods and services as well as the purchasing power of consumers." When these are adversely affected, food and nutrition security of hundreds of millions of the poor like marginal farmers, small farmers and rural labour is lost, including in terms of price instability. So, the point to remember is that trade liberalisation is not some sort of manna from heaven, which is nothing but pure good. It is not.* Also, let us look at the consumption patterns in India. We produce about 210 million tonnes of foodgrains. Pending any enlightened diversification of our eating and nutrition habits, a shortfall in our need of rice is very difficult to make up because in terms of world production of rice, it is simply not available to the extent we need, for love or money. Even money, on which is based trade, cannot buy rice at will in the world market. This is one basic scenario. The other is: what happens when, say, both China and India enter the world market for foodgrains at the same time–not necessarily for rice, even for wheat whose surpluses are a lot more certain? What happens to prices and their stability? Which trade can ensure supplies based on predictability, either in terms of quantities or in terms of price? The question "why grow food when we can import" could mean application of a freeze to efforts at enhancing food production in deficient nations or in deficient areas within a nation like India so that the cash-rich, industrialized, developed countries can and will export food to the food-insecure countries based on a billion dollars a day subsidies to their farmers, till it suits their convenience. The three-way consequences of such dependence are obvious (i) World food prices will be depressed affecting exports of nations that do not have the cash to subsidize their own exports to remain competitive in international market making nonsense of rule based trade; (ii) Depressed prices make national food production in the developing world unremunerative threatening food security over all and especially of the poor and (iii) once food producers in developing nations have no market incentive to grow food because of depressed prices, depleted production in the developing world exposes them to dependence on the developed world even more, who thereafter enjoy the freedom of hiking up the prices of their production to further endanger the developing world's food security. Egypt is an outstanding example of having its agriculture ruined because of this ill-informed dependence. India should guard against this possibility. Subversion of agriculture would lead inevitably to subversion of employment avenues for the large masses of our people. The fallacy in the import-based food security argument can be further seen from the implicit condemnation of the resources and resourcefulness of the small and marginal farmers engaged in dryland agriculture in the developing countries of the world like India. There are any number of examples, most notably in the work being done in dryland agriculture in our own State in the Pastapur area of Zaheerabad in Medak district by the Deccan Development Society under P. V. Satheesh, which demonstrates the traditional wisdom and resourcefulness and therefore the self-reliance of our small and marginal farmers. These farmers have demonstrated their capacity to emancipate themselves from hunger through the cultivation of traditional coarse cereals, using environment-friendly organic fertilizers and pesticides, mixed cropping strategies as against monocropping, establishment of gene banks to store and supply seed and use of traditional storage technologies that safeguard the shelf life of these seeds, which run into some 20 varieties, preserving our rich bio-diversity. In this area hunger has been banished and there have been no farmers' suicides. There is little doubt that neither hunger nor poverty will be eliminated in 70 per cent of this nation's geography if the problems of agriculture in these dry-land, drought-prone and desert prone areas and the resource-poor tribal areas of India are not tackled using strategies like the ones used in Pastapur. However, when taken up on a large scale, which we have to, the effort would call for large investments including subsidies in aggregate terms, not to mention the need for production credit and remunerative Minimum Support Prices (MSP). Is it going to be any body's case that we will not support these farmers and help them realize their own potential and achieve their own food security, their own enhanced levels of employment and wages and thus reduction of their poverty, by agreeing to a trade-based food security?

And won't these Pastapur strategies enhance the nutrition security of the people in these vast tracts of our country not only because of new food production, employment and wages but more significantly also because of the nutritive values of these dryland-specific crops such as jowar, ragi, bajra and numerous other small millets? Are we to give up this kind of security in the name of an uncertain and unproven food security predicated on international trade-led growth? The answers are obvious.

7. In the context of Food and Nutrition security of the kind I have alluded to above the following are the essential policy needs in India:

(i) An Agriculture policy that recognizes the need for *Decentralized Agriculture,* which aims at raising levels of productivity across agro-climatic zones right down to the village level which would mean:

   1. *Support to Dryland Agriculture,* including mixed cropping.

      (a) An inputs policy that incorporates Moisture Conservation, Discipline in Ground Water management and closely regulated use of chemical inputs and enhanced use of bio-fertilization and integrated pest control methodologies.

   2. *Public-funded Research* in evolving drought resistant seeds.

      (a) Price incentives through remunerative MSPs for coarse cereals also known as nutritious cereals.

      (b) Purchase mechanisms for local procurement through local institutions.

      (c) A *credit policy* that unambiguously supports these efforts.

All this should be aimed at producing marketable surpluses of nutritious 'coarse' cereals.

Surplus in this context primarily, and to begin with, to mean for food consumption needs (as against industrial raw material needs) with recognition of the primacy of palatability and taste preferences as also storage technologies to enhance shelf life, including, in particular, in the locale of production.

- Decentralized Agricultural strategies should thus lead to easy, local availability of food needs both in terms of price and physical access. In regard to price State intervention should be on both the MSP front for the farmer and the affordability front for the poor through sensitive price interventions.
- Access to the poor must be the result of a combined strategy of affordable prices through public distribution and creation of enhanced purchasing power for the working poor through guaranteed employment - an Employment Guarantee Scheme (EGS) that incorporates the principle of a living wage as provided for in Article 43 of the Constitution.

(ii) *The twin concept of the Right to Work and the Right to Food to a poor household regardless of its purchasing power is the basis for Food and Nutrition security.* The latter principle would embrace classes of people that cannot and should not work and these are infants, children in the age group of 0-6, children at school, adolescent girls, pregnant women, nursing mothers, the old and the infirm and the disabled of all categories. The programme design for a household should integrate these classes of people with the class that is capable of work so that together the household as a unit accesses its full food requirements, with due allowance for menarche, pregnancy etc. These must come from a variety of nutrition programmes and social defence and family benefit measures. *The validity of the successful implementation of this entire concept should be constantly evaluated by the State through concurrent monitoring of levels of hunger at the household level, with the village as the unit.*

(iii) The National Policies on Agriculture, Health, Nutrition, the Public Distribution System, Labour and Women and Child Development should all be viewed as an integrated whole so that the quantitative and qualitative food and nutrient needs of different sections of our people are rationally met. *Nutrition Education* should be deemed as a life skill and built into livelihood concerns of the people so that policies reflect support for the positive needs of the people and discourage undesirable and negative practices. *The Right not to be infected (in a variety of ways) is as much part of the Right to Health and therefore to Life as anything we may conceive under Article 21 of the Constitution. Infection and Nutrition insecurity go hand in hand.*

(iv) The above imperatives would, if brought to bear upon the process of macro policy decision making in the country, will start to act as correctives to the kind of negative policies promoted in the past 15 years in all relevant areas such as Agriculture, the Public Distribution System, Rural Employment, Living Wages, Social Welfare and defence, outlays on Health and Education etc.

The key factors in this strategy are:

DECENTRALIZATION

A. Autonomy

A policy mix that helps the poor access their needs, which are really their fundamental rights, from the general economy on the one hand and the alternate mechanisms that substitute the market for them on the other. At one level an example of this is to make a people-implemented Public Distribution System (PDS) play an integrative, infrastructure role in the delivery of the foodgrains entitlement in the PDS, nutritional and real wage components of the employment programmes and the nutrition component in the ICDS and MDM programmes so that it acts as a delivery mechanism for Food and Nutrition Security, till enlightened integration of macro policies can make a delivery-based Food and Nutrition Security system redundant as we strive for a decentralized, autonomous system of food security.

In all this we have to look at Food and Nutrition Security at the National as well as household level and also ensure inter-personal equity within the household, with particular reference to the needs and rights of children and women.

Our goal should therefore, be autonomous food and nutrition security based on self-sufficiency. This is not some dogma or food fundamentalism. There is nothing fanatic or romantic about it. It is just that we have to be unconditionally free of hunger as a nation and as a people. It is at once the right of a sovereign nation and the sovereign duty of a nation State to itself and its people, especially its poor. This does not mean that we will never import food, that we will never trade in food, or that we will not develop the capacity to import what we want. It only means that in the name of liberalizing trade, we will not become a dependant nation for food on others but will retain the choice to diversify our agriculture to value add and export to the developed world.

8. The issue also is: what kind of social action needs to be generated to compel the powers that be to act as if Food and Nutrition Security of the nation and the poor mattered to them at all?

9. Having stated this bottom line, I acknowledge that we would need additional expenditures and additional financial outlays for all these strategies to be put in place. *This leads us to the question: do we have enough leeway in the WTO framework negotiations to ensure autonomy and freedom in regard to our agriculture and food and nutrition security for our country and for our poor on the lines I have advocated above? The answer is in the positive, as I shall presently show.*

10. The most significant aspect of the Marrakesh Agreement that established the WTO is its preamble which clearly mentions and recognizes the importance of the conduct of the WTO negotiations with a view to raising the

standards of living, ensuring full employment and allowing for the optimal use of the world's resources in accordance with the objectives of sustainable development consistent with the respective needs of countries and concerns at different levels of economic development. Again, in the preamble to the Agreement on Agriculture (AOA) it has been clearly laid down that the commitments made under trade reforms programmes should be equitable, having regard to non-trade concerns, including Food Security and the need to protect the environment, having regard to non-trade concerns and with due regard to the agreement that Special and Differential Treatment (SDT) for developing countries is an integral element of the negotiations, taking into account the possible negative effects of the implementation of the reforms programmes on the least developed and net food-importing developing countries. The reference to SDT is reiterated in clause 1 of Article 15 of the AOA. Admittedly, India is not a least developed country (LDC). However, India is a country of continental proportions. There are vast dry land areas in India that are "least developed and in the domestic context "net food importing" in the sense that 70 per cent of the cultivable land in India is rain-fed and without any kind of assured irrigation facilities. And, thanks to the Green Revolution strategies of the 1960s, just two and half States of the northwest of India alone produce any worthwhile surpluses and consequently "export" food to the rest of the country through state purchases made by the Food Corporation of India. In the vast, poorly endowed areas of the country the human development indices (HDI) are so low that they can be compared with the conditions obtaining in sub-Saharan Africa and other LDCs of the world. Therefore, the principles incorporated in the AOA are eminently applicable to the Indian context. Clause 2 of Article 6 of the AOA refers to Government measures of assistance, direct or indirect, to encourage Agriculture and Rural Development as being an integral part of the development programmes of the developing countries and that, therefore, investment subsidies available to agriculture in developing countries and agricultural input subsidies available to low income or resource-poor producers in developing countries shall be exempt from domestic support reduction commitments expected under the WTO regime. This provision thus totally exempts India from reducing any of the subsidies it currently provides to its farmers such as indirect input subsidies for power, fertilizers and irrigation and direct, product-specific domestic support like Minimum Support Prices (MSP). In any event the level of minimum support prices the Government offers to farmers in India is generally, if not always, below market prices (otherwise, nobody would part with their grains in favour of the Government agencies). Our Aggregate Marketing Support (AMS) is well below the *de minimis* percentage.

11. Annex 2 to the AOA deals with the basis for exemption from the reduction commitments in regard to domestic support. Exemptions can be claimed for Government Service Programmes that benefit agriculture and the rural communities such as research relating to particular products and research in connection with environmental programmes; general and product-specific pest and disease control measures; training services including specialist training facilities; extension and advisory services and the transfer of information and results of research to producers and consumers; expenditures on marketing and promotion services, including market information, advice and promotion relating to particular products and infrastructure services including electricity reticulation, roads and other means of transport, market facilities, water supply facilities, dams and drainage schemes; holding of stocks of products which form an integral part of a food security programmeme identified in national legislation, which may include Government aid to private storage of products; and domestic food aid to sections of the population in need where eligibility is

subject to clearly-defined criteria related to nutritional objectives enabling eligible recipients to buy food at subsidised prices. Footnotes to Annex 2 clarify that expenditures in regard to Government stock holding programmes for food security purposes conducted in accordance with officially published objective criteria or guidelines and provision of foodstuffs at subsidised purposes with the objective of meeting the food requirements of urban and rural poor in developing countries on a regular basis would be in conformity with the WTO exemptions. The same goes for expenditures on Governmental crop insurance participation and environmental programmes that include production methods. There is also specific reference to exemption for payments under regional assistance programmes to clearly designated contagious geographical areas with definable economic and administrative identity, considered as disadvantageous on the basis of objective criteria–a provision directly relevant to the agriculture and food security strategies of the entire vast dryland tracts of India.

12. Para 13 of the Doha Ministerial Declaration of November 2001 in its reference to Agriculture and to Article 20 of the AOA, which is a commitment to further comprehensive negotiations agrees that Special and Differential Treatment (SDT) for developing countries shall be an integral part of all elements of the negotiations so that concessions can be negotiated "to enable developing countries to effectively take account of their development needs, including food security and rural development.... non-trade concerns will be taken into account in the negotiation as provided for in the Agreement on Agriculture". This was further clarified in Clause 44 to make provisions for Special and Differential Treatment "stronger, more precise, effective and operational".

13. Thus, while the AOA of 1994 may be the basic structure, Article 20 of the AOA recognizes the on-going nature of the process of the negotiations, because of the long-term objectives of trade corrections. *Therefore, the point that the enlightened public opinion in India should force the Government of India to recognize and acknowledge publicly is that further negotiations are provided for in the WTO structure, that we now have the principles of the Doha Declaration to defend the interests of India and further the interest of the requirements of the marginalized sections of the Indian society in the forthcoming December 2005 negotiations and therefore it is up to the Government of India and its negotiators to learn about what the poor people's needs are and their rights are and realize the tremendous leeway that is available in the WTO regime to protect those rights by honestly presenting them and fighting for them in the forthcoming negotiations in Hong Kong.*

14. The kind of strategies that I have enumerated in para 8 being the requirement for food and nutrition security for the Indian people, raise wide ranging issues such as financial outlays relating to surface irrigation and watershed programmes; dryland agriculture based on seed sovereignty, public-funded research related to this and other connected aspects like the shelf life of seeds and coarse/nutritious dryland cereals in terms of storage and palatability; remunerative minimum support prices for coarse cereals and private storage subsidies at the community level; subsidies for drilling for ground water in dry land areas and associated capital expenditure for equipment like casing and pipes, sprinklers, subsidies for power for lift irrigation; easy institutional credit availability, including interest subsidies; input subsidies for seeds, bio-fertilizers, bio-pesticides and other chemical inputs; provision of marketing yards with facilities for the farmers including advance payments against storage of grains; crop insurance programmes

with subsidy for the premium payable; consumer subsidies for the targeted poor in the Public Distribution System, ICDS and the Mid Day Meal (MDM) scheme to make food and nutrition security affordable; subsidies to state agencies involved in food procurement and distribution for staff costs, storage costs, transport costs and marketing costs in the context of procurement especially of nutritious coarse cereals; a universal employment guarantee scheme with guaranteed living wages for the participating poor. *All these are consumption stimulating and trade enhancing and not trade-distorting and all these are, therefore, permissible under the WTO regime as shown by me earlier. Only the case for these strategies and the methods for protecting these should be clearly thought out and presented by the Government of India's negotiators at the WTO negotiations for them to be internationally accepted as part of the goals of rule-based trade. It is, therefore, entirely the responsibility of the Government of India to formulate pro-poor strategies for agriculture and agricultural productivity and design and defend distribution programmes that safeguard and promote the food and nutrition security of the poorer sections of the Indian people, including through appropriate programmes that enhance the purchasing capacity of the poor. Often we hear official excuses that the country cannot have such pro-poor programmes because they would fall foul of the WTO regime. This is not so at all. To argue that such enlightened programmes for the poor are hit by the WTO is actually a red herring designed to deny domestically the Indian poor their rights. Enlightened public opinion in India should, therefore, make the marginalized people aware of these facts relating to the WTO and the right kind of policies needed in the Agriculture and Food sectors so that food and nutrition security become a reality for the Indian people and remain so for all time to come.*

15. What are the facts that affect the interests of the farmers and the poor in the WTO context? Today in WTO, we have a basic Agreement on Agriculture. Of the three pillars or blocks of this Agreement on Agriculture, export competition is one. As for export subsidies, since we are not a cash-rich country, there is not much we can do, at least at the present time. Since we had given no worthwhile subsidies at the relevant base period (1986) there is nothing for us to reduce either, in any case. We have no role in this, more or less, at least at the present time. The second block refers to Domestic Support, which includes non-product specific support or input subsidies like those for credit, fertilizers, agriculture marketing, water, power, etc., and product specific support for crops in the form of Minimum Support Prices (MSP). The combination of both represents the Total Aggregate Marketing Support (AMS). We should defend these to whatever the extent necessary to protect our agriculture and our farmers. If we look at the available leeway in the AOA there is no objection whatever to this. This is practically an internal matter for the country and at the present levels of subsidies we are giving we are well within the WTO stipulated limits. That we need internal reforms in this is a fact e.g. ensuring that fertilizers subsidies go to the farmers and not to the manufacturing middlemen. *The Government of India should provide all the support the farmer needs in all these areas domestically and negotiate hard at the WTO, giving up nothing and making no concessions in the negotiations.* Under Domestic Support will also come areas like Extension, Research, stockholding for food security, domestic food aid, Insurance, Environmental protection programmes etc. and these are all Green Box measures i.e. measures which are not trade distorting or only minimally distorting. On this score, there is no obligation on the part of India to reduce support to the farmers since base total measurement of support is below *de minimis* (10 per cent). In fact, public funded research

and strengthening of extension services are the crying need of the hour to stem the onslaught of the dysfunctional effects generated by unregulated, unethical marketing practiced by the inputs trade in India, cheerfully egged on by the liberalizing leaders and Governments of certain States in India which have led to the large scale suicides of farmers. Moisture conservation expenditures will greatly serve environmental protection and dryland agriculture. *Our Government should fight for these and there can be no serious threat to these measures from the Governments of the developed world in the ongoing negotiations. In fact, the threats to these measures are coming internally from some of our own leaders who have no understanding of these issues. That is why I say that we need domestic social action to defend the interests of the farmers' vis-à-vis those of the vested interests. The globalising economists and their friends in the Government who are allied to them need to be countered through organised, social action because it is they who are at the service of the multinational, global capital interests that are dictating priorities in research and scuttling extension efforts by pre-empting public agencies through misleading promotional activities in regard to inputs using fiscal incentives through the informal credit system.* It bears repetition that as far as Aggregate Marketing Support (AMS), that is, Domestic Support is concerned, India has no obligations to reduce it, as our Marketing Support to Agriculture at the relevant, base period was *de minimis*.

16. In the Food and Nutrition context for which protection of our Agriculture is most relevant, the third pillar, namely, Market Access, in other words Tariffs, is the most important lever for India. We have a comfortable position in regard to this and we need to leverage this to the maximum extent possible to our advantage. Tariffs give India the most significant protection. And that is exactly the reason why the industrialized, developed world is bringing to bear upon us all their sophistry for

reduction. India needs to stand firm and not give in to the unreasonable demands of the West in this regard. In fact, of all the developing countries of the world we have the highest bounded tariffs, up to 300 per cent in the case of edible oils, for example. I know that on ground we are imposing only 60 per cent on edible oil but the point is we have the slack to play with. And edible oils are very important for our nutrition security. As we expand our consciousness about what an ideal public distribution system should be and plan how to make Nutrition security as the most essential aspect of the Public Distribution System's goals, dryland agriculture where higher incomes would also be predicated on high value food crops like oilseeds will take centre stage, in addition to the coarse nutritious cereals. So tariffs are important for us. I should also flag the point that time was when in 1948 we had bounded to a 0per cent tariff for rice, wheat and dairy products. That was needed then. However, subsequently in 1999-2000 we negotiated this up to around 80 per cent. We should stick by these limits and ensure that we balance the interests of our producers as well as our consumers. The only antidote from the Indian side to heavy subsidies in the developed world is tariffs. Higher the subsidies in the West, higher should be the tariffs that we should impose against commodities that would jeopardize our food sovereignty and food security.

17. A basic point I want to make is that given all the constraints we are called to face in a globalising world, the central issue for Indian Agriculture and the food and nutrition security of the Indian people is that we have to re-appraise our approach to agriculture on the lines I have outlined earlier. To be competitive abroad and to stimulate consumption by our own people and our poor, our Agriculture needs to become cost effective. Our agriculture is so high cost that even if the European Union reduces its tariffs to 0 per cent, countries of the developing world themselves like Brazil and Argentina

would out bid us in those markets. Therefore, enhanced domestic market support to our farmers by way of increased infrastructure investments, for which there is no objection, is the answer. In other words, we should recognize the important lesson that the three pillars of the AOA and WTO negotiations are inter-twined and inter-dependant. Not that the Indian Government's negotiators do not know this but they should be made to know that the ordinary citizen also knows this and knowing this, the ordinary Indian citizen should hold the Indian Government accountable in terms of how the Government are calibrating the negotiations on these three pillars, leveraging our strengths and not compromising on our Agriculture and Food and Nutrition Security needs. If the ordinary citizens do not organize themselves to do this, surely the Government is going to be indifferent to these needs. Considering that neither the average farmer nor the poor have a lobby with the Commerce Ministry and, what is worse, the emerging powerful, non-agriculture interests may persuade the Commerce Ministry to trade off at the negotiating table these vital interests in return for concession in non-agricultural areas that benefit only certain elite and already advantaged interests of the country, there is absolute need for social action based on organization of the small and marginal farmers and dry land farmers and the poor every where in the context of Agriculture and Food and Nutrition Security.

18. I am optimistic that a seminar like the one we are having here can organize this mobilization. The reasons for optimism also stem from the fact that the Doha Mandate, approved by the Ministers after nine long months of negotiations, has emphasized India's major concern relating to Food and Livelihood securities. Also, we have in the WTO Agreement a call for taking note of non-trade concerns, as already noted. Rural environment protection is one such non-trade concern and obviously it can be no body's case in the West that agriculture is not friendly

to the environment vis-à-vis industries and especially the kind of ecology-friendly dryland agriculture advocated by me here. *Only, we do not know if the Indian State believes in such an agriculture policy. Hence my submission regarding the Social Action we need to ensure that the voice of India in the negotiating chambers in Hong Kong articulates the essential needs and interests of the common people of India, its marginalized farmers and the poor.* The position as it now stands is that we have in the July 2004 Framework for agriculture opportunities for further negotiations through which we can defend and enhance our commitment to poverty reduction strategies, Food and Nutrition Security and livelihood concerns. Though India has itself been demanding that Product Specific Support be capped, AMS is cumulatively negative for all our agriculture production. Therefore, there will be no need for us to be worried if we decide to enhance our MSPs for coarse cereals etc., and even maintain and enhance our MSPs for rice and wheat. That way there should be no danger to our food security. However, the danger will come from market access and demand for lowering of our tariffs to agricultural products from the developed countries. That is where tariffs are a matter of life and death for us and we should defend them at all costs. Why should we be frightened or fight shy of standing up to the illogic of a $360 billion subsidy–a billion a day–and refuse to bring down our tariffs on agricultural products? *It all boils down to their subsidies versus our tariffs.* Further, in regard to market access, there are commodities that are called "sensitive products", the meaning of which is to be defined in the future through negotiations. The United States believes sugar to be a sensitive product and will agree only to the absolute minimum reduction of tariff in the case of sugar. Now, here is our opportunity. Let us identify what, from our point of view of food and nutrition security, are sensitive products and refuse to bring down our tariffs. Also, under what is called the principle of "Special Products" for developing countries India can nominate these products e.g., cereals and edible oils based on our rural development and food security needs and agree to only minimal reduction in tariffs. The framework for agricultural negotiations has clearly given the flexibility for developing countries to designate appropriate number of special products based on the criteria of Food Security, Livelihood Security and Rural Development. *Let us bring into the negotiations all the dimensions of these concerns.* Also, there is the Special Safeguard Mechanism that can be set in motion whenever there is a "surge in imports" that affects our agriculture adversely, provided we can prove injury to our agriculture. *Our farmers are poorly organised no doubt for this entire contingency, but appropriate organization and social action led by intellectuals can remedy this.* Meanwhile, India can show during negotiations how unlimited volumes of import can endanger and injure our agriculture and our future food security. Hand in hand, we should keep the pressure on to make the developed countries stick to their commitment to reduce their subsidies, direct and indirect.

19. To conclude, the opportunity is available to us to protect our Food and Nutrition Security, though as we meet here today it is certainly not guaranteed. *The entire WTO regime has clearly recognized Food and Nutrition security and Livelihood Security as fundamental to the ongoing negotiations but it is entirely up to those in power in India to define comprehensively and in detail what these should mean to the people of India and make the country's negotiators use it during the further negotiations provided for in the existing AOA. The mandate clearly exists now for the Government of India to negotiate an autonomous Food and Nutrition Security for our people. The ball is squarely in the Government of India's court.* I commend my submissions made in this paper to you in furthering that mandate, both as a challenge and an opportunity.

The essence of the challenge is this: trade is a game that involves competition and moves and counter-moves. There is inequality between nations and the more powerful ones obviously are looking for domination over the rest in the name of a rule-based world. What is at stake is the very right to life of the poorer citizens of the developing world. The primary responsibility for defending and promoting this right of the poor rests with the Governments of these countries. India's political leadership, therefore, has a huge responsibility in the context of the WTO regime to safeguard and promote the Food and Nutrition Security of the nation and its more disadvantaged citizens. This it can do if it honestly makes the right choices and shows a willingness to confront the industrialized rich countries of the world in regard to the interests of its people using every avenue available in the framework. Conviction born of the inalienable rights of the poor and a willingness to display courage to fight for them even if it involves confrontation with the rich and the powerful of the world is the need of the hour. The opportunity to show principled courage is always one that should be welcomed.

IMPACT OF GLOBALISATION ON SMALL SCALE INDUSTRY IN INDIA —A STUDY

A. Annadurai

India has a long entrepreneurial tradition with craftsmen of different hues catering to a variety of needs of the people at the village level for centuries. The indispensable role of such decentralised industrial activities for employment generation and achievement of local self sufficiency in certain types of essential consumer goods was recognised and emphasised upon in the Industrial Policy Resolutions of 1948 and 1956 as well as in the Industries (development and Regulation) Act of 1951. Organised development of the small scale sector (SSI) can be said to have begun with this.

If a sector were to contribute more than 40 per cent of the gross turnover in manufacturing activities and exports of manufactured products in a country, it deserves all encouragement to play its rightful role in industrial development. The small scale industries can lay claim to this with over 36 lakh units providing employment to 20 million persons and producing goods worth over Rs. 7,42,021 crore of which Rs. 80,919 crore worth are exported.

The small scale industry has played a very important role in the socio–economic development of our country over the period of 50 years. The SSI is given a special emphasis, as they are the vehicles of creating additional employment through low capital investment. SSIs have very important role in the national economy offering scope for individual, village or cooperative enterprises and means for rehabilitation of displaced persons. These industries are particularly suited for the better utilisation of local resources and for the achievement of local self-sufficiency in respect of certain essential consumer goods. They offer a method ensuring more equitable distribution of national income and facilitate effective mobilisation of resources of capital and skill, which might otherwise remain uncivilised.

The Government of India has made considerable efforts to develop this sector since the planning era. A number of measures such as package of incentives, launching development programmes, enhancing plan allocation and financial support through the network of financial institution has been continuously taking place.

The role of the SSI sector becomes crucial in this context, because small enterprises by their very nature have a strong a local content and relevance. They utilise local resources and skills and meet the needs of local markets. Being dispersed all over the country, the sector can network the local industries into the national economy. It can correct regional imbalances in economic development and help transform traditional skills into industrial ventures and thus give a boost to swedesh.

The small scale industry sector, which is an important segment of the Indian economy accounts for more than 90 per cent of the industrial units, 40 per cent of the manufacturing sector output, 34 per cent of exports, 6.75 per cent of GDP and provides direct employment to 20 million persons in around 3.6 million registered SSI units in our nation.

Therefore, massive benefits are obtained from this sector and it is right time to analyse the impact of globalisation in this sector.

OBJECTIVES

The objectives of the present study are:

1. To study the present status of SSI in India.
2. To examine the growth of SSI during the pre-economic and post-economic reform period.
3. To examine some performance indicators such as value of output, employment and export for the period under study.

METHODOLOGY

The present study aims at a detailed analysis on the impact of Globalisation in SSI. The study is based on secondary data from DC (Small Scale Industry), Government of India. Compound Growth rate and percentages have been used for the purpose of analysis of trend in the post and pre-reform period for the SSI.

The plan outlay of Small Scale Industries are presented in Table 1

Table 1
Allotment of Funds in Small Scale Industries in India Under Five-Year Plan

Five-Year Plans	*Period*	*Plan Outlay*	*SSI Outlay*	*Share of per cent*
First	1951-1956	3,870	5.02	0.13
Second	1956-61	7,900	56.00	0.71
Third	1961-66	11,600	113.06	0.97
Fourth	1967-74	24,850	96.19	0.39
Fifth	1974-79	53,410	227.74	0.42
Sixth	1980-85	158,710	661.10	0.42
Seventh	1985-90	348,150	1120.00	0.42
Eighth	1992-97	8,71,000	2862.10	0.33
Nineth	1997- 02	28,69,728	3319.42	0.12

Note: Figures in bracket indicate percentage growth over the previous year.

Source: DC (SSI) Government of India, New Delhi.

It is noticed that there is an increasing trends in the absolute value of outlay over the plan period. But, it is noteworthy point i.e. not even one per cent in any plan period.

Even then, the notable contribution from this sector is derived in our nation.

It is inferred here that, the allocation of outlay for this sector should be increased atleast one per cent, which is the need of the hour for occupying better position under the globalisation era.

The growth of small-scale industries on the basis of number of units has been presented in Table 2.

Table 2
Growth Performance of Small Scale Industries in India (Pre and Post-Reform Period)

Pre-Reform			*Post-Reform*		
Years	*No. of units (in lakhs)*	*Growth Rate percent*	*Years*	*No. of units (in lakhs)*	*Growth rate percent*
1979-80	8.05		1991-92	20.82	6.88
1980-81	8.74	8.57	1992-93	22.35	7.35
1981-82	9.62	10.07	1993-94	23.84	6.67
1982-93	10.53	9.67	1994-95	25.71	7.66
1983-84	11.50	9.00	1995-96	26.58	3.86
1984-85	12.42	8.00	1996-97	28.03	5.46
1985-86	13.56	9.18	1997-98	29.44	5.03
1986-87	14.64	7.96	1998-99	30.80	4.62
1987-88	15.86	8.33	1999-00	32.12	4.29
1988-89	17.12	7.94	2000-01	33.12	3.11
1989-90	18.26	6.66	2001-02	34.12	3.91
1990-91	19.48	6.68	2002-03*	35.72	4.69
Average Growth Rate		8.37			5.29

Note: Figures in bracket indicate percentage growth over the previous year.

Source: DC (SSI) Government of India, New Delhi.

Projections are worked out by taking average of last three years growth rate.

The growth performance of SSI Units has been increased in both pre and post-reform period in absolute number. But, the average growth rate performance was 8.37 per cent in

Pre reform period and the average growth rate of performance is 5.29 per cent in Post-reform period.

There has been a continuous increase in the number of small scale industries during the study period. This number increased by two times during the pre-reform period, that is, 8.05 lakh in 1979–80 to 19.48 lakh in 1990-91, while it has increased from 20.82 lakh in 1991-92 to 35.72 lakh in 2002–2003.

While comparing, the performance on the basis of growth rate, the pre-reform period is quite satisfactory than the post-reform period. It is also alarming to note that, the annual growth rate of SSI is on the decline in recent years. The reason for this declining trend is due to changes in the government and their policies.

Table 3
Employment Opportunities From Small Scale Industries in India (Pre and Post-Reform Period)

Pre-Reform			*Post-Reform*		
Years	*Employment (in lakhs)*	*Growth Rate percent*	*Years*	*Employment (in lakhs)*	*Growth rate percent*
1979-80	8.05		1991-92	20.82	6.88
1979-80	6.70		1991-92	13.00	3.75
1980-81	7.10	5.97	1992-93	13.40	3.08
1981-82	7.50	5.63	1993-94	13.90	3.73
1982-93	7.90	5.33	1994-95	14.60	5.04
1983-84	8.40	6.33	1995-96	15.26	4.52
1984-85	9.00	7.14	1996-97	16.00	4.85
1985-86	9.60	6.67	1997-98	16.72	4.50
1986-87	10.10	5.21	1998-99	17.16	2.63
1987-88	10.70	5.94	1999-00	17.85	4.02
1988-89	11.30	5.61	2000-01	18.56	3.98
1989-90	12.00	6.19	2001-02	19.22	3.66
1990-91	12.50	4.17	2002-03*	19.97	3.90
Average Growth Rate		5.84			3.98

Note: Figures indicate percentage growth over the previous year.
Source: DC (SSI) Government of India, New Delhi.
*Projections are worked out by taking average of last three years growth rate.

The employment scenario during pre-and post reform period is shown in Table 3.

With regard to employment opportunities provided by the small scale industries in the post reform period the average growth rate is 5.84 per cent as compared with pre-reform period which was 3.98 per cent. It is observed from after the reform period that the employment opportunities from SSI sector are not satisfactory.

The Table shows the continuous increase in the number of persons employed in small scale industries. The Table also reveals that in the pre-reform period the employment growth rate was more than 5 per cent, low rate of 4.17 per cent in 1990-91.

Table 4
Value of Output in Small Scale Industries in India (Pre And Post-reform Period)

Years	*Value of Output (in crore)*		*Years*	*Value of Output (in crore)*	
1979-80	21635		1991-92	178699	15.00
1980-81	28060	29.70	1992-93	209300	17.12
1981-82	32600	16.20	1993-94	241648	15.46
1982-93	35000	7.40	1994-95	298886	23.69
1983-84	41620	18.90	1995-96	362656	21.34
1984-85	50520	21.38	1996-97	411858	13.57
1985-86	61228	21.20	1997-98	462641	12.33
1986-87	72250	18.00	1998-99	520650	12.54
1987-88	87300	20.83	1999-00	572887	10.03
1988-89	106430	21.88	2000-01	639024	11.54
1989-90	132320	24.36	2001-02	690316	8.03
1990-91	155340	17.40	2002-03*	742021	7.49
Average Growth Rate		19.75			14.00

Note: Figures indicate percentage growth over the previous year.
Source: DC (SSI) Government of India, New Delhi.
*Projections are worked out by taking average of last three years growth rate.

A trend of the low growth is seen in the post- reform period, while it shows highest rate of 5.04 per cent in 1994-95.

Further, this growth rate has been at a level of 2.63 per cent during the year 1998–99. This is seen as the lowest rate in employment for the entire period of study.

The output value of small scale Industries has been furnished in Table 4.

The value of output from SSI post-reform period is at 19.75 per cent, in the pre reform period it was 14 per cent. When we compare the output value from this sector after the reform period is dissatisfactory.

It is noticed that there is a fluctuating trend in the absolute value of output of small scale industries both in pre and post-reform periods. In the pre-reform period the production value of small scale industries have been increased from Rs. 21635 crore in 1979-80 to Rs.155340 crore in 1990-91, i.e. seven times.

In the post-reform period the value of production of small scale Industries has increased from Rs. 178699 crore in 1991-92 to 742021 crore in 2002-03 i.e. four times.

From the above analysis it may be concluded that the post-reform period is dissatisfactory when compared to the pre-reform period.

It is observed from the Table 5 that the export performance of SSI during the pre-reform period is 21.25 per cent and Post-reform period it is 19.60 per cent. It is also observed from the table the export performance is satisfactory because the export performance is showing increase in the absolute value during the study period.

Where exports value is concerned, there was fluctuation in export in the first five years of pre-reform period. However, there has been an increasing trend in the next five years.

During post-reform period the years 1991-92 and 1993-94 have shown high growth rates. However, in the following years there has been a declining trend. The reason for this declining trend is due how to the SSI sector relates to adequate and timely bank credit and low capacity utilisation and variety of operational problems related to demand, power, finance and so on.

Table 5
Value of Exports From Small Scale Indsutries in India
(Pre and Post-reform Perod)

Years	*Value of Export (in crore)*	*Growth Rate percent*	*Years*	*Value of Export (in crore)*	*Growth Rate percent*
1979-80	1226		1991-92	13883	(38.48)
1980-81	1643	(34.00)	1992-93	17784	(28.10)
1981-82	2071	(26.05)	1993-94	25307	(42.30)
1982-93	2045	(-1.26)	1994-95	29068	(14.86)
1983-84	2164	(5.82)	1995-96	36470	(25.46)
1984-85	2541	(17.42)	1996-97	39248	(7.62)
1985-86	2769	(8.97)	1997-98	44442	(13.23)
1986-87	3643	(31.56)	1998-99	48979	(10.21)
1987-88	4372	(20.00)	1999-00	54200	(10.66)
1988-89	5489	(25.55)	2000-01	69797	(28.78)
1989-90	7625	(38.91)	2001-02	71244	(2.07)
1990-91	9664	(26.74)	2002-03*	80919	(13.58)
Average Growth Rate		21.25			19.60

Note: Figures indicate percentage growth over the previous year.
Source: DC (SSI) Government of India, New Delhi.
*Projections are worked out by taking average of last three years growth rate.

The Table 5 shows that the growth rate of export has not been any clear trend. The rate has been widely fluctuating over the study period of 24 years.

In terms of growth rate, the pre-reform period was showing the export value as increasing from Rs. 1226 crore in 1980-81 to Rs. 9664 crore in 1990-91, i.e. eight times.

As shown in the post–reform period the export value as increasing from Rs. 13883 crore in 1991-92 to Rs. 80919 crore in 2002-03, i.e. more than five times.

The foregoing analysis clearly indicates that the growth rate of export value in both the pre-reform period and the post–reform periods are encouraging and also there is a scope for further improvement of export volume. Therefore, the government may take appropriate measures for this area.

Table 6
Small Scale Industry Exports as Percentage of Production and Small Scale Industry Share in Total Exports in India (Pre and Post Reform Period)

	Pre-Reform				Post–Reform		
Years	*Value of Exports (in crore)*	*SSI Exports as a percent age of production*	*SSI Share in total Export*	*Years*	*Value of Exports (in crore)*	*SSI Exports as a percent age of production*	*SSI Share in total Export*
1979-80	1226.30			1991-92	13883.40	7.77	29.70
1980-81	1643.20	5.86	24.50	1992-93	17884.80	8.50	31.50
1981-82	2070.60	6.35	24.50	1993-94	25307.10	10.47	33.50
1982-93	2045.00	5.84	26.50	1994-95	29068.20	9.89	36.40
1983-84	2164.00	5.20	23.00	1995-96	36470.20	10.24	35.20
1984-85	2540.80	5.03	21.90	1996-97	39248.50	9.51	34.30
1985-86	2769.10	4.52	22.10	1997-98	44442.20	9.55	33.40
1986-87	3643.70	5.04	25.40	1998-99	48979.20	9.28	35.20
1987-88	4373.00	5.01	29.00	1999-00	54200.50	9.20	34.60
1988-89	5489.60	5.16	27.80	2000-01	69776.50	10.90	34.00
1989-90	7625.70	5.76	27.00	2001-02	71244.00	10.30	34.50
1990-91	9664.10	6.22	27.50	2002-03 *	80919.00	10.90	34.30

Note: Figures indicate percentage growth over the previous year

Source: DC (SSI) Government of India, New Delhi.

·Projections are worked out by taking average of last three years growth rate.

As observed from Table 6 export as a percentage of production of SSI has been studied for the pre-reform and post-reform periods.

The export percentage from SSI sector production and SSI share in total production have increased is both pre-reform and post-reform period.

In the pre-reform period, the export percentage from SSI sector production and SSI share in total production ranged between 4 to 6 per cent and 19-29 per cent, respectively.

In the post-reform period, the export percentage from SSI sector and SSI share in total production ranges between 7 to 11 and 30-37 respectively.

It is also clearly reveals that a significant contribution is provided by SSI after the globalisation also which is remarkable. It is high time to make hay while the sun shines.

The foregoing facts, figures and analysis clearly reveals that under globalisation era, there are a lot of challenges to face in order to harvest the opportunities.

CONCLUSION

The study concludes that, the SSI has shown that it is strong enough to grow in an era of globalisation, with its attendant competition. The number of SSI units has risen from 20.82 lakhs in 1991-92 to 35.72 lakhs in 2002-03. During this period the value of production has risen from Rs. 178,648 crore to Rs. 742,021 crore, employment from 13 million to 20 million and exports from Rs. 13,883 crore to Rs. 80,919 crore.

The SSI sector is capable of producing goods for mass consumption at competitive prices. Hence, the units should be encouraged to manufacture branded goods of large companies by providing suitable exercise concession. The SSI makes an important contribution to industrial production and exports. It has been felt that the Index of Industrial Production (IPP) should have a fair representation of the SSI sector and to help improve the quality of SSI products, testing facilities at the clusters of SSI concentrations by the SSI Associations with a one-time grant from the Government.

The Government can act quickly to provide necessary requirements for this sector and the Central Government budgetary allocation and plan outlay have been very low. It is right time to allocate more funds. These are the requirements of the sector under remedial steps to promote. This augurs well for the future of the SSI sector.

REFERENCES

Rama, Prasad M.V. "WTO and its implications on Indian SSI" Indian Economic Panorama, p. 4-7.

Venugopa, K., "Challenges of Small-Scale Industries in Era of Economic Reforms." *Indian Economic Panorama,* p. 1-6.

Sreeramulu, D. "Growth & Overall Performance of Indian Small Scale Enterprises" *Indian Economic Panorama,* p. 20-21.

Renu Verma, "Performance of Small Scale Industries (pre and post reform period) *Economic Affairs* Vol. 49 Qr. 3 Sept.' 04, p. 174-180.

Jaya Singh, "SSI Small Industries, Big Scope" *Kisan World,* August 03, p. 26 & 27.

Pankaj Jain, "SSI Sector in the Tenth Plan Leveraging on Competitiveness" *Loghu Udyog Samachar,* April-Sep. 2002, p. 27-32.

GLOBALISATION AND TRADE IN SERVICES EMERGING TRENDS AND IMPLICATIONS FOR INDIA

M.V. Lakshmi & B. Meena Rao

INTRODUCTION

The services sector is an important driving force in economic development, competitiveness, and productivity. And, the expansion and globalisation of services is of great significance due to the inter-linkages of services with other sectors of the economy. Part 1 of this paper gives a brief introduction to the emerging trends in the service economies and the growing potential for international trade in services. Part 2 ponders a little on the issues of defining and measuring services. Part 3 briefly discusses the World Trade Organisation GATS framework; GATS classification of the services sectors and modes of service supply; and the ongoing negotiations for liberalisation of trade in services. In Part 4 the performance of India's services sector; and the sectors and modes of service delivery in which India has a competitive advantage are discussed. Some concluding remarks are made in Part 5 on the challenges and opportunities for India under the impact of emerging trends in the competing global environment and the ongoing GATS negotiations.

GLOBALISATION AND THE SERVICE ECONOMY

Over the past two decades, the services sector is playing an increasingly important role in the economies of all industrialised and most developing countries. The services sector encompasses a wide range of areas and activities-from traditional areas such as transport, communication, and tourism to new and dynamic areas like software, environmental, and educational services. In 1997, service sector output was valued at $6.6 trillion or about 60 per cent of global output of goods and services. Although the developed countries have dominated this expansion, accounting for three quarters of world services output, the contribution of services has increased significantly in developing countries as well. (Rupa Chanda, 2001). Moreover, infrastructural services (transportation, communication, financial services) give the support necessary for any type of business. Increasingly even in the production of goods, the major proportion of value added (up to 70per cent) comes from services inputs-(UPSTREAM–such as feasibility studies, and research and development activities); ONSTREAM–such as accounting, engineering, administrative and other business services); DOWN-STREAM–such as advertising, warehousing and distribution).

The sector constitutes close to 70 per cent of production and employment in the OECD countries. Services output and employment have also witnessed rapid growth in developing countries during the past two decades. In some developing countries, services today constitute over 50 per cent of economic activity, significantly more than traditional sectors such as agriculture. (Rupa Chanda, 2002a).

INTERNATIONAL TRADE AND INVESTMENT IN SERVICES

The services sector is the fastest growing area in international trade. There has been considerable expansion in service sector trade and investment flows. World exports of services are substantial at an estimated $1.4 trillion, or about one-quarter of global merchandise exports. The developed countries account for the bulk of trade in services. Between 1990-2000, world exports of commercial services kept pace with the growth in merchandise exports, at an average rate of 6 per cent per year. Recent estimates indicate that the service sector accounts for some 40 per cent of the global annual stock of foreign direct investment (FDI), at about $30 billion, and for 50 per cent of world annual FDI flows, with the developed countries again accounting for the majority of this FDI.(Rupa Chanda, 2002a). The huge potential of the services trade both as an engine of domestic and export growth cannot be overlooked as services account for two-thirds of world's economic activity and WTO statistics reveal that during 1990-2002 export world-wide of services trade rose by 190.8 per cent to USD 1540 billion and about 60 per cent of service trade is concentrated among the 10 developed nations of the world. World exports of commercial services has increased from USD Billion 940.6 in 1993 to USD 1796.5 Billion in 2003. World imports have increased from USD 958.3 Billion in 1993 to USD 1782.4 Billion in 2003. (WTO, 2004b).

World merchandise exports rose by 16 per cent to $7.3 trillion and commercial services exports by 12 per cent to $1.8 trillion in 2003. For both merchandise and services trade, this was the strongest annual increase in nominal terms since 1995. (See Table 1).

Table 1
World Exports of Merchandise and Commercial Services, 1990-2003

	Value	*Annual Percentage Change*			
	2003	*1990-2000*	*2001*	*2002*	*2003*
Merchandise	7,274	6	-4	4	16
Commercial services	1,763	7	0	6	12

Source: WTO, 2004.

Several developing countries too, have participated in the globalisation of services. For example, India and the Philippines have carved a niche for themselves in the global market and have emerged as leading exporters of software services. In several services sectors, that include construction and engineering, audio-visual, health-related services and education services, developing countries have considerable export potential, mainly due to the availability of skilled and abundant labour. In recent times India has also become a leading player in high-end knowledge-based services.

In services like insurance, transport, and telecommunications, many developing countries are increasingly becoming important destination markets for investment, due mainly to their huge capital and technology requirements in these areas. Since many developing countries have embarked on ambitious reform and privatization programmes in various service sectors, the importance of services trade and FDI is bound to increase further.

DEFINING AND MEASURING SERVICES: SOME ISSUES

Most of the theoretical and conceptual interest in international trade in services dates back no further than the 1970s. Before then services were commonly considered as typical non-traded activities, involving production for the domestic market, and by domestic factors only. In a similar vein many economists defined services as necessarily involving simultaneous production and consumption, defining away the possibility of an internationally tradable service product. Macro economic definitions typically describe services as 'residual' economic activities which are not agricultural, mining and or manufacturing activities. There is no single universally agreed definition of services although a number of alternatives do exist.

SOME UNIQUE QUALITIES OF SERVICES

The difficulty in defining services and measuring service activity is the result of their unique qualities like:

Experience based and intangible: Frequently customers receiving services are not certain of what they will receive until the services is actually performed.(e.g. abdominal surgery).

Simultaneous: Services are often delivered as they occur face-to-face with the customer (e.g. during a live music performance).

Location specific: Because of this simultaneity services frequently need to be delivered at the point of consumption. (e.g., restaurants, colleges etc.)

Unable to be stored: Most services cannot be stored. Each time they are produced, services provided may involve significant variation.

REDEFINING SERVICES IN THE ERA OF GLOBALISATION

Each of the above characteristics creates particular difficulties and challenges in the provision and export of services. Hence, it is difficult to provide a universal definition for services which captures the heterogeneity and range of activities within this sector. Also, the traditional definition of services, which focuses on the three distinguishing features of non-storability, non-tradability, and intangibility, is too static. And also inappropriate in a world where transnational corporations and rapid advances in information and communication technologies have transformed and globalized the service sector (Rupa Chanda,2002a). *And services trade is now commonly considered as involving the international movement of factors of production, products and consumers.*

TRADE IN SERVICES: GATS FRAMEWORK

One of the most important achievements of the Uruguay Round was the General Agreement on Trade in Services (GATS) which for the first time brought the services trade under the discipline of WTO. GATS is one of the 28 Accords agreed upon in the Uruguay Round and embedded in the Final Act. The GATS architecture consists of three main elements, namely: general rules and principles; commitments in specific sectors and across sectors; and sectoral annexes and various attachments to the agreements. The WTO General Agreement on Trade in Services (GATS) establishes rules on trade and investment in services consisting of a core set of disciplines including most favoured nation (MFN) treatment, market access, and national treatment[1]. GATS also identifies four modes of service delivery based on the territorial presence of supplier and consumer at the time of the transaction.

GATS: CLASSIFICATION OF SERVICES

The entire gamut of trade in services is divided into 12 sectors (see Box. 1) and further sub-divided into 161 sub-sectors.

Box 1
GATS Classification of Services (By Sector)

Business services (including professional services, IT-related services, R & D)	Financial services (banking, insurance and all services related to security.
Communication services Construction and related engineering services	Health-related and social services Tourism and travel-related services
Distribution services	Recreational, cultural and sporting services
Educational services	Transport services
Environmental services	Other services not included elsewhere (the "catch all" category)

GATS: 4 MODES OF SERVICE SUPPLY

The GATS identifies four modes of supply. The four modes of supply classify transactions depending on the territorial presence of supplier(service provider) and consumer(service user) at the time of the transaction.

MODE 1: CROSS-BORDER TRADE/SUPPLY

In this mode the service is embodied in transportable media such as a paper document, computer diskettes, or digitized and transmitted via telecom links. Cross border trade in services is analogous to trade in good.

MODE 2: CONSUMPTION ABROAD

This, mode 2 refers to services trade where the consumer of the service moves to the country that produces the services, as in the case of tourism.

MODE 3: COMMERCIAL PRESENCE

Commercial presence occurs when there is establishment of service operations in the consuming country, such as setting up of a bank branch offices or law offices overseas. It is analogous to foreign direct investment.

MODE 4: MOVEMENT OF NATURAL PERSONS

Movement of natural persons involves the delivery of the services through the movement of service suppliers through the presence of natural persons in the territory of the consumer, E.g. physical movement of professionals, skilled and unskilled labour for temporary period, etc. not covering permanent migration.

Thus, the above GATS classification of four modes of service supply reflects a novel approach and addresses the complexity in the nature of international transactions in services; the diverse forms–goods, human capital, information-in which services are embodied as also in terms of consumption, production, and distribution related activities. Such a classification also brings into the purview of GATS regulatory issues relating to investment policies and immigration and labour market legislation that were earlier outside the domain of the multilateral trading system.(Rupa Chanda, 2002a, 2003).

GATS: BUILT-IN AGENDA

The GATS mandate has called for a fresh round of comprehensive negotiations for obtaining specific commitments starting from 1 January 2000. Under Article XIX of GATS, Member-nations "shall enter into successive rounds of negotiations beginning not later than five years from the date of entry into force of the WTO Agreement, and periodically thereafter, with a view to achieving a progressively higher level of liberalisation." The main objective is to achieve a greater degree of liberalisation in all the 12 service sectors in the GATS' Services Sectoral Classification list, and four modes of services delivery recognized by GATS.

ONGOING NEGOTIATIONS AND EMERGING ISSUES

The complexities of services trade are such that the scope of trade liberalisation that could be negotiated in the Uruguay Round was limited. Most of the national commitments - including India-annexed in the schedules are unbound in four modes of supply of services. Under the mandated negotiations, the most important decision so far taken was the Agreement on Guidelines for Services Negotiations on 28 March 2001 in the special session of the Council of Trade in Services. And the Doha Ministerial declaration provides for recogniging the work already undertaken under the mandated negotiations initiated in January 2000 as the basis for future negotiations. The method of negotiations that had been adopted in the case of services under the WTO is the request-offer approach. The Doha Ministerial Declaration had required members to submit initial requests by June 30, 2002, and make initial offers by March 31, 2003 in order to further the negotiations under GATS.

Services negotiation during the Uruguay Round did not go beyond establishing the basic framework or rules and disciplines and resulted in a preliminary set of commitments that were neither deep nor extensive. Today, there has been much criticism about the failure to realise meaningful liberalisation under the GATS. For most developing countries and even for developed countries, there is a wedge between the existing degree of openness to services trade and investment and the level of binding in commitments made by countries. Most recently, the initial offers that have been made under the GATS 2000 discussions indicate a continued unwillingness on the part of countries to lock in their policies on market access and national treatment for foreign service providers. The failure to achieve meaningful commitments is in large part due the voluntary and flexible nature[2] of the commitment structure under the GATS.

INDIA'S SERVICE SECTOR

The services sector in India is growing rapidly and the share of services in India's GDP increased to 54.2 per cent in 2000-01 from 51.5 per cent in 1998-99. During the 1990s the Indian services sector grew at more than 17 per cent per annum compared to the world average growth rate of 5.6 per cent. Most of the rapid growth has been in the information technology and business process outsourcing services. However the telecommunications, financial sector and the tourism and travel industry have also shown an encouraging growth curve.

INDIA'S SERVICE EXPORTS

India has participated in the globalisation of services. In 1999-2000, India's trade in services was estimated at about $30 billion (Rupa Chanda, 2001). While India's share in global merchandise trade is around 0.9 per cent, the share of Indian services exports is slightly higher at 1.4 per cent of the total world trade in services. The WTO statistics show that India has emerged as one of the dynamic suppliers of services in the world and is ranked 21st in export of services and 27th in service imports. However, the need to move faster assumes greater importance, considering that even countries like Hong Kong, Singapore and the Republic of Korea have a share of 2.9 per cent, 1.8 per cent and 1.9 per cent respectively in the global services trade. (Srivastava, 2004). India's export of commercial services grew from USD

5034 million in 1993 to USD 25043 million in 2003 and imports from USD 6356 Million in 1993 to USD 21593 in 2003 (WTO, 2004b).

GATS: INDIA'S COMMITMENTS

Though India has strong reservation to open up all service sectors to foreign competition on MFN basis and to extend national treatment, it has submitted a comprehensive list of commitments to the GATS liberalising its services trade. In total, India has made commitments in 33 activities, compared with an average of 23 for the developing countries. These commitments generally bind India's existing policy framework, though in some cases applied policy may be more liberal than the binding commitments. India has not made any commitments on services relating to distribution, education, environment, recreational, cultural and sporting, transport etc. India has further liberalized its commitments in the basic telecommunication services in early 1998. Along with the list of commitments, India also submitted a list of services, for which it wants exemptions from MFN treatment. The areas of services are: telecommunication services, audio-visual services, shipping services and recreational services.

In most of the service sectors included in the schedules, India's commitments are unbound in all modes of supply with some exceptions. This may be market access (MFN) and national treatment (Article III). A few sectors are discussed below.

TELECOMMUNCATION SECTOR

In voice telephone services, which is limited to local/long distance for public use over a public telecommunication transport network, the limited market access is permitted under Mode 3, it is provided only after the operator gets a license from the Designated Authority (DA) who shall determine the need, if any, for issuance of new licenses. The DA or government or the prevailing laws in the country will lay down the terms and conditions of the license. On electronic mail, voice mail, on-line information and database retrieval and value added facsimile, market access is permitted only through incorporation with a foreign equity ceiling of 51 per cent (mode 3) and unbound (mode 4). On the cellular mobile telephone services, market access through mode 3 is permitted only after the operator gets a license from the DA who shall determine the need, if any, for issuance of new licenses. Only digital (GSM) technology will be permitted and this will only be terrestrial based. There will be two cellular service operators in each service area. The position will be reviewed after 10 years. The right of DoT/MTNL to enter into each service area is reserved. The private operator should be a company registered in India in which total foreign equity must not exceed 25 per cent. The detailed terms and conditions for providing services are as per the license conditions. Under mode 4, market access is unbound except very stringent horizontal commitments (commercial presence allowed , presence of natural persons not allowed).

In the Telecommunications sector, under the GATS India has allowed 25 per cent and 51 per cent FDI investment for wire based/cellular services and data/message transmission services, respectively. In February 2005 the government increased the FDI limit in telecom service providers from 49 to 74 per cent. A competitive market structure (with the presence of both domestic and foreign firms) in the telecom sector has also been instrumental in high IT related growth.

BANKING AND FINANCIAL SERVICES

In banking and other financial services, market access commitments are limited to mode 3 supply, i.e., commercial presence only. Sectors like financial services, construction and related engineering services, health and air transport services are examples of areas where the policy regime is moderately liberal with some explicit barriers. In the Banking and other financial services (except insurance) FDI is permitted up to 49 per cent. Foreign sector participation in the insurance sector is limited to 26 per cent and foreign firms can only set up firms through partnerships or joint ventures. Nine foreign firms (both in the life and non-life segments) have started operating insurance joint ventures in India.

At present there are 18 foreign banks operating in India and this sector has attracted USD 1.25 billion of FDI between 1991-2002 i.e. 4.4 per cent of total FDI approvals. India's commitments on market access under mode 3 are: (a) only through branch operations of a foreign bank licensed and supervised as a bank in its home country (b) grant of license as permissible under existing laws, (c) a limit of twelve licenses per year both for new entrants and existing banks (d) banks are allowed to install ATMs at branches and at other places identified by them. Installation of ATM at a place other than in licensed branches is treated as a new place of business and requires a license. Licenses issued for ATMs installed by foreign banks will not be included in the ceiling of twelve licenses, and (e) investments in other financial services companies by branches of foreign banks licensed to do banking business in India individually not to exceed 10 per cent of owned funds or 30 per cent of the invested company's capital whichever is lower. As regards limitations on national treatment is concerned, foreign banks are required to constitute Local Advisory Boards[3] consisting inter alia of professionals and persons having expertise in areas such as small scale industry and exports. Public sector enterprises can invest surplus funds in term deposits only with scheduled commercial banks incorporated in India. All these commitments are in mode 3. India is gradually opening up service sectors to domestic operators who can tie up with foreign participants with a maximum 26 per cent equity participation. This kind of an arrangement is made in case of insurance. Thus, banking services, which have been under state monopoly until recently, are now open to foreign participations on fixed number of licenses offered by the RBI. This arrangement is made on reciprocal basis.

IT SECTOR

In the IT sector although GATS commitment allows only investment up to 51 per cent, India has autonomously liberalised itself to permit 100 per cent FDI through the automatic route with the exception of B2B electronic commerce where FIPB approval is required and the foreign promoters are required to disinvest 26 per cent of ownership. Between 1991-2002, India could attract substantial FDI investment in this sector i.e. USD 1.8 billion which account for 6.4per cent of the total FDI approvals within this period.

OTHER SECTORS

FDI is not permitted in the real estate sector. The construction sector growth is restricted because of complex tenancy laws, rent control, high stamp duties and poor enforcement of building regulations. Issues like minimum acreage development (100 acres), minimum capitalisation requirements ($ 10 million) and a three year lock-in period before repatriation of proceeds limit the attractiveness of this sector to foreign firms. There is no cap on FDI in the health sector but foreign individuals are prohibited from providing services for profit and are subject to the registration requirements of the respective medical associations in India. Professional services like accountancy, legal and other service sectors like retail distribution, postal and rail transport services are closed to foreign participation. Foreign service providers are not allowed to undertake statutory audit of companies and restrictions on use of advertising and foreign brand names also exist. In the legal sector, the services can only be provided by a natural person who is a citizen of India and not a firm. In order to be eligible to practise a natural person has to be enrolled as a member of the Bar Council and a foreign service provider so enrolled must belong to a country which allows Indian nationals to practise in their country. FDI is not permitted in this sector and international law firms are also not authorised to open their offices in India. Foreign service providers may be engaged as employees or consultants in local law firms but they cannot sign legal documents or represent clients or appointed as partners.

India has one of the highest retail outlet densities in the world but the distribution sector is highly fragmented, protected and skewed towards the counter stores rather than the supermarket concept prevalent elsewhere in the world. However, no FDI is permitted in the retail distribution business. Requirements regarding RBI/FIPB approval for wholesale trade and franchising services (which do not have a FDI cap) coupled with restrictions in the transportation and warehousing area limit the potential of this sector for foreign service providers.

INDIA'S MAJOR INTERESTS AND CONCERNS

Cross-border supply (Mode 1) and presence of natural persons (Mode 4) are the two key modes of service delivery in which India has comparative advantage. In these modes India is interested in market access under Mode 1 and Mode 4 on a horizontal basis in all the sectors. However significance of other modes i.e. Mode 2 for health, tourism and educational services and Mode 3 for IT and banking related activities is not to be undermined.

Cross border supply faces few explicit restrictions but the significant expansion of Indian services and the perceived exodus of white collar jobs from importing countries is increasingly translating itself into protectionist measures viz. legislations preventing outsourcing of government contracts etc., especially in the United States. (Aaditya Mattoo and Sacha Wunsch, 2004).

There is overwhelming evidence to indicate the growing importance of cross-border supply in service sector trade. This is in stark comparison to the time of the Uruguay Round discussions when this mode did not receive much attention and its scope was largely unrecognised. And in fact many countries left commitments in this mode unbound on the ground of technical feasibility. However, today, improvements in information and communication technology and in telecommunications infrastructure and lower connectivity costs have made it technically and economically viable to trade many services through cross-border supply.

Like the earlier migration of labour-intensive manufacturing jobs to the developing countries, today there is migration of service jobs from the developed to the developing countries, which in turn is facilitating cross-border trade in services.

Also, Mode 4 faces serious restrictions in all countries and the issue is examined more from the immigration legislation and labour market policy rather than international trade perspective. Burdensome visa formalities, imposition of quotas, wage parity conditionalities and non-recognition of professional qualifications are few areas which do not allow free movement of temporary service providers. Mode 2 consumption of health services in India is restricted because of the limited insurance coverage available for services consumed abroad.

India is much interested in pushing through its agenda on mode 4 supply of services, i.e. movement of natural persons. So far, developed countries did not provide any commitment in this area. All their commitments on mode 4 supply are unbound and horizontal, which are subject to discrimination. India's one–point in the requests made is to ensure effective market access to its professionals and skilled labour force to industrialised countries and bring about symmetry in the movement of labour and capital. In particular, the GATS has failed to liberalise the movement of natural persons, the key mode of export interest to developing countries with significant developmental implications for their economies. Specific commitments on movement of natural persons are virtually non-existent. At three formal meetings in 2003, the council held discussions on the implementation of Article VII of GATS (Recognition) based on a submission from India (WTO, 2004a).

INDIA'S RECENT 'REQUESTS' AND 'OFFERS'

Under the ongoing negotiations, India has submitted 'requests' to its trading partners in computer related services, architecture services, health services, audio-visual services, tourism services, maritime services and financial services.

On the other, hand, India has received requests from 22 countries. However, the initial offer has no legal status and can be withdrawn or amended at any time if the Member feels that the trading partner's offers are not satisfactory or adequate. In June 2002, India made specific requests on medical, dental and health services to the quad countries–the EC, the US, Japan and Canada (mode 1 and mode 4), Far-East countries (all four modes), West Asia and certain African countries (all four modes).[7]

To bring about greater market access for its professionals and skilled personnel in proportion to the capital that it allows into its economy, India has been suggesting the following steps to be taken:

1. Elimination of the Economic Needs Test (ENT), at least in a certain specified categories. India views issues like "economic needs test", "local market tests "and management needs tests" conducted by the developed countries to ascertain the need for entry as well as the number to be allowed to enter a foreign market as barriers set up to prevent entry of labour. It finds that the conditions on which these tests are based provide complete discretion to the developed countries in their application leaving room for arbitrary interpretations. Such discriminatory ENT is seen to be widespread; it is noted that only in 3 out of a total of 54 cases, have the criteria been specified. In this area, it seeks transparency and the application of objective criteria;
2. India holds that there should not be any insistence on Social Security Contributions from temporary resident workers and professionals. The logic here is that there is no point in asking migrant workers and professionals to contribute to the Social Security Fund when their presence in the host country is on a temporary basis, or they are not eligible to receive the benefits of their contributions on some domestic grounds;
3. The visa regime should be made transparent. In this regard, India has suggested that a separate GATS visa

be conceived for personnel whose contracts are governed by the commitments made by a Member-country. A GATS visa would thus be simple and easily procurable, compared to the normal immigration visa;

4. The needs of the developing countries for specific sectoral commitments from developed ones should be appreciated. For that purpose, India feels further detailed sub-classification of categories of personnel and their inclusion in sectoral/horizontal commitments might be required; and
5. Article VII of GATS provides for Mutual Recognition Agreements (MRAs), and also gives opportunities to the Members to participate in negotiations. But the provisions of Article VII have largely remained unused. Developing countries have normally been kept outside the ambit of such MRAs. India holds that qualifications of personnel of the developing countries should be recognised by the developed countries. At present, this is not being done, thereby creating a serious impediment to the entry of professionals from the developing countries to the developed ones. India believes that minimum international standards and criteria for recognition should be arrived at under GATS to eliminate this kind of barrier, and also that there should be a mechanism to oversee the conduct of nations in the matter of mutual recognition of qualifications.

India circulated its initial offer in ongoing services negotiations under the WTO General Agreement on Trade in Services (GATS) in January 2004. The offer indicated India's commitment to liberalising its economy in certain modes of supply in sectors such as professional businesses, engineering, tourism and transport. The services negotiations are currently in their request-offer phase. The 'July Package' of the General Council mandates that initial offers must be submitted by all member-countries by May 2005.

CONCLUDING REMARKS

The services sector is fast growing and expanding not only in the developed countries but also in some developing countries. The services sector is complex in nature. Hence, much progress has not been made in the ongoing GATS negotiations. And it is argued that the "bottom-up" scheduling approach is too lacking in ambition and, therefore, commercial impact. However, "in certain circumstances, a GATS approach would be an appropriate alternative–in developing new disciplines–to a plurilateral negotiation". (WTO, 2004c).

The focus on Mode 1 service supply is necessitated by its rising importance in global trade in services. In recent years, there has been rapid growth in global outsourcing and off shoring of many services to developing countries by companies in developed countries, across a wide range of sectors. Advances in information and communication technologies and the internet revolution, pressures to cut costs and remain competitive and demographic factors in developed countries have fueled this growth. As a result, the role of cross-border supply in services trade has increased, particularly, in labour-intensive services such as software, consulting, design and accountancy services where movement of natural persons is also important. India along with other developing countries in a recent joint statement submitted to the WTO Secretariat in May 2004 have suggested that the Mode 4 concessions need to be de-linked from the commercial presence condition (Mode 3). Moreover, more horizontal commitments need to be made across all sectors in order that the market access commitments become more meaningful to the developing countries. The growing potential for services exports and the protectionist tendencies towards outsourcing in particular, calls for a determined and innovative GATS negotiation and export promotion strategy.

Also India needs to gear up to withstand competitive pressures from other countries. Lower wage costs in countries like China, Brazil, Vietnam etc., territorial proximity of certain countries like Mexico/Brazil to US and being in a similar time zone, familiarity with desired standards of service in US by certain countries like Philippines etc. are some of the probable reasons for exportable services to be provided by other countries. The need to identify newer export sectors in services trade based on the comparative advantage and professional competence available in India assumes greater importance in view of the challenging global environment.

NOTES

1. MFN means treating one's trading partners equally. A special element of GATS is individual countries lists showing where countries are temporarily not applying the MFN principle of non-discrimination. As an example: if a government commits itself to allow foreign banks to operate in its domestic market, that is a market access commitment. And if the government limits the number of licenses it will issue, then that is a market access limitation. If it also says foreign banks are only allowed one branch while domestic banks are allowed numerous branches, that is an exception to the national treatment principle.
2. Countries can not only choose the sectors they want to schedule, but can also choose the level of commitment they undertake (full, partial, or unbound) across the four modes of supply, for individual activities and sub-sectors. They can also choose the sectoral and horizontal limitations they wish to inscribe in their schedules on individual modes of supply and for specific activities and sub-sectors. Thus , there is a high level of discretion and flexibility in the GATS commitment structure, which while allowing countries to address their particular sensitivities and concerns also slows down the process of liberalisation and undermines the value of many of the commitments made.
3. Local Advisory Board must be Indian nationals except for the chief executive office who may be a foreign national. The appointment of chairman and members of the Board requires RBI's approval.
4. Information collected from Government of India, Ministry of Commerce website and several business newspapers.

REFERENCES

Aaditya Mattoo and Sacha Wunch (2004), "Preempting Protectionism in Services: The GATS and Outsourcing", January.

Government of India, "Consultation document on the WTO negotiations under the general agreement on Trade in Services GATS" Ministry of Commerce & Industry: Department of Commerce, Trade Policy division *http://commerce.nic.in/wto_counsel_paper.htm.*

http://commerce.nic.in/IndiaSchedules.doc.

http://www.itu.int/osg/spu/wtpf/wtpf98/cases/info/infodoc.pdf

"Country case studies of the changing international telecommunications environment".

http://www.ciol.com/content/news/2005/105020202.asp

http://www.indiabandwidth.com/dir1/bandwidth90.html.

MVIRDC (1995), *GATT Agreements: Results of the Uruguay Round*, World Trade Centre, Bombay.

Rupa Chanda (2001), "India and GATS 2000: Negotiating Strategies and Domestic Reforms" ICRIER Paper, September

——— (2002a), *Globalisation of Services: India's Opportunities and Constraints*, Oxford University Press, New Delhi.

——— (2002b), *GATS and its implications for developing countries: Key issues and concerns*, ST/ESA/2002/DP 25, DESA Discussion Paper No. 25.

——— (2003), *Cross border supply and movement of natural persons: Complementary approaches to liberalisation* July 29-31. Prepared for the UNCTAD Expert Meeting on Movement of Natural Persons.

Srivastava, Ajay, (2004), Gats–The Indian Scenario "Business for Development" Challenges and Options for Government and Business After the Adoption of the WTO "July Package" Manila, Philippines, 21-22 October.

WTO (2004), http://www.wto.org/english/news_e/pres04_e/pr373_e.htm.

WTO (2004a), *WTO Annual Report,* Geneva.

WTO (2004b), *World Trade Organization, International Trade Statistics*, Geneva

WTO (2004c), *The Future of the WTO–Addressing Institutional Challenges in the New Millennium*, Report by the Consultative Board to the Director-General Supachai Panitchpakdi.

IMPACT OF GLOBALISATION ON WORKERS, SPECIALLY IN INDIA

K.L. Mahendra

The Director-General of International Labour Organisation, Mr. Somara, presenting his report, entitled "Working out of Poverty" at the 91st Session of L.L.O. in 2003, observed that the global efforts, aimed at cutting poverty by half by 2015 would fail, unless new ways were found to create opportunities for the world's poor to earn a decent living. Painting a grim picture to poverty affecting the global population in every country in the world, he reported that nearly 3 billion people are living on less than 2 U.S. dollars a day; about a billion (about 23 per cent) of the developing world) struggle on 1 U.S. dollar or less. The report estimates unemployment at 180 million and under-employment at 1 billion, amidst a global labour force increasing by 50 million every year, and the disparity of wealth amongst nations deepending. The income gap between the wealthiest and poorest fifth of the world population is growing. In 1960, it was 30 : 1; by 1999, it had widened to 74: 1. Needless to say that the gap has worsened since then. Two-thirds of the women workers are employed by the informal sector in extremely low wages and subjected to multiple exploitation and harassment.

The global economy, according to I.L.O. Director-General, was not organised enough to absorb and make full use of one billion young people, who will attain working age in the near future. In the most indutrialised countries, more than 10 per cent of the population lives below the poverty line of less of less than 50 per cent of the meridian income.

According to Human Development Report, economic growth and poverty alleviation is not automatic, as is evident from the deepening poverty in Indonesia, Poland, Sri Lanka, despite their higher rates of growth.

Data of 155 countries shows that 30 had an annual per capita growth rate of more than 3 per cent while 54 countries experienced an average income drop and the remaining 71 countries failed to reach 3 per cent income growth.

A study conducted by the I.L.O. under the World Commission on Social Dimension of Globalisation found that "the global trade has expanded faster than global G.D.P. over the last two decades. Yet, it is not uniform. The share of low income countries in the global exports is only 3-4 per cent, whereas the high income countries accounted for 75.2 per cent. Even the F.D.I. inflow into the 12 developed countries during 1990s has been of the order of 75.7 per cent while the rest of 176 countries had to be contented with a meagre share of 25.3 per cent. These anomalies have not only accentuated unemployment and poverty, but also raised a question on the sustainability of globalisation itself."

"Global unemployment has increased to 180 million in 2003 with higher incidence of unemployment in Asia and Sub-Saharan Africa. We are reminded of the Philadelphia Declaration that 'poverty anywhere is a threat to prosperity everywhere'."

The All China Federation of Trade Unions (ACFTU), the World Federation of TradeUnions (WFTU), the Organisation of Africa Trade Union Unity (OATUU), the International Confederation of Arab Trade Unions (ICATU) and the General Confederation of Trade Unions of (GCTU) of CIS countries, meeting in Beijing jointly launched the "International Forum of Economic Globalisation and Trade Unions."

Participants noted that three is a growing trend towards neo-liberal globalisation. On the one hand, with the rapid advance of science and technology, globalisation has, to a certain extent, optimised the allocation of resources, deepened the international division of labour and promoted income growth and economic development world-wide. On the other hand, with the free cross-border movement of capital, globalisation has aggravated economic inequalities and social justice across the world. This has brought immense pressures and challenges to workers all over the world in the sphere of employment, social security and workers' rights.

The AFL, CIO is propagating in U.S.A., that in the U.S.A., the unemployment is there due to the F.D.I. in developing countries, and because of outsourcing of jobs. But the fact is that of 2.7 million jobs lost over the last three years, only 300,000 have been lost to the outsourcing, whereas one per centage point increase in productivity is estimated to have created a loss of 1.3 million jobs. Such are the estimates of Forester Research in U.S.A. Thus, instead of rousing the working class against the neo-liberal policies, the workers are misled into mobilisation against developing countries.

In most of the developed countries, the prople's wrath is directed against ethinic minorities and the immigrant workers. Not content with that, the leaders of ICFTU and AFL, CIO, in collaboration with the employers and the governments of developed countries moved a resolution that there should be a ban on import of goods in the manufacture of which child labour has been used in the I.L.O. conference. The trade union representatives from India. Morocco, Nigeria and Iran opposed it as non-tariff protectionist policy. Representatives of 113 developing countries also opposed the proposal, and it had to be dropped. In the subsequent year, a resolution was moved that sanctions could be imposed on the countries saw to it that the resolution does not come for consideration in the plenary. So far, L.L.O. follows the method of persuasion and creates public opinion but does not take any punitive measures. The developed countries and the I.C.F.T.U. tried to subordinate I.L.O. to the policies of neo-liberalism being pursued by the I.M.F., the World Bank and the W.T.O.

The Millennium declaration of heads of states stated that would poverty shall be reduced by half by the international efforts, by 2015. But, after the 11th September, Bush declated that immediate task is global war against terrorism and hence, the problem of poverty alleviation will have to wait.

India initiated the process of globalisation in the eighties when there was a feeling that excess control and over-protection of domestic market in India has resulted in slow economic development and unsatisfactory performance of the Indian economy in the post-Independence period. The introduction of some structural reforms in the economy defined as liberalisation, privatisation and globalisation, as prescribed by the Bank and the Fund were considered to be essential to bring about macro economic stability and put the economy on higher path of growth.

The main findings of the study conducted by the Global Policy Network and the Ford Foundation are as follows:

Unemployment rate as measured on C.D.S. basis has increased significantly from 6 per cent in 1993-94 to 7.3 per cent in 1999-2000. The total volume of unemployed persons has touched the figure of about 27 million in 1999-2000. Seventy four per cent of them are in rural areas and about 60 per cent of them are educated. The main reason for increase in unemployment is a decline in the job-creating capacity of Indian economy since 1993-94.

The employment growth per annum dropped from 2.7 per cent during 1983-94 to 1.7 per cent during 1994-2000, in spite of an increase in the G.D.P. growth rate from 5.9 per cent during 1983-94 to 6.1 per cent during 1993-2000.

The agriculture-led growth in India can only lead to employment generation. But, it did not happen. The share of agriculture in G.D.P. declined. The rate of growth of employment in agricultural sector was slowed down. In fact, the annual rate of growth of employment in agriculture sector became negative (-0.34 per cent) during 1994-2000. So much so that absolute number of persons in agricultural sector declined from 242.46 million in 1993-94 to 237 million in 1999-2000. The decline in the agricultural growth had a negative effect on the rate of growth of the total employment and the country had grown without jobs in the nineties.

The National Council of Applied Economic Research (N.C.A.E.R.) report, commenting on wage employment stability in India, estimates the duration of agricultural and non-agricultural wage employment at 137 and 152 days, respectively. The average days of wage employment for females is about 15 per cent less than for males in agriculture, and 18 per cent less in non-agricultural workers.

The World Health Report says that there are over 50,000 high net worth individuals in India with financial assets of more than one million dollars, more than Rs. 5 crore in terms of Indian currency, representing a rise by 5,000 in one single year of 2001. Thirteen more families have been additionally added to the billionaires' club in 2002 benefiting from the process of economic reforms. UNCTAD report, 1998, stated that the gap between the rich and the poor within and between the countries is increasing fast, leading to civil strife.

Tax revenue is on the decline, having a drop of more than Rs. 1,05,000 crore in 2002-2003.

India lags behind all the developing countries in respect of public expenditure on social services; the share of the allocation for education is lower than in East Asian countries; the spending on health in India is lowest among the South Asian countries.

Most of the foreign monies either flow into stock market or used up to take over Indian firms; least goes into green field projects.

The process of disinvestments and privatisation has caused colossal loss to the exchequer. Balcon was handed over to Sterlite for Rs. 500 crore, though the assets are around Rs. 5,000 crore. The VSNL is now a joint sector with Tatas. The undertaking was handed over for Rs. 1,400 crore while it had a reserve fund of Rs. 1,200 crore, which the Tatas transferred to its company immediately after taking over. The Centaur Hotel was sold to a party which immediately sold to another party, making a clean profit of Rs. 8 crore. The N.D.A. government held the philosophy that government has no business to be in business. It wanted to privatise Nalco; but the resistance by the people and the working class prevented it. It wanted to privatise two oil companies; but the Supreme Court held that they were nationalised by an act of the Parliament, so Parliament alone can decide whether to privatise them. The proceeds of privatisation or of offering of disinvestments were used to meet the budgetary deficit which means selling family silver to meet the revenue account deficit. It is the world which pressurises that there should be zero deficit, and there be no inflation, and the previous government worked this framework.

In 1930s economic crisis, Lord Keynes suggested deficit financing for revival of the economy. Since then deficit financing for demand push growth was being followed. But since the developed countries have surpluses, they want to follow the neo-liberal policies. They stress on market-driven growth on the basis of competition and free market economy. The developing countries, with labour-intensive technology, need to protect their nascent industry as against the products of multinational companies. But the trio pressurise to follow the policies of provatisation, liberalisation and globalisation.

Recently, the U.P.A. government has decided to disinvest up to 49 per cent in the profit-making public sector enterprises and the proceeds to be deposited in a fund which will be utilised to revive the viable PSUs and for the social sector such as education and health.

The government wanted to privatise banks, but could bot do so, because of the organised resistance. But, they allowed opening of the private banks and already some of them are closed. The Global Bank, which was, as most efficient, has collapsed, and all big depositoes withdrew their money before it collapsed, and it is the small depositors who have suffered.

Now the government has announced that foreign banks will be allowed to have 74 per cent equity in the private banks. Further, the government is toying with the idea of merger of public sector banks to create megabanks and would like them to go global.

In spite of the N.P.A. of more than one lakh crore rupees, the public sector banks have so far managed well. But, under the new policies of competing with the multinational financial institutions, they have to adopt new methods, which may have adverse effect on customers.

The workers in the unorganised sector constitute 92 per cent of the workforce. But, they have no security of service of service and are not covered by social security scheme which looks after health care, delivery period and old age, etc. A comprehensive scheme for agricultural workers was drafted by a Parliamentary Committee. But the same is not enacted so far. Now, under the neo-liberal policies, more jobs are passed on to the unorganised sector. The Second Labour Commission has recommended; but, no scheme is so far finalised and security of service or decent wage provided. The government announced Rs. 65 as a floor level wage. But large number of workers in the unorganised sector do not get even that meagre wage and the government has not provided any machinery to get the same implemented. In Kerala, Tamil Nadu and West Bengal, some schemes are being implemented. But it is necessary that a comprehensive legislation is enacted for agricultural workers and a social security scheme for the whole unorganised sector, including the self-employed, be enacted.

There is much hype about the IT sector. The salaries are high. But the work is at nights when the staff in U.S.A. is aleeping so that by the time they go to office, the matter is on their table. The persons have to work for twelve hours continuously at night. They cannot talk to each other and the manager will be able to see what every individual is doing from the glass fixed above. The tension is such, the highly qualified workforce is not able to work beyond three or four years. There is no legislation for their service conditions.

The capital formation in the country is low, at 24 per cent of the G.D.P.

There is a rise in the profits of corporate sector, downsizing of labour force and decline in the real wages.

A survey of 100 large corporations has shown that their aggragate devidend pay outs increased by a massive 29.4 per cent in one year from 2001-2002 to 2002-2003. Their net profits have increased by 28 per cent. Even 226 companies have left losses behind in 2002-2003, benefiting from lowered interest rate and earning from other sources, making speculative investment in stock market. The net profit has also improved because of lowering of taxes.

According to a survey conducted by a financial daily, 125 companies whose comparable data were available, had in a year 2001-2002, slashed down labour force by 53,998 heads. In five years, SAIL reduced its manpower by 20 per cent, BHEL by 27 per cent. The output per employee has increased, but not the wages commensurate with it. More than one lakh bank employees accepted. VRS within three months. The downsizing, called right-sizing, mergers, closures and so-called voluntary retirement scheme, all these have led to reduction of labour force of one crore since the beginning of reforms. About five lakh industries were closed as a result of liberalisation. As per the reports of Ahulwalia Committee, Rakesh Mohan Committee, there are attempts to contracualise certain jobs in government departments, railways and PSUs and there is no recruitment at all. Apart from this, there is attempt to privatise certain sections in the railways, defence industries and PSUs. For instance, in public sector, canteens and guest house catering, transport, i.e., jobs except direct production, are being contractorised. In Roukela the power plant has been privatised. Apart from these employment of persons on time-bound contract basis is restored to, for a period of three years, on consolidated pay, without any facility for D.A., or leaves or gratuity and provident fund. Not only workers, but doctors, paramedical staff, lecturers and professors are being appointed on the basis of individual contracts. All this is done with a view to reducing the labour cost. To make the industry competitive and increase profits of the corporate sector at the cost of workers is the socalled policy of 'structural adjustment.' The workers have been resisting amendment of Industrial Disputes Act with a view to legalising the policy of hire and fire. Flax labour laws is the goal under the capitalist globalisation. The watch word is no security of service, but security of income.

Prime Minister Manmohan Singh said that they will not adopt the policy of hire and fire. But, immediately Chidambaram, the Finance Minister, said that industry will require labour when there are more orders, but the labour will have to be reduced when the orders are reduced. Even on the guaranteed employment scheme, the bill drafted by the Coordination Committee, has been diluted by the government. There is resistance from the Planning Commission that the scheme will require huge amount and is not possible to implement, even though the Prime Minister said that it has to be implemented.

The Prime Minister has agreed to raise the interest on provident fund amounts at 9½ per cent interest which was the demand of the Central Trade Union Organisation. But, immediately, the Finance Ministry sources said that they will not provide any subsidy to cover the deficit of Rs. 940 crore due to the increase in interest rate.

The trade unions have been stressing that every year, the difference between the estimate and actuals is being deposited seperately and the amount at present stands at Rs. 8,000 crore.

Actually, those who opted for voluntary retirement in the hope that they can sustain on 12½ per cent interest that was available, are facing difficulty in making two ends meet, because the bank interest on deposits has come down to 7 per cent. They are all above fifty years of age and cannot opt for any other vocation at this age.

In the wake of globalisation and the neo-liberal policies, even the outlook of the judiciary is influenced. Earlier, the Supreme Court ruled that labour working under contractors on perennial jobs should sbe treated as permanent employees. Further, when contract labour is abolished, as per notification, the workers under the contractor should be absorbed on permanent jobs. But, subsequently, in another case, the Supreme Court held that there is no employer-employee relation between the principal employer and the contractor's labour, and hence there is no question of absorbing the contractor's workers in perminent vacancies.

The Kerala High Court ruled that bandhs are illegal and against the Constitution. The Supreme Court held, in appeal, that bandhs are illegal, but general strikes and hartals are not illegal. In reality, general strikes and hartal, if simultaneous, become bandhs. Bandhs have been a form of struggle during the freedom movement.

In the case of Tamil Nadu strike of 7 lakh employees and teacher services of one and a half lakh were terminated. The Supreme Court argued that it causes inconvenience to the public and advised that the employees should work hard so that government may feel sympathy and concede their demands.

This reflected the feudal mindset of the judiciary. They held that the government employees have no legal or moral right to go on strike and based themselves on a clause in service rules which were drafted during the colonial regime, and were not even amended after the adoption of the secular, democratic Constitution.

The Calcutta High Court passed orders that processions and rallies on roads are banned between 8 A.M. and 8 P.M.

The Karnataka High Court held that an employee, even an office-bearer of a union, cannot critise the corruption or mismanagement of the management in the press, and held a dismissal as valid. The bench held that if an employee wants to exercise his Fundamental Right, he should resign from service.

The head-load workers in the Tata Yard went on strike in Maharashtra, which was held as illegal. The consumer court held that the losses suffered be recovered from their future earnings. Even the protection under Trade Union Act for collective bargaining was ignored.

Resistance to the neo-liberal policies of capitalist globalisation is growing throughout the world. The workers in France, Spain and Italy have gone on general strike twice and the German workers once, again the privatisation and attacks on the social security. The old age pension and the unemployment allowance are being reduced. In United Kingdom, there is agitation against privatisation of education and medicare.

In South Africa, there were two general strikes against privatisation. In South Korea, there have been struggles and trade union leaders were imprisoned. In India, since the beginning of the 'economic reforms' there have been six country-wide general strikes and the financial sector employees are continuously agitating againsprivatisation.

In Latin America, through democratic elections, governments against U.S. imperialists attempt to impose economic domination, have come into existence in Venezuela, Brazil, Argentina, Peru and Urguary, and there is firment in other countries. Hug Chavez survived as President of Venezuela with mass support in spite of three attempts to dethrone him by the U.S. imperialists and local reaction.

The U.S. imperialists wish to dominate over the world through the economic policies and through war. There have been bombings of Yugoslavia, Afghanistan and Iraq, rendering thousands of civilians, specially women and children, either dead or maimed. The U.S. imperialists, ignoring United Nations assert that they have the right to take preemptive action, Iran, Cuba, North Korea, Syria, Vietnam etc., are on their hit list.

But the anti-war demonstrations against aggression in Iraq were unprecedented.

Apart from the working class and the peasantry, the civil society is also raising its voice against the capitalist globalisation. The world social forum, at its meet in Mumbai, said that another world isd possible. The same slogan is repeated at its recent meeting in Brazil where, again more than 1,00,000 people from all walks of life participated.

Already, France, Germany, Russia, China and India, have declared that they want a multipolar world. The developing countries, at the initiative of Brazil, South Africa, India and China formed a group of 21 and stood firm against the subsidies for agricultural products in European Union and U.S.A. at the Cancun conference, which dispersed without any decision.

Thus, if the working class and the developing countries can unitedly oppose the imperialist forces, their policies can be defeated.

GLOBALISATION OF CORPORATE POWER AND WATER PROBLEM

A. V. Nachane

"There is little doubt that 'globalisation' is the buzzword of the moment, the most talked about and perhaps the least understood concept of this new millennium". This observation by Wayne Ellwood sums up the present situation.

This globalisation is far beyond exchange of people, products, plants, animals, technologies and ideas. The rules for running the global economy laid down at Bretton woods after the Second World War specifically sought to control finance capital and contain it within national borders. Keynes was Britain's delegate to the meeting and he warned that unregulated flows of international capital would remove power from elected politicians and put it into the hands of the rich investors. The ultimate allegiance of investors, he said, is to their own self-interest.

Keynes' prediction has come true. The deregulation of global finance coupled with the micro-electronics revolution since the 1970s has sparked unrestricted, uncontrolled flows of finance capital which has replaced long-term productive investment by speculative investments. The unregulated flows of capital- more than $ 1.5 Trillion changing hands daily on global currency markets-is turning the world, into a global '*financial casino.*'

As surveyed by C.P. Chandrasekhar and Jayati Ghosh, a whole new category of altogether different kind of businessmen came up in this period, mostly in the nature of upstairs, international racketeers, fixers, middlemen linked to NRIs or smuggling and arms trade. They had not much of a production base and their parasitic intermediary nature helped them to prosper in an 'open economy'.[1]

What is dangerous and has gone mostly unnoticed is that this kind of globalisation is destroying the well-presserved ethnic and local cultures substituting them with a new global 'commercial' culture which is reflected in Disney movies, Barbie dolls, fast-food restaurants, hip-hop music and corporate-driven American-style culture alongwith dazzling variety of 'ethnic' foods. The multiplex and shopping malls we now see in cities like Mumbai and Bangalore and the changing face of Kolkata are a part of this process. One does not find world-wide emergence of Shakespeare theatres, Einstein clubs or rainbows of classical western and Indian music. The 'knowledgeable' western world knows neither Kalidasa nor Gurudev Tagore. There is 'fusion of cuisine' (with a dazzling varieties of 'ethnic' food - Thai, Mexican, Indian) but there is no fusion of the rich ethnic and tribal cultures prevailing in various parts of the world. The extremely rich treasure of art, music and literature built over several centuries is being destroyed and this sinful act is going unnoticed.

Michel Chossudovsky has pointed out in several details[2], how, as the recession continues to deepen, the world economy is overshadowed by a handful of international banks and global monopolies and how 'competition' has in practice supported a wave of corporate merger and acquisitions as well as the planned bankruptcy of small and medium-sized enterprises.

Even after the bursting of the bubble of progress made by the 'Asian tigers' in 1997 and mass protects thereafter in Seattle (1999) and Prague (2000), the world capital, with G-7 as its nucleus, is trying to conjure up a futuristic vision of our universe with electronic currency, information highways and so on. To the workers fighting for wage-rise they now say: "If you win, you will be flooded by cheaper goods from overseas or see your factories transplanted abroad by owners in search of lower labour costs and should you try to resist on a national scale, you will be brought to ruin and forced to surrender by the flight of capital, foreign capital and domestic as well.[3]

In the background of this scenario an attempt is being made here to examine the consequences of globalisation in the case of water problem.

The growing financialisation of the economy with primacy of finance over industry, privatisation of the information industry and services along with shrinking of politics and the public space and the explosion of internet have facilitated the entry of financial sharks into the sphere of water management. Till recently, water remained one of the last goods and services to be touched upon by the wave of privatisation roaring in the last 25 years engulfing banks, insurance companies, gas, electricity, railways, postal services, hospitals and so many other fields. However, today water, the source of life, is in danger of becoming one of the principal sources of profit, perhaps the last area to be conquered for the accumulation of private capital.

Today we hear of Global Water Partnership, World Water Council and several statements from the different bodies of United Nations and World Trade Organisation on water. The trade in water today is of 400 Bn dollars and is expected to rise upto 1000 Bn dollars. The 'value' of total services for conservation and supply of water (including governmental and municipal services) is estimated at about 7000 Bn dollars. So far, only 10 per cent of it has been commercialised. Multinationals want that the rest should also be commercialised, privatised. The condemned companies like Enron, Bachtel, Monsato have entered the trade as Vivandi of France, Suez International, Byewater and various 'Cola' companies are rushing ahead. Vivandi's annual income has exceeded 1000 crore dollars while Pichtel, a Swiss Bank, has started Unit Trust Company linked to the share prices of 80 water companies. The big sharks in the world trade have discovered that trade in water will expand very fast (with no fear of recession) and here is an opportunity for making unprecedentedly high profits.

Is there any basic problem of shortage of water? According to Herman Bouwer, a water expert, a renewable water supply of 2000m³ is enough for one person in a year. Thus, there is enough water for at least three times the present world population[4].

This view is shared by Prof. H. M. Desarda who points out: "Requirement of potable water to cater to the drinking and domestic water use is 40 Bn cubic metre (bcm) of the total 4000 bcm water we get on Indian land mass through precipitation (rainfall). This means that just one per cent of the total rainfall and around 2.5 pc of the total usable water resources are sufficient"[5].

It is true that such statistical averages do not always reveal the complete picture. In recent years, water-rich countries like China, California and South Africa were hit by water shortage affecting defferent social groups and regions within the country defferently, regardless of its overall water resource level. The same was the experience in the water-rich Soviet Union in the 1980s.

Then what is the problem? It is true again that rainfall continues to be an important factor and it is not uniform all over the world, all over India and in all years. But there have been traditional systems of water shortage which has a Cherapunji as well as a Jaisalmer, there were two million water structures before the British came. Society created these structures using its own resources. There was no Zilla Bank or World Bank but the village community, that invisible and invincible structure for water management.

Rejender Singh gives an interesting example. In 1995-96, Alwar in Rajasthan received more than twice its average rainfall. The surplus water was trapped and it seeped into the earth and the river Aravali began to flow after a long, long time. In the next six years, Alwar received less than half of normal rainfall but the excess water trapped in 1995-

96 sustained the needs of the population.[6] That did not require great skills sof engineering. It was done through traditional old methods.

In contrast was the experience in England. Towards the end of November 2003 came a warning that England would have serious water shortage unless there was 120 per cent of the average rainfall in 2004. Raingods obliged them.[7] Why could not England sustain water shortage due to insufficient ráinfall? Because water management was in the hands of private companies which relied on increasing abstraction from rivers and groundwater and building more reservoirs. They still had perhaps no knowledge of water harvesting.

There are some other important factors relevant to the subject under consideration.

Deforestation: The reckless deforestation in the name of industrial progress has affected the rainfall. In India, the National Forest Policy of 1952 had prescribed one-third of the country's total land area to be under forests while the forest area prescribed for the mountainous regions like the Himalayan region was €0 per cent of the total geographical area. By 1990, the actual area under forests as shown by satellites was no more than 10 per cent.[8] It is an illusion that the deforestation of sub-tropical countries and land degradation affecting Asia, Africa and Latin America will have only local consequences.

Inequitable distribution of water: In South Africa, six lakh white farmers practising irrigation consume 60 pc of the available water in the country while 15 million blacks have no direct access to water at all.

Favours to multinationals: The IBM in France pumps 2.7 million cubic metres of water every year from the Neocomian strata. To produce its 64 megabyte microchips, IBM factory needs pure water such as one finds only in ancient reserves of this kind. Although these reserves are protected by official provisions, the government gave the go-ahead for exploitation of this water table instead of compelling the IBM to use surface water. The question came of maintaining and creating job opportunities. IBM is one of the largest employers in the computer industry in France and its position is quite simple: all its competitors tap the same ancient reserves of underground water, so it has to do the same to remain in the technological race.

It may not be out of place to mention here that it takes four lakh litres of water to make one car and most of the 50 million cars produced every year by the multinationals are bought and used by the people in the countries of the North.

Loot of available water: Water wars are raging everywhere on the issue of available water. There are as many as 5.60,000 swimming pools in California which were draining fresh water from the mountains of Nevada (around the population of Arizona and Nevada). After forty years of continuing dispute, the local authorities in Los Angeles have accepted that they are responsible for exccessive depletion of water from Lake Owen and for the devastating effects which this has produced on the lake and the surrounding region. They have also recognised - together with big farmers - their responsibility in relation to the Colorado river (one of the few in the world that does not carry water to the sea). An agreement has been signed among the concerned parties. In India, the conflicts over sharing of river waters between different states are aggravating year by year.

In spite of such realities, misleading theories are trotted out. It is said that the enormous waste in the use of water is due to the fact that most of our societies have hitherto considered water as a social asset rather than a commodity. This has kept the prices of water very low and thus encouraged careless, wasteful and inefficient use (more so in agriculture) and so, we must get away from the notion that water is a free good. The market will lead to efficient distribution and use of water. The privatised regimes of ownership, of infrastructural construction and management, of distribution and purification, offer a better solution than regimes of public, national, state or municipal ownership. That will also provide the best services to the poor at the most favourable cost.

The idea being sold out is that since the water crisis has reached serious proportions, gigantic projects alone can save us. The multinationals and transnationals have started pursuing their interests in making water a commodity by lobbying with multilateral funding agencies. In 'cooperation' with World Bank and IMF, they are trying to influence governments of the third-world countries to open the control of water to private companies. This explains the emergence of various privately funded bodies like World Water Council, World Water Commission etc. Corruption has accompanied the spread of private water.

With so much depending upon political decisions and contract negotiations, there has come an incentive to offer bribes. The world's largest multinationals were convicted on three occasions for paying bribes to obtain water contracts in France.

It is an essential feature of the market that one can choose among several goods of the same or a different nature. Using for that choice such criteria as price and quality. To have access to water, however, is not a matter of choice. Everyone needs it. The very fact that it cannot be replaced by anything else makes water a basic asset that can not be subordinated to a single sectoral principle of regulation. This is precisely what is called a social asset, a common good, basic to any human community. The transformation of water into a commodity along the lines of oil is an aberration bound up with the thinking of market fundamentalism which reduces everything to a commodity and every value to market exchange value.

Access to water for the satisfaction of the vital needs of every human being is a basic obligation for human society, whatever the cost. The choice intervenes only in relation to the forms of access or use: surface water versus groundwater, appropriation and distribution of water supplies, water for industry, agriculture or household needs, tap water or bottled water etc. Every society has to cover collectively all the costs of collection, purification, storage, distribution, utilisation and recycling necessary to guarantee basic access to water for all. That is a fundamental right which cannot be bought and sold, quoted on the stock exchange, traded or swapped.

NOTES AND REFERENCES

1. The Market that Failed-A Decade of Neo-liberal Economic Reforms in India.
2. The globalisation of poverty-Impact of IMF and World Bank Reforms.
3. "Whose millennium? Theirs or ours?" - Daniel Singer.
4. Herman Bouwer (US Water Conservation Lobaratory),-Agricultural Research, 8 March 2000.
5. Speech at Seminar conducted by Groundwater Surveys and Development Agency, Government of Maharashtra-Pune, 27-28 September 1981.
6. Civel Society-Sept./Oct. 2004.
7. Press Association, London-26 November 2003.
8. Man versus Ecology-Anil Rajimwate.

GLOBALISATION AND WOMEN: CHALLENGES AND OPPORTUNITIES

Naierossadat Daneshvar

While one interpretation of globalisation has to do with equal exchange and sharing of goods and services between countries and cultures, the reality of a globalized world is much different. Globalisation is a phenomenon that crosses and erases geographical and political borders and makes all countries start to look the same. As a result of globalisation, local products, services, and cultures disappear into a global culture, a culture defined not by the global citizenry but rather the world's economic and political super powers-mostly North America-owned corporations. Because of globalisation, people on every continent are exposed to and consumed by a North American culture defined by Nike running shoes, MTV, Coca Cola, and McDonald's. Some people have re-named the process of globalisation and called it McDonaldization or CocaColonization.

WOMEN AND GLOBALISATION

The issue of women and globalisation is one that concerns all mankind, men or women. The subject of globalisation and its impact on women has been of considerable interest in most countries. Tackling this question reveals that there are two views. The first considers that globalisation has been a source of more pressures and responsibilities on women, while the second views globalisation as a source of several advantages for women. In fact, both trends are bearing non-negligible traits of reality. The primary results of studies about globalisation and women reveal two divert directions:

The first believes that globalisation will put more pressure and responsibilities on women, while others, believe that there are many positives or advantages for women. In the political field, some studies concluded that women's political role will be marginalised in the developing countries, on the contrary others concluded that political participation of women will be increased and that women's issues will be in the centre of human rights issues. As for the economic side, women will be excluded from the market because of their lack of skills and experience; and because of strong competition women will be marginalised and impoverished. On the contrary in western countries, where women have more experience and qualifications, they are expected to have more opportunities to compete in the market. Some social studies empathise that the role of women in raising up children will shrink causing family system to break- down. Other social studies come to the opposite conclusion.

GLOBALISATION, CULTURE AND GENDER INEQUALITY

In regard to culture there are three main issues concerning women and globalisation. The first concerns the relationship between the particularity of the national culture and the international thought, because of the growing international concern of women's issues and which dealt with this relationship and the different national identities. There is a contradiction between the two extremes, some consider international thought and culture as a kind of alienation; others look at the cultural identity as a kind of self -inclusion. This contradiction is considered as one of the wide gaps that need to be overcome and reconciled. The second issue is how to encourage the moderate and open-minded elucidation of the religious scripts. It is important to find continuous motives and incentives for religious interpretations in women issues. The third issue is the relationship between the future perspective of women's issues within the framework of globalisation and the process of modernisation of the society in a comprehensive way.

In some countries, globalisation has resulted in serious gender imbalances. The extent of this imbalance depends largely on the level of gender equality prevailing in the norms, institutions and policies of a country at the time when integration into the global economy takes place. In addition, women from different social groups in a particular country are affected differently. Nevertheless, in many developing countries deep-rooted and long-standing gender inequalities have meant that the social cost of globalisation has fallen disproportionately on women.

There is a growing body of evidence illustrating the ways in which substantial numbers of women have been adversely affected by globalisation, both absolutely as well as in relation to men. For instance, trade liberalisation has often allowed the import of subsidised agricultural products and consumer goods that have wiped out the livelihoods of women producers. The increased entry of foreign firms has often had a similar effect through, for example, displacing farming women from their land or out-competing them for raw materials essential to their productive activities.

At the same time, women producers face formidable barriers to entry into new economic activities generated by globalisation. This is often because of biases, either against women directly or against the micro-and small enterprise sector in which they predominate, in the policy and regulatory environment.

WOMEN AND CONSUMPTION PATTERN

Globalisation inherit a lot of contradictions such as, spreading the culture of consumer entertainment through television, films and advertisements, which serves the big companies and destroy the social values and traditions.

Globalisation, changes the consumption patterns of the family life and creates a tendency for unilateral consumption pattern. The problem of unlimited consumption is faced by households all over the world, even in the developed countries, therefore the question is how we can rationalise the consumption behaviour of the household, because unlimited consumption will deprive the next generations from their rights in consumption. Therefore, women can play a very important role in the rationalisation of consumption as they are responsible for household expenditure and budget, but of course women alone cannot do this. This emphasises the importance of the role of all sectors of the state to help women rationalise domestic consumption and raise domestic savings to be able to finance economic development.

WOMEN IN AGRICULTURAL SECTOR

Economic globalisation-the process of opening up regional markets for global consumption-has played a major role in the transformation of agriculture from family gardens to a huge industry characterised by agri-businesses. Globalisation has stressed production for export-free trade agreements have encouraged this export. Commercialized agriculture relies just as heavily on the work of women as did the family farm. Women are cogs in the machine of a globalised agriculture industry: picking tomatoes in Mexico, harvesting rice in India, planting tea in Uganda, packing peaches in Ontario and fish in Nova Scotia. But while women still play a role in agricultural production, women's control over the means of food production has been significantly weakened. The forced migration, environmental contamination, and hunger that have resulted from this transformation, have been devastating.

Globalisation has also severely impacted women's relationship to food and the production of food. The liberalisation of trade and the subsequent global spread when inequalities between countries become greater, of a market economy has forced many impoverished countries to stop growing food for themselves in favour of growing food for export. As mentioned this has led to greater food insecurity, reduced nutrition, and has moved women in exporting countries into low-paying, undervalued agricultural work.

WOMEN IN INDUSTRIAL SECTOR

The increase of industrial exports in developing countries was accompanied by an increase in the demand for female employment, because industrialisation under the present international conditions in the developing countries depended on female labour. Therefore, the new female employment opportunities depended on the expansion of industrial export. The participation of women in the industrial sector was much higher than on the national level in the formal sectors, and in the industrial sector female employment was concentrated in the export sector. Empirical evidence proved that industrialisation in low income countries depended on women, just like export production; and that the increase in the income of many women is due to the expansion of trade. The expansion of export industries was the main reason for women to enter the market economy. For example, the number of the fabric factories in Bangladesh, increased from four in 1978 to 2400 in 1995, with 1.2 million workers, 90per cent of them women under the age of 25 years. Many other countries share the same experience such as , Indonesia, Tunisia, Taiwan and others.

WOMEN IN THE SERVICE SECTOR

Service sector offers regular paid contract jobs to women more than any other sector. This increases women's employment opportunities, this is strongly connected to their contribution in family expenses especially of education and health for women and children, which support the creation of new human resources and raise the level of human development.

The service sector is considered one of the strongest sectors at the present time, as it clearly expanded very rapidly to the extent that it is getting more similar to the progress achieved by the industrial sector, especially in the field of communication and information technology The service sector includes a lot of activities, starting from domestic services and small trade, government administration, social service sector (education and health), project services (accounting, counselling services, law and information processing). This sector is considered the largest sector of all the economic sectors in terms of its output, and the employment opportunities which it provides in many countries. Working in the service sector especially small businesses is considered the most important income source for the poor women.

Modern information and communication technology, specially the Internet, and the growing trans-continental employment opportunities gave a lot of new opportunities for women. However, women who will benefit from these advantages are mostly those who are well educated and who belong to high-income classes, while women who are not well educated or are illiterate, are marginalised, usually they are over 35 years old and are working in sectors which suffer from declining demand.

Although technology is increasing the number of women working in the information and communication, and the rapid development of this technology in all possible languages means that poor people, especially women in developing countries face the danger of being left out of production or knowledge and information exchange, and in many other aspects of life.

A negative impact is the very limited employment opportunities this sector offers to the poor women who are not educated, compared to those offered by the industrial and the agricultural sectors. On the other hand, the picture is different, if we focus on the gender gap in earnings in open semi-industrialised economies. Economic growth was higher where the gender gap in earnings was higher. This shows that some types of growth do not diminish gender gaps in the labour market, even though the absolute incomes of women may increase. Again in open economies where capital is highly mobile, policies that successfully promote greater autonomy for women can lead to an increase in national income; but those that increase women's bargaining power in the workplace can have a negative impact on national output if the response of capital is to move to other locations.

The International Monetary Fund and the World Bank encourage developing countries to use export-led growth to expand their economies. Such globalised economies require a labour force of a size that must include women, but women's employment varies greatly by region. For example, 74 per cent of women are in the work force in East Asia, the greatest proportion among all regions of the world, and they participate for the longest part of their lives in comparison to other regions. In the Middle East and North Africa, however, only about 34 per cent participate, while women in the Middle East drop out of the labour force in great numbers when they marry and have children. In many cases, cultural barriers, especially in the relationship between women and men within households, impede increased economic participation, or undermine the quality of that participation. For example, even women who do work face differential treatment such as wage gaps and segregation into traditionally female industries. Women have historically borne the burden of non-monetised labour, such as child care and domestic work. Increased participation in the work force also implies increased hazards for women, however. Women's jobs outside the home tend to be the worst compensated, least secure, and most dangerous available in the economy, especially in periods of recession in most developing countries. For example, gaps in labour laws, or ignorance and lack of enforcement of the labour codes in practice, allow for the exploitation of women. Women have only a precarious claim on the rights to minimum wage, work-week length, leave time, health care under the national social security system, and privacy protections. Often, they are subject to physical and/or sexual abuse, according to Human Rights Watch. Unfortunately, even the global nature of business does not confer universal rights for these women.

WOMEN IN INFORMAL SECTOR

In most developing countries there is a large informal economy, where economic activity lacks recognition and protection under formal legal or regulatory frameworks. It typically consists of small-scale manufacturing, services or vending in urban areas, domestic work or agricultural work on small plots of land. In many of the lowest-income countries it accounts for the large majority of workers. There is often a high proportion of women workers. This work is very diverse, from small enterprises to survival activities, including not only the self-employed and family workers but also wage labour in many forms. Typically such activities are of low productivity, and poverty levels among informal workers are high. But there is also a large reservoir of entrepreneurship and innovation.

Informal work is less prominent in industrialised countries, but by no means absent, and includes the informalisation of previously secure wage employment. Like poverty, the informal economy long predates globalisation. But it is growing. In many parts of the world today the bulk of new employment, both self-employment and wage work, is informal and the increased competitive pressures in global markets have not made informality easy to control. At the same time, while some informal workers provide low-cost inputs to global production systems, the majority are excluded from the opportunities of globalisation and confined to restricted markets.

At the Lisbon European Council in March 2000, the European Union set itself a new strategic goal for the next decade: to become the most competitive and dynamic knowledge-based economy in the world, capable of sustainable economic growth with more and better jobs and greater social cohesion The goal must be to make these informal activities part of a growing formal sector that provides decent jobs, incomes and protection, and can trade in the international system. This will be an essential part of national strategy to reduce poverty. That means increasing assets and productivity, appropriate regulatory frameworks, raising skills and ensuring that policy biases are removed. Policies to deal with the lack of recognition of qualifications and skills, and the exclusion of informal workers from social security and other protections are particularly important. The same are policies to improve the distribution of assets, and especially to increase access for self-employed women and men and small businesses to financial resources, technology and markets, and to increase opportunities for investment. But most workers and economic units in the informal economy have difficulty accessing the legal and judicial system to enforce contracts, and their access to public infrastructure and benefits is limited. A variety of bureaucratic and other restrictions create barriers and difficulties which hinder formalisation, growth and sustainability.

The relation between both formal and informal sectors is explained by the fact that small workshops produce production inputs to the big factories. The scope of this cooperation and integration is very difficult to evaluate as it varies from time to time and from one industry to another and from one season to another.

Many argue that in the process of globalisation demand for female employment has increased in the informal sector, through sub-contracts with the formal sector. The role and importance of the informal sector in economic activity has increased in the developing countries especially for women, however a high ratio of these women are working without any contracts.

WOMEN AND FLEXIBILITY AT WORK

While flexibility can be attractive for workers when it meets the needs desire of the workers, in reality this flexibility is far from benefiting women workers. because it has created an environment of part-time work sub contracting, temporary and casual employment. These forms of work are increasing in industrialised countries and although they affect both men and women, it is substantially women who are employed in this insecure sector. Far from legislating to protect workers from such insecurity, some governments have actually encouraged this type of flexibility as being good for industry. This requirement for flexibility also extends to working hours where in practice it means that women are often required to meet unreasonable attendance schedules at short notice.

CONCLUSION

Globalisation offers women unprecedented opportunities, but equally new and unique challenges. Gender inequality exacerbated by the effects of globalisation.

The paper argues that globalisation creates many challenges for women in different economic sectors and substantial numbers of women have been adversely affected by globalisation, both absolutely as well as in relation to men.

Women have additional vulnerabilities, especially malnutrition, sexually transmitted diseases, pregnancy complications, domestic violence, sexual abuse, In many cultures, women are the first to take care of the vulnerable, sick, and dying and the last to receive preventative or life saving treatment. In order to alleviate these problems, public education programmes can promote healthy-lifestyles, eliminate gender discrimination, access to services, and prioritise the help for women.

The paper argues that for many women, globalisation has resulted in an improvement in their economic and social status. Many women workers have been absorbed into the global production system and the wage employment gives them higher incomes than their previous situations and a greater potential economic independence and often raises social status.

Progress towards eliminating gender inequality in the future depends on finding and embracing the occasions, mostly in the political and legal realm, where the global approach strengthens women's security and welfare, and fighting the issues, mostly in the economic realm, where women are made worse off by the new global system.

REFERENCES

Allmendinger, J. (1989), "Educational System and Labour Market Outcomes." *European Sociological Review* 3. 231-250.

Scott, Catherine V. (1995), *Gender and Development.* Boulder, Colorado: Lynne Rienner.

UNDP (1999), *Human Development Report,*1 New York, Oxford University Press.

UNIFEM (2000), *Progress of The World's Women,* UNIFEM Biennial Report. Dianne Elson, Coordinator. New York.

UNCTAD (1999), *Trade, Sustainable Development and Gender.* UN, New York and Geneva.

National Council for Women (2001), Women and Globalisation Seminar, Cairo, May 2001.

INTERNET REFERENCES

European Commission (2001),Employment in *Europe report,* European Commission, Brussels, Belgium, *http://europa.eu.int/comm/dgs/employment_social/pub_en.htm.*

ILO (2001), *World Employment Report,* International Labour Office, Geneva, Switzerland.

www.ilo.org

ILO (2001) *Decent Work for Women,* Bureau for Gender Equality Breaking through the glass ceiling, International Labour Office, Geneva, Switzerland, *www.ilo.org/public/english/bureau/gender.*

UNI (2001) *UNI for People in the Changing Economy,* Union Network International (UNI), Nyon, Switzerland, *www.union-network.org.*

UNDP(2001), *Human Development Report,* United Nations Development Programme, New York, USA, www.undp.org.

World Bank (2001), *Gender and the Digital Divide,* The World Bank Group, Gender and the Digital Divide Seminar Series, *www.worldbank.org/gender/info/digitaldivide.*

WTO'S GLOBALISATION REGIME AND INDIA'S NEW TRADE POLICY 2004–2009

M. Sundara Rao

In recent years, there have been intense discussions in the academic as well as policy circles regarding the second-generation economic reforms in our country. It must be recognised that while the first generation economic reforms in July 1991 was initiated as per the conditionality of the IMF loan that we took at that time to salvage India's credibility in the world financial market, the second generation economic reforms at the turn of the 21st century has been guided by our compulsions to confirm to the norms set by the WTO in matters of trade policy, to which India committed herself at the conclusion of the Uruguay Round of GATT negotiations. Accordingly, Indian Government aligned EXIM procedures with WTO norms.

India being a founder-member of the WTO has been following the WTO policies through its trade policies, so that, certain effects on the Indian economy have become evident. In this context, an attempt is made in this study to examine the impact of WTO policies on the Indian trade policy regime. This study is divided into three sections. Aligning EXIM procedures with WTO norms are presented in the first section. The highlights of the Trade Policies of 2004-09 and the impact of WTO policies on new trade policies of Indian economy are presented in the second section and conclusions are presented at the end.

ALIGNING EXIM PROCEDURES WITH WTO NORMS:

Prior to the 1991 crisis the foreign trade sector of India suffered heavily from highly restrictive bureaucratic control. Thus, reducing controls, simplify procedures and creating a congenial environmental for trade became an objective of subsequent policy- makers even to date. On August 13, 1991 the Government made a statement on trade policy in the Parliament ushering in a new era in the foreign trade policy of India. From then on the focus shifted to promotion and development of foreign trade by facilitation instead of controls and regulations.

India did not remove quantitative restrictions (QRs) on its imports fully with respect to consumer products and certain agricultural imports in view of its balance of payment difficulties. India negotiated with a large number of countries and agreed to phase out QRs by 2003. However, the US Government lodged a complaint with the World Trade Organisation and the appellate body upheld the US position. Consequently, India has been requested to speedily remove QRs .EXIM Policy (2000) has, therefore, removed QRs on 714 items out of 1,429 items (nearly 50 per cent items) by moving them from Special Import List (SIL) to Open General License (OGL). In view of our commitment as a member of the WTO, EXIM Policy (2001-02) announced by the Commerce Minister, decided to dismantle quantitative restrictions on the remaining items at one stroke, giving clear signals to the domestic producers to face competition with international players.

Due to pressure of USA, which carried on a crusade against QRs by India, a case was filed by USA in WTO to direct India to lift QRs. The dispute panel of WTO gave its verdict against India in 1997. The Government of India filed an appeal, but the verdict of the appellate body of WTO also went against India. India was thus forced to lift QRs. The government, taking a leaf out of the US book, will make available government funds for market research and development. This is considered to be a positive step. The critics, however, feel that the government has opened the doors of the Indian market for a variety of consumer goods used by the upper and Indian middle classes. USA and other advanced countries had an eye on 250 million members of the middle class who are prone to follow foreign styles.

A second side effect of the withdrawal of QRs will be felt by artisans, marginal and small farmers and small-scale industries. There is a strong fear that by opening the floodgates of imports in all kinds of goods, India may be faced with the prospect of closure of lakhs of small production units, which produce consumer items of every day use. Already reports of desperation among weavers and farmers committing suicides are mounting in evidence of the backlash of removal of QRs. Union Commerce and Industry Minister announced the EXIM policy for the 5-year period (2002-07) on March 31, 2002. The main thrust of the policy is to push India's exports aggressively by undertaking several measures aimed at augmenting exports of farm goods, the small scale sector, textiles, gems and jewellery, electronic hardware etc. Besides these, the policy aims to reduce transaction cost to trade through a number of measures to bring about procedural simplifications. In addition, the EXIM policy removes QRs on exports, except a few sensitive items. The Medium Term Export Strategy for 2002-2007 provided a vision for creating a stable policy environment with indicative sector- wise targets aiming at achieving one per cent share for India in world trade by 2007. The EXIM policy 2002-07 also sought to usher in an environment free of restrictions and controls.

The present government replaced the EXIM policy 2002-07 with National Foreign Trade Policy 2004-2009, which encompasses Free Trade Agreements and Regional Trade Agreements along with EXIM policy components. The synergy between government and market participants expected to realise India's high export potential by enhanced overall competitiveness and faster economic growth. Another important feature of the EXIM Policy is to promote Market Access Initiative by the exporters. In addition, the EXIM Policy removes QRs on exports, except a few sensitive items. Through new trade policy of 2004-2009, India has cooperated with WTO commitments and even removed all the remaining quantitative restrictions on imports, which is likely to harm our agriculture and small-scale industries further and more so after China joined WTO.

IMPACT OF WTO REGIME ON INDIA'S NEW TRADE POLICY 2004-09

The foreign trade policy 2004-09 is intended to double India's share of global trade to 1.5 per cent in the next five years. In a major relief to exporters the policy does away with the service tax on exports while seeking to give a push to employment generation by outlining a special package for agricultural exports. Other key elements include the creation of free trade warehousing zones, the setting up of a Services Export Promotion Council and biotechnology parks while providing special focus initiatives in the handicrafts, handloom, jewellery and leather sectors. The import of second-hand capital goods will also be allowed without any age restrictions.

The new policy comes at a time when India's foreign trade is growing robustly. The impressive growth of merchandise exports, by no less than 20.3 per cent in dollar terms has continued. There has been a better than 25 per cent rise in imports too, reflecting a market review in industrial activity. Oil will dominate the import bill, underlying the need for a further boost to exports. Finally, while fashioning a trade policy, issues connected with WTO and the free trade agreements between India and other countries must be factored in. A frame work agreement for the Doha round has recently been worked out in Geneva and Indian negotiators face the challenge of devising modalities in a number of critical areas.

To implement the WTO guidelines like achieving the higher exports, the Indian Government has relied on some established strategies like: loosen controls and create an atmosphere of trust; simplify procedures and reduce transaction costs, neutralises the incidence of levies and duties on inputs used in export products; facilitate technological and infrastructural up gradation in all sectors of the economy. Agriculture and services now get their due share in the export promotion framework. The Duty Entitled Pass Book Scheme will be persisted with until an alternative WTO compatible scheme is put in place. The new trade policy does not suffer from a lack of vision. Further, it signals continuity with EXIM policy. Finally, with the WTO rules coming into play, fiscal concessions and other sops are no longer in the exclusive domain of national trade policies.

The new foreign trade policy takes an integrated view of the overall development or India's foreign trade and essentiality provides a roadmap for the development of this sector. It is built around two major objectives of doubling India's share of global merchandise trade by 2009 and using trade policy's an effective instrument of economic grownth with a thrust on employment generation. Key strategies to achieve these objectives, include unshackling of controls and creating an atmosphere of trust and transparency, simplifying procedures and bringing down transaction costs, neutralising incidence of all levies on inputs used in export products, facilitating development of India as a global manufacturing trading and services while identifying and nurturing special focus areas to generate additional employment opportunities particularly in semi-urban and rural areas. Facilitating technological and infrastructural upgradation of the Indian economy, especially through import of capital goods and equipment, avoiding inverted duty structure and ensuring that domestic sectors are not disadvantaged in trade agreements, upgrading the infrastructure network related to the entire foreign trade chain to international standards, revitalising the Board of Trade by redefining its role and inducting into it experts on trade policy and activating Indian embassies as key players in the export strategy.

The trade policy 2004 has identified certain thrust sectors having prospects for export expansion and potential for employment generation. These thrust sectors include agriculture, handlooms and handicrafts, gems and Jewellery and leather and footwear sector. Sector-specific policy initiative for the thrust sectors includes for agriculture sector, introduction of a new scheme called Vishesh Krishi Upaj Yojana i.e. Special Agricultural Prudence products. Under this scheme, exports of these products qualify for duty-free credit entitlement for importing inputs and other goods. Other components for agriculture sector include duty-free import of capital goods under export promotion capital goods this scheme permitting the installation of capital goods imported under EPCG for agriculture anywhere in the Agri. Export Zone (AEZ), utilising funds from the Assistance to States for Infrastructure Development of Exports(ASIDE) scheme for development of AEZs, liberalisation of import of seeds, bulbs, tubers and painting material, plants and herbal products. The special focus initiative for handlooms and handicraft sectors include extension of facilities like enhancing duty-free import of trimmings and embellishments for handicoms and handicrafts, exception of samples from countervailing duty (CVD), authorising handicraft export promotion council to import trimmings, embellishments and samples for small manufacturers, and establishment of a new handicraft special economic zone.

Major policy announcements under gems and jewellery sector encompass permission for duty-free import of consumables for metals other than gold and platinum up to 2 per cent value of exports increase in duty free import of commercial samples of jewellery to Rs. 1 lakh, and permission to import of gold of 18 carat and above under the replenishment scheme. Special policy initiatives in leather and footwear sector are mainly in the form of reduction in the incidence of customs duties on the inputs and plants and machinery. The major policy announcements for this sector include increase in the limit for duty free entitlements of import trimmings,embellishments and footwear components for leather industry to 3 per cent of value of exports and that for duty free import of specified items for leather sector to 5 per cent of value of exports, import of machinery and equipment for efficient treatment plants for leather industry exempted from customs duty and export of unsuitable imported materials has been permitted. The threshold limit of designated towns of export excellence has also been reduced from Rs. 1,000 crore to Rs. 2.50 crore in the above thrust sectors.

A new scheme to accelerate growth of exports called Target Plus has been introduced. Under the scheme, exporters achieving a quantum growth in exports are entitled to duty-free credit based on incremental exports substantially higher than the general actual export target fixed rewards are target based on a tiered approach for incremental growth of over 20 per cent 25 per cent and 100 per cent, the duty-free credits are 5 per cent, 10 per cent and 15 per cent value of incremental exports. Another new scheme called Vishesh Krishi Upaj Yojana has been introduced to boost exports of fruits, vegetables, flowers, minor forest produce and their value added products. Export of these products qualify for duty- free credit entitlement equivalent to 5 per cent value of exports. The entitlement is freely transferable and cannot be used for import of a variety of inputs and goods.

To accelerate growth in export of services so as to create a powerful and unique 'served from India brand instantly recognised and respected the world over, the earlier duty-free export credit (DFEC) scheme for services has been revamped and re-cast into the Served from India' scheme to the individual service providers who earn foreign exchange of at least Rs. 5 lakh. The other service providers who earn foreign exchange of at least Rs. 10 lakh are eligible for a duty–credit entitlement of 10 per cent of total foreign exchange earned by them in the case of stand alone restaurants. The entitlement is 20 per cent, whereas in the case of hotels it is 5 per cent hotels and restaurants can use their duty credit entitlement for import of food items and alcoholic beverage. To make India into a global trading hub, a new scheme to establish Free Trade and Warehousing Zone (FTWZs) has been introduced to create trade related infrastructure to facilitate the import and export of goods and services with freedom to carry out trade transactions in convertible currencies. Besides permitting FDI up to 100 per cent in to development and establishment of these zones each zone would have minimum amount of Rs. 100 crore and five lakh sq.mts built up area.

EPCGF scheme has been further improved upon by providing additional flexibility for fulfilment of export obligation, facilitating and providing incentives for technological upgradation, permitting transfer of capital goods to group companies and managed hotels, doing away with the requirement of certificate from central excise and improving the viability of specified projects by calculating their export obligation based on confessional duty permitted to them import of second hand capital goods without any restriction on age has been permitted and the minimum depreciated value for plant and machinery to be re-located into India has been reduced from Rs. 50 crore to Rs. 25 crore. The new policy which has allowed transfer of the import entitlement under duty free replenishment certificate scheme will continue until replaced by a new scheme to be drawn up in consultation with exporters. Additional benefits have been provided to export oriented units including exemption from service tax in proportion to their exported goods and services. Permission to retain 100 per cent on plant and machinery to DTA units, which convert into electronic hardware technology park (EHTP), software technology park (STP) and biotechnology park (BTP) units allowing import of capital goods on self-certification basis and permission to dispose of leftover materials and fabrics up to 2 per cent value or guarantee of import payment of duty on transaction value only . Minimum investment criteria have been also waived for brass hardware and handmade jewellery EOUs. The trade policy proposes setting up of BTPs by granting all facilities of 100 per cent EOUs. The trade policy 2004 has introduced a new rationalised scheme of categorisation of status holders as Star Export Houses, with benchmark for export performance varying from Rs/ 15 crape to Rs. 5000 crore (for Five Star Export House). The new scheme is likely to bestow status on a large number of hitherto unrecognised small exporters. Such Star Export Houses will be eligible for a number of privileges including fast track clearance procedures, exemption from furnishing of bank guarantee, eligibility for consideration under Target Plus Scheme etc.

Following the WTO provisions, the Government of India introduced different policy measures to further rationalise/ simplify the rules and procedures. They include exemption for exporters with minimum turnover of Rs. 5 crore and good track record from furnishing bank guarantees in any of the schemes. Service tax exemption for exports of all goods and services, increase in validity of all license entitlements issued under various schemes uniformly to 24 months, reduction in number of returns and forms to be filed, delegation of more power to zonal and regional offices, and time-bound introduction of electronic data interface. Institutional measures proposed in the trade policy 2004 include revamping and revitalising the Board of Trade, setting up of an exclusive Services Export Promotion council to map opportunities for key services in key markets and setting up of common facility centers for use of professional home-based service providers in state and district level towns. Pragati Maidan in Delhi is proposed to be transformed into a world class complex, with state-of the–art, environmentally controlled, visitor friendly exhibition areas and marts. The trade policy 2004 also proposes provision to deserving exporters, on the recommendation of the Export Promotion Councils, of financial assistance for meeting the costs of legal expenses connected with trade related matters.

CONCLUSION

The above presented highlights of the new trade policy 2004-09 indicate that the Government of India has introduced the different provisions of the WTO for fastening up the process of globalisation programmeme. To conclude, there is no escape from the implementation of WTO agreements whatsoever the cost is incurred on Indian economy. It may be in terms of mergers and acquisition of Indian companies by the multinationals, closure of small and medium level industries and the displacement of workers both in the rural and urban areas. India has cooperated with WTO commitments and even removed all the remaining quantitative restrictions on imports, which is likely to harm our agriculture and small-scale industries further and more so after China joined WTO .

The impact that WTO–membership would make on the Indian economy is an issue of paramount national importance. It is little pre-mature to make a judgment, at this stage, essentially because things have just started evolving. A neat picture will emerge well after all agreements are implemented world–wide, net of neutralisations and modifications that might come off because of the voices being raised by the developing economies, including India, and the countervailing strategies to be unleashed by the vested trade interests. Recently, India herself has completed the last bit of the opening–up on April 1, 2004. Furthermore, this is hardly the stage at which we can scientifically delineate the effect of a particular agreement, or a specific aspect of the same, on the concerned sector, free of other inters–connections. Hence, the best we can do is to make some conjectures on the basis of what has been going on in the recent past. Indeed, this is our only analytical choice, since the kind of economic regime that may emerge in the next few years would be only a reaffirmation, and a gradual extension, of the globalisation policies set afloat during the first half, and comprehensively expanded during the second half of the 1990s when WTO came.

REFERENCES

Bhattacharya, B. and Mogo, L.D. (1998), "Trade and Environment Issue in the WTO-Indian Experience", Foreign Trade review, ILFT, New Delhi.

Government of India (1991), "India's New Economic Policies".

Government of India (2000-02) Economic Survey.

Gulati, Ashok et.al, (1999), "From Marakkesh to Seattle–Indian Agriculture in Globalsing World", *Economic and Political Weekly*, Vol. XXXIV, Oct., 9-15.

Gulati, Ashok (2000), "Indian Agriculture and the WTO: Preparing for the New Millennium", IEA Conference (83rd), Volume of the Millennium, Jammu.

Mukhopadhya, S. (2000), "The Uruguay Round and India's Export Response", IEA Conference (83rd0 Volume of the Millennium, Jammu.

O.E.C.D. (2000), "Agricultural Policies in O.EK.CK.D. Countries. Paris.

Pursell, Gary (1999), "Some Aspect of the Liberalisation of South Asian Agricultural Policies. How can the WTO help ? In Blarel, B. and et.al.(ed).

Implications of the Uruguay Round Agreement for South Asia–the Case of Agriculture, World Bank, 1999.

Singh Sukphal (2000), "New Barriers to Trade under WTO: Implication of TBT and SPS Measures for India's Agro-food Industry and Agro-Exports".

GLOBALISATION AND EDUCATION: CHALLENGES AND OPPORTUNITIES

Sadegh Bakhtiari

Globalisation is a complex phenomenon that has had far-reaching effects. Not surprisingly, therefore, the term "globalisation" has acquired many emotive connotations. At one extreme, globalisation is seen as an irresistible and benign force for delivering economic prosperity to people throughout the world. At the other, it is blamed as a source of all contemporary ills.

To different scholars, the definition of globalisation may be different. According to Cheng (2000), it may refer to the transfer, adaptation, and development of values, knowledge, technology, and behavioural norms across countries and societies in different parts of the world. The typical phenomena and characteristics associated with globalisation include growth of global networking (e.g. internet, world wide e-communication, and transportation), global transfer and interflow in technological, economic, social, political, cultural, and learning areas, international alliances and competitions, international collaboration and exchange, global village, multi-cultural integration, and use of international standards and benchmarks.

UNDP in Human Development Report (1999) describes globalisation as the increasing interdependence of the world's inhabitants, on an economic, technological, cultural, as well as political level. It is seen as a general tendency towards the liberalisation of economic trade, a wider circulation of capital, goods and products, and a quasi-abolition of national borders. The speed of communication and the relatively low cost of processing information have caused distances to be eliminated. The categories of time and space have been completely overturned. Models of consumption, values, and standardised cultural products thus tending to make behaviours and attitudes more similar and wipe out differences across the globe.

GLOBALISATION, EDUCATION AND LIFE-LONG LEARNING

People can only contribute and benefit from globalisation if they are endowed with knowledge, skills and with the capabilities and rights needed to pursue their basic livelihoods. They need employment and incomes, and a healthy environment. These are the essential conditions which empower them to participate fully as citizens in their local, national and global communities. These goals, can only be reached if national governments allocate adequate resources to education, basic infrastructure and the environment, and create the institutional framework which ensures broad access and opportunity.

Ensuring that all children have adequate access to education is an essential public sector function for countries at all income levels. Education not only benefits the individual, but society as a whole. When children remain sufficiently long in school, and in particular when girls receive adequate schooling, this increases economic growth rates, lowers fertility rates, leads to a reduction in child mortality and so on. Adequate primary and secondary education is more than the empowerment of the individual; it is the empowerment of the society.

Education is a major concern for all societies. As the foundation and essential driving force of economic, social and human development, education is at the heart of the change that is dramatically affecting our world in the areas of science, technology, economics, and culture. It is the reason behind social change and scientific progress, and in its turn, it is subjected to the results of progress that it itself has engendered, both with regard to content as well as methods and established aims.

In spite of the aforementioned facts, some people argue that education systems no longer seem to take into account the new needs confronting people everywhere in the world. For example, René Bendit and Wolfgang Gaiser make the following observation on the education system in the United States of America, which could be applied to many countries in the world:

> "The education system has failed to meet current social challenges. The increase in youth problems such as a problematic transition to the working world, increasing poverty, teenage pregnancies, drug abuse, intolerance towards minorities, juvenile delinquency and violence, are treated as a reflection of the fact that schools no longer have any connection with the real life world."

In order to integrate into the world economy, people must not only acquire the knowledge and tools of traditional knowledge, but above all, they must be capable of acquiring new skills demanded by a knowledge society. Indeed, the resulting rapid change in technological and scientific knowledge make learning a permanent process, a life-long learning process in the words of the Report of the International Commission on Education for the 21st Century to UNESCO, entitled: Learning, the treasure within.

Life-long learning is based on the following four fundamental precepts:

1. Learning to know, by combining a sufficiently broad general knowledge with the opportunity to work indepth on a small number of subjects. This also means learning to learn, so as to benefit from the opportunities education provides throughout life.
2. Learning to do, in order to acquire not only an occupational skill but also, more broadly, the competence to deal with

a large number of situations and work in teams. It also means learning to do in the context of young people's various social and work experiences which may be informal, as a result of the local or national context, or formal, involving courses alternating study and work.

3. Learning to live together, by developing an understanding of other people and an appreciation of interdependence-carrying out joint projects and learning to manage conflicts–in a spirit of respect for the values of pluralism, mutual understanding and peace.
4. Learning to be, so as to develop better one's personality and be able to act with increasingly greater autonomy, judgment and personal responsibility. To that end, education must not disregard any aspect of a person's potential: memory, reasoning, aesthetic sense, physical capacities and communication skills.

SOME POSITIVE AND NEGATIVE IMPACTS OF GLOBALISATION

Although globalisation seems to be unavoidable to many countries and numerous initiatives and efforts have been made to adapt to it with aims at taking the opportunities created from it to develop their societies and people, in recent years there are also increasing international concerns with the dangerous impacts of globalisation on indigenous and national developments. Various social movements have been initiated against the threats of globalisation particularly in developing countries. The negative impacts of globalisation include various types of economic, political and cultural colonisation by advanced countries on those developing and under-developed countries. Inevitably, how to maximize the opportunities and benefits from globalisation to support local developments and reduce the threats and negative impacts of globalisation will be the major concerns of developing countries.

As mentioned above, globalisation is creating opportunities for sharing knowledge, technology, social values, and behavioural norms and promoting developments at different levels including individuals, organizations, communities, and societies across different countries and cultures. In particular, the advantages of globalisation may include the following:

- Global sharing of knowledge, skills, and intellectual assets that are necessary to multiple developments at different levels;
- Mutual support, supplement and benefit to produce synergy for various developments of countries, communities, and individuals;
- Creating values and enhancing efficiency through the above global sharing and mutual support to serving local needs and growth;
- Promoting international understanding, collabouration, harmony and acceptance to cultural diversity across countries and regions.
- Facilitating communications, interactions, and encouraging multi-cultural contributions at different levels among countries.

At the same time, globalisation, potentially creating serious negative impacts for developing and under-developed countries. This is also the major reason why there have been so many ongoing social movements in different parts of the world against the trends of globalisation particularly in economic and political areas. The potential negative impacts of globalisation are various types of political, economic, and cultural colonization and overwhelming influences of advanced countries to developing countries and rapidly increasing gaps between rich areas and poor areas in different parts of the world. In particular, the potential negative impacts include the following:

1. Increasing the technological gaps and digital divides between advanced countries and less developed countries.

2. Creating more legitimate opportunities for a few advanced countries for a new form of colonisation of developing countries.
   - Increasing inequalities and conflicts between areas and cultures; and
   - Promoting the dominant cultures and values of some advanced areas.

GLOBALISATION AND UNEQUAL ACCESS TO EDUCATION

Many people believe that, education is one of key local factors that can be used to moderate some impacts of globalisation from negative to positive and convert threats into opportunities for the development of individuals and local community in the inevitable process of globalisation. How to maximise the positive effects and minimize the negative impacts of globalisation is a major concern in current educational reform for national and given the phenomenon of "globalisation", economic growth of the last decades has been accompanied by a worsening of inequalities in the world and in particular, inequalities of access to knowledge.

Integration into today's world economy implies not only mastery of traditional knowledge but also the capacity to acquire the new skills required by a knowledge society. It is therefore evident that an unequal sharing of the new communication and information technologies only serves to reinforce existing inequalities.

While education deficits are obviously greater in developing countries, this is a major issue in developed countries as well. In many industrialised countries there is a persistent problem of illiteracy and low skills, which is an important source of social exclusion. Unequal access to education also fuels growing wage inequality and worsens the income distribution. The uneducated and unskilled in industrialized countries face severe disadvantage in an increasingly competitive global market.

However, the provision of both primary and secondary schooling increased during the 90s across the globe, but progress is inadequate and hides the differences between countries and regions. The OECD countries, for example, spend 100 times more per pupil in primary and secondary education than low-income countries. There are many evidences which indicate that the more rapid progress is possible if the political will and the resources exist, in high- and low-income countries alike.

All countries which have benefited from globalisation have invested significantly in their education and training systems. Today women and men need broad-based skills which can be adapted to rapidly changing economic requirements as well as appropriate basic skills which enable them to benefit from information technology, increasing their ability to overcome barriers of distance and budgetary limitations. While Internet technology is not particularly capital-intensive, it is very human capital-intensive. Sound education policy also provides an important instrument to offset the negative impacts of globalisation, such as increasing income inequalities, with effects which may ultimately be stronger than labour market policies.

Education is a core element of society, and the foundation of democratic choice. The large differences in opportunities in education between countries are one of the basic causes of global inequality. Furthermore, international migration allows rich countries to benefit from the investments in human capital made in poor countries–giving them a responsibility to support the education systems where those investments are made.

The development of a national qualifications framework is also an important foundation for participation in the global economy, since it facilitates life-long learning, helps match skill demand and supply, and guides individuals in their choice of career. Access to training and skills development for women is often hindered by family commitments, indicating a need for childcare facilities and possibilities for distance learning. Other priorities include recognition and upgrading of skills for workers in the informal economy and the adaptation of training to accommodate workers with no formal education.

GLOBALISATION, EDUCATION AND TECHNOLOGICAL GAP

In today's global economy and information society, knowledge and information are the keys to social inclusion and productivity, and connectivity is the key to global competitiveness. Yet in our unequal world the networked economy is able to incorporate all that it regards as valuable, but also to switch off people and parts of the world that do not fit the dominant model.

Technological capability is essential. Countries need the communications infrastructure and the production system which can process and use information for development; and people must have access to the knowledge and the ability to use it, in order to participate, take advantage of and be creative in the new technological environment. That puts education and skills at the centre of a fair and inclusive globalisation.

Online distance learning could become a powerful tool for developing countries–reducing the need for expensive physical infrastructure for tertiary and vocational educational facilities and enabling investments to be made instead in communications equipment, with curricula and teaching provided through regional initiatives. The Global Distance Learning Network (GDLN) is one such initiative. It is a world-wide network of institutions which are developing and applying distance learning technologies and methods with a focus on development and poverty reduction. Such networks are likely to play an important role in building technological capabilities.

Increasing the technological gaps and digital divides between advanced countries and less developed countries that are hindering equal opportunities for fair global sharing Global sharing of knowledge, skills, and intellectual assets that are necessary to multiple developments at different levels . Creating more legitimate opportunities for a few advanced countries to economically and politically colonise other countries globally. Mutual support, supplement and benefit to produce synergy for various developments of countries, communities, and individuals. Exploiting local resources and destroying indigenous cultures of less advanced countries to benefit a few advanced countries Creating values and enhancing efficiency through the above global sharing and mutual support to serving local needs and growth Increasing inequalities and conflicts between areas and cultures.

ILO argues that promoting international understanding, collabouration, harmony and acceptance to cultural diversity across countries and regions Promoting the dominant cultures and values of some advanced areas. Facilitating multi-way communications and interactions, and encouraging multi-cultural contributions at different levels among countries Clearly, the management and control of the impacts of globalisation are related to some complicated macro and international issues that may be far beyond the scope of this paper.

The increase in poverty in the world is the most tragic phenomenon in this era of abundance. It is the cause of marginalization and the exclusion of increasingly bigger groups of the world population and in particular, affects children, the young and women. As a consequence, we see the development of cultures of poverty and marginalisation that lock the same people into the cycle of poverty and reinforce their exclusion.

But it is still the inequality with regard to knowledge that constitutes one of the biggest challenges of our societies. The traditional raw materials and non-renewable natural resources under threat of extinction no longer occupy the most important place in the process of production and development. It is knowledge in itself that has become one of the key resources of economic growth. We thus see a new category of workers appearing on the scene, "knowledge workers". Without knowledge, you are subject to marginalisation and progressive exclusion, but the corollary is also true. "The higher the level of education and training of a country's population, the more chances a nation has of seizing opportunities and minimising the social cost of technological change and the transition towards a more open economy."

GLOBALISATION, EDUCATION AND HUMAN RIGHTS

Education has been proclaimed as an integral part of human rights: "It must be free and compulsory with regards to basic, elementary teaching. Vocational and technological teaching must be widely available and access to higher education available to all equally, on the basis of merit" Education is also the driving force behind economic growth and human and cultural development. The application of policies of compulsory basic education for all and investment in quality teaching have meant governments and experts have been able to measure the impact on populations and the society as a whole. That impact can be seen in improvement in health, lowering of the rate of demographic growth, reduction of child mortality and increase in life expectancy. Education also means that populations become aware of their rights and obligations as citizens and are thus able to participate actively in the construction and management of life in their communities.

According to studies undertaken by UNESCO as well as by UNDP, the world economic crisis, which dominated the eighties, spread in virtue of the constraints imposed by economic globalisation. It was also pointed out that "the process of restructuring and social adjustment that have taken place in most countries and are still taking place in some, seem to have had a lasting effect on national politics at the expense of education".

The education sector has not yet acquired the right to benefit from special treatment or to be exonerated from the application of policies limiting public expenditure in general.

CONCLUDING REMARKS

This paper tries to highlights the fact that economic policies in most of the world rarely considered education as investment for the future or as a key to development, and even less as a fundamental right of human beings. The repercussions of these policies at all levels of education systems in the world, with the exception of a few industrialised countries, have been sorely felt. Such repercussions include the worsening of teaching conditions; insufficient numbers of school establishments and increase in numbers per class, particularly in developing countries experiencing strong demographic growth; the loss of teaching quality often due to the qualification level of the teacher's and the material conditions in which they carry out their profession; and finally, the loss of relevance regarding the education programmes themselves. But still remains many questions, such as:

> What is education for the 21st, century? The present-day crisis in conventional education systems is only the syndrome of a society undergoing profound change. Its political, economic, and cultural institutions and the values and symbols at the heart of those institutions, have become inoperable and obsolete in their regulatory and integrating function concerning the same individual members of the society in question.

How can education respond to the challenges of increasing poverty, unemployment, and exclusion in the world and to those of intolerance and violence that affect all societies and are even to be found within schools themselves?

How can education answer the needs of a multicultural society which, in virtue of the cultural and ethnic diversity of that society's people, requires recognition of that diversity and of the people's own particular needs, and at the same time favour their social and economic integration into the majority culture?

How can the trends towards globalisation, standardisation, and the homogenisation of cultural models be conciliated? And how can we conciliate the increasingly strong claims for cultural diversity which, in their most extreme form, can be seen as a relinquishment of identity, the violent rejection of the other, and fundamentalism of all kinds?

"In its new guise, continuing education is seen as going far beyond what is already practiced, particularly in the developed countries, namely, upgrading and refresher training, retraining and conversion or promotion courses for adults. It should open up learning opportunities for all, for many different purposes–offering a second or third chance, satisfying the thirst for knowledge, beauty, or the desire to surpass oneself, or making it possible to broaden and deepen strictly vocational forms of training, including practical training."

REFERENCES

Altbach, P.G. (Ed.) (1999), Private Prometheus: Private Higher Education and Development in the 21st Century. *Contributions to the Study of Education No. 77*. Connecticut: Greenwood Press.

Argyris, C., Putnam, R., & Smith, D.M. (1985), *Action science*. San Francisco: Jossey-Bass.

Ayyar, R.V.V. (1996), Educational Policy Planning and Globalisation. *International Journal of Educational Development, 16*(4), 347-354.

Bendit, R. and W. Gaiser (1995), "Integration and Segregatio of Young People in a Changing World", *Prospects,* Vol. XXV, No. 3, Sept.

Brown, P., & Lauder, H. (1996), Education, globalisation and economic development. *Journal of Education Policy, 11* (1), 1-25.

Brown, T. (1999), Challenging globalisation as discourse and phenomenon. *International Journal of Lifelong Education, 18*(1), 3-17.

Cheng, Y.C. (2000), A CMI-Triplization Paradigm for Reforming Education in the New Millennium. *International Journal of Educational Management* 14 (4), 156-174.

Cheng, Y.C., Ng, K.H., & Mok, M.M.C. (2002). Economic Considerations in Education Policy Making: A Simplified Framework. *International Journal of Educational Management,* 16(1), 18-39.

Fowler, F.C. (1994), The International Arena: The Global Village. *Journal of Education Policy, 9*(5-6), 89-102. Green, A. (1999). Education and Globalisation in Europe and East Asia: Onvergent and Divergent Trends. *Journal of Education Policy, 14* (1), 55-71.

Henry, M., Lingard, B., Rizvi, F., & Taylor, S. (1999), Working with/ Against Globalisation in Education. *Journal of Education Policy, 14*(1), 85-97.

Holmes, W. (1999), The Transforming Power of Information Technology. *Community Coledge Journal,* 70 (2), pp. 10-15.

ILO (2004), *A Fair Globalisation: Creating Opportunities for All,* Geneva, International Labour Office.

James, E. (1994), Public-private division of responsibility for education. In T. Husén & T.N. Postlethwaite (Eds.), *The international encyclopedia of education* (2nd ed. Vol. 8,) Oxford, England/New York: Pergamon/Elsevier Science.

Jones, P.W. (1999), Globalisation and the UNESCO mandate: Multilateral prospects for Educational Development. *International Journal of Educational Development,* 19 (1), 17-25.

Klor de Alva, J. (2000), Remaking the Academy in the Age of Information. *Issues in Science and Technology,* 16 (2), 52-58.

Lick, D.W. (1999), Transforming Higher Education: A New Vision, Learning Paradigm, and Change management. *International Journal of Innovative Higher Education 1999, Fall,* 13.

Little, A.W. (1996), Globalisation and Educational Research: Whose Context Counts? *International Journal of Educational Development*, 16 (4), 427-438.

McGinn, N.F. (1996), Education, Democratization, and Globalisation: A Challenge for Comparative Education. *Comparative Education Review,* 40 (4), 341-357.

UNESCO (1996), *Learning the Treasure Within,* Paris, Co-Publication Unesco/odile Jacob Publishers.

UNESCO (1998), World Report on Education, Paris, Unesco Publications.

Wang, Y. (2000), (ed.) Public-private Partnerships in the social sector. Tokyo: Asian Development Bank Insitute. Waters, M. (1995). *Globalisation.* London: Routledge.

DEHUMANISED EDUCATION IN A GLOBALISED SOCIETY: OPPORTUNITIES AND CHALLENGES OF GLOBALISED EDUCATION

M.K. George

INTRODUCTION

It might look too sentimental to begin a scientific presentation on Education, with a reference to an Engineering girl student in Kerala, who a few months ago jumped down from a multi-storeyed building because she couldn't apparently afford to pay the exorbitant fee in a private/self-financing engineering college. However, this event is symbolic of the theme this paper wants to present. Does globalised education lead to such de-humanisation that young students will be forced to take their own precious lives? The paper is a preliminary search into the all-pervasive globalisation trends, how it affects the educational efforts particularly at the higher education levels, whether it leads to humanisation or de-humanisation and finally concludes with suggestions for a humanising response to globalised education.

CLARIFYING THE CONCEPTS

The two major concepts that are used are Globalisation and Humanisation. In this paper, globalisation is understood as a process of growing and intensifying interaction at all levels of society, in world trade, foreign investment, capital markets, abetted by technological advances in transport and communications and by rapid liberalisations and deregulation of trade, capital and labour flows, both nationally and internationally leading to one market. It also means the removal of national boundaries as impediments to the free flow of capital, of goods and of services. The entire system is crafted, of course, mostly by and for the great Multinational Corporations, who are increasingly in the business of raising capital in one part of the world, investing it in another, to produce something that can be sold in a third (Adam Hoschschild, 1998).

In this sense, globalisation has always been part of the modern world. What makes contemporary globalisation distinctively different is the unprecedented intensification and acceleration of an ever open flow of communication and movement of people, capital, technologies, goods, images and knowledge, through and beyond national borders. A global market now controls the whole process.

Forces of neo-liberalism power globalisation, which is so much a driving force that some even treat it as synonymous with globalisation. Added to the values of neo-liberalism, the ideological revolution of egalitarianism, the technological and scientific revolution, the cybernetic and electronic information revolution and the market economy have together constituted this phenomenal experience of globalisation in the contemporary society (Louis Xavier, 1997).

The all-pervasive effects of modern day globalisation trends have been highlighted by economists, sociologists, geographers, and even by religion. However, responses to globalisation have at best been ambiguous or ideologically committed. (Odozor, I, 1999; A.R. Roy, 1999; Hussain, Abid, 2005). Two major trends have characterised the responses to globalisation: looking at it as a neo-colonial strategy to conquer the under developed world and looking at it as a massive opening to future growth opportunities. Whichever be the position one subscribes to, one cannot avoid the fact that education will be one of the primary institutions that will be affected by globalisation trends. And, that is the theme of this paper.

Humanisation is a value-loaded term. Using Freirean concepts (1968, 1972, 1985) it is seen as a basic faith in ontological vocation of man to be a subject who acts upon the world, transforming the world and thus makes the world a pro-human world. In a humanized world all are subjects, who think for themselves, act and dialogue. In the process a just world emerges. In contrast, a de-humanised world is characterised by objects that are acted upon, thought for by others and are subjected to monologues. The net result would be an unjust world.

Education is seen as an instrument of humanisation by all traditions of education. The critical question is whether in a globalised world, education can still be a humanising agent.

GLOBALISED EDUCATION

The clearest manifestation of the impact of globalisation on education is the growing concern with what is called Internationalisation of education. "It is a process of systematic integration of an international dimension into the teaching, research and public service function of a higher education institution" (Watcher, 1999).

It refers to the activities of higher educational institutions often supported or framed by multilateral agreements or programmes, to expand their reach over national borders. Internationalisation of activities and policies can serve a broad variety of objectives, such as the diversification and growth of financial input by the recruitment of fee-paying foreign students, the broadening of curricula and educational experiences for domestic students in foreign partner-institutions, regional net-working in order to allow a more cost effective use of resources and to provoke a process of collective institutional learning and development or the enhancement of the quality of education and research by bringing students and staff in the realm of international competition. Activities in this context include joint research projects, student exchange programmes, staff mobility projects, specially designed programmes, aimed at foreign students, joint curriculum development initiatives, specific initiatives in the context of university development, policies etc. (Damme Dirk Van, 2003).

The GATS and WTO agreements immediately affect higher education, allowing foreign universities to market their education in this country. In fact information technology is altogether eliminating the concept of jurisdiction of a university.

IMPACT OF GLOBALISATION ON EDUCATION

To the layman, globalisation of education is manifested by simple indicators like increased number of students migrating to foreign countries to study, easier loan facilities, a student can get up to Rs. 15 lakhs as loan, increasing number of foreign universities operating in India, increased reservation for NRIs and foreign students in professional colleges and so on. In fact, these are indicative of the deeper and more substantive changes that are taking place.

COMMODIFICATION OF EDUCATION

Education is now considered a marketable commodity, a multi-billion dollar business. From a social good to a marketable commodity, education has become so different in its ideological and practical domains.

"A revolution is taking place in Education. Education is becoming an internationally traded commodity. No longer is it seen primarily as of skills, attitudes and values required for citizenship and effective participation in modern society– a key contribution to the common good of any society. Rather, it is increasingly seen as a commodity to be purchased by a consumer in order to build a "skill set" to be used in the market place or a product to be bought and sold by multinational corporations. Academic institutions have transmogrified themselves into business, and other providers. Nowhere is this trend more clearly exemplified than in the current debate about GATS, the General Agreement on Trade in Services, now taking place internationally within the world trade organization" (Altbach, Philip, 2002).

1. Global Competitiveness: With globalisation of education, the challenge is to raise standards to make it globally competitive, locally relevant and offer a marketing paradigm appropriate for the developing societies.

2. Higher costs of education: The unit cost of education, particularly of professional education, is quite high and has gone out of reach of the Indian middle and lower classes. The whole debate on subsidy of higher education is relevant in this context. There is tremendous pressure on India and other developing countries to stop subsidising higher education and shift to primary education. However, Ren Borwon, former U S commerce secretary, when asked about whether the free education available from 19th century to 1970s was good for the economy, he responded:" It was great for the economy. It was one of the best things that the U S Government did at that time in American history-building institutions of higher education, which were accessible to the masses of the people. I think it is one of the reasons why our economy grew and prospered, one of the ways in which the U S was able to close some of its social gaps. So people who lived in rural areas would have the same kind of access to higher education as people living in other parts of the country. It was one of the reasons for making America strong" (Dinesh Mohan 1998).

3. The fact is that more than 95 per cent of the Indians will need assistance to go to university. And hence, raising the cost of higher education retards upward mobility. To cite the example of America once again, the proportion of Blacks attending university has remained static or gone down in recent periods as the cost increased.

(a) Student Mobility: According to UNESCO estimates, in 1994-95 there were 1.5 million foreign students in the top 50 host countries. Over the last 25 years, international student mobility has risen by more than 300 per cent. It is estimated that by 2010 there will be 2.8 million students studying abroad. In 2025 it would be 4.9 million, of which 2.9 million would be from Asia. Indian students number around 30,000 paying Rs 400 crore as fees.

(b) Teaching Staff Mobility: There is increasing staff mobility, which is characteristically called brain drain. However, there have been two opinions about brain drain, one group arguing that in a globalised world the concept of brain drain does not arise, as they bring precious resources to the home country as well as some return to the home country, more professional and committed. Some also argue that brain drain is better than 'brain in the drains'. But the fact is that developing countries and countries in Eastern Europe face the problem of emigration of researchers and academics to the global centres of research.

(c) Internationalisation of Curricula: An obvious impact of internationalisation of education is the internationalisation of curricula. For credibility as well as marketability there is the need for standardising curricula on par with international standards. While it looks a challenging and profitable impact, the impact on those who cannot cope with English language and the international levels of curricula remain a problem.

(d) Branch campuses: It is amazing the speed at which branch campuses are emerging for universities and other institutes.

(e) Mutual recognition agreements: Whether it is in the form of franchisees or twinning, mutual recognition and acceptance of degrees have become very common too.

(f) Transnational University networks and trans-national virtual delivery of higher education have become realities.

(g) Threat to indigenous arts and culture: One major fall-out of internationalisation of education is the almost total neglect of indigenous culture and arts. In fact while critiquing globalisation, it has been observed that " in some ways, the effects of free trade in images and information are more far-reaching than those of trade in tangible objects, for here we are talking about forces that mould minds, tastes and values." (Hoschchild 1998).

GLOBALISED EDUCATION AND DE-HUMANISATION TENDENCIES

Globalised education per se is not de-humanizing. In fact, there are innumerable benefits like improvements in the quality of education, greater choice of agencies, use of information and communication technologies for domestic and cross-border delivery of programmes, greater access to knowledge, reduction in the knowledge gap between the rich and poor countries and so on. However, there are specific dimensions, which can cause a de-humanising effect.

The first and foremost factor is that globalisation brings amnesia of the poor. In the rat race of market economy, the poor are forgotten. There is an eclipse of the social consciousness. One of the most conspicuous evidences for this is the fact that in spite of all globalisation efforts, not even six per cent of the relevant population is in the higher education.

The costs of education are escalating. Simultaneously, there is the pressure to reduce subsidy. The result of all these are that a substantial number of the poor will never be able to benefit higher education. The instance of Indian IITs has been pointed out. When the fee was raised to Rs. 25,000/-

per year, 30-50 per cent of drop in admission were reported. (Dinesh Mohan, 1998).

There is little interest in the humanities and social sciences among the youth. The professional courses are the most sought after. Through these efforts, it is as though globalised higher education is 'forming faithful acolytes at the altar of globalisation and liberalisation".

"Open markets, at least in higher education, reinforce the inequalities that already exist. If educational borders are completely open, the strongest and the wealthiest education providers will have unrestricted access. Countries and institutions that cannot compete will find it difficult to flourish. This means that developing countries and smaller industrialized nations will be at a considerable disadvantage" (Altback, 2002).

MAKING GLOBALISED EDUCATION A HUMANISED ONE

The challenge to all concerned is how we can move towards a globalisation based on equality rather than a new neo-colonialism. Or, how do we create a global academic environment that recognises the need to ensure that academic relationships are as equal as possible.

The response must begin by recognising the inequality and the consequent possibilities of discrimination and de-humanisation. It entails a challenge to create a world that ameliorates these inequalities. This would of course require institutional safeguards and policy strictures. Most important, monitoring processes of educational practices and institutions also need to be established.

The task is not easy. H.G. Wells once remarked, "History becomes more and more a race between education and catastrophe". Today, globalised education itself will become a catastrophe unless proactive steps are initiated.

REFERENCES

Dinesh Mohan (1998), Education and its Market Value in *Seminar* No. 461.

Freire Paulo (1968), Pedagogy of the Oppressed. New York: Seabury Press.

——— (1972), Cultural Action for Freedom. Harmondsworth.

——— (1985), The Politics of Education. London: Macmillan.

Hussain, Abid (2005), Impact of Globalisation. Talk delivered at Trivandrum.

Muralidharan, K. (2002), 'Values in Education: A Changing Perspective' in *University News*. Vol. 40, No. 1. Jan. 7-13.

Odozor, I.P. (1999), 'Emerging African Alternatives to Globalisation ' in *Vidyajyoti Journal* Vol. 63. No. 7, July 1999. New Delhi.

Oommen M.A. (2000), The Context of Globalisation. Talk Delivered at Kottayam.

Shukla and Kaul (1998), 'Education, Development and Underdevelopment. New Delhi: Sage.

Takwale, Ram (2003), 'Challenges and Opportunities of Globalisation for Higher Education in India–Alternatives through e-education ' in *New Frontiers in Education* Vol. XXXIII No. 4, Oct-Dec.

Xavier Louis (1997), Response of Jesuit Higher Education to Globalisation.

NATIONAL SECURITY ISSUES IN POST LIBERALISATION ERA

U.P. Thakur, K. Soma Sekhar and V. Divya Thejomurthy

INTRODUCTION

The collapse of the erstwhile Soviet Union in the early 1990s, shattered the political equilibrium that had sustained the international community in the aftermath of the Second World War and led to substantial and marked shifts, adjustments, readjustments and transformations in the domain, range and scope of India's security imperatives. Though conflicts in the cold war period were centered on posturing in various fields, there was no real reason for the two blocks to go to war because of nuclear deterrence. The two blocks were in their own world, while other countries were being supported by one of them, and thus maintaining a semblance of peace.

The dissolution of the Soviet Union coupled with the financial crisis of 1991 compelled India to liberalize her economic policy and undertake major reforms and market economy to integrate herself with the global system. This liberalisation of Indian market and various economic reforms launched under the philosophy of globalisation have raised issues that have direct and indirect bearing on India's security. It is therefore, necessary to identify the issues that need to be considered for defining a national security paradigm in the changed context and drawing up a strategy.

The extent to which globalisation has altered the nature and direction of prevailing theories and paradigms of India's national security requires to be examined. We must inquire whether globalisation has circumvented the "nation-state" concept and to what extent it has impacted the security concerns. How security communities are articulating the anxieties and interests in the complex process of globalisation necessitate an analysis for their import to national security.

NATIONAL SECURITY

Security of a nation-state is a multi-dimensional concept involving various concepts. While Morton Berkowitz and P.G. Bock, describe it as the ability of a nation to protect its internal values from external threats", and "the preservation of its core values critical to the nation-state from external and internal threats", Water Lipman emphasizes that, "a nation has security when it does not have to sacrifice its legitimate interests to avoid war and is able, if challenged, to maintain them by war". Henry Kissinger opines that, national security, comprises every action by which a society seeks to assure its survival or realizes its aspirations internationally", and asserts that the basic factors that govern it are political, social, technological, economical and psychological; while Jaswant Singh, calls it as the preservation of the core values of our nation, the political, economic and social well-being and preservation of our state, the inviolability of our territorial boundaries and the maintenance of national interest within the strategic frontiers of India". For Rathy Sawheny, of the Institute for Defence Studies and Analysis, Delhi, it is the nation's ability to effectively safeguard its internal values and legitimate national interests against external threats including externally fostered internal subversion and if challenged attain or maintain them even by recourse to war". Frank N. Trager, and Frank L. Simonie, describes national security as that part of the government policy which aims to create favourable national and international conditions for the protection or extension of national interests against existing or potential enemy threats, both external or internal or externally fostered internal threats.

These definitions quoted above identify national security as the ability of a nation to protect its core values and interests from internal and external threats, capability to pursue and promote its legitimate interests. The nation has security when it does not have to sacrifice its legitimate interests to avoid war and is capable to maintain its interests if challenged by war. It also means the country should be able to assure its survival and realize its aspirations internally as well as internationally and security covers political, social, technological, economic and psychological factors. National Security stands for inviolability of territorial boundaries, protection from externally fostered internal subversion and is a part of the government policy aimed to create favourable national and international conditions for the protection or extension of national interests against existing or potential enemy threats, both external or internal or externally fostered internal threats. The subject of discussion here is which of these points are impinged by the forces of liberalisation and to what extent liberalisation has altered these security formulation and how these elements of national security and to what degree, have been influenced by the factors and forces brought into play due to liberalisation.

SECURITY PARADIGMS

Definitions apart, it is necessary to examine the various ways in which security theorists and practitioners look at security and its importance. A number of concepts like security community, collective security, cooperative security and securitization has been proposed. It is also suggested that cooperative security cannot function effectively due to the divergence of threat perception among the ruling elites belonging to different nations. It has been said that geopolitical perceptions of the cold war period are yielding to geo-psychological perceptions. It may not be wrong, to quite some extent, that psychic responses especially ethno religious conflicts and crisis are assuming far more importance than ever before. Security analysts like Buzan, Waver and Wilde talk of security within the framework of social processes whereas the Copenhagen Group asserts that unless social problems are addressed, a composite security is not possible.

Cooperative security on the one hand, is based on a set of common ideals and goals, which can be realized by recognizing the mutual necessities, the concept of "security complex" on the other, introduced by Barry Buzan talks of a group of states whose primary security concerns are so closely linked together that their national securities cannot be considered different from one another. It will be worthwhile to watch the shift in security paradigm because of the forces of liberalisation and the bearing they have on Indian security view.

EVOLVING THREAT PERCEPTIONS

In the globalised and dynamic context a broader conceptualization of security is necessary so that totality of national spectrum is visualized. Ensuring the security of any country or society requires that the conditions be created that would contribute to India's politico-social consolidation and territorial integrity, that would sustain such conditions which would guarantee its existence and survival and, safeguard the freedom of options and capacities of the country to survive in a changing volatile international environment. Security is therefore not a static but dynamic concept. Ensuring security, therefore, goes beyond strategic and military factors, and involves political, economic, social, technological, and environmental factors and inputs and everything that has a bearing directly or indirectly on the health of the nation, physical as well as psychological. This thinking is particularly relevant in the post-Cold War period because of the incremental trend of international regulatory regimes being put in place. They control the activities in the areas of technology, space, nuclear energy, human rights and the environment. These regimes have not been formulated by consensus or through detailed deliberation at the UN but have been mostly created by the great powers and the industrially and technologically advanced countries. They are discriminating and are mostly against Indian interest and Indian security view. This is the background in which India's new security concerns and threat perceptions are evolving, and are the vital ingredients in India's changing defence and foreign policy orientation, and economic and social policy formulation.

Security issues arising out of India's territorial integrity, adversarial relations with neighbours, internal centrifugal forces that affect India's geo-political unity including the demands for secession from various segments of the population must enter into security calculation in the backdrop of globalisation. So also is another thinking, and very disturbing for India, after the breakup of the USSR and the ethnic, linguistic divisions of Eastern Europe and Central Asia, is the recurrent refrain of some foreign countries and foreign think tanks questioning the very practicability of India's survival as a polity because of the religious, ethnic and the linguistic plurality. While this new trend must be countered effectively, thinking and policy of US and military presence in the neighbourhood of India, the Indian ocean and the Arab and African littoral countries and the China's overwhelming nuclear capabilities and the presence of nuclear weapons in the Asian and Indian ocean region are the issues that influence India's maritime security and must be considered in security analysis.

LIBERALISATION MEASURES AND NEW DIMENSIONS OF SECURITY

The financial crisis in 1991 forced India to adopt the path of economic liberalisation and structural adjustment. The three major elements of the IMF–dictated conditions were, India had to deregulate and liberalise all markets, there had to be increased competitiveness in all spheres of economic activity, and that the government would have to learn to live within its means of a strong budget constraints, the fiscal austerity. All aspects of license and control too were to be given up.

India's adjustment policy was worked out to enter the global economy, through the "exploitation of benefits that accrue from economic independence", and to win political maneuvering room. The government, in such a free market economy were to provide regulatory institutions to implement policies with regard to competition, while protecting "people from negative, predatory externalities". Import liberalisation was undertaken with a view to promoting efficient export production, leading to improved export earnings–all laudable contemplation.

The assault on the government expenditure led to the curtailment and downsizing of social programmes. The amount of public investment declined; subsidies reduced and poor suffered. The execution of market oriented economic policies should have gone hand-in-hand with measures that strengthen the social sector to fight poverty, illiteracy, malnutrition, and ill-health. But none of them happened and the employment really declined and social sectors suffered. Reforms were supposed to protect the economic and social interest of the public, but poor have suffered and widespread corruption has been siphoning whatever money is available. The State bureaucratic apparatus remains unresponsive and unconcerned to the public necessity. Recent developments in the telecommunication sector reveal the need for public scrutiny and surveillance to avoid undue exploitation of liberalisation. It is felt that the relationship between the means and outcome of liberalisation and security needs are to be better understood, the parameters identified and correct equation established.

As we globalise, we also globalise to new issues of security, that includes internal and external terrorism, internal destabilization, environmental degradation, depletion of resources, fundamentalism, social tension and fissures, ethnic discordance, linguistic narrowism, religious dogmas, cultural and economic barriers and sanctions and restrictions of all kinds. While liberalisation may be intentioned at creating more wealth, more opportunities, more prosperity and economic strength of the nation, the very democratic route of achieving this also springs up voices of dissonance and disruption and gives rise to forces that weaken the nation's defence. India already had enough of them and liberalisation has fuelled further these dimensions of security where attempts at liberalizing human enterprises are leading to internal and external security issues. The Indian security paradigm for the new and emerging world must be evolved and formulated that would assure not only survival as a nation but one that would help harmonise these forces and exploit the environment creatively.

Thus, the concept of security has to be enlarged to encompass military as well as non-military, conventional as well as non-conventional threats and challenges to the state and to the society. Security is increasingly being construed as "security of the people, not just territory; security through development, not just arms; security of all people everywhere– in their home, on their jobs, in the streets, in their communities, and in their environment. It is also being realized that the "security and development" are two faces of the same coin and security must be seen as a feedback process in a national responsive system with global perspective.

Issues of national security in the backdrop of liberalisation can therefore be examined under three categories; one, the internal security that includes challenges of food, energy and environment, human rights, social harmony and tension, insurgency and growing insecurity at the root of rising expectation of people amidst economic deprivation and rising political expectation; two, the external security involving the external threats across the border, cross-border terrorism, drug traffic, diffusion of small arms, money laundering, illegal migration across the border and refugee influx, and others and; three, global security that influences and has impact on India's internal and external security environment, that includes global treaties and cooperation, diplomatic parleys and factors, energy and environmental issues, global economic and technology regimes and development, globally oriented transformations of society, culture and economy, inimical postures of cyber crimes and terrorism and many others. How liberalisation under the philosophy of globalisation is going to affect these security parameters, the orientation and direction required and the policy framework to be designed need examination.

Does participation in the global economy threaten India's sovereignty by liberating its markets to international environment? Will globalisation lead to a situation where Indian state will lose control of its economy and state power? What are the implications for India's security in inviting foreign investments–opening the internal market and becoming–part of the global community? Through the door of liberalisation, will Indian business monopolists and many others exploit Indian economy to their advantage to the detriment of people's and national interest. It has to be examined if the foreign governments through MNCs or MNCs themselves could create or damage India not only economically but even socially and culturally, biologically or chemically that remain unnoticed with the complicity of internal agents. The atmosphere of "laissez faire"–free-for-all, under the liberalized environment may encourage internal antinational and unsocial elements to create disturbances and anxieties which may pose a serious threat to national integrity. Security environment must be assessed in its entirety to exclude possibility of overlooking any significant factor. Though foreign direct investment could be significant, there is every possibility that MNCs in the name of supplying critical and strategic technology may use the liberalized environment for transferring ecologically harmful products and processes putting the society to risk. In the days of regulated economy we were told that we needed to protect internal markets from outside interference and to promote technology development. Today we are opening the markets again to promote technology development through competition. This contradiction is an issue that directly impact the national security. How long shall we take to compete the western products, processes and services and will liberalized atmosphere help India achieving a technological status? What will happen to India's current account balance and the resulting effect on the State economy and security? The stabilization measures and structural reforms were intended to transform the country into a more market oriented economy, but it has left a void of uncertainty in social, political, technological arena impacting the national security in various ways and giving rise to different security apprehensions. These issues need to be discussed to focus the main components of national security so that a calibrated security measure can be programmemed.

INTERNAL SECURITY

The very process of liberalisation sets in the environment of higher expectation for better living and an urge of equality. A society where there is a large gap between poor and rich for centuries, where information flow is causing aspirations to catch up but lack of opportunities find frustrations, is bound to have social tensions, agitations and violent expression for achieving their desire. And it is a major security issue. Conflicts that also emanate from social injustice, from the forces of cultural nationalism and ethnic consciousness are being further fuelled by liberalisation. Diverse conflicts–political, social, economic and cultural, psychological and civilizational conflicts, borne out of self-consciousness, aspirations and self-identity in the backdrop of globalisation of values, freedom and democracy are appearing in different forms throughout the country. If this freedom is not channelised constructively, it becomes the national security issue. Then there are non-conventional and non-military threats which are aiding the forces of terrorism, ethnic conflicts, fundamentalism, natural disasters, etc. all of which are getting energy and momentum from the liberation unleashed in the society.

The break-up of the Soviet Union and Yugoslavia seem to have eroded the sanctity or legitimacy of pluralistic societies as well as multi-ethnic, multi-lingual and multireligious states. And India has enough of fissiparous tendencies on these counts. Also, rising levels of political consciousness, due to the information revolution, have accentuated the economic expectations beyond the resource capacity of the Indian state leading to tension and instability. This frustration has led to the emergence of sub-regional ethno linguistic centrifugal trends in Indian politics. Caste-based parties, religion-based parties, ethnic and linguistic parties are already challenging the consolidation of the Indian Republic in political as well as territorial terms. Liberalisation and globalisation are making this still more difficult.

Liberalisation has increased the demand for restructuring relation between the Central and the state governments with a view to delegating more power and jurisdiction to the state setting the Centre-State relations under strain. Rapid economic reforms and modernization undertaken by India since June 1991, has also created regional imbalances in development, employment, income and industrialization with poor becoming poorer and the rich becoming richer. All these trends portend the likelihood of coalition governments based on temporary multiparty equation, which would lead to political instability.

The national consensus on security, defence and foreign policy is missing today. Liberalisation has added to the voices of discordance on international equations, defence capability acquisition, regional security alliance and on nuclear non-proliferation. All are not one on what is nationalism, what are national priorities, what are the issues of national security and what should be done to strengthen India. There are people who question, poor don't have a stake in Indian security, first feed them, defence comes later. The way different and divergent views are expressed by different Indian political and NGO groups at international forums exhibits the ill effects of globalisation and liberalisation and this is acquiring security dimension.

Liberalisation has pushed the debate of defence vs development to a new level without dealing with the core issues of security. If nations are economically weak and they also have a substantial external security threat, the authority of such nation is diminished both internally and internationally. Such nations have a tendency to divert more and more of their meagre resources into the military sector, resulting in declining investment in production which leads to slower growth, heavier taxes, increased external debt and finally lead to weakening of the defence forces. India faces the difficult task of balancing defence and developmental requirements neither of which can be ignored. Liberalisation that promotes imbalance between defence and economic growth, the one that ignores either and doesn't emphasise economic strength as an input to military strength, is a security issue.

ECONOMIC ISSUES

Economic reforms that do not thus address the problems in respect of development of society and nations are faulty and security risk. Economic primacy also stems from the competitive global environment. How far they meet our security needs? The rush for gaining competitive edge is leading to the commercialization of intellect, and of thinking process that gives birth to various conflicts and uncontrolled violent world order. The way multi-nationals are dictating terms and controlling government policies and programmes is a matter of security. It won't be out of place to think then how our entire planet would look like if multi-nationals are given a free run to take over national economies of States under their control, and to decide upon everything government in accordance with their concept guided solely by their economic wisdom. In a globalised world, it would be "survival of the fittest". The economy of the poor and developing countries would suffer, increasing the condition of deprivation and poverty if liberalisation is given as a fodder to MNCs. It is argued that globalisation is a strategy coined, propagated and ensured implementation by those powers who want to rule through the back door and rule by proxy of globalisation, jeopardizing the national interests and security. What happens to the sovereignty of the state then? Should globalisation allow multinationals to outstrip the nation-state? Should we not measure the globalisation programmes on our scale of national security?

Liberalisation was ostensibly meant to prop up the economic growth, to put the inefficient public sector to economic use, to remove rampant corruption, and to match the growth that meet the growing aspiration of the common man and bridge the chasm between the political and economic development and eliminate economic and political frustration and social fragmentation. However, the developments since the reforms were launched indicate it otherwise. The various implicit and explicit fiscal subsidies of the Central and state governments to a large number of interest groups have gone to mostly relatively rich. Many state governments are near bankruptcy whereas Central government has ways of parking its additional deficits in the public financial sector. Small-scale industries are crippled because they do not have much access to the equity markets and don't know where to go. Social expenditure has declined (not adequately compensated by rise in private investment). Capital expenditure of the central and state government together too has also been decreasing. The fact that it would be cheaper to import wheat in South India from Australia than from Punjab is a worrying point for economic security.

How liberalisation has faced in social sectors? Development index figures exhibit mixed performance after the liberalisation began. But the moot point is, how far these figures reflect the measure of equity, equality and distributive justice that determine the social cohesion, and well-being and security. Is liberalisation not meant to liberate the poor and the deprived and is it only aimed at meeting the revenue requirement of business? How have we performed socially?

Another question that haunts security thinkers is: the way India was almost aligned to Soviet ways of thinking in cold war days and killed its entrepreneurship because of its over dependence on Soviet Union for arms supply, will not liberalisation era India find itself aligned to multinational thinking and get carried away by the immediate foreign glory and glare putting national security to great risk? Is it not happening already?

National autonomy depends on the domestic political process and the national economic strength. If India's exports grow rapidly and its economic growth is high, there is no reason to suspect that India's sovereignty will be sacrificed by opening its markets to international competition. But then the point is, are you competitive, are your products, processes and services competitive.

Manipulation of economic policies and economic exploitation have been a subtle and often not so subtle method to subjugate countries. Economic aggression has been precursor to military takeover. Corporate multinationals have started dictating national policies and international alliances. The crisis of Korea, Malaysia and the worst of all, Indonesia are all too recent. The root cause of the economic collapse of these nations was their over-dependence on external powers, external aid and international loans. Only an economically strong nation can resist such measure. The SE Asian crisis is a lesson for India to avoid the economic abyss it may head for.

Foreign direct investment no doubt could be a significant source for advanced technology. But the country has to be careful that it is not used to transfer economically harmful and chemically and biologically dangerous products and processes to India, causing security threat. But will any country allow advanced technology to come to India? One may also ponder. Foreign savings used not for investment and growth but to finance consumption is security risk. Although capital inflows to India are much smaller than those in China, Mexico, Malaysia and other emerging markets, India must guard against situation of the type of the Mexican Peso crisis and be cautious, particularly of volatile short term portfolio inflows in quest of high returns. Large current account deficits are just not sustainable, and capital inflows in the mode of foreign direct investment are preferable to other forms of capital inflows.

RURAL INDUSTRIALIZATION

Economic reforms that leave small-scale, rural industrialization and invigoration untouched give room to uneven development and social unrest. Rural non-farm employment grew at a much slower rate in the 90's than in the 80's. Reforms are totally silent about human development, education, health, child nutrition, drinking water, women's welfare and autonomy, and are unusually preoccupied with problems of the foreign trade regime, fiscal deficits, and the constraints on industrial investments in the factory sector, and they believe that once these are handled right, trickle-down will take care of the issues that concern the masses. One may note that trickle down of benefits never take place in India. It is only the liabilities and losses that go down to hit the poor. Issues of illiteracy, gender and regional gaps in access to education, public health needs to be probed in relation to liberalisation. Economic reforms that increase the efficiency of enterprise and investment could help the poor by creating new jobs. But that has not happened. There are vast inter-regional differences in the level of human development and the forces of production. Both the differences have increased. Reforms that are oblivious of rural reality and do not address their problems and growth are security risk.

Rural areas throughout India remain less developed. Opportunities for personal and social advancement for people living in the rural areas are also limited. Food security remains one of the most important issues in India's economic management. However, the state schemes meant for public welfare, like the public distribution system, have not benefited the poor. While liberalizing the agricultural sector could be beneficial to farmers, it need to be designed with the support to poor farmers since the capacity to purchase food is a matter of life and death. A minimum of social safety net has not yet been constructed. If the administrative mechanism of delivery of public services in the area of human development remains seriously deficient, as it is today in most states, chances of constructing a minimum social safety net are low, and without such a safety net any large-scale programmeme of economic reform will remain politically unsustainable.

Reforms not implemented in letter and spirit may create havoc to social and economic fabric of the nation. It is difficult to expect reform to be carried out by an administrative set up that for many years has functioned as an inert, arbitrary, heavy-handed, corrupt and uncoordinated monolith. Economic reform is about competition and incentive, and a governmental machinery that does not itself allow them in its own backyard is an unconvincing proposition. Economic reforms without reforms in the delivery of public administration won't carry the message and would be a security risk.

TECHNOLOGICAL ISSUES

The present is witnessing a march of technology driving not only war-fighting doctrines and defense strategies but also the economy and the entire spectrum of national and global processes and entities. Technology is the enabler of liberalisation process as well as of the security. Technology has revolutionalised military thinking, political dialogues and social and economic activities. Operation "Enduring Freedom" and the recent war in Iraq remind us of this truth. Liberalisation has to a great extent made it possible for commercial technology to be within the reach of common man. This has brought in a revolutionary change in the thinking and in the way people do things, and in their hopes and aspirations. Those who have the technology have security, those who don't, can't ensure it. The meaning and implication of technologies of knowledge age must be understood. Since both technologies and strategies naturally transform each other, it is essential to include technology as the significant element of security thinking. Things become simpler if you recognize technology as a liberator as well as a defender, as an equalizer as well as an aggressor.

In the liberalized environment, the role of private sector in defence preparedness need to be examined along with the question if government controlled defence R & D is capable of meeting the diverse and fast changing needs of the country. If economy can be liberalized, why military technology remain shackled to government control and regulation. Why can't development of military hardware and software be open to private and individual enterprise? Why military technology be an exclusive preserve of the government of the day?

The liberalisation process under the globalisation philosophy has permitted western suppliers of lethal weapons to Pakistan to enjoy commercial access also in India. All technological deals between USA and India seem to ultimately tilt the tactical balance in favour of Pakistan. If USA is worried over use of dual technology, should not India too be worried over the supply of critical technology to Pakistan, while the same being denied to India and commercial technology being dumped in India by the same company for commercial gains? Threat to India's security from the new concept of the "danger of dual technologies falling into the hands of irresponsible states" is basically a techno-security threat that need to be faced headlong. A continuing handicap in updating and sustaining India's technological capabilities is a significant hurdle to ensuring Indian security. As long as this policy continues, our security will remain only in theory. We must guard against the tendency to globalize national security and remain open to all risks, manipulation and exploitation from within and outside the country.

Liberalisation under globalisation philosophy has more restrictions, selective controls and denial of important resources like oil, energy, technology and technical equipment beyond a certain degree of sophistication and is the tactic that bigger powers employ to keep a nation dependent, thereby ensuring technological and economic deprivation as well as holding the nation's security to ransom. Even technology for civil use of nuclear power has been under sanction. Can India be secure without securing emerging military and non-military technology? If technology determines our security status, it is a serious issue and we must create and develop leading edge technologies. Shall we keep complaining and bemoaning on what is given to Pakistan while we ourselves do nothing to compete? Is it the way to seek security for India? Do we still hope to get technology from somewhere to meet the challenge posed by the same powers who preach us about "dual technologies", and keep sitting idle? The post cold war scenario of globalisation has left India alone and made it urgent and essential to look into technological aspects of Indian security. There is no doubt that technology must enter into our strategic planning.

Technologies have had been the guarantor of security of nations in all areas–economy, politics, social and diplomacy. They determine the economics and military might, the social well-being and diplomatic strength of a nation and therefore are the ensurer of security. The present age, which is being referred to as post-modern age or knowledge age, is unfolding an unprecedented revolution in technology, and has initiated a revolution in military affairs (RMA). Technology as an enabler of security, politics, economy and diplomacy is emerging as one of the greatest tools in world affairs. Technology must form the backbone of our security framework. Technology has changed the traditional thought processes on military effectiveness and national security and must be factored into any security formulation.

ENERGY, ENVIRONMENT, FOOD AND COMMERCE

In the mainstream security studies, the object to be secured is state. The threats are either external, military ones or internal insurgencies each trying to violate the boundaries of the state, physical or psychological. In the environmental security, the referent object to be secured is the ecology that includes people, society and the total eco-system. The ecology is not a closed system like the state (though globalisation has breached that boundary), but is an open system, global system interacting with the neighbouring state and beyond. So environmental security is a global issue, and concerns everybody, transcending the national geographical boundaries.

Environment and security are interrelated. We use environment to get air, water, earth and her resources to produce things for our living and convenience and in the process while we deplete her resources we also pollute her. The processes used by modern civilization are such that we don't replace what we consume, leaving less and less for our children, deforesting it, desertifying it, emptying it. This is the issue of survival. Food, energy, population, consumption, technology are thus the interrelated security issues. Any security analysis without environment entering into it would be meaningless.

Another way to conceptualise environmental security is to match the trends of globalisation, population growth and urbanization and relate them to the economic, environmental and politico-military aspect. While globalisation may lead to the dumping of harmful products, larger population leads to larger consumption, larger pollution and urbanization lead to concrete jungles–desertification–all three cause environmental degradation. One of the main ingredients in all these three is the technology that we use for our living. The very technology that we use degrade the environment.

While, it is natural and just for developing countries to rapidly industrialise and make lives of people better, the developed countries are the major producer of pollution and are refusing to compromise their lifestyle. Rather than reducing emissions as agreed upon in the Kyoto Protocol, they are emitting pollutants which have long-term damage potential. This pollution by rich nations harms developing countries which may get submerged as a result of rich countries lifestyle and historic usage resulting in rise of the sea level due to global warming. It is axiomatic that to cope with the global warming will be easier for the rich rather than the poor. Liberalisation has downed the voice of the poor countries, making the pollution a major security issue.

Environmental degradation because of higher exploitation of environment (habitat) by increasing world population is leading to scarcity of resources, causing environmental stress and violent conflicts. After the collapse of Soviet Union, the only super power- the United States and some of the other advanced countries are bent on controlling the resources of the world on global scale, as was evident in the case of Iraq and elsewhere. This has certainly brought environment, energy and resources into focus for any security consideration. In the name of globalisation, what is being attempted is to gobble up the resources of poor, and defenceless countries.

No wars have broken out between nations directly as a result of environmental reasons. But as the unrest indicate about water scarcity, about rivers flowing between and among two or more nation states, that day is not far off. At least Indian states are already fighting over river-water issues. The scarcity of water in the middle-east is cited as one reason for worsening of Arab-Israeli conflict and a future war. The principle that might is right in the globalised world is making the poor nations pay for their weakness.

Wars have scorched the earth. Vietnam, the two World wars and Hiroshima and Nagasaki are the glaring examples. Environmental warfare like changing the weather is often quoted as a secret weapon. Environmental degradation as a threat to human health and wellbeing of people is not seen in correct perspective. National security is paramount, but its attainment is linked more and more with human society, whose eco, social and health security depend on the environment. In cold war time, war was out of question. Now for every issue the threat of war is shown as a possibility. In fact, globalisation that is understood for one country, one value system has made war very probable.

Poverty forces people to suffer from environmental impact. The rich can ward off the threat. The very fundamental rights are at stake. For example, availability of war is at stake, its pollution and potability is the environmental security issue. Degradation of land and reduced food crop, pollution of air in the big cities and the disease as a result of the polluted environment, acid rain which affects crops and health, vanishing and withering of forests, biodiversity losses like herbal plants, birds, animals, vultures and peacock all lead to the increased suffering of people. Economic reforms and the liberalisation measures are unleashing forces that have launched onslaught on the environment in various ways affecting the security of individuals and societies.

Environmental imbalance is causing climatic change and geographic changes leading to unpredictable behaviour. The environment also shifts the old neo-realistic security paradigm by about 180 degrees. From securing a state from external military threat, now the state has to be secured against threat to its natural environment and ecology. Most of the threats are within and our own creation. The threat is by forces and cycle of nature as a result of humans induced economic activities, activities that don't follow energy process of nature. Thus, issues which have been defined as transcending national boundaries are energy security, environmental management, safeguarding communication systems of the world rooted in new information technology and securing stable international environment for international trade and economic transactions. But which MNC follows these guidelines of security?

Policies of the US and other major powers on issue of energy security and economic trade and technological relations are aimed at ensuring US/Western dominance in the spheres of access and control of natural resources, assuring discriminatory access to the markets of the developing countries and ensuring that the technological superiority of the US, and its close allies is maintained to the exclusion of other countries. International regimes governing transfer of technologies, prevention of horizontal proliferation of nuclear weapons and missiles confirm this assessment. This is also underpinned by politico-strategic concepts like "Axis of Evil" and the selective and arrogant definitional identity of states "irresponsible or "rogue" states. India need to evolve its strategy to counteract such security threats.

Energy and Power which are the main drivers of economy and so of security are important for strategic objective of national security and industrial growth. A growing India has to examine its energy sources alternatives and future dependence on other nations factored into national security concern, safeguarding its energy sources against the rising cult of violence, militancy and terrorism and sabotage. While self-sufficiency may be illusive, conventional as well as unconventional energy sources may be explored. India must evolve multiple energy fronts requiring multiple strategies. In addition to Middle East, other areas: Central Asia, Bangladesh and South East Asia can be explored, which will require new alliances, secure routes and transportation. India must gear up its naval forces for constant maritime surveillance for steady and secure supply of energy from Gulf and elsewhere. Exploration activities in Iran, Egypt, Tanzania, Vietnam and Abu Dhabi are other possibilities.

It is also necessary to move away environment as a security issue from the strategic and security studies that are based on the western model and develop indigenous model that is representative of the Indian situation and takes care of the Indian resources and necessity. Even energy security that is an important discipline of environment security need a different approach–away from simply ensuring hydrocarbon imports from western and eastern Asian neighbours.

Liberalisation measures that cause India's major environmental problems of drought, desertification of soil quality, waste disposal and management, excessive and inappropriate use of fertilizers and pesticides, destruction and exploitation of fisheries, flora and fauna have often been ignored in the ecological analysis for the development in India. The lack of attention for the environment in project planning and implementation is visible. The ecological fragility affects the lives of millions of Indians requiring the state to take suitable measures to protect India's environment and livelihood of people dependent on sustainable environment. There is a need to structure economic liberalisation based on ecologically sound development strategy.

POLITICAL PERCEPTIONS

There is nothing wrong if globalisation theorists focus upon the world as a system and devote most of the attention to the global processes that transcend or operate more or less autonomously from individual societies or nations. It is also not wrong if globalisation is viewed in terms of cultural, economic, political, psychological, strategic and institutional forms. But flaw comes when, Thomas L. Friedman, The New York Times columnist, finds "globalisation system as a replacement of the cold war system", and talks about the emergence of a global market place and the rise of "homogenous" global culture that is essentially the spread of "Americanisation on a global scale". The 1999 Human Development Report, defines globalisation as "global markets, global technology, global ideas and global solidarity, enriching the lives of people everywhere, and involves new markets, new actors, new rules and norms and new tools of communication. For Hans–Hendrick Holm and George Sorensen globalisation is "the intensification of economic, political, social and cultural relations across borders, and is "interregional of intercontinental in scope". It has intensified the levels of interaction and interconnectedness within and between states and societies. Naturally the fears of cultural invasion, Americanisation, market capitalization, technological onslaught, civilizational clash, loss of national, ethnic, linguistic and religious identity are stalking the nation states and fear of danger to their security. India has to find a political security response to this aspect of globalisation.

Huntington hypothesises, that "fundamental source of conflict in this new world will not be primarily ideological or economic, but cultural has been criticized by peace theorists and activists, who advocate the emphasis on "a dialogue of civilization" instead of "clash of civilizations". Huntington argues in another article titled, "A Lonely Super Power?" for the need of the American Global leadership to save the world community from total anarchism, with a view to maintaining "western predominance" and "protect" western interests and promote western political and economic values.

After the establishment of the WTO in 1995, a kind of new war is perceptible–a trade cold war between and among developed and between developed and developing nations. Proceedings of the WTO at Geneva exhibit the persisting controversy among WTO members over the social chapter, that include the environment, human rights, and labour standards. If we want to have an equitable world order, then it hardly requires any explanation that the world order should be based on equity, equality and distributive justice. But that is not happening. If globalisation means free flow of ideas, knowledge, goods and services, why barrier to technology, why patent? Are these not barriers to diffusion that globalisation aims at?

While globalisation is being promoted, why naked power is displayed by the strategic coalition of the United States and Britain against the so-called rogue states–Iran, Iraq, Libya and North Korea? The misuse of the world community to serve their national interests, the use of stick policy to penalize those who threaten American strategies and economic interests in the Middle East, Gulf or elsewhere is something India should guard against. The bombing of the Republic of Yugoslavia by the NATO forces was an open flexing of power muscles, caring least for the UN body. Without seeking the fresh mandate either in the case of Iraq or in Kosovo, the US led forces attacked them. It can happen anywhere. Though international relations theorists argue that nature of power politics has changed and it is through the "collective security" approach that big powers take punitive action to maintain peace and security in the world there does not seem to be any basic difference in the power value, may be individual or collective. What is the security response to this unilateralism? Such attitudinal changes in globalised world are major security issues that require strategic response.

EMERGING WORLD ORDER

Liberalisation and its security implication have to be approached in the background of the end of cold war between two blocks led by Warsaw pact and the NATO that has led to an entirely different canvas on international scene and security of nation-states, especially, India, which was not comfortably placed with NATO. Any examination of the emerging perspectives on Indian security has to note certain developments and attitudinal changes that have occurred the world over in the last decade and should be investigated for an assessment of the unfolding facets of Indian security. A democratization of international relations has resulted in not only the nation state but also non-state actors from civil societies influencing international politics. The information revolution has caused more interaction among nations, both in sociological and economic terms. An erosion of state sovereignty can be observed due to technological onslaught and the changes in power equation, with the US emerging as the overwhelming hub of power. A new kind of multilateralism is being pursued where the UN and its agencies are now playing a subsidiary role to multilateral economic and security arrangements being put in place under the guidance of the US. And India is not finding it easy in the changed context because of its past ideological postures and the present strategic requirement. One trend that is very much perceptible is the linking of the issues of human rights, good governance and management of environment to security issues by the international community. There is also the focused concern about countering terrorism that poses a threat to entire state structure, both domestically and across national frontiers.

India's prime security concern is to cope with this complex and competitive international situation which has been compounded by unipolar world with the US as power centre, dominated by the consensus among the great powers on important issues in the UN under the leadership of the USA, pressure on conformance to economic and technological regimes which are considered necessary by the great powers for ensuring stable new world order. Now with the leverage of a stable political equation with one of the super powers gone, new political relationships, strategic ties and defence equation have to be explored and forged. Diversified economic and technological links need to be established with a number of countries given the erosion of arrangements which existed earlier, particularly the USSR and the Eastern European Countries.

How we look at Indian Security in view of the talk about "New World Order" as against the "Old World Order" dominated by cold war? State security, which at the most comprehensive level, involves territorial integrity, internal unity and cohesion, sovereignty in fashioning policies, and the ability to choose options related to foreign relations, defence and social-economic development–all these criteria affecting the autonomy of nation-state are under question and are in the process of erosion. What course correction is required to face the challenge posed by these new trends?

The notion of new world order in the western concept as based on peace, justice, cooperation, collective security system, rule of law, human rights, democracy and good governance, is flawed on the ground that these do not take cognizance of the key notions such as equality, equity and sovereignty. There are also theorists who feel that the concept of sovereignty in the globalisation process has lost much of its relevance given the inevitable global interdependence. But the question is, can we ignore state's sovereign character, that too when state systems are absolutely indispensable to the international relations. Kevin P. Clements of "International Alert" writes that state systems are absolutely indispensable to the peace building process and cannot be performed by non-state actors. The meaning and concept of globalisation cannot be extended to the level where it itself becomes a security threat.

With the dissolution of the Soviet Union, India feels friendlessness in most of the East European countries today with telling effect on our economic and political security. This is also the reason for the advocacy of multipolar world based on equality and sovereignty. While economic, political, and cultural boundaries of the weak are being broken, the strong are protecting their technological and political boundaries to the detriment of the developing countries. It is a grave security issue.

State sovereignty itself is now subject to what one would call neo-multilateralism being evolved under the guidance of the United States. The United States articulation of a new framework for international security to fashion security consultations and informal defence cooperation under Article 51 of the Chapter which allows countries of different regions to put in place regional defence and security arrangements on their own initiative outside the framework of the United Nations and its Security Council is putting countries like India in a very awkward position. In reality it advocates a kind of "Pan Americana", where such arrangements would be put in place both institutionally and operationally under the guidance of the United States and its close allies. This approach need to be examined also in the context of a thesis propounded by President Jimmy Carter's National Security Advisor Zibignew Brezenski on USA's relations with the rest of the world, with US as the centre of global power where in the rest of the world was divided into three categories of nation states, namely, the Vassal states, the tributary states and a few countries which might pose a challenge to US domination of world politics. India has no doubt limited options in the irreversible globalisation process but can certainly make serious attempt to expand it and find a maneuvering space to avoid irrelevancy. There is no single model or paradigm in international relations that can explain the complex nature of emerging world order. Nor is there any uncontested security model that can fit in the interconnected and interdependent but unipolar world. India has to evolve one.

CONCLUSION

The dramatic dissolution of the Soviet Union and the financial crisis of 1991 forced India to go for a liberal economic ideology to integrate itself with the global economy with the express purpose of achieving a higher growth rate. The paper has brought out the significance of liberalizing the economy for national security. Security issues have been identified, examined and their interrelationships discussed to offer insights into the underlying theme on which India could act to have a sound, fool-proof security strategy. A review of different ideas and concepts on national security has been made, bringing out its major elements that have bearing on Indian security. Various security paradigms, their relevance and strength and weaknesses have been considered for a critical appraisal of current world situation and evolving threat perceptions. India's measures of liberalizing its markets, their impacts on thought processes of people, society and culture, economy, political perceptions and human and rural issues, and their links with the national security have been deliberated. Energy security, food security, population, the environment and the commerce and their relationships with the security are analysed to fine-tune the security measures for India. Role of technology of knowledge age, its influence on the mode of war, on the economics and politics, the very concept of it and doctrine has been highlighted along with the way it is changing the direction of every facet of internal, national and international security. The problems are investigated and issues deciphered. Macrolevel development and attitudinal changes that have occurred the world over, the talk of new world order and their security implication for India have been inquired into to specify the issues confronting India in the new environment.

REFERENCES

Bardhan, P. (1998), "The Political Economy of Development in India", Oxford University Press, New Delhi.

Barry Buzan (1995), "The post-Cold War Asia-Pacific Security Order: Conflict or Cooperation?" In Andrew Mack and John Ravenhill, eds., Pacific Cooperation Building Economic and Security Regime in the Asia-Pacific region, Boulder, Westview, pp. 130-151.

Barry Buzan (1991), "People, States and Fear", An Agenda for International Security Studies in the post-Cold War Era, London, p. 192.

Barry Buzan (1998), "Liberation and Security. The contradiction of the Liberal Leviathan", Keynote Address Paper Presented at the Vilnius Conference on Regionalism and Conflict Resolution, Sep 24-27.

Baruah, Bonita (2004), "The India We don't know", Sunday Times of India, Hyderabad, October 10, p. 11.

Beaufre, Andre (1965), "Deterrence and Strategy", Faber and Faber, London, pp. 54-59.

Chaturvedi, Geeta (2004), "Globalisation and Social re-engineering : Human Rights, An Instrument of Empowering Women", Security in South Asia : Trends and Directions", Ed. Vandana A and Ashok C. Shukla, APH Publishing Corporation, New Delhi, pp. 289-305.

Dadwal Shebonti Ray (1997), "India's Energy Security Policy: A case for Nuclear Power", Strategic Analysis, November, pp. 1301-1313.

David Held (1997), Democracy and Globalisation", Global Governance, Vol. 3, No. 3, Sept.-Dec. p. 253.

Friedman (1999),"The Lexus and the Olive Tree", New York, p. 7.

Global Environmental Review TERI, June 2000, pp. 2-9.

Globalisation with a Human Face (1999), United Nations Development Programmeme (UNDP), Human Development Report.

Holm and Sorensess (ed.) (1995), Whose World Order? Uneven Globalisation and the End of the Cold War, Boulder, West View.'

Jain B.M., "Globalisation in the New World System: Reinterpreting the Theoretical Paradigm" in the book "India's Security in 21st Century", pp. 95-11.

Jalan, Bimal (1996), "India's Economic Policy: Preparing for the Twentyfirst Century", Penguin Books, New Delhi.

Mahbub-ul-Haq (1997), Development in South Asia, Karachi, p. 94.

Mian Zia, "The Search for Military Security as Self Destruction in South Asia", Sustainable Development by DD Khanna, pp. 393-394.

Mishra, Brajesh (2003), "India, United States, and the New World Order: Prospects of Cooperation", Address at the Council of Foreign Relations, New York, May 07.

Narsimha Rao, P.V. (2004), "Post-Cold War Tasks", The Hindu, Hyderabad, March 23, p. 10.

New World Coming : American Security in the 21st Century, The United States Commission on National Security / 21st Century, part I: Analysis of Mid-1970s Era Future Studies, Sep 15, 1999, from Internet.

Quoted in Vincent, Wei-Chenge Wang, Op. Cit. p. 65.

Roy-Chaudhury, Rahul (1996), "Strategic Trends in the Indian Ocean", Strategic Analysis, Vol. XIX, No. 6, Sept. pp. 892-897.

Sharma, Harvir (2004), "Security Imperatives for India in the Emerging Geo-Political Environment", India's Security in 21st Century : Challenges and Responses Ed Rajendra Prasad, Dominant Publishers and Distributors, New Delhi, Reprint Ed. pp. 220-262.

Singh, Shri Arvindar (2003), "40th Anniversary of the Sino-Indian conflict : A Historical Perspective", Journal of the United Services Institution of India, Vol. CXXXIII, No. 551, January-March, pp. 128-135.

Subrahmanyam, K. (2000), "Challenges to Indian Security", Journal of the United Services Institution of India, Vol. CXXX No. 542, October-December, pp. 541-562.

Suri R.B. (1995), "Maritime Dimensions of India's Security", Agni, Vol. I, No. 2, November, pp. 111-117.

Toffler, Alvin, Future Shock, (New York: Random House, 1970).

Vidhyar, Rakesh (2003), "Managing Technology –A challenge for the Future", Journal of the United Services Institution of India, Vol. CXXXIII, No. 552, April-June, pp. 233-252.

Vasudeva P.K. (2003), "World Trade Organization : Its Implications on Indian Economy", Journal of the United Services Institution of India, Vol. CXXXIII, No. 553, July-September, pp. 445-457.

Verma, N.M. (2001), "Dynamics of National Security: Essential Dimensions and Perspectives", Jaico Publishing House, Mumbai, First Jaico Edition.

VALIDICTORY ADDRESS

S.P. Shukla

For more than a decade, the term Globalisation has acquired such wide currency in our print and electronic media, in our speech-making and statements, in our discussions and dialogues and in our cyber-space that we do not pause to question whether this term has a well-defined and commonly understood meaning-content. There is also a vague but widely prevalent feeling that it is benign in character.

It is worth remembering that the expression "Globalisation" was not in vogue only a decade and a half ago. Other terms such as "International" and "Internationalism" were in use: One talked of "Universal" charter of human rights etc. And these terms had clearer, definite connotations: they stood for approaches, movements and commitments inspired by universal concerns of humanity, by a vision of more just, equitable and peaceful world. They were concepts that evolved historically, and the historical reality associated with them was transparent. In contrast, the way the term "Globalisation" is being widely used in the contemporary discourse, tends to obfuscate the historical process of which it is a part; and, such usage seems to provide a studied ambiguity, if not a misleading veneer , to its meaning and attributes. To quote from Michel Beaud's 'A History of Capitalism': "Plump and round, smooth and slippery, the word "globalisation" is an all-purpose word. It can be substituted for terms such as "imperialism" "world capitalism" or "dependence", as well as for the whole group of phrases, which express forward progress toward a unified and happy humanity. Nonetheless, the growing use of the term is not neutral, but takes place within the neo-liberal flood, where, once again, extreme positions are being stated. Within this context, the word is used to justify certain choices and to cover up certain sacrifices."

Globalisation is not a phenomenon; much less the destiny of humanity, as some would like to present the concept. It is also not a moral or social goal to strive for. In these days when it has become fashionable in certain quarters to resurrect ancient concepts or adages, totally out of their context, only to justify certain untenable or unjust propositions, some have tried to discern the message of *"Vasudhaiva Kutumbakam"* in "Globalisation"! Others are content with imagining the realization of the dream of a "global village" in it. Such romantic verbiage need not detain us here. A casual look at the long queues at the consulates of the countries like USA and UK in the metropolitan cities of the Indian subcontinent; the guns and electric fences that guard the borders of USA from Mexico; nearer home, the chauvinism palpable in dealing with the alleged immigrants from a neighbouring country, which, only a few decades ago, was part of the one and the same sub-continental entity to which we belonged: and, the overwhelming reality of the "local" and the "national" for the large masses of humanity all over the third world : these are sharp enough reminders to wake up anyone to the reality of a fragmented world.

But there are many that would like to see the process of "globalisation" as simply and entirely, a by-product of technological progress. For them, "Globalisation " has arrived riding piggyback on the revolutionary changes in technologies of telecommunications and informatics. Nobody will dispute the tremendous leaps that these technologies have made in the recent decades. But it would be unhistorical to forget that technological leaps of this order or perhaps, even greater order, had been accomplished in the earlier era too. Railroad, Steam-ship, Telegraph including undersea cables, Telephone, Electricity, Gasoline, Internal Combustion Engine, Automobile, Airplanes–things we now take for granted: If we put them in the context of the pre-existing technologies, the quantum leaps would be perceptible. And all these technologies brought the world together much earlier, for good as well as bad.

The only way we can understand "Globalisation" is to see it as part of the historical process, which started long ago. How long ago? It depends on where we place the origin of capitalism. If we include the phases of mercantile and manufacturing capitalisms that preceded the phase of industrial capitalism as we know it and in which we live today, the beginnings of the process may date back to five hundred years. If we restrict ourselves to industrial capitalism, the process would be two hundred years old. To recall Paul Sweezy, it is the logic of capitalism that, once it takes root, it grows internally and expands externally. It cannot remain static over time nor confined in a geographic space.

And the imperialist domination is its logical necessity. Among its various contradictory characteristics as pointed out by Michel Beaud, it has this one: it is national as well as global at the same time. And, therefore, its expanding urge launches it on the global trajectory. Indeed Samir Amin has gone to the extent of saying that imperialism is not a 'stage' but the 'state 'of capitalism !

In all its history the expanding phase of capitalism has been imperialistic. It is characterized by polarizing growth and hierarchical expansion. Technological progress provided the process its form and muscle and the process, in turn, facilitated the development of technologies furthering its growth and expansion. The logic of accumulation which is the essence of the capitalist process is exploitative and its successful practice implies subordination or hierarchical ordering. The colonialism was but one stage in that process. With the emergence of modern industry, banking and finance, tendency towards centralization and concentration of capital accentuated. Finance tended to dominate the capital. Competitive capitalism of the earlier era gave way to monopoly capitalism at the national level. Which led to repeated crises of realization in the system, on the one hand, and, the imperialist era of capitalist expansion, on the other. This was also characterized by intensified inter-imperialist rivalry, which eventually led to two imperialist wars of unprecedented proportions in the twentieth century. The process of global expansion (or, if you wish, "globalisation") of the capitalist-imperialist system was already proceeding apace in the preceding century. According to Karl Polanyi, an authority on the process of " The Great Transformation" that was brought about by capitalism, by the last couple of decades of the nineteenth century, globalisation was already an accepted feature of the contemporary economic reality. "World commodity prices were the central reality in the lives of millions of Continental peasants; the repercussions of the London market were daily noted by the businessmen all over the world; and governments discussed plans for the future in the light of the situation on the world capital markets. Only a madman would have doubted that international economic system was the axis of the material existence of the human race."

And to see directly this global inter-connections in our own context in those times, we need only recall that the industrial house that laid the foundation of industrial capitalism in India accumulated its capital through fortunes it made out of the boom in cotton markets consequent upon the cessation of supplies from cotton-exporting states of America (on account of the America's civil war) to England's textile mills ! And the American civil war itself was a product of direct tension between two tendencies in the developing capitalism of America: one in the South in favour of continuing the role of dependent economy supplying raw materials to England; and the other in the New England territories wanting to develop national industrial capitalism in America.

In short "Globalisation" is no wonder of the yesteryear. We have lived with it for over a hundred and twenty-five years.

It may appear that this process of capitalist–imperialist expansion changed its spots in the brief period of close to twenty-five years of the so-called " Golden Age of Capitalism", that is to say, the period between the end of the second world -war and the oil-prices rise that took place in the nineteen seventies. But it was more of a short-lived aberration or an exception to the rule, a specific historical conjecture, brought about by a combination of a number of special circumstances, not the least of which was the coming of age of a powerful alternative system to capitalism in the shape of the USSR and the emergence of the People's Republic of China. Others included: massive reconstruction of the post - war Western Europe; the emergence of greater mobility of capital beyond national borders; growth of trans-national processes and organizations of production; strengthening of oligopolistic and monopolistic trends; leeway available to European nations to follow auto-centric macro-economic expansionary policies; a perceived need to accommodate labour in the system at the domestic level, on the one hand, and to provide the newly emerging nations from the erstwhile colonial world, some space for industrialization, on the other, so that they remain outside the sphere of influence of the alternative system; and consequent success, though short-lived in hindsight, of the three projects: the social democracy in Western Europe; the welfare state everywhere; and the weakly autonomous national development project in the third world.

With the American economy facing troubles, partly of the systemic nature and partly created by its own adventurous policies in relation to what it considered to be its arch-enemy because of the systemic alternative it seemed to offer and thus challenge the very existence of capitalism, USA abandoned the role of providing the anchor to the system which it had done during this brief period after the second world-war. This was followed by the period when the reconstructed Western Europe and Japan started offering tough competition to the leading economy of USA in different vital areas including agriculture, aircraft, steel, automobiles, integrated circuits. And new competitors threatened to emerge from among the third world, at least in some lines of manufacture.

The danger of slowdown, if not stagnation in the system, was palpable. Intra -system rivalries were resurfacing. Here was the alarm ringing for the leading power of the capitalist system. New offensive was launched by USA to change the rules of the game in its favour. So was born in the 1980s the Uruguay Round of Trade Negotiations with emphasis on liberalisation of Services trade (which included financial services like banking and insurance; among others), where Americans perceived their superior competitive edge. Initiatives were launched to prise open the protected markets of goods and services the world over. And ways were found to enhance the monopoly hold and profits of big corporations by legislating a New World regime strengthening private rights in intellectual property rights. These initiatives implied a severe intrusion into the autonomous space of economic decision- making, particularly of the third world countries, signifying the beginning of the end of their autonomous development project. They also signified, in conjunction with other developments in the global financial system, severe erosion of the space for pursuit of autonomous expansionist macroeconomic policies at the level of all nations, except USA. With the trade and financial liberalisation that was being pushed, the pressures for attaining and retaining global competitiveness eventually resulted in attempts to unravel the welfare state project and the compromise that the system was compelled to strike in the post- war years in favour of labour.

The global capitalist-imperialist process was once again manifesting its true characteristics: strengthened monopolistic tendencies; intensified intra-system rivalries; a tendency towards a long -term downward phase; and increasing domination of finance capital. If these tendencies were, in essence, more or less abiding characteristics of the process throughout its history, the response of the system to the crisis was also typical: to launch new offensives to expand its field of operation, to avail itself of new opportunities of appropriation and to increase the rate of exploitation.

II

We have been through a decade and a half of this latest and intensified phase of the so-called "globalisation" of the Indian economy. The process was triggered by the balance of payment crisis faced by the Indian economy in 1990-91 which was partly due to the extraneous causes. The emergency operation to meet the crisis, was soon turned, under the encouragement and pressure of IMF and World Bank, into a full-fledged process of deregulation in trade and investment sectors; the opening -up of the economy and its progressive integration with the global economy; withdrawal of the state from various spheres of economic activity; drastic cuts in public sector outlays on social sectors; dis-investment and privatization of the public sector enterprises; retrenchment of labour-force in the name of improving operational efficiency and market taking the central place in economic decision-making. The complex of these policies was given a benign label: "Economic Reforms."

The proponents of the reforms were promising a definite turnaround in five years' time and India's entry into the new millennium on a strong base, with a high rate of growth, rising employment, globally competitive industries, accelerating exports and balanced budgets. And incidentally, faster eradication of poverty, as a by-product of accelerated growth. All these promises have remained undelivered. On the contrary, what we are witnessing is a modest and uneven rate of growth, burgeoning unemployment, debilitating competition from abroad, stagnating industries, retrenchments and closures, and persisting and large revenue deficits. What is more, agriculture has been starved of public investment, the policy of state intervention to guarantee remunerative prices has been virtually abandoned, and agricultural products have been exposed to unfair and sudden import competition resulting in widespread and unprecedented distress in the rural hinterland. To compound the misery of the common man, the public distribution system has been rendered meaningless for vast sections of the low-income population in urban and semi-urban areas. The increasing costs of electricity, transportation, kerosene, cooking gas, staple food and accommodation have made the life of even the lower middle classes an unending, losing marathon to make both ends meet. And there is direct evidence that contrary to the official claims that the proportion of population living below the poverty line has gone down substantially as a byproduct of the growth engendered by the economic reforms, the proportion of population not having access to the minimum nutrition levels has, in fact, increased to as high levels as 74 per cent in rural areas and 55 per cent in urban areas.

More than a decade of these "globalising reforms" has increased the vulnerability of the economy and deepened the duality within the polity. Finance, food and agriculture and energy typically illustrate the increasing vulnerability. As a result of a deliberate policy, the ratio of direct tax revenues to the GDP has been brought down. The saving potential of the economy has not been fully tapped. The globalisation of economy and increasing incomes and wealth in the hands of the richer sections of the population have resulted in widening the trade gap. Full convertibility of rupee for current account transactions; a unified, market-determined exchange rate of the rupee; and a series of other measures "liberalizing" the financial sector have considerably reduced the policy options of the government. The situation thus created is being met through increasing dependence on largely speculative inflows of external capital, propitiating which has become a major, if not the main, objective of financial policy. The burgeoning inflows of essentially speculative, short-term and reversible foreign financial capital have put increasing strains on the sound management of monetary and exchange rate policies. The warning was recently sounded by no less a person than the Governor of the Reserve Bank in this regard. But the spectacle of a hasty retraction (obviously under the pressure of the Finance Ministry) is symptomatic of the situation where policy options have been severely circumscribed. The relative isolation of the Indian financial system (which itself was a significant deviation from the policies of full financial integration advocated by the proponents of "globalising reforms" and "financial liberalisation") had played a major role in saving the Indian economy from the fate of the South-East Asian tigers a few years ago. But the advocates of financial integration have not yet given up their zeal for capital account convertibility; and indeed they seem to be succeeding in pushing the policies towards that goal surreptitiously and gradually.

Agriculture, which was, for long, insulated from the forces of the notoriously volatile global market, has been exposed to global competition. The effective tool of imposing quantitative restrictions on imports as necessary has been abandoned. In the last few years, distress seized various sectors such as cotton, oilseeds, horticulture, sugarcane, plantation crops such as tea, coffee and coconut; the problem does not seem to be far off in respect of staple food crops of rice and wheat. Un-remunerative prices and heavy indebtedness have driven thousands of peasants to suicide. In the name of reducing fiscal deficit, subsidies on the food supplied through the public distribution system have been reduced or eliminated. The off-take has naturally slackened and the Food Corporation, the central procuring agency, is reluctant to procure food-grains for want of adequate finances. The faith of the farmers in the procurement system, which was the cornerstone of the policy aimed at food self-sufficiency, has been shaken. This, coupled with the declining rate of public investment in agriculture and drying up of the credit flows, which again was a direct consequence of the deliberate policy of reducing government expenditure and investment, is threatening the food and livelihood security of millions of small and marginal peasants.

The official long-term perspective is that of "corporatisation" of our agriculture. The paradigm set out by the Agreement on Agriculture in WTO is being accepted despite its dangerous implications for our agricultural and rural economy. That paradigm was constructed by the two cross- Atlantic agri- business giants viz. USA and EU, mainly to serve their own mutual interests. It implies corporate, capital-intensive, export–oriented, agribusiness- centred, peasant-insensitive and mass–livelihood- endangering agriculture. Its total inappropriateness to our agriculture is too obvious to bear any elabouration. But the catastrophic implications of aligning our agriculture to it are not receiving serious attention of our policy makers. In the environment of "globalising economy" and "globally competitive industries" there will be no way to absorb the massive displacement of workforce it will cause. And the "sponge" character of our agriculture to absorb the increases in the workforce has already vanished thanks to the policies followed during the decade and a half of the "economic reforms" and the increasing demographic pressures on land over the years. In the circumstances, the alignment of our agriculture to the WTO paradigm will mean inconceivably massive displacement from the rural hinterland with no hope of alternative means of livelihood.

The energy sector has been subjected to fundamental changes, institutional, technological and economic. Increasing dependence on imported energy has been accepted as the basis of perspective planning. Dependence on imported capital and management in the energy sector has been encouraged. One third of the extractive capacity is lying unutilized in the oil sector. The hydroelectric potential is not being fully tapped. The alternative of bio-mass produced energy is not even being seriously explored. The pricing of electricity is being determined to guarantee high returns to private producers, both indigenous and foreign. The state electricity boards which, over the years, have created a reservoir of technical and managerial competence, and which were denied financial support they were entitled to under the statute, are being decimated systematically. The indigenous power equipment industry is being starved of orders and rendered helpless in the face of unfair and state-aided competition from the multinationals. The developing crisis in the power sector in the wake of the so-called reforms will impact our agriculture the most adversely.

Economic reforms have deepened the duality within the Indian polity. There has emerged a class, of not more than seven to eight per cent of the Indian population, which has never had it so good. They have experienced an unprecedented rise in their income and wealth, thanks to the entry of multinationals, particularly in the financial sector. Another contributing factor has been the boom in the information technology industry. The tax reliefs generously bestowed on the rich in the name of new economic policy ensured that rising income remained in their hands. And the liberalized import regime provided them with imported goodies. The inevitable counterpart was the increased burden of indirect taxes, including inflation, on the poor and not-so-well-off sections. Closures and retrenchments, which followed in the wake of the pursuit of "efficiency" and "open markets" under the reforms, have added to their misery. With growing casualization of employment and encouragement of lax implementation of labour laws, the quality of employment has deteriorated. Women workers have been the worst hit. The withdrawal of the State from a number of economic activities, the slow-down of social sector expenditure and privatization of public sector enterprises– all spell stagnation, if not decline, of employment opportunities, particularly for the weaker sections.

The direct result of the slowdown of the social sector expenditures has been a marked deterioration in the vital public services of education and health. As it was, these services were never of high quality and universal in reach, particularly in the rural areas. But in the decade of reforms, the reach has been severely compromised and the quality has gone down drastically. On the other hand, there has been conscious encouragement of the "health care industry" in metropolitan centres, where the rich can avail of state-of-the-art health care. The urban and semi-urban areas are witnessing a spurt of private schools promising high quality education for those who can afford to pay steep admission and tuition fees. For the rest, we have poorly equipped inadequately staffed apologies for schools.

The brunt of the process is being borne by the working people. The artisan class and the self-employed poor, drawn predominantly from amongst the backward and minority communities and women are the worst victims of the ongoing mass annihilation of the small, cottage and tiny sectors of industry. Poor fisher-folk are being deprived of their means of subsistence as rapacious fishing by big multi-national companies is being encouraged in the name of export promotion. Farmers, plantation workers and landless labourers are facing the assault of the unfolding integration of Indian agriculture with world agriculture. Dispossession of agricultural land is being expedited through amendment of the Land Acquisition Act. Liberal grant of prospecting and mining leases in forestlands is threatening the survival of tribal population. Construction of mega projects of dams is given green signal, without even pretence at rehabilitation of hundreds of thousands of tribal people and rural poor facing ouster and destitution.

The ruling elite is never tired of projecting the vision of India emerging as a great technological and economic power in the coming years. The media is doing a high-pressure salesmanship job for them. The language itself is being distorted and appropriated: systematic deprivation of the poor masses is described blandly as "liberalisation"; handing over of the people's productive assets to the powerful capitalist clique is called simply "dis-investment"; onslaught of the neo-colonial forces is heralded as "globalisation"; and ruthless furtherance of these tendencies is christened "the next generation of reforms". The stark contrast that India of the working and deprived poor masses presents is sought to be obliterated by the elite architects and beneficiaries of the process through the media jugglery and, even worse, the attempts at diversion of public discontent into divisive and revivalist agendas.

III

But the scenario on the ground is not bleak. The mighty forces of globalisation have unleashed powerful protests in India. Anti-globalisation sentiment is gathering strength in factories and fields. The trade unions are gearing up and are launching united all-India protests and industrial actions. From the organised left to autonomous social activists and radical Gandhians, covering a broad spectrum of communists and socialist forces and democrats of various schools, an Indian rainbow in numerous shades is in the making against the challenge of globalisation.

The revivalist and divisive forces have been thrown out of power and the agenda of "economic reforms" pursued diligently by governments of different political hues during the last fourteen years has been called in question. The ruling elite has made a tactical move of partly recognizing the adverse effects of the process of globalisation. It has started using wishy- washy, qualifying phrases such as the need to provide "a human face" to the process of economic reforms. The popular pressure has made it accept, in principle, the need to provide a national employment guarantee programmeme, the need to provide larger allocations for social services such as health and education, and the need to review the new "Electricity Act". But the implementation of these promises is being substantially diluted. On the other hand, there is no let up in its ardour to continue the decade -old policies in financial and other important spheres. The moves to relax or remove the limits for foreign capital investment in crucial spheres such as telecommunication, banking and insurance, the recent Ordinance amending the Patent Act and the repeated policy statements being made that the process of "economic reforms" will be continued with vigour only go to show that the ruling elite has not yet digested the lessons of the last General Elections. The current scenario only underlines the paramount need for effective regrouping and reinforcement of the popular forces opposed to the process of globalisation.

The opposition to globalisation is growing not only in India and other third world countries, but also in large parts of Europe and North America. Wide arrays of political forces have participated in these protests. These protests have primarily targeted the key institutions of global capital, namely, WTO, World Bank, IMF.

The recent re-emergence of solidarity of the poor nations of the South at the Cancun Ministerial Meeting of WTO, in the shape of the formation of G-20, (a group of twenty important developing countries including Argentina, Brazil, China, India and South Africa) constituted a definite advance for the movement of resistance to globalisation. The movement had first manifested itself dramatically at Seattle in 1999. It then proceeded to secure a tactical victory of sorts at Doha meeting of WTO in 2001 in the shape of the Declaration on TRIPS and the Public Health which recognized, in principle, the need to adopt a flexible and people- oriented stance towards patent-monopolies in respect of essential drugs. And then at Cancun in 2003, the combined economic might of the two economic giants failed to force their expansionist and one-sided agenda on the unwilling poor countries. When the negotiations deadlocked in Cancun were resumed in Geneva in July 2004, the global capital had to agree to give up some of its expansionist agenda. But, on the other hand, it did succeed in engaging the emerging coalition of developing countries in negotiations on agriculture within the broad paradigm set by them. This paradigm of corporate, capital-intensive, export-oriented, agri-business-centered, peasant-insensitive and mass livelihood-endangering agriculture which informs the US-EU approach to the international discipline on agriculture has posed unprecedented challenge to the very survival of the three billion strong third world peasantry. The possibilities of the mobilization of the South on this issue in the WTO are considerable. This is a likely terrain that can yield successful results in preventing further aggravation of the inequity of the global system. One important condition for such mobilization is that G-20 must creatively explore with the rest of developing countries an alternative paradigm for South-South trade and economic cooperation on agriculture. And in this exercise, India must play a leading role. As we have seen earlier, the ruling elite in India is not interested in such an initiative. But the vast masses of the Indian peasantry, if properly mobilized, can force the ruling establishment to change its stance. And here the global and domestic interfaces of the resistance to the process of globalisation can coalesce and collabourate most effectively.

The formidable challenge of globalisation is generating its antithesis in the shape of worldwide movements strengthening people's solidarity. During the last few years, such movements have emerged all over the world, in the South as well as North, confronting the onslaught of the global capital. Massive anti-war demonstrations all over the globe constituted a most powerful and moving expression of this trend confronting the worst manifestation of the contemporary process of globalisation. At the global level, we have witnessed the emergence and rapid growth of the World Social Forum which recently held its fifth global meet in Porto Alegre in Brazil The resistance to the anti-democratic onslaught of global capital is building up. It remains to be seen how the structured political formations and processes respond to these developments, recast and sharpen their strategies and make a decisive intervention both at the nation-state level as well as in the international fora.

The globalisation offensive is all pervasive and well orchestrated. To meet it effectively and defeat it decisively, the vigorous but scattered struggles, intensive but sporadic protests need to acquire a more unified expression. What is needed is a movement forward from mere criticism of this or that aspect of globalisation to determined opposition and resistance to the forces propelling globalisation. Struggles against particular impacts of globalisation need to coalesce into a broader and coordinated confrontation with the process of globalisation itself, its dynamics and its manifestation in various forms. The terrain of such a struggle will be primarily national. But the emerging coalition of the peoples' movements of the North and South to resist the onslaught of the global capital will provide the struggle a powerful impetus and a vital global dimension. Such a coalition will launch the movement on the trajectory of establishing the foundation of a truly global society, which is just, harmonious and peaceful.

INDEX